A JOURNEY FROM PRINCE OF WALE'S FORT, IN HUDSON'S BAY, TO THE NORTHERN OCEAN. UNDERTAKEN BY ORDER OF THE HUDSON'S BAY COMPANY. FOR THE

A JOURNEY FROM PRINCE OF WALE'S FORT, IN HUDSON'S BAY, TO THE NORTHERN OCEAN. UNDERTAKEN BY ORDER OF THE HUDSON'S BAY COMPANY. FOR THE

Samuel Hearne

www.General-Books.net

Publication Data:

Title: A Journey From Prince of Wale's Fort, in Hudson's Bay, to the Northern Ocean. Undertaken by Order of the Hudson's Bay Company. for the Discovery of Copper Mines, a North West Passage, c. in the Year 1769, 1770, 1771, 1772
Author: Hearne, Samuel, 1745-1792
Reprinted: 2010, General Books, Memphis, Tennessee, USA
Publisher: Dublin, Printed for P. Byrne and J. Rice
Publication date: 1796
Subjects: Indians of North America
Natural history

A JOURNEY FROM PRINCE OF WALE'S FORT, IN HUDSON'S BAY, TO THE NORTHERN...

SAMUEL WEGG, Efq. Governor,
  Sir JAMES WINTER LAKE, Deputy Governor,
  THE REST OF THE COMMITTEE
  OF THE HONOURABLE
  HUDSONS BAT COMPANT,
  HONOURABLE SIRS,
    AS the folloving Journey, vas undertaken at your Requeft and Expence, I feel it no lefs my Duty than my Inclination to ad-drefs it to you; hoping that my humble Endeavours to relate, in a plain and unadorned Style, the various Circumflances and Remarks a vrhich which occurred during that Journey, will meet with your Approbation.
    I am, with much Efteem and Gratitude,
  HONOURABLE SIRS,
  Your moll obedient, and moft obliged humble Servant,
  SAMUEL HEARNE.
  PREFACE.
    MR. Dalrymple, in one of his Pamphlets relating to Hudfons Bay, has been fo very particular in his obfervations on my Journey, as to remark, that 1 have not explained the con-ftrud: ion of the Quadrant which I had the misfortune to break in my fecond

Journey to the North. It was a Hadley's Quadrant, with a bubble attached to it for an horizon, and made by Daniel Scatlif of Wapping. But as no inftrument on the fame principle could be procured when I was fetting out on my laft Journey, an old Elton's Quadrant, which had been upwards of thirty years at the Fort, was the only inftrument I could then be provided with, in any refpecl proper for making obfervations with on the land.

Mr. Dalrymple alfo obferves, that 1 only in-ferted in my laft Journal to the Company, one obfervation for the latitude, which may be true; but I had, never-thelefs, feveral others during that journey, particularly at Snow-bird Lake, Thelwey-aza-yeth, and Clowey, exclufive of that mentioned in the Journal taken at Conge-catha-whachaga. But when I was on that Journey, a 2 anc and for feveral years after, I little thought that any remarks made in it would ever have attracted the notice of the Public: if I had, greater pains might and would have been taken to render it more worthy of their attention than it now is. At that time my ideas and ambition extended no farther than to give my employers fuch an account. of my proceedings as might be fatisfacto-ry to them, and anfwer the purpofe which they had in view; little thinking it would ever come under the infpeclion of lo ingenious and indefatigable a geographer as Mr. Dalrymple muft be allowed to be. But as the cafe has turned out otherwife, I have at my Icifure hours rccopied all my Journals into one book, and in fome inftan-ces added Xo the remarks I had before made; not fo much for the information of thofe wlio are critics in geography, as for theamufement of candid and indulgent readers, who may perhaps feel them. felves in fome meafure gratified, by having the face of a country brought to their view, which has hitherto been entirely unknown to every European except myfelf. Nor will 1 flatter myfelf, a defcription of the modes of living, manners, and cuftoms of the natives, (which, though long known, have never been defcribed.) be lef3 acceptable to the curious.

I cannot help obferving, that I feel myfelf rather hurt at Mr. Dairymple's rejeding my latitude in fo peremptory a manner, and in fo great a proportion, portion, as he has done; becaufe, before I arrived at Conge-cathawhachaga, the Sun did not fet during tlie whole night: a proof that I was then to the Northward of the Arctic Circle. I may be allowed to add, that when I was at the Copper River, on the eighteenth of July, the Sun's declination was but 2 i ', and yet it was certainly fome height above the horizon at midnight; how much, as 1 did not then remark, I will not nozv take upon me to fay; but it proves that the latitude was confiderably more than Mr. Dalrym-ple will admit of. His altertion, that no grafs is to be found on the (rocky) coaft of Greenland farther North than the latitude of 6y is no proof there ihould not be any in a much higher latitude in the interior parts of North America. For, in the firft place, I think it is more than probable, that the Copper River empties itfelf into a fort of inland Sea, or extenfive Bay, fomewhat like that of Hudfon's: and it is well known that no part of the coafi of Hudfon's Straits, nor thofe of Labradore, at leaft for forae degrees South of thenfi, tiuy more than the Eail coaft of Hudfon's Bay, till we arrive near Whale R. iver, have any trees on them; while the Weft coaft of the Bay in the fame latitudes, is well clothed with timber. WHiere then is the ground for fuch an altertion? Had Mr. Dalrymple conil-dered this circumftance only, I flatter myfelf he would not fo haftily have objecled to woods and grafs being feen in iimilar fituations, though in a much higher latitude. Neither can the reafon-

VIll

PREFACE.

ing which Mr. Dalrymple derives from the error I committed in eftimating the diftance to Cumberland Houfe, any way affeisl- the quellion under confideration; becaufe that diftance being chiefly in longitude, I had no means of correcting it by an obfervation, which was not the cafe here.

I do not by any means wifli to enter into a dif-pute with, or incur the difpieafure of Mr. Dalrymple; but thinking, as 1 do, that I have not been treated in fo liberal a manner as I ought to have been, he will excufe me for endeavouring. to convince the Public that his objections are in a great meafure without foundation. And having done fo, 1 fhall quit the difagreeable fubjeft with declaring, that if any part of the following flieets ftiould afford amufement to Mr. Dalrymple, or any other of my readers, it will be the higheft gratification I can receive, and the only recompence I defire to obtain for the hardfliips and fatigue which I underwent in procuring the information contained in them.

Being well aflured that feveral learned and curious gentlemen are in poffeftion of manufcript copies of, or extracts from, my Journals, as well as copies of the Charts, I have been induced to make this copy as corredt as pofllble, and to pub-lilh it; efpecially as 1 obferve that fcarcely any two of the publications that contain extracts from my Journals, agree in the dates when I arrived at, or departed trom, particular places. To rectify thofe difagreements 1 applied to the Governor and

Committee

Committee of the Hudlon's Bay Company, fof leave to perufe my original Jou nau. Ibis as granted with the greateft affability and polite-nefs; as well as a fight of all my Charts relative to this Journey. With this affiftance 1 have been enabled to rectify fome inaccuracies that had, by trufting too much to memoryj crept into this copy; and I now offer it to the Public unde authentic dates and the beft authorities, howevef widely fome publications may differ from it.

I have taken the liberty to expunge fome paffa-ges which were inferred in the original copy, as being no ways interefting to the Public, and fe-. veral others have undergone great alterations; fo that, in fa(5t, the whole may be faid to be new-modelled, by being blended with a variety of Remarks and Notes that were not inferted in the original copy, but which my long rcfidence in the country has enabled me to add.

The account of the principal quadrupeds and birds that frequent thofe Northern regions in Summer, as well as thofe which never migrate, though not defcribed in a fcientific manner, may not be entirely unacceptable to the moft fcientific zoologifts; and to thofe who are unacquainted with the technical terms ufed in zoology, it may perhaps be more ufeful and entertaining, than if I had defcribed them in the moft claflical manner. But I muft not conclude this Preface, without acknowledging, in the moft ample manner, the affiftance I have received from the peru- fal of Mr. Pennant's Ardic Zoology; which has enabled me to give feveral of the birds their proper names; for thofe by which they are known in Hudfon's Bay are purely Indian, and of courfe quite unknown to every European who has not refided in that country.

To conclude, I cannot fufeciently regret thelofs of a coniiderable Vocabulary of the Northern Indian Language, containing fixteen folio pages, which was lent to the late Mr. Hutchins, then Correfponding Secretary to the Company, to copy for Captain Duncan, when he went on dif-coveries to Hudfon's Bay in the year one thou-fand feven hundred and ninety. But Mr. Hutchins dying foon after, the Vocabulary was taken away with the reft of his effects, and cannot now be recovered; and memory, at this time, will by no means ferve to replace it.

CON-

at Seal River, kill two deer; partridges plenty. Meet ajlra7igenorther?! Indian, accompany him to his tent, uage received there; wy Indians ajjiji in killing fame beaver. Proceed toward home, and arrive at the Fort.-Page i

CHAP II.

Tranfactions from our arrival at the Factory, to my leaving it again, and during the Firft Part of my Second Journey, till I had the misfor-tune to break the Quadrant.

Tranfactions at the Fad ory. Proceed on my fecond journey. Arrive at Seal River. Deer pkntiful forfome time. Method of angling fjh under the ice. Stt ourfijhing-nets. Meihod offetting nets under the ice. My guide propofes to Jlay till the gecfe Jhoidd begin to fly; his reafons accepted. Pitch our tent in the beji manner. Method of pitching a tent in Winter. Fijh plentiful for fome time; grow veryfcarce; in great want of provifiom. Manner of employing my time. My guide killed two deer. Move to the place they were lying at; there killfe-veral more deer, and three beavers. Soon in want of provflons again. Many Indians joiri us from the Weftward. We began to move towards the barren ground. Arrive at She-than-nee, therefuffergreat diflrefs for ivant of provifions. hidians kill two fwans and three geefe. Geefe and other birds of pajfageplentiful. League She-than-nee and arrive

CHAP.

CHAP. III.

Tranfa(ftions from the Time the Quadrant was broken, till I arrived at the Faclory.

Several fir ange Indians join us from the Northward, They plunder me of all I had; but did not plunder the Southern Indians. My guide plundered. We begin our return to the Fadory. Meet with other Indians who join our company. Coded deer-Jkins for clothing. but could not get them dreffed Suffer much hardfhip from the want of tents and warm clothing, Moji of the Indians leave us. Meet with Matonabbee So? ne account of him, and his behaviour to me and the Southern Indians. We remain in his company fame time. His ob- fervations on my two unfuccefsful attempts. We leave him, and proceed to a place to which he di-reded us, in order to make fnow-flooes andjledges. "-Join Matonabbee again, and proceed towards the Factory in his company. Ammunition runs jhort. Myfelf and four Indians fet off poftfor the Fadory, Much bewildered in afnowjtorm; my dog is fro-en. to death; we lie in a bufh of willows. Proceed on our journey. Great difficulty in crcffing a jumble of rocks. Arrive at the Fort. Page 47

CHAP.

CHAP. IV.

Tranfaclions during our Stay at Prince of Wales's Fort, and the former Part of our third Expedition, till our Arrival at Clowey, where we built Canoes, in May 1771.

Preparations for our departure. Refufe to take any of the home-guard Indians with me, By fo doing, I offend the Governor. Leave the Fort a. third time. My injiruclions on this expedition. Provi-Jtons of ail kinds very fear ce. Arrive at the woods where we kill fome deer. Arrive at Iland Lake Maionabbee taken ill. Some remarks thereon. yoin the remainder ef the Indians' families. Leave Jfland Lake. Defcription thereof Deer plentiful. Meet a firange Indian. Alter our courfe from Wefi North Wefi to Wefi by South. Crofs Catha-whachaga River Coffed Lake, Snow-Bird Lake and Pike Lake. Arrive at a tent ofjlrangers, who are employed infnaring deer in a pound. Defcription of a pound. Method of proceeding. Remarks thereon. Proceed on our journey. Meet with federal parties of Indians; by one of whom I fent a letter to the Governor at Prince of Waless Fort. Arrive at Theweyazayeth. Employment there. Proceedto thenorthnorthwefi andnorth. Arrive at Clowey. One of the Indians wives taken in labour.

hour. Remarks thereon, Cujioms obferved by the Northern Indians on thofe oc-cafions. Page 60

CHAP. V.

Tranfaaions at Clowey, and on our Journey, till our Arrival at the Copper-mine River.

Several Jirange Indians join us. Indians employed in building canoes', defcripiion and ufe of them. More Indians join us, to the amount of fame hundreds, Leave Clowey. Receive intelligence that Kcdjhies was near us.—Two young men difpatched for my letters and goods.–Arrive at Pcfloew Lake; crofs part of it, and make a large fmoke. One of Maionabbte's wives elopes, Some remarks on the natives. Keeljhies joins us, and delivers my letters, but the goods were all expended. A Northern In-dianwifhes to take one of Matonabbee's wives from him; matters compromifed, but had like to have proved fatal to my progrefs. Crofs Pefiew Lake, when I make proper arrangements for the remainder of my journey. Many Indians join our party, in order to make war on the Efquimaux at the Copper River. Preparations made for that purpofe while at

join us. Indians propofe to go to the Athapufcow Country to kill moofe. Leave Point Lake, and arrive at the wood's edge. Arrive at Anawd Lake. Tranfadions there Remarkable infiance of a man being cured of the palfey by the conjurors. Leave Anawd Lake Arrive at the great Athapufcow Lake. 189

CHAP. VIII.

Tranfactions and Remarks from our Arrival on the South Side of the Athapufcow Lake, till our Arrival at Prince of Wales's Fort on Churchill River.

Crofs the Athapufcow Lake. Defcription of it and its produbions, as far as could be difcovered in Winter, when the fnow was on the ground. Fifh found in the lake. Defcription of the buffalo; of the moofe or elk, and the method of drejjing their fkins. Pind a woman alone that had not feen a human face for more than feven months. Her account how Jhe came to be in thatfituation; and her curious method of procuring a livelihood. Many of my Indians wrejlled for her. Arrive at the Great Athapufcow River. Walk along the fide of the River for fever al days, and thenjirike off to the Eafi-ward. Difficulty in getting through the woods in many places. Meet with fome firange Northern Indians on their return from the Fort. Meet more Jir angers, whom my companions plundered, and from whom they took one of their young women, Curious manner of life which thofe Jlrangers lead, and the reafon they gave for roving fo far from their ufual refidence. Leave the fine level country of the Atha-pufcows, and arrive at the Stony Hills of the Northern Indian Country. Meet fome firange Northern Indians, one of whom carried a letter for me to Prince of Wales' s Fort, in March one thoufandfeven hundred and feventy-one, and now gave me an an-fwer to it, dated twentieth of June following. Indians begin preparing wood-work and birch-rind for canoes.- The equinoctial gale very fevere. Indian method of running the inoofe deer down by fpeed of foot. Arrival at Theeleyaza River. See fome fir angers. The brutality of my companions. A tremendous gale and ftiow-drift. Met with more Jirangers; remarks on it. Leave all the elderly p(ople and children, and proceed dire6lly io the Fort. Stop to build canoes, and then advance. Several of the Indians die through hunger, and many others are obliged to decline the journey for want of ammunition. A violent fiorm and inundation, that forced us to the top of a high hill, where we fuffcred great dijlrefs for mere than two days.

-Kiu -Kill feveral deer. The Indians method of pre-fefving the flejh without the ajfijlance qffa't.- See feve nil Indians that were going to Knapp's Bay. Ga? ne of all kinds retnarkably plentiful. Arrive at the Fadory Page 247

CHAP. IX.

A (hort Defcription of the Northern Indians, alfo a farther Account of their Country, Manufactures, Cuftoms, Isfc.

An account of the perfons and tempers of the Northern Indians. They pojfefs a great deal of art and cunning. Are very guilty of fraud when in their power, a7id generally exad more for their furrs than any other tribe of Indians. Always dijfatisfied. yet have their good qualities. The men in gefieral jealous of their wives. Their marriages. Girls always betrothed when children and their reafonsfor it. Great care and confinement of young girls from the age of eight or nine years. Divorces common among thofepeople.–The women are lefspro-I fie than in warmer countries. Remarkable piece of fuperfiition obferved by the women at particular periods. Their art in making it an excufe for a temporary feparation from their hufbands on any little quarrel. Reckoned very unclean on thofe occafi-ons. The Northern Indians frequently, for the want of firing., are obliged to eat their meat raw.

b 2 Some

Some through necejjity obliged to boil it in veffels made of the rind of the birch-tree, A remarkable difij among thofe people, The young animals always cut out of their dams eaten, and accounted a great delicacy. The parts of generation of all animals eat by the men and boys. Manner of pajjlng their time, and method of killing deer in Summer with hows and arrows Their tents, dogs, fledges, c. Snowfhoes. Their partiality to domeftic uermin. Utrnqft extent of the Northern Indian country. Face of thfi country. Species of fijh, A peculiar kind of mofs ufeful for the fupport of man, Northern Indian method of catching fjh, either with hooks or nets. Ceremgny obferved when two parties of thofe people meet. Diverfions in common ufe. Afingular diforder which attacks fome of thofe people, heir fuperftition with refped to the death of their friends. Ceremony obferved on thofe occafi-ons. Their ideas ofthefirji inhabitants of the world, Noformof religion amongthem. Remarks on that circumftance- The extreme mtjery to which old age is expofed. Their opinion of the Aurora Borealis, 5jc. Some account of Matonabbee, and his fervi-ces to his country, as well as to the Hudfon's Bay company, Page 304

CHAP.

CONTENTS.

CHAP. X.

jn Account of the principal ladriipeds found in the
Northern Parts ofhudforhs Bay. The Buffalo.,

Moofe, Mujk-ox, Deer, and Beaver.-A capital Mijiake cleared up refpeding the We-was-kijh.

Animals with Canine Teeth. The Wolf

Foxes of various colours Lynx, or Wild Cat Polar, or White Bear Black Bear Brown Bear Wolverene Otter- Jackafi Wejack Skunk Pine Martinermine, or Stote.

Animals with cutting Teth. The Mufk Beaver Porcupine Varying Hare American Hare Common Squirrel-Ground Squirrel Mice of various Kinds, and the Cajior Beaver.

The Pinnated adrupeds with jinlike Feet, found in Hudfons Bay, are but three in nu? nber viz. the Warlus, or Sea-Horfe, Seal, and Sea-Unicorn.

The Species of Fifn found in the Salt Water of Hud-fon Bay are alfo few in number; being the Black Whale White Whale Salmon a? id Kepling.

Shell-jifh, and empty Shells of fever al kinds, fotmd on the Sea Coaji near Churchill River.

Frogs of various Jizes and colours; f. lfo a great vari ety of Grubbs, and other Infecls, always found in a frozen fate during Wi? iler, but when expofed to the heat of ajl: w fire, arefoon re-animaied.

xxin ; xxiv CONTENTS.

yin Account of fotne of the principal Birds found in the Northernparts ofhudfons-bay; as well thofe that ori ly migrate there in Sum?? ier as thofe that are known to brave the coldefi Winters: Eagles of various kinds Hawks of varicusfi-z. es and plumage

White or Snowy Owl Grey or moitlcd Owl Cob a-dee- cooch Raven Cinerious Crozu Wood Pecker

Ruffed Groufe Pheafant–Wood Partridge

Willow Partridge R ock Partridgepigeon Red- hreafted Thrufh Grojbeak Snow Bunting

White-crowned Bunting Lapland Finch two forts Lark Tiimeufe Swallow Martin-hopping Crane Brown Crane Bitron Carlow, two forts Jack Snipe Red Godwart Plover Black Guuemet iorthern Diver Black-throated Diver Bed-throated Diver White Gidl–Grey Gull-Black-headpelicangoofander– Swojis of Hwo fpeciescommon Grey Goofe Canada Goofe White or Snow Goofeblue Goofehorned Wavylaughing Goofebarren Goofebrent Goofedunter Goofe- Bean Goofe.

The Species of Water-Fowl ufually called Duck, that refort to thofe Parts annually are in great variety; but thofe that are mofi efteemed are the Mallard Duck Long-tailed Duck, Wigeon and Teal.

Of the Vegetable Produions as far North as Churchill River, particularly the mofi ufeful; fuch as the Berry-bearing Bufhes, c. Goofeberrycranberry Heathberry Dewater- berry– Black Cur-ran s–funiper-berry–Partridge berry-Strawber- ryeye-berryblue-Berryand a fmallfpecies of Hips,

Burridgecoltsfoot Sorrel Dandelion, Wijha-capucca Jackajhey-puck Mofs of various forts Grafs of feveral kinds and Vetches.

The Trees found fo far North near the Sea, con-ftji only of Pines Juniper Small Poplar Bufh-nxillows and Creeping Birch.- Page 358 INTRODUCTION.

FOR many years it was the opinion of all ranks of people, that the Hudfon's Bay Company were averfe to making difcoveries of every kind; and being content with the profits of their fmall capital, as it was then called, did not want to in-creafe their trade. What might have been the ideas of former members of the Company re-fpedling the fir ft part of thefe charges I cannot fay, but I am well aflfured that they, as well as the prefent members, have always been ready to embrace every plaufible plan for extending the trade. As a proof of this affertion, I need only mention the vaft fums of money which they have expended at different times in endeavouring to eftablifh fifheries, though without fuccefs: and the following Journey, together with the various attempts made by Bean, Chriftopher, Johnfton, and Duncan, to find a North Weft paitage, are recent proofs that the prefent members are as de-firous of making difcoveries, as they are of exend-ing their trade.

That air of myftery, and affedation of fecrecy, perhaps, which formerly attended fome of the

Company's.

Company's proceedings in the Bay, might give rife to thofe conjectures; and the unfounded ac-fertions and unjuft afperlions of Dobbs, Ellis, Robfon, Dragge, and the American Traveller, the only Authors that have written on Hudfon's Bay, and who have all, from motives of intereft or revenge, taken a particular pleafure in arraigning the conduct of the Company, without having any real knowledge oi their proceedings, or any experience in their fervice, on which to found their charges, muft have contributed to confirm the public in that opinion. Mod of thofe Writers, however, advance fuch notorious abfurdities, that none except thofe who are already prejudiced againft the Company can give them credit.

Robfon, from his fix years refidence in Hud-fon's Bay and in the Company's fervice, might naturally have been fuppofed to know fomething of the climate and foil immediately round the Factories at which he refided; but the whole of his book is evidently written with prejudice, and dictated by a fpirit of revenge, becaufe his romantic and inconfiftent fchemes were rejected by the Company. Befides, it is well known that Robfon was no more than a tool ip the hand of Mr. Dobbs.

The American Traveller, though a more elegant.

Since the above was written, a Mr. Umfreville has published an ac-i oiuit of Hudfon's Bay, with the fame ill-nature as the former Authors; and for no other reafon than that of being difappointed in fucceeding to a command in the Bay, though there was no vacancy for him.

gant writer, has ftill lefs claim to our indulgence, as his aftertions are a greater tax on our credulity. His faying that he difcovered feveral large lumps of the fined virgin copper, is fuch a palpable falfehood that it needs no refutation. No man, either tnglifli or Indian, ever found a bit of copper in that country to the South of the fe-venty. firft degree of latitude, unlefs it had been accidentally dropped by fome of the far Northern Indians in their way to the Company's Factory. The natives who range over, rather than inhabit, the large track of land which lies to the North of Churchill River, having repeatedly brought famples of copper to the Company's Factory, many of our people conjectured that it was found not far from our fettlements; and as the Indians informed them that the mines were not very diitant from a large river, it was generally fuppofed that this river muft empty itfelf into Hudfon's Bay; as they could by no means think that any fet of people, however, wandering their manner of life might be, could ever tra-verfe fo large a track of country as to pafs the Northern boundary of that Bay, and particularly without the afliftance of water-carriage. The following Journal, however, will fliew how much thefe people have been miftaken, and prove alfo the improbability of putting their favourite Scheme of mining into practice.

American Travellers, page 23.

The accounts of this grand River, which fome have turned into a Strait, together with the fam-ples of copper, were brought to the Company's Factory at Churchill River immediately after its fird eiiabiifhment, in the year one thoufand feven hundred and fifieen; and it does not appear that any attempts were made to difcover either the rivex or mines till the year one thoufand feven hundred and nineteen, when the Company fitted out a fliip, called the Albany Frigate, Captain George Barlow, and a floop, called the Difco- very,

Captain Barlow was Governor at Albany Foit vvlien the French went over land from Canada to befiege it ia the 1704. The Canadians and their Indian guides luikcd in t! le ntighboiiihood of Albany for feveral days before ihey made the attack, and killed many of the cattle that were graz-inc in the maifhes. A faithful Home-Indian, who was on a hunting ex. ct; rf; on, difcovering thofc Grangers and fuppofing them to be enemies, i. Tsmediateiy letiirned to the Fort, and informed the Governor of the cir-cumdance, vvho gave little credit to it. However, every meafure was taken for the defence of the Foit, and orders were given to the Mafterof a floop that lay at fome diflance, to come to the Fcrt with all pofttble expedition on hearing a gun fitcd.

Accordingly, in ih. e middle of the night, or rather in the morning, the French came before the Fort, marched up to the gate, and demanded entrance. Mi. Bailow, who was then on the watch, told them, that the Oovernor was afleep, but he would get the keys immediately. The French hcarrng this, expe. ed no oppofition, and. flocked up to the gte as clofe as they could (land. Bailow took tlie advantage of this opportunity, and inflead of opening the gate, only opened two port holes, where two fix-pounders flood loaded with grape (liot, vhich were inflantly fiied. This Jiloharge killed gieat numbers of the French, and among tjiem the Com-iinndtr, who was an (riiliman.

Such an unexpected reception made the remaindir retire with great precipitation; and the Matter of the flocp hearing the guns, made tlje he it of his way up to the Fort; but fome of the Fitnch who lay concealed uixier the Lcnks of the liver killed him, and all the boat crew.

INTRODUCTION. xxxi very. Captain David Vaughan. The fole com-inand of this expedition, liowever, was given to Mr. James Knight, a man of great experience in the. Company's fervice, who had been many years Governor at the different Factories in the Bay, and Vvho had made the firft fettlement at Churchill River. Notwithftanding the experience Mr. Knight might have had of the Company's bufinefs, and his knowledge of thofe parts of the Bay where he had refided, it cannot be fup-pofed he was well acquarnred with the nature of the buhnefs in which he then engaged, having nothing to direct him but the flender and imperfect accounts which he had received from the Indians, who at that time were little known, and lefs underftood.

Thofe difadvantages, added to his advanced age, he being then near eighty, by no means dif-couraged this bold adventurer; who was fo pre-poffeffed of his fuccefs, and of the great advantage

The French retired from this place with rekiclance; for fome of them weie heard rtioonng in the neighbourhood of the Fort ten days after they were rcpalfed; and one man in paiticular walked up and down the platform leading from the gate of the Fort to the Launch for a whole day. Mr. Ftiuarton, who was thengoverrior at Albany, fpoke to him in French, and offered him kind quarters if he chofe to accept them: hat to thofe propofals he made no reply,-and only (hook his head. Mr. Fusiartoa tiien told him, that unlefs he would refign himfelf up as a prifoner, he would moft aduredly (hoot him; on which tlie man advanced nearer the Fort, and Mr. Fullarton (hot him out of his chamber window. Perhaps the hardlhips this poor man fxpefted to encounter in his return to Canada, made him prefer death; but his refufing to receive quarter from fo humane and generous an enemy as the Engliib, is aftonilhing.

xxxii INTRODUCTION.

tage that would arife from his difcoveries, that he procured, and took with him, fome large iron-bound chefts, to hold gold duft and other valuables, which he fondly flattered himfelf were to be found in thofe parts.

The firft paragraph of the Company's Orders to Mr. Knight on this occafion appears to be as follows:

To Captain James Knight.

"SIR, 4th June, 1719.

"From the experience we have had of your " abilities in the management of our affairs, we " have, upon your application to us, fitted out " the Albany frigate, Captain George Barlow, " and the Difcovery, Captain David Vaughan " Commander, upon a difcovery, to the North-" ward; and to that end have given you power " and authority to acl and do all things relating " to the faid voyage, the navigation of the faid " fhip and floop only excepted; and have given orders and inftrudions to our faid commanders " for that purpofe.

"You are, with the firft opportunity of wind " and weather, to depart from Gravefend on your " intended voyage, and by God's permiflion, to " find out the Straits of Anian, in order to difco-" ver gold and other valuable commodities to the " Northward, c, ifc: INTRODUCTION. xxxiii

Mr. Knight foon left Gravefend, and proceeded on his voyage; but the fliip not returning to England that year, as was expected, it was judged that file had wintered in Hudfon's Bay; and having on board a good ftock of proviiions, a houfe in frame, together with all neceftary mechanics, and a great affortraent of trading goods, little or no thoughts were entertained of their not being in fafety: but as neither fhip nor floop returned to England in the following year, (one thoufand feven hundred and twenty,) the Company Avere much alarmed for their welfare; and, by their fhip which went to Churchill in the year ane thoufand feven hundred and twenty-one, they fent orders for a Hoop called the Whale Bone, John Scroggs Mafter, to go in fearch of them; but the fliip not arriving in Churchill till late in the year, thofe orders could not be put in execution till the fummer following (one thoufand feven hundred and twenty-two).

The North Weft coaft of Hudfon's Bay being little known in thofe days, and Mr. Scroggs finding himfelf greatly embarrafled with fhoals, and rocks, returned to Prince of Wales's Fort without making any certain difcovery refpecling the above fnip or floop; for all the marks he faw among the Efquimaux at Whale Cove fcarce-ly amounted to the fpoils which might have been made from a trifling accident, and confequently could not be confidered as figns of a total fliip-wreck.

The: xxxiv I N T R O D U C T I O f.

The ftrong opinion which then prevailed in Europe refpecting the probability of a North Weft paflage by the way of Hudfon's Bay, made many conjecture that Meffrs. Knight and Barlow had found that paflage, and had gone through it into the South Sea, by the way of California. Many years elapfed without any other convincing proof occurring to the contrary, except that Middleton, Ellis, Bean, Chriftopher, and John-fton, had not been able to find any fuch paflage. And notwithftandins: a floop was annually fent to the Northward on difcovery, and to trade with theefquimaux, it was the iiimmer of one thoufand feven hundred and fixty feven, before we had po-fiiive proofs that poor Mr. Knight and Captain Barlow had been loll: in Hudfon's Bay.

The Company were now carrying on a black whale fiflery, and Marble Ifl-and was made the place of rendezvous not only on account of the commodioufnefs of the harbour, but becaufe it had been obferved that the whales were more plentiful about that ifland than on any other part of the coaft. This being the cafe, the boats, when on the look-out for fifli, had frequent oc-caflon to row clofc to the ifland, by which means they difcovered a new harbour near the Eaft end of it, at the head of which they found guns, anchors, cables, bricks, a fmith's anvil, and many other articles, which the hand of time had not defaced, and which being of no ufe to the natives, or too heavy to be removed by them, had INTRODUCTION. xxxv not been taken from the place in which they were originally laid. The remains of the houfe, though pulled to pieces by the Efquimaux, for the wood and iron, are yet very plain to be feen, as alfo the hulls, or more properly fpeaking, the bottoms of the (hip and floop, which lie funk in about five fathoms water, toward the head of the harbour. The figure-head of the fhip, and alfo the guns, Iffc. were fent home to the Company, and are certain proofs that Meffrs. Knight and Barlow had been loft on that inhofpitable ifland, where neither ftick nor ftump was to be feen, and which lies near fixteen miles from the main land. Indeed the main is little better, being a jumble of barren hills and rocks, deftitute of every kind of herbage except mofs and grafs; and at that part, the woods are feveral hundreds of miles from the fea-fide.

In the Summer of one thoufand feven hundred and fixty-nine, while we were profecuting the fifh-ery, we faw feveral Efquimaux at this new harbour; and perceiving that one or two of them were greatly advanced in years, our curiofity was excited to afk them fome queftions concerning the above fhip and floop, which we were the better enable to do by the affiftance of an Efquimaux, who was then in the Company's fervice as A linguill, and annually failed in one of their velfels in that character. The account which we received from them was full, clear, and unre- c ferved, xxxvi INTRODUCTION.

ferved, and the fum of it was to the following purport:

When the veffels arrived at this place (Marble Illand) it was very late in the Fall, and in getting them into the harbour, the largeft received much damage; but on being fairly in, the Englifli began to build the houfe, their number at that time feeming to be about fifty. As foon as the ice permitted, in the following Summer, (one thou-fand feven hundred and twenty,) the Efquimaux paid them another vifit, by which time the number of the Englifh was greatly reduced, and thofe that were living feemed very unhealthy. According to the account given by the Efquimaux they were then very bufily employed, but about what they could not eafily defcribe, probably in lengthening the long-boat; for at a little diftance from the houfe there is now lying a great quantity of oak chips, which have been moft affuredly made by carpenters.

Sicknefs and famine occafioned fuch havock among the Englifh, that by the letting in of the fecond Winter their number was reduced to twenty. That Winter (one thoufand feven hundred and twenty) fome of the Efquimaux took up their abode on the oppofite fide of the harbour to that on which the Englilh had built their houfes, and frequently fupplied them with fuch provifions as they I have feen the remains of thofe boufcs fereral times; they are on the Weft fide of the harboutj and in all probability will be difcernible for jnany years to come. It INTRODUCTION. xxxvii they had, which chiefly confiftcd of whale's blubber and feal's flefli and train oil. When the Spring advanced, the Efquimaux went to the continent, and on their viiiting Marble llland again, in the Summer of one thoufand feven hundred and twenty-one, they only found five of the Englifli alive, and thofe were in fuch diftrefs for provifions that they eagerly eat the feal's flefh and whale's blubber quite raw, as they purchaf-ed it from the natives. This difordered them fo much, that three of them died in a few days, and the other two, though very weak, made a fhift to bury them. Thofe two furvived many days after the reft, and frequently went to the top of an adjacent rock, and earneftly looked to the South and Eafl, as if in expectation of fome veffels coming to their relief. After continuing there a coniiderable time together, and nothing appearing in fight, they fat down clofe together, and wept bitterly. At length one of the two died, and the other's ftrength was fo far exhauft-ed, that he fell down and died alfo, in attempting to dig a grave for his companion. The fcuus It is rather furprifing, that neither Middleton, Ellis, Chriftopher, Johnfton, not Garbet, who have all of them been at M. irblc Ifland, and fome of them often, ever difcoveted this harbour; particularly the laft- mentioned gentleman, vho alually failed qhiteround tlie Illland in a very fine pleafant day in the Summer oi 1766. B. it this difcovery wasrcfrv-td for a Mr. Joftph Stephens! a man of the kaft merit I ever kt. w, though he then had the command of a veftel called the Succe "s, employed; n the whale-fifliery; and in the year 1769, had the command of the Charlotte given to him, a fine biijj of one hindred tons; when 1 wakl. is mate.

xxxviii INTRODUCTION.

and other large bones of thofe two men are now lying above-ground dole to the houfe. The longeft liver was, according to the Efquimaux account, always employed in working of iron into implements for them; probably he was the armourer, or fmith.

Some Northern Indians who came to trade at Prince of Wales's Fort in the Spring of the year one thoufand feven hundred and fixty-eight, brought farther accounts of the grand river, as it was called, and alfo feveral pieces of copper, as Ianiples of the produce of the mine near itj which determined Mr. Norton, who was then Governor at Churchill, to reprefent it to the Company as an affair worthy of their attention; and as he went that year to England, he had an opportunity of laying all the information he had received before the Board, with his opinion thereon, and the plan which he thought mod likely to fucceed in the difcovery of thofe mines. In confequence of Mr. Norton's reprefentations, the Committee refolved to fend an intelligent perfon by land to obferve the longitude and latitude of the river's mouth, to make a chart of the country he might walk through, with fuch remarks as occurred to him during the Journey; when I was pitched on as a proper perfon to conduct the expedition. By the Ihip that went to Churchill in the Summer of one thoufand feven hundred and fixty-nine, the Company fent out fome aftro-nomical inllruments, very portable, and fit for fuch INTRODUCTION. xxxix fuch obfervations as they required me to make, and at the fame time requefted me to undertake the Journey, promifmg to allow me at my return, a gratuity proportionable to the trouble and fatigue I might undergo in the expedition.

The conditions offered me on this occafion cannot be better expreffed than in the Company's own words, which I have tranfcribed from their private letter to me, dated ajth Ma 1769.

"From the good opinion we entertain of you, and Mr. Norton's recom- mendation, we have agreed to raife your wages to, per annum

"for two years, and have placed you in our Council at Prince of Wales's " Fort; and we ftiould have been ready to advance you to the command of the Charlotte, according to your requeft, if a matter of more immedi. " ate confequence had not intervened.

"Mr. Norton has propofed an inland Journey, far to the North of Chnichill, to promote an extenfion of our trade, as well as for the difcg-" very of a North Weft

Paftage, Copper Mines, c.; and as an undertak- ing of this nature requires the attention of a peifon capable of taking " an obfervation for defermining the longitude and latitude, and alio di-" ftances, and the courfe of rivers and their depths, we have fixed upon " you (efpecially as it isreprefented to us to be your own inclination) to " conduft this Journey, with proper ahiftants.

"We therefore hope you will fecondour expectations in readily perform- ing this fervice, and upon your return we fhall willingly make you any acknowledgment fuitable to your trouble therein.

We highly approve of your going in the Speedwell, to aflifl on the whale filhery lafl year, and heartily wi(h you health and fuccefs in the prefsnt expedition.

We lemain your loving Friends,

"BiuYE Lake, Dep. Gov. " James Winter Lake.

"John Anthonv Merle. Herman Berens.

"Robert Merry. " Joseph Sfurrel.

"Samuel Wegg, "James Fitz Gerald."

The Company had no fooncr perufed my Journals and Charts, than they ordered a handfome fum to he placed to the credit of my account; xl INTRODUCTION.

I did not helitate to comply with the requeft of the Company, and in the November following, when fbme Northern Indians came to trade, Mr. Norton, who was then returned to the command of Prince of Wales's Fort, engaged fuch of them for my guides as he thought were moft likely to anfwer the purpofe; but none of them had been at this grand river, I was fitted out with every thing thought neceltary, and with ammunition to ferve two years. I was to be accompanied by two of the Company's fervants, two of the Home-guard (Southern) Indians, and a fufficient number of Northern Indians to carry and haul m. y baggage, provide for me, V. But for the better and in the two (irft paragraphs of ihcir letter to me, datea I2th May I'i, lliey expieis themfelves ia the following words.

"Mr. Samutll Hearne,

"SIR,

Your letter of the i3th Auguf: lafl gave us the agreeable pleafure t3 " hear of your fafe return to our Fa(ftorv. Your Journal, and the two " charts you lent, fuffitiently convinces us of your veiy judicious re-" marks.

"We have maturely confidered your great affiduity in the various acci-" dents which occuied in your feveral Journies. We hereby return " you our grateful thanks; and to manifcil our obligaiion vie have con-" fented to allow you a gratuity of for thofc fervices."

As a farti. fr proof of the Company's being peile(ftly fatisfied with my conduct while on that Journey, the Committee unanimoully appointed me Chief of Piincc of Wales's Fort in the Summer of 1775; and Mr. Bibye Lake, who was then Governor, and feveral others of the Committee, honoured me with a legular correfpondence as long as they lived.

By the Home-guard Indians we are to onderlland certain of the natives who are immediately employed under the pioteftion of the Company fervants, refide on the plantation, and are employed in hunting for liic Fadlorv, INTRODUCTION. xli ter ftating this arrangement, it will not be im. proper to infert my Inftruclions, which, with fome occafional remarks thereon, will throw much light on the following Journal, and be the beft method of proving how far thofe orders have been complied with, as well as fliew my reafons for negleding fome parts as unneceflary, and the impoffibility of putting other parts of them in execution.

"ORDERS and INSTRUCTIONS for Mr. Samuel Hearne, going on an Expedilion by " Land iawards the Latitude 70 North, in order to gain a Knowledge of the Northern Indiam Country, he. on Behalf of the Ho- nourable Hudfons Bay Co?)ipany, in the Tear " 1769.

Mr. Samuel Hearne, "SIR, Whereas the Honourable Hudfon's Bay " Company have been informed by the report " from Indians, that there is a great probability " of confiderable advantages to be expected from " a better knowledge of their country by us, " than what hitherto has been obtaijied; and as it is the Company's earneft delire to embrace " every circumftance that may tend to the bene-" fit of the faid company, or the Nation at large, " they have requefted you to condud this Expe-" dition; and as you have readily confented to " undertake the prefent Journey, you are here- xlii INTRODUCTION.

by defired to proceed as foon as poflible, with William Ifbefter failor, and Thomas Merriman landfman, as companions, they both being wil-' ling to accompany you; alfo two of the Home-" guard Southern Indians, who are to attend " and ailift you during the Journey; and Cap-" tain Chawchinahaw, his Lieutenant Nabyah, " and fix or eight of the bell Northern Indians we can procure, with a fmall part of their families, are to conduct you, provide for you, and af-" lift you and your companions in every thing that lays in their power, having particular or- ders fo to do.

"2dly, whereas you and your companions are " well fitted-out with every thing we think ne-" ceflary, as alfo a fample of light trading goods; " thele you are to difpofe of by way of prefents (and not by way of trade) to fuch far-off Indi-" ans as you may meet with, and to fmoke your " Calimut of Peace with their leaders, in order to eftablifli a friendfhip with them. You are " alfo to perfuade them as much as poflible from " going to war with each other, to encourage " them to exert themfelves in procuring furrs " and other articles for trade, and to aflure them ' of good payment for them at the Companys Factory.

The Calimut is a longoinamented ftem of a pipe, much in ufe among all the tribes of Indians who know the ufe of tobacco. It is particularly v. red in all cafes of ceremony, either in making war or peace; at all public itt! tainmtucs, orations, c.

INTRODUCTION. xlili

"It is fincerely recommended to you and your " companions to treat the natives with civiiity, " fo as not to give them any room for complaint " or difguft, as they have ftricl orders not to give " you the leaft offence, but are to aid and affifi: " you in any matter you may requeft of them " for the benefit of the undertaking.

"If any Indians you may meet, that are com-" ing to the Fort, fhould be wdjiing to trufl you " with either food or clothing, make your agree-" ment for thofe commodities, and by them fend " me a letter, fpecifying the quantity of each ar- tide, and they fhall be paid according to your agreement. And, according to the Company's orders, you are to correfpond with me, or the " Chief at Prince of "Wales's Fort for the time be-ing, at all opportunities: And as you have ma- thematical inftruments with you, you are to " fend me, or the Chief for the time being, an " account of what latitude and longitude you may be in at fuch and fuch periods, together with the heads of your proceedings; which ac-" counts are to be remitted to the Company by " the return of their fhips.

"3dly, The Indians who are now appointed " your guides, are to condudl you to the borders " of the Athapufcow Indians country, where

Captain

No convenient opportunity oftered during my lafv Journey, except one on the 22d March 1771; and as nothing material had happened during that part of my Journey, I thought there was not any neceflity for lending an extradtof my Journal; I theiefore only fent a Letter to the Governor, informing him of my fituation with refped to latitude and longitude, and feme account of the ufage which I received from the native, c.

f By miflake in iry former Journal and Diaft called Arathapefcow.

xliv INTRODUCTION.

Captaim Matonabbee is to meet you in the Spring of one thoufand feven hundred and fe-" venty, in order to conduct you to a river re- prefented by the Indians to abound with cop- per ore, animals of the furr kind, c. and which is faid to be fo far to the Northward, " that in the middle of the Summer the Sun does " not fet, and is fuppofed by the Indians to emp- ty itfelf into fome ocean. This river, which is called by the Northern Indians Neetha-fan-" fan-dazey, or the Far Off Metal River, you are, " if poffible, to trace to the mouth, and there de-" termine the latitude and longitude as near as " you can; but more particularly fo if you find " it navigable, and that a fettlement can be made " there with any degree of fafety, or benefit to the Company.

"Be careful to obferve what mines are near " the river, what water there is at the rivers mouth, how far the woods are from the fea-" fide, the courfe of the river, the nature of the foil, and the productions of it; and make any other remarks that you may think will be ei-

"ther f This wa5 barely probable, as Matonabbee at that time had not any in- foiniation of this Journey being fet on foot, much lefs had he received oi-(Seis to join n. e at the place and time here appointed; and had we accidentally met, he would by no means have undertaken the Journey without firft going to the Faftory, and tliere making his agreement with the Governor; for no Indian is fond of performing any particular fervice for the Englifh, without firft knowing what is to be his reward. At the fame time, had I taken that rout on my out-fet, it would have carried me fome hundreds of miles out of my road. Sec my Track on the Map in the Winter 1770, and the Spring 1771.

INTRODUCTION. xlv

"ther neceflary or fatisfadory. And if the faid " river be likely to be of any utility, take poitef-" Con of it on behalf of the Hudfons Bay Com-" pany, by cutting your name on feme of the " rocks, as alfo the date of the year, month, life When you attempt to trace this or any other " river, be careful that the Indians are furniflied " with a fufficient number of canoes for trying " the depth of water, the ftrength of the current, c. If by any unforefeen accident or difafter " you fiiould not be able to reach the beforc-men-" tioned river, it is earneftly recommended to you, " if poffible, to know the event of Wager Straitj; " for it isreprefented by the laft difcoverers to ter-" minate

in fmall rivers and lakes. See how far the woods are from the navigable parts of it j
" and whether a fettlement could with any pro-" priety be made there. If this fhould
prove un-

"worthy I vvasnot provided with inftrumcnts for cutting on (lone; but for form-fake,
I cut my name, date of the year, c. on a piece of board that had been one of the Indian's
targets, and placed it in a heapof ftones on a fmall eminence near the entrance of the
river, on tlie South fide.

f There is certainly no harm in makingout all Inrtruiftions in the fulleft manner, yet
it muft be allowed that thofc two parts might have been omitted with great propriety;
for as neither Middleton, Ellis, nor Chriftopher were able to penetrate far enough up
thofe inlets to difcover any kind of herbage except mos and grals, much lefs woods,
it was not likely thofe parts were fo materially altered for the better fince their times,
as to make it worth my while to attempt a farther difcovery of them; and cfpecially
as I had an opportunity, during my fecond Journey, of proving that the woods do not
reach the fea-coa(l by fome hundreds of miles in the parallel of Cheftei field's Inlet.
And as the edge of the woods to the Northward always tends to the Weflward, tiie
diflance mud be greatly increafed in the latitude of Wager Strait. Thofe paits have
long fince been vifitcd by the Company's fsrvants, and aie within the known limits of
their Charter; confefjiuently require no ether form of poocftion.

xlvi INTRODUCTION.

"worthy of notice, you are to take the fame me- thod with Baker's Lake, which is
the head of Bowden's or Chefterfield's Inlet; as alfo with any other rivers you may
meet with; and if likely to be of any utility, you are to take pof-" feflion of them, as
before mentioned, on the behalf of the Honourable Hudfon's Bay Com-" pany. The
draft of Bowden's Inlet and Wager Strait I fend with you, that you may have a bet-"
ter idea of thofe places, in cafe of your vifiting " them.

"4thly, Another material point which is re-" commended to you, is to find out, if
you can, " either by your own travels, or by information " from the Indians, whether
there is a paflage " through this continentf. It will be very ufeful " to clear up this
point, if pollible, in order to. prevent farther doubts from arifmg hereafter

"refpecl-

See the preceding Note.

f The Continent of America is much wider than many people imagine, particularly
Robfon, who thought that the Pacific Ocean was but a few days journey from the
Weft coall of Hudfon's Bay. This, however, is fo far from being the cafe, that when
I was at my greateft Weftern diftance, upward of five hundred miles from Prince of
Wales's Fort, the natives my guides, well knew that many tribes of Indians lay to the
Weft of us, and they knew no end to the land in that direoion; nor have I met with
any Indians, either Northern or Southern, that ever had fcen the fea to the Weftward.
It is, indeed, well known to the intelligent and well-informed part of the Company's
fervants, that an extenfive and numerous, tiibe of Indians, called E-arch-e-thinnews,
whofe country lies far Weft of ariy of the Company's or Canadian fettlements, muft;
have traffic with the Spaniards on the Well fide of the Continent; becaufe fome of the
Indians who formerly traded to York Fort, when at war with thofe people, frc-iiuently

found faddles, bridles, mulkets, and many other articles, in their pofteflion, which were undoubtedly of Spanifh raanufadory.

I have INTRODUCTION. xlvii

"refpe5ling a paffage out of Hudfon's Bay into " the Weftern Ocean, as hath lately been repre- fented by the American Traveller. The particu-" lars of thofe remarks you are to infert in your " Journal, to be remitted home to the Company.

"If you fliould want any fupplies of ammuniti-" on, or other neceffaries, difpatch fome trufty " Indians to the Fort with a letter, fpecifying the " quantity of each article, and appoint a place " for the faid Indians to meet you again.

"When on your return, if at a proper time of " the year, and you fliould be near any of the " harbours that are frequented by the brigantine " Charlotte, or the floop Churchill, during their " voyage to the Northward, and you fliould chufe " to return in one of them, you are defired to " make frequent fmokes as you approach thofe " harbours, and they will endeavour to receive " you by making fmokes in anfwer to yours; " and as one thoufand feven hundred and feven-" ty-one will probably be the year in which you " will return, the Mailers of thofe veffels at that

"period I have feen fcveral Indians who have been fo far Weft as to crofs the top of that immenfe chain of mountains which run from North to South of the continent of America. Beyond thofe mountains all rivers lun to the Weftward. I muft here cbferve, that all the Indians I ever heard lelate their excutfions in that country, had invaiiably got fo far to the South, that they did not experience any Winter, nor the lead appeatancc of either froft ot fnow, though fometimts they have been abfent eighteen months, or two years.

As to a paflage through tlie continent of America by the way of Hudfon's Bay, it has fo long been exploded, notwithftanding what Mt Ellis ha? urged in its favour, and the place it has found in the vifionary Map of the American Traveller, that any comment on it would be quite unneceflary. My huitudeonly will be afufficient proof that no fuch paltage isin exillence- xlviii INTRODUCTION.

"period hall have particular orders on that head " It will be pleafing to hear by the firft oppor-" tunity, in what latitude and longitude you meet " the Leader Matonabbee, and how far bethinks = it is to the Coppermine River, as alfo the pro- bable time it may take before you can return. " But in cafe any thing ftiould prevent the faid " Leader from joining you, according to expecla-" tion, you are then to procure the beft Indians " you can for your guides, and either add to, or ' diminifh, your number, as you may from time to time think moft neceffary for the good of " the expedition.

"So I conclude, wifliing you and your compa-" nions a continuance of health, together with a " profperous Journey, and a happy return in " fafety. Amen.

"MOSES NORTON, Governor.

Dated at Prince of Wales's Fort, Churchill River, Hudfon's Bay, North America, November 6lli, 769-"

Ifbefter and Merriman, mentioned in my In-ftruaions, adually accompanied me during my firft fliort attempt; but the Indians knowing them to be but common men, ufed them fo indifferently, particularly in fcarce times, that I was under fome appre-henfions of their being ftarved to death, and 1 thought myfelf exceedingly happy when

I got them fafe back to the Factory. This extraordinary behaviour of the Indians made me determine not to take any Europeans with me on niy two lafl expeditions.

With regard to that part of my Inftruclions which directs me to obferve the nature of the foil, INTRODUCTION. xlix the produftions thereof, c. it muft be obferved, that during the whole time of my abfence from the Fort, I was invariably confined to ftony hills and barren plains all the Summer, and before we approached the woods in the Fall of the year, the ground was always covered with fnow to a confi-derable depth; fo that I never had an opportunity of feeing any of the fmall plants and flirubs to the Weftward. But from appearances, and the flow and dwarfy growth of the woods, c. (except in the Athapufcow country,) there is undoubtedly a greater fcarcity of vegetable productions than at the Company's moft Northern Settlement; and to the Eaftward of the woods, on the barren grounds, whether hills or vallies, there is a total want of herbage except mofs, on which the deer feed; a hw dwarf willows creep among the mofs; fome wifh-a-capucca and a little grsfs may be feen here and there, but the latter is fcarcely fufecient to ferve the geefe and other birds of paffage during their fliortftayin thofe parts, though they are always in a ftate of migration ex-cept when they arebreeding andina moultingftate. In confequence of my complying with the Company's requeft, and undertaking this Journey, it is natural to fuppofe that every neceflary arrangement was made for the eafier keeping of my reckoning, r. under the many inconveniences I muft be unavoidably obliged to labour in fuch an expedition. I drew a Map on a large Ikin of parch-ment, that contained twelve degrees of latitude North, and thirty degrees of lonjritude Weft, of Churchill Factory, and flecched all the Weft coaft INTRODUCTION.

coaft of the Bay on it, but left the interior parts blank, to be filled up during my Journey. 1 alfo prepared detached pieces on a much larger fcale for every degree of latitude and longitude contained in the large Map On thofe detached pieces 1 pricked off my daily courfes and diftance, and entered all lakes and rivers, c. that I met with; endeavouring, by a ftricl enquiry of the natives, to find out the communication of one river with another, as alfo their connections with the many lakes with which that country abounds: and when opportunity offered, having corrected them by obfervations, 1 entered them in the gene-ral Map.- Thefe and feveral other neceffary preparations, for the eafier, readier and more correctly keeping my Journal and Chart, were alfo adopted; but as to myfelf, little was required to be done, as the nature of traveuing long journies in thofe countries will never admit of carrying even the moft common article of clothing; fo that the traveller is obliged to depend on the country he paffes through, for that article, as well as for provifions. Ammunition, ufeful ironwork, fome tobacco, a few knives, and other in-difpenfable articles, make a fufficient load for any one to carry that is going a journey likely to laft twenty months, or two years. As that was the cafe, I only took the fnirt and clothes I then had on, one fpare coat, a pair of drawers, and as mucli cloth as would make me two or three pair of Indian ftockings, which, together with a blanket for bedding, compofed the whole of my flock of clothing. A JOUR-

Alyo. TSXHlsjeSr A"j."W i JftkIPTO: f 'JL.1.   SS IFOlitim B. mb S OivSB. OirineA3v3KKICAlbfii:4Jlatii777

JOURNEY

NORTHERN OCEAN.

rranfaclions from my leaving Prince of Wales's Fort on my firft expedition, till our arrival there again.

Set off from the Fort. Arrhe at Fo'Co-ree-kif-co River, One of the Northern Indians defert. Crof Seal River, and walk on the barren grounds. Receive wrong information concerning the difiance of the woods. Weather begins to be very cold, proviji-ons all expended and nothing to be got.-Strike to the Weftward, arrive at the woods, and kill three deer. Set forward in the North Weft quarter, fee the tracks of mufk-oxen and deer, but killed none. Very fjort of provifions. Chawchinahaw wants lis to return. Neither he? ior his crew contribute to our maintenance. Fie influences feveral of the Indians to defert. Chawchinahavj and all his crew B leave leave us,- Begin our return to the factory; kill a few partridges ihefrfi meal we had had for fever al days. Villany of one of the home Indians and his wife, who was a Northern Indian woman, Arrive at Seal River kill two deer; partridges plenty. Meet a flrange Northern Indian, accompany him to his tent, ufage received there; my Indians afjifi in killing foine heaver. Proceed toward home, and arrive at the Fort.

AVING made every neceflary arrangement for rny departure on the fixth of November, I took leave of the Governor, and my other friends, at Prince of Wales's Fort, and began my journey, under the falute of feven cannon.

The weather at that time being very mild, made it but indifferent hauling, and all my crew being heavy laden, occafioned us to make but fhort days journeys; however, on the eighth, 8th. we croffed the North branch of Po-co-ree-kif-co River, and that night put up in a fmail tuft of woods, which is between it and Seal River. In the night, one of the Northern Indians defert-ed; and as all the reft of my crew were heavy laden, I was under the ncceffity of hauling the fledge he had left, which however was not very heavy, as it fcarccly exceeded iixty pounds.

The weather ftill continued very line and plea-fant: vve direded our courfe to the Weft North

Weft,

The colder the weather is, the eafier the flejges fiide over the fnow.

Weft, and early in the day crofled Seal River. In, 5 the courfe of this day's journey we met feveral Northern Indians, who were going to the fadlory th. with furs and venifon; and as we had not killed any deer from our leaving the Fort, I got feveral joints of venifon from thofe ftrangers, and gave them a note on the Governor for payment, which feemed perfectly agreeable to all parties.

When on the North Weft fide of Seal River, I afked Captain Chavchinahaw the diftance, and probable time it would take, before we could reach the main woods; which he altured me would not exceed four or five days journey. This put both mie and my companions in good fpirits, and we continued our courfe between the Weft by North and North Weft, in daily expectation of arriving at thofe woods, which wc were told would furnifh us with every thing the country affords. Thefe accounts were fo far from being true, that after we had walked double the time here mentioned, no figns of woods were to befeen in the direction we were then fleering; but we had frequently feen the looming of woods to the South Weft.

The cold being now very intenfe, our fmall ftock of Englifii provifions all expended, and not theleaft thing to be got on the bleak hills we had for fome time been walking on, it became neceflary to ftrike miore to the Weftward, which we accordmgly did, and the next evenmg arrived at fome fmall patches of low fcrubby woods, B 2 where where we favv the tracks of feveral deer, and killed a few partridges. The road we had tra-verfed for many days before, was in general fo rough and flony, that our fledges were daily breaking; and to add to the inconveniency, the land was fo barren, as not to afford us materials for repairing them: but the few woods we now fell in with, amply fupplied us with necef-faries for thofe repairs; and as we were then enabled each night to pitch proper tents, our lodging was much more comfortable than it had been for many nights before, while we were on the barren grounds, where, in general, we thought ourfelves well off if we could fcrape together as many flirubs as would make a fire; but it was fcarcely ever in our power to make any other defence againft the weather, than by digging a hole in the fnow down to' the mofs, wrapping ourfelves up in our clothing, and lying down in it, with our fledges fet up edgeways to windward. ift. On the twenty-firfl:, we did not move; fo the Indian men went a hunting, and the women cut holes in the ice and caught a few HQi in a fmall lake, by the fide of which we had pitched our tents. At night the men returned with fome venifon, having killed three deer, which was without doubt very acceptable; but our number being great, and the Indians having fuch enormous ftomachs, very little was left but fragments after the two or three firfl: good meals. Having devoured devoured the three deer, and given forae necef- g fary repairs to our fledges and fnovv flioes, which c-v-

J 1 November.

only took one day, we again proceeded on to- zbih. ward the North Weft by Weft and Weft North Weft, through low fcrubby pines, intermixed with fome dwarf larch, which is commonly called juniper in Hudfon's Bay. In our road we frequently faw the tracks of deer, and many mufk-oxen, as they are called there; but none of my companions were fo fortunate as to kill any of them: fo that a few partridges were all we could get to live on, and thofe were fo fcarce, that we feldom could kill as many as would amount to half a bird a day for each man; which, confidering we had nothing elfe for the twenty-four hours, was in reality next to nothing.

By this time I found that Captain Chawchin-ahaw had not the profperity of the undertaking at heart; he often painted the difficulties in the vorft colours, took every method to difhearten me and my European companions, and feveral times hinted his defire of our returning back to the factory: but finding I was determined to proceed, he took fuch methods as he thought would be moft likely to anfwer his end; one of which was, that of not adminiftering toward our fupport; fo that we were a confiderable time without any other fubfiftence, but what our two home-guard (Southern) Indians procured, and the little that I and the two European men could kill; which was very difproportionate to j5g our wants, as we had to provide for feveral wo- r–J men and children who were with m.

Chawchinahaw finding that this kind of treatment was not likely to complete his defign, and that we were not to be ftarved into compliance, at length influenced feveral of the bell: Nojthern Indians to defert in the night, who took with them feveral bags of my ammunition, fome pieces of iron work, fuch as hatchets, ice chiftels, files c. as well as feveral other ufeful articles. 30th. When I became acquainted with this piece of villany, I alked Chawchinahaw the reafon of fuch behaviour. To which he anfwered, that he knew nothing of the affair: but as that was the cafe, it would not be prudent, he faid, for us to proceed any farther; adding, that he and all the reft of his countrymen were going to ftrike off another way, in order to join the remainder of their wives and families: and after giving us a fhort account which way to fteer our courfe for the neareft part of Seal River, which he faid would be out bed way homeward, he and his crew delivered me moft of the things which they had in charge, packed up their awls, and fet out toward the South Weft, making the woods ring with their laughter, and left us to confider of our unhappy lituation, near two hundred miles from Prince of Wales's Fort, all heavily laden, and our ftrength and fpirits greatly reduced by hunger and fatigue.

Our fituation at that time, though very alarming ing, would not permit us to fpend much time in 1769. reflection; fo we loaded our fledges to the beft J – November.

advantage, (but were obliged to throw away fome bags of fhot and ball,) and immediately iet out on our return. In the courfe of the day's walk we were fortunate enough to kill feveral partridges, for which we were all very thankful, as it was the firft meal we had had for feveral days: indeed, for the five preceding days we. had not killed as much as amounted to half a partridge for each man; and fome days had not a Angle mouthful. While we were is this diflrefs, the Northern Indians were by no means in want; for as they always walked foremoft, they had ten times the chance to kill partridges, rabbits, or any other thing vhich was to be met with, than we had. Befides this advantage, they had great flocks of flour, oatmeal, and other Englifli pro-viflons, which they had embezzled out of my ftockduring the early part of the journey; and as one of my home Indians, called Mackachy, and his wife, who is a Northern Indian woman, always rcforted to the Northern Indians tents, where they got amply fupplied with provilions when neither I nor my men had a fmgle mouthful, I have great reafon to fufpecl they had a principal hand in the embezzlement: indeed, both the man and his wife were capable of committing any crime, however diabolical.

This day we had fine pleafant weather for the December. feafon of the year: we fet out early in the morning.

1760. K- nd arrived the fame day at Seal River, v-.,,-. along which we continued our courfe for fe- Tti? veral days. In our way we killed plenty of partridges, and faw many deer; but the weather was fo remarkably ferene that the Indians only killed two of the latter. By this time game was become fo plentiful, that all apprehenlions of ftarv-ing were laid afide; and though we were heavily laden, and travelled pretty good days journeys, yet as our fpirits were good, our ftrength gradually returned, 5th. In our courfe down Seal River we met a ftran- ger, a Northern Indian, on a hunting excuriion; and though he had not met with any fuccefs that day, yet he kindly invited us to his tent, faying he had plenty of venifon at my fervice; and told the Soutliern Indians, that as there were two or three beaver houfes near his tent, he fhould be glad of their afliftance in taking them, for there was only one man and three women at the tent.

Though we were at tliat time far from being in want of provifions, yet we accepted his offer, andfet off with our new guide for his tent, which, by a comparative diftance, he told us, was not above five miles from the place vhere we met him, but we found it to be nearer fifteen; fo that it was the middle of the night before we arrived at ir. When we drew near the tent, the ufual fjgnal for the approach of ftrangers was given j by firing a gun or two, vhich was immediate- ly anfwered by the man at the tent. On our 1760. arrival at the door, the good man of the houfe v.v-vj came out, fhook me by the hand, and welcomed us to his tent; but as it was too fmall to contain us all, he ordered his women to afiift us in pitching our tent; and in the mean time invited m, c and as many of my crew as his little habitation could contain, and reraled us with the bed in the houfe. The pipe went round pretty brifldy, and the con-verfation naturally turned on the treatment we had received from Chawchinahaw and his gang; which was always anfwered by our hofl with, "Ah! if I had been there, it fhould not have been " fo!" when, notwithftanding his hofpitality on the prefent occafion, he would moft affuredly have acled the fame part as the others had done, if he had been of the party.

Having refrefhed ourfelves with a plentiful fup-per, we took leave of our hoft for a while, and retired to our tent; but not without being made thoroughly fenfible that many things would be expecled from me, before I finally left them.

Early in the morning, my Indians altifted us in-taking the beaver houfes already mentioned j but the houfes being fmall, and fome of the beavers efcaping, they only killed fix, all of which were cooked the fame night, and voracioufly devoured under the denomination of afcad. I alfo received from the Indians feveral joints of venifon, to the amount of at leaft two deer; but notwith-llanding I was to pay for the whole, I found that Mackachy and his wife got all the prime parts of

December.

io A JOURNEY TO THE the meat; and on my mentioning it to them, there was fo much clanfhip among them, that they preferred making a prefent of it to Macka-chy, to felling it to me at double the price for which venifon fells in thofe parts: a fufficient proof of the fmgular advantage which a native of this country has over an Englifhman, when at fuch a diftance from the Company's Factories as to depend entirely on them for fubliftence.

7tii. Thinking I had made my ftay here long enough, I gave orders to prepare for our departure; and as I had purchafed plenty of meat for prefent ufe while we were at this tent, fo I like wife procured fuch a fupply to carry with us, as was likely to laft us to the Fort.

Stiu Early in the morning we took a final leave of our hoft, and proceeded on our journey homewards. One of the ftrangers accompanied us, for which at firft I could not fee his motive; but foon after our arrival at the Faclory, I found that the purport of his viiit was to be paid for the meat, faid to be given gratis to Mackachy while we were at his tent. The weather continued very fine, but extremely cold; and during this part of my journey nothing material happened, till we arrived fafe at Prince of Wales's Fort on the eleventh of December, to my own great mortifica-tino, and to the no fmall furprife of the Governor, who had placed great confidence in the abilities and condu6l of Chavchinahaw.

CHAP.

NORTHERN OCEAN. n

CHAP. II.

Tranfaclions from our arrival at the Facflory, to my leaving it again, and during the firft part of my fecond journey, till I had the misfortune to break the quadrant.

Tranfaclions at the Fasfory, Proceed on my fecond journey. Arrive at Seal River. Deer plentiful forfome time. Method of anglitigfijh under the ice. Set our fifhing nets. Method of fetting nets under the ice.-My guide propofes to flay till the geefe began to fly; his reafons accepted. Fitch our tent in the hefl manner. Method of pitching a tent in winter. Fifh plentiful for fome time; grow very fcarce; in great want of provifions. Manner of employing my time, My guide killed two deer. Move to the place they were lying at; there killfe-veral more deer, and three beavers. Soon in want of provfions again. Many Indians join us from the Wefiward. We begin to move towards the barren ground Arrive at She-ihan-nee, and there fuffer great difirefs for want of provifions. Indians kill twofwans and three geefe. Geefe and other birds of paffageplentiful. Leave She-ihan-nee, and arrive at Beralzone. One of my companions guns burlsy andhatters his left hand. Leave Beralzofie, and get on the barren ground, clear of all woods. Throw away away ourjledges andfnowjhoes. Each peron takes a load on his back; 7ny part of the luggage. Ex-pofed to many hardjJjips. Several days without viduals. Indians kill three 7imjk oxen, but for wa7it of fire are obliged to eat the meat raw. Fine weather returns; make afire; effects oflongfafling; flay a day or two to dry fome meat in the fun. Proceed to the Northward, and arrive at Cathawhac-haga; there find fome tents of Indians. A Northern leader called Keelchies meets us; fend a letter by him to the Governor. Tranfaclions at Cat haw-hachaga; leave it, and proceed to the Northward. Meet feveral Indians. My guide not willifig to proceed; his reafons for it. Many more Indians join us. Arrive at Doobaunt Whoie River, Mangier of ferrying over rivers in the Northern Indian canoes. No rivers in thofe parts in a ufeful diredi-onfor the natives. Had nearly Iqi the quadrant and all the powder. Some refiedions on our fituation, and the condud of the Indians. Find the quadrant and part of the powder. Obferve for the latitude. adrant broke. Refolve to return again to the Fadory.

DURING my abfence from Prince of Wales's Fort on my former journey, feveral Efebruary. jsjqrfnem Indians arrived in great diftrefs at the Fadory, and were employed in (hooting partridges for the ufe of our people at the Fort. One of thofe Indians called Conne-e-quefe faid, he had been very near to the famous river I was engaged to go in queft of. Accordingly Mr. Norton engaged hini and two other Northern Indians to accompany me on this fecond attempt; but to avoid all incumbrances as much as poffible, it was thought advifable not to take any women, that the Indians might have fewer to provide for. I would not permit any European to go with me, but two of the home guard (Southern) Indian men were to accompany me as before. Indeed the Indians, both Northern and Southern, paid fo little attention to Ifbefter and Merriman on my former journey, particularly in times of fcarcity, that I was determined not to take them with me in future; though the former was very defirous to accompany me again, and was well calculated to encounter the hardfhips of fuch an undertaking. Merriman was quite fick of fuch excurfions, and fo far from offering his fervice a fecond time, feemed to be very thankful that he was once more arrived in fafety among his friends; for before he got to the Factory he had contracted a moft violent cold.

Having come to the above refolutions, and finally determined on the number of Indians that were to accompany us, we were again fitted out with a large fupply of ammunition, and as many other ufeful articles as we could conveniently take with

This was a propofal of the Governor's, though he well knew we could not do without their afliftance, both for hauling our baggage, as well as tlrcffing fkins for clothing, pitching out tent, getting filing, c.

j-Q US, together with a fmall fample of light trading V goods, for prefents to the Indians, as before.

My inftruclions on this occafion amounted to no more than an order to proceed as faft as pof-fible; and for my conduct during the journey, I was referred to my former inftruclions of November 6th, 1769.

Every thing being in readinefs for our depar-, ture, on the twenty-third of February I began my fecond journey, accompanied by three Northern Indians and two of the home-guard (Southern) Indians. I took particular care, however, that Mackachy, though an excellent hunter, fliould net be of our party; as he had proved himfelf, during my former journey, to be a fly artful villain.

The fnow at this time was fo deep on the top of the rampartsj that few of the cannon were to be feen, other wife the Governor would have fa-iuted me at my departure, as before; but as thofe honours could not poflibly be of any fervice to my expedition, I readily relinquifhed every thing of the kind; and in lieu of it, the Governor, officers, and people, infilled on giving me three cheers.

After leaving the Faory, we continued our courfe in much the fame direction as in my former journey, till we arrived at Seal River; when, inftead of croffing it, and walking on the barren grounds as before, we followed the courfe of the river, except in two particular places, where the bends tended fo much to the South, that by crolting two necks of land not more than five or fix miles wide, we faved the walking of near twenty-miles each time, and ftill came to the main river 8th. again.

The weather had been fo remarkably boifterous and changeable, that we were frequently obliged to continue two or three nights in the fame place. To make up for this inconveniency, deer were fo plentiful for the iirft eight or ten days, that the Indians killed as many as was neceffary; but we were all fo heavy laden that we could not pollibly take much of the meat with us. This I foon perceived to be a great evil, which expofed us to fuch frequent inconveniences, that in cafe of not killing any thing for three or four days together, we were in great want of provifions; we feldom, however, went to bed entirely fuppcrlefs till the eighth of March; when though we had only walked about eight miles that morning, and expended all the remainder of the day in hunting, we could not produce a fmgle thing at night, not even a partridge! nor had we difcerned the track of any thing that day, which was likely to afford us hopes of better fuccefs in the morning. This being the cafe, we prepared fome hooks and lines ready to angle for fifh, as our tent was then by the fide of a lake belonging to Seal River, which feemed by its Situation to aflford fome profpect of fuccefs.

Early in the morning we took down our tent, and moved about five miles to the Wefl by South, !9th.

2clh.

A JOURNKY TO THE to a part of the lake that feemed more commodious for fifhinc than that where we had been the night before. As foon as we arrived at this place, fome were immediately employed cutting holes in the ice, while others pitched the tent, got firewood, Sec.; after which, for it was early in the morning, thofe who pitched the tent went a hunting, and at night one of them returned with a porcupine, while thofe who were angling caught feveral fine trout, which aflforded us a plentiful fupper, and we had fome trifle left for breakfaft.

Angling for fifh under the ice in winter requires no other procefs, than cutting round holes in the ice from one to two feet diameter, and letting down a baited hook, which is always kept in motion, not only to prevent the water from freezing fo foon as it would do if fuffered to remain quite flill, but becaufe it is found at the fame time to be a great means of alluring the fifh to the hole; for it is always obferved that the nfh in thofe parts will take a bait which is in motion, much fooner than one that is at reft.

Early in the morning we again purfued our angling, and all the forenoon being expended without any fuccefs, we took down our tent and pitched it again about eight miles farther to the Weflvvard, on the fame lake, where we cut more holes in the ice for angling, and that night caught feveral fine pike. The next day we moved about five miles to the South Weft, down a fmall river where we pitched our tent; and having fet four fifhing iifiiing nets, in the courfe of the day we caught many fine fifh, particularly pike, trout, tittymeg, and a coarfe kind of fih known in Hiidfon's Bay by the name of Methy.

To fet a net under the ice, it is firft neceffary to afcertain its exact: length, by ftretching it out upon the ice neir the part propofed for fetting it. This being done, a number of round holes are cut in the ice, at ten or twelve feet diftance from each other, and as many in number as will be fufkcient to ftretch the net at its full length. A line is then, paffed under the ice, by means of a long light pole, which is firft introduced at one of the end holes, and, by means of two forked fticks, this pole is eafily conducted, or paited from one hole to another, under the ice, till it arrives at the laft. The pole is then taken out, and both ends of the line being properly fecured, is always ready for ufe. The net is made fall to one end of the line by one perfon, and hauled under the ice by a fecond; a large ftone is tied to each of the lower corners, which ferves to keep the net expanded, and prevents itrifingfrom the bottom with every waft of the current. The Europeans fettled in Hudfon's Bay proceed much in the fame manner, though they in general take much more pains; but the above method is found quite fufecient by the Indians.

In order to fearch a net thus fet, the two end G holes

The Methy arc generally caught with a hock; and the bed time for that fijort is in the night; aad if tlie night be dark, the better.

March.

holes only are opened; the line is veered away by one perfon, and the net hauled from under the ice by another; after all the fifli are taken out, the net is eafily hauled back to its former ftation, and there fecured as before. 2Tft As this place feemed likely to afford us a con- flant fupply of fifh, my guide propofed to flay here till the geefe began to fly, which in thofe Northern parts is feldom before the middle of May. His reafons for fo doing feemed well founded: "The weather, he faid, is at this time too cold to walk on the barren grounds, and " the woods from this part lead fo much to the " Weftward, that were we to continue travelling in any tolerable fhelter, our courfe would not " be better than Weft South Weft, which would " only be going out of our way; whereas, if we " fhould remain here till the weather permit us " to walk due North, over the barren grounds, " we fhall then in one month get farther ad-" vanced on our journey, than if we were to " continue travelling all the remainder of the " winter in the fweep of the woods."

Thefe reafons appeared to me very judicious, and as the plan feemed likely to be attended with little trouble, it met with my entire approbation. That being the cafe, we took additional pains in building our tent, and made it as comm. odiousas the materials and iituation would admit.

To pitch an Indian's tent in winter, it is firft neceilary to fearch for a level piece of dry ground; which which cannot be afcertalned but by thrufting a flick through the fnow down to the ground, all over the propofed part. When a convenient fpot is found, the fnow is then cleared away in a circular form to the very mofs; and when it is propofed to remain more than a night or two in one place, the mofs is alfo cut up and removed, as it is very Hable when dry to take fire, and occafion much trouble to the inhabitants. A quantity of poles are then procured, which are generally proportioned both in number and length to the fize of the tent cloth, and the number of perfons it is intended to contain. If one of the poles fhould not happen to be forked, two of them are tied together near the top, then raifed erect, and their buts or lower ends extended as wide as the propofed diameter of the tent; the other poles are then fet round at equal diftances from each other, and in fuch order, that their lower ends form a complete circle, which gives boundaries to the tent on all fides: the tent cloth is then faftened to a light pole, which is always raifed up and put round the poles from the weather fide, fo that the two edges that lap over and form the door are always to the leeward. It muft be underftood that this method is only in ufe when the Indians are moving from place to place every day; for when they intend to continue any time in one place, they always make the door of their tent to face the South.

The tent cloth is ufually of thin Moofe leather, C 2 drelted drefled and made by the Indians, and in fhape It nearly refembles a fan-mount inverted; fo that when the largeft curve inclofes the bottom of the poles, the fmauer one is always fufficient to cover the top; except a hole, which is defignedly left open to ferve the double purpofe of chimney and window.

The fire is always made on the ground in the center, and the remainder of the floor, or bottom of the tent, is covered all over with fmall branches of the pine tree, which ferve both for feats and beds, A quantity of pine tops and branches are laid round the bottom of the poles on the out-fide, over which the eves of the tent is fl: aked down;. a quantity of fnow is then packed over all, which excludes great part of the external air, and contributes greatly to the warmth within. The tent here defcribed is fuch as is made ufe of by the Southern Indians, and the fame with which 1 was furnifhed at the Faclory; for that made ufe of by the Northern Indians is made of different materials, and is of a quite different ihape, as fhall be defcribed hereafter.

The fituation of our tent at this time was truly pleafant, particularly for a fpring refidence; being on a fmall elevated point, which commanded an extenfive profpec?:

over a large lake, the Hiores of which abounded with wood of different kinds, fuch as pine, larch, birch, and poplar; and in many places was beautifully contrafted with a variety of high hills, that lliewed their fnowy fummits

March.

NORTHERN OCEAN. an lummits above the talleft woods. About two 1770. hundred yards from the tent was a fall, or rapid, which the fwiftnefs of the current prevents from freezing in the coldell winters. At the bottom of this fall, which empties itfelf into the above lake, was a fine (heet of open water near a mile in length, and at leaft half a mile in breadth; by the margin of which ve had our fifhing nets fet, all in open view from the tent.

The remaining part of this month paittd on without any interruption, or material occurrence, to difturb our repofe, worth relating: our fih-ing nets provided us with daily food, and the Indians had too much philofophy about them to give themfelves much additional trouble; for during the whole time not one of them offered to look for a partridge, or any thing elfe which could yield a change of diet.

As the time may now be fuppofed to have Iain heavy on my hands, it may not be invproper to inform the reader how I employed it. In the firft place, I embraced every favourable opportunity of obferving the latitude of the place, the mean of which was 58" 46 30" North; and the longitude by account was 5 i Weft, from Prince of Wales's Fort. I then corresfled my reckoning from my laft obfervation; brought up my jour-nal, and filled up my chart, to the place of our refidence. I built alfo fome traps, and caught a iz" martins; and by way of faving my ammunition, fet fome fnares for partridges. The former 1770. performed by means of a few logs, fo arranged-nj that when the martin attempts to take away the " bait laid for him, he with very little ftruggle pulls down a fmall poft that fupports the whole weight of the trap; when, if the animal be not killed by the weight of the logs, he is confined till he be frozen to death, or killed by the hunter going his rounds.

To fnare partridges requires no other procefs than making a few litrle hedges acrofs a creek, or a fewfhort hedges projecting at right angles from the fide of an ifland of willows, which thofe birds are found to frequent. Several openings muft be left in each hedge, to admit the birds to pafs through, and in each of them a fnare muft be fet; fo that when the partridges are hopping along the edge of the willows to feed, which is their ufual cuftom, fome of them foon get into the fnares, where they are confined till they are taken out. I have caught from three to ten partridges in a day by this fimple contrivance; which requires no farther attendance than going round them night and morning.

I have already obferved that nothing material jj happened to diflurb our repofe till the firft of April, vvhen to our great furprife the fioiing nets did not afford us a fin2: le fifh. Ihougrh fome of the preceding days had been pretty fuccefsful, yet my companions, like true Indians, feldom went to fleep till they had cleared the tent of every article of provifion. As nothing was to be caught caught in the nets, we all went out to angle; but in this we were equally unfuccefsful, as we could not procure one fi(h the whole day. This fudden change of circumftances alarmed one of my companions fo much, that he began to think of refuming the ufe of his gun, after having laid it by for near a month.

Early in the morning we arofe; when my guide Conne-e-quefe went a hunting, and the reft attended the nets and hooks near home; but all with fuch bad fuccefs, that we could not procur enough in one day to ferve two men for a fuppcr. This, inftead of awakening the reft of my companions, fent them to fleep; and fcarcely any of them had the prudence to look at the filhing nets, though they were not more than two or three hundred yards from the tent door.

My guide, who was a fteady man, and an excellent hunter, having for many years been ac-cuftomed to provide for a large family, feemed by far the moft induftrious of all my crew; he clofely purfued his hunting for feveral days, and feldom returned to the tent till after dark, while thofe at the tent paffed moft of their time in fmoking and iieeping.

Several days pafled without any figns of relief, till the loth, when my guide continued out Ion- loth. ger than ordinary, which made us conjedlure that he had met with ftrangers, or feen fome deer, or other game, which occafioned his delay. We all therefore lay down to ileep, having had but little refrelh- refrefhment for the three preceding days, except a pipe of tobacco and a draught of water; even partridges had become fo fcarce that not one was to be got; the heavy thaws had driven them all out towards the barren grounds. About midnight, to our great joy, our hunter arrived, and brouoht with him the blood and fra2; ments of two deer that he had killed. This unexpected fuccefs foon roufed the fleepers, who, in an in-ftant were bufily employed in cooking a large Jietrle of broth, made with the blood, and fome fat and fcraps of meat Hired fmall, boiled in it. This might be reckoned a dainty dilli at any time, but was more particularly ih in our prefent almoft famiflied condition.

After partaking of this refrefhment, we refum-ed our reft, and early in the morning fet out in a body for the place where the deer were lying. As we intended to make our ftay but (liort, we left our tent ftanding, containing all our baggage. On our arrival at the place of deftination, luh. fome were immediately employed in making a hut or barrocado, with young pine trees; while one m. an ikinned the deer, the remainder went a hunting, and in the afternoon returned to the hut, after having killed two deer.

Several days were now fpent in feafting and gluttony; during which the Indians killed five more deer and three fine beavers; finding at laft, however, that there was little profpett of procuring either more deer or beavers, we determined mined to return to our tent, with the remains of what we had already obtained.

The fiefli of thefe deer, though none of the largetl, might with frugality have ferved our fmall number, (being only fix) for fome time; but my companions, Uke other Indians, feafted day and night while it lafted; and were fo indolent and unthinking, as not to attend properly to the fifhing-nets; fo that many fine fiih, which had been entangled in the nets, were entirely fpoiled, and in about twelve or fourteen days we were nearly in as great diftrefs for provilions as ever.

During the courfe of our long inaftivity, Saw-fop-o-kifliac, commonly called Softop, my principal Southern Indian, as he was cutting fome birch for fpoons, diihes, and other neceflary houfehold furniture, had the misfortune to cue his leg in fuch a manner as to be incapable of walking; and the other Southern Indian, though a much younger man, was fo indolent as not to be of any fervice to me, except hauling part of our luggage, and eating up part of the provifions which had been provided by the more indullrious, part of my companions.

On the twenty-fourth, early in the day, a great 24th. body of Indians was ieen to the South Weft, on the large lake by the fide of which our tent ftood. On their arrival at our tent we difcovered them to be the vives and families of the Northern Indian gcofe-hunters, who were gone to Prince of Wales's

Wales's Fort to attend the feafon. They were bound toward the barren ground, there to wait the return of their hufbands and relations from the Fort, after the termination of the goofe-feafon.

My guide having for fome days paft determined to move toward the barren ground, this morning we took down our tent, packed up our luggage, and proceeded to the Eaftward in the fame track we came; but Softop being fo lame as to be obliged to be hauled on a fledge, I eafily prevailed on two of the Indians who had joined us on the 24th, and who were purfuingthe fame road, to perform this fervice for him. 29th. After two days good walking in our old track, we arrived at a part of Seal River called She-than-nee, where we pitched our tent and fet both our fifhing-nets, intending to flay there till the geefe began to fly. Though we had feen feveral fwans and fome geefe flying to the Northward, it was the thirteenth of May before we could pro-May. 13th. cure any. On that day the Indians killed two fwans and three geefe. This in fome meafure alleviated our diftrefs, which at that time was very great; having had no other fubfiftence for five or fix days, than a few cranberries, that we gathered from the dry ridges where the fnow was thawed away in fpots; for though we fet our fifliing-nets in the beft judged places, and angled at every part that was likely to afford fuccefs, we only caught three fmall fifh during the whole time.

time. Many of the Northern Indians, who had joined us on the 24th of April, remained in our company for fbme time; and though I well knew they had had a plentiful winter, and had then good (locks of dried meat by them, and were alio acquainted with our diftrefs, they never gave me or my Southern companions the leali fupply, although they had in lecret amply provided for our Northern guides.

By the nineteenth, the geefe, fwans, ducks, 19th. gulls, and other birds of paflage, were fo plentiful that we killed every day as many as were fuffici-ent for our fupport; and having flopped a few days to recruit our fpirits after fo long a fail, on the twenty-third we began once more to pro- 23d. ceed toward the barren ground. Soltop having now perfeclly recovered from his late misfortune, every thing feemed to have a favourable appearance; efpecially as my crew had been augmented to twelve perfons, by the addition of one of my guide's wives, and five others, whom I had engaged to aflift in carrying our luggage; and I well knew, from the leafon of the year, that hauling would foon be at an end for the fum-mer.

The thaws having been by this time fo great a to render travelling in the woods almofl impracticable, we continue our courfe to the Eall on Seal River, about fixteen miles farther, when we came to a fmall river, and a firing of lakes con-isefled with it, that tended to the North.

ss A JOURNEY TO THE

The weather for fome time was remarkably-fine and pleafant. Game of all kinds was exceedingly plentiful, and we continued our courfe to the Northward on the above river and lakes j(. till the firft of June, when we arrived at a place called Beralzone. In our way thither, befide killing more geefe than was neceffary, we iiiot two deer. One of my companions had now the mif-fortune to ihatter his hand very much by the burfting of a gun; but as no bones were broken, I bound up the wound, and with the ailiftance of fome of Turhngton's drops, yellow bafdicon, c. which I had vith me, foon reftored the ufe of his hand; fo that in a very fhort time he feemed to be out of all danger.

After Hopping a few days at Beralzone, to dry a little venifon and a few geefe, we again proceeded to the Northward on the barren ground; for on our leaving this place we foon got clear of all the woods.

ith. The fnow was by this time fo foft as to render walking in fnow-fliocs very laborious; and though the ground was bare in many places, yet at times, and in particular places, the fnow-drifts viere fo deep, that we could not poilibly do with- c. H, out them. By the fixth, however, the thaws were fo general, and the fnows fo much melted, that as our fnow-fiioes were attended with more trouble than fervice,. we 11 confented to throw xcth. them away. Till the tenth, our fledges proved ferviceable, particularly in croiling lakes and ponds ponds on the ice; but that mode of travelling now growing dangerous on account of the great thaws, we determined to throw away our fledges, and every one to take a load on his back.

This I found to be much harder work than the winter carriage, as my part of the luggage confided of the following articles, viz. the quadrant and its ftand, a trunk containing books, papers, kc. a land-compafs, and a large bag containing all my wearing apparel; alfo a hatchet, knives, files, c. befide feveral fmall articles, intended for prefents to the natives. The aukwardnefs of my load, added to its great weight, which was upward of lixty pounds, and the exceitive heat cf the weather, rendered walking the moft laborious t3. ik I had ever encountered; and what confiderably increafed the hardfiiip, was the bad-nefs of the road, and the coarfenefs of our lodsr-ing, being, on account of the want of proper tents, expofed to the utmoh: feverity of the weather. The tent we had with us v-as not only too large, and unfit for barren ground fervice, where no poles were to be got, but we had been obliged to cut it up for fhoesj and each perfon carried his own fhare. indeed my guide behaved both negligently and ungeneroufly on this occaiion; as he never made me, or my Southern Indians, acquainted with the nature of pitching tents on the barren ground; which had he done, we could eailly have procured a fet of poles before we left the woods. He took care, however, to procure procure a fct for himfelf and his wife; and when the tent was divided, thougjh he made fliift to s: et a piece large enough to ferve him for a complete little tent, he never afeed m. e or my Southern Indians to put our heads into it.

Belide the inconvenience of being expofed to the open air, night and day, in all weathers, we experienced real diftrefs from the want of vidu-als. When proviiions were procured, it often happened that we could not make a fire, fo that we were obliged to eat the meat quite raw; which at firft, in the article of fifli particularly, was as little relifhed by my Southern companions as myfelf.

Notwithftanding thcfe accumulated and complicated hardfhips, we continued in perfect health and good fpirits; and my guide, though a per-fect: niggard of his provifions, efpecially in times of fcarcity, gave us the ftrongeft allurance of foon arriving at a plentiful country, which would not only afford us a certain fupply of provifions, but vhere we fhould meet with other Indians, who probably would be Vvilling to carry part of our luggage. This news naturally gave us great confolation; for at that time the weight of our conflant loads was fo great, that when Providence threw any thing in our way, we could not carry above two days provifions with us, which indeed was the chief reafon of our being fo frequently in want.

From the twentieth to the twenty-third we walked 2ld.

walked every day near twenty miles, without any other fubfiftence than a pipe of tobacco, and a drink of water when we pleafed: even partridges and gulls, which fome time before were in great plenty, and eafily procured, were now fo fcarce and fhy, that we could rarely get one j and as to geek, ducks, c. they had all flown to the Northward to breed and molt.

Early in the morning of the twenty-third, we fet out as ufual, but had not walked above feven or eight miles before we faw three mulk-oxen grazing by the fide of a fmall lake. The Indians immediately went in purfuit of them; and as fome of them were expert hunters, they foon killed the whole of them. This was no doubt very fortunate; but, to our great mortification, before we could get one of them fkinned, fuch a fall of rain came on, as to put it quite out of our power to make a fire; which, even in the fineft weather, could only be made of mofs, as we were near an hundred miles from any woods. This was poor comfort for people who had not broke their faft for four or five days. Neceffity, however, has no law; and having been before initiated into the method of eating raw meat, we were the better prepared for this repaft: but this was by no means fo well relifhed, either by me or the Southern Indians, as either raw venifon or raw fifli had been: for the flefli of the niufk-ox is not only coarfe and tough, but fmells and taftes fo ftrong of mufk as to make it very difa- agreeable greeable vvhen raw, though it is tolerable eating wheij properly cooked. The weather continued fo remarkably bad, accompanied with conftant heavy rain, ihow and fleet, and our necelllties were fo great by the time the weather permitted us to make a fire, that we had nearly eat to the amount of one buffalo quite raw,

Notwithiianding I muftered up all my philofo-phy on this occalion, yet 1 muft confefs that my fpirits began to fail me. Indeed our other misfortunes. were greatly aggravated by the inclemency of the weather, which was not only cold, but fo very wet that for near three days and nights, I had not one dry thread about me. When the fine weather returned, we made a fire, though it was only of mofs, as I have already obferved; and having got my cloaths dry, all things feem-ed likely to go on in the old channel, though that was indifferent enough; but I endeavoured, like a failor after a llorm, to forget paft misfortunes.

None of our natural wants, if we except thirft, are fo diftreffing, or hard to endure, as hunger; and in wandering fitu, ations, like that which I now experienced, the hardfhip is greatly acrgra-vated by the uncertainty with refpecl to its duration, and the means moft pro'ier ro be ufed to remove it, as well as by the hbour and fatigue we muft necefiarily undergo for that purpofe and the difappointments which too frequently fruftrate our beft concerted plans and moft ftre- nuous nuous exertions: it not only enfeebles the body, but i. epreites the fpirits, in fpite of every effort to prevent it. Belidess, for want of action, the fio-mach fo far lofes its digeluve powers, that after long fafling it relumes its office with pain and. reluctance. During this journey I have too frequently experienced the dreadful effects of this calamity, and more than once been reduced to fo low a ftate by hunger and fatigue, that when Providence threw any thing in my way, my fto-mach has fcarcely been able to retain more than two or three ounces, without producing the mod oppreffive pain. Another difagreeable cir-cumftance of long faffing is, the extreme difficulty and pain attending the natural evacuations for the fiift time; and which is fo dreadful, that of it none but thofe who have experienced can have an adequate idea.

To record in detail each day's fare fince the commencement of this journey, would be little more than a dull repetition of the fame occurrences. A fufficient idea of it may be given in a few words, by obferving that it may juffly be faid to have been either all feafting, or all famine: fometimes we had too much, feldom juft enough, frequently too little, and often none at all It will be only neceffary to fay that we have hiled many times two whole days and nights; twice upwards of three days; and once, while at She-than-nee, near feven days, during which we taft-ed not a mouthful of any thing, except a few

D cran- cranberries, water, fcraps of old leather, and burnt bones. On thole prelhng occaiions I have frequently feen the Indians examine their wardrobe, which conlifted chiefly of fkin-clothing, and conlider what part could beft be fpared 5 fometimes a piece of an old, half-rotten deer fkin, and at others a pair of old fhoes, were facrificed to alleviate extreme hunger. The relation of fuch uncommon hardftiips may perhaps gain little credit in Europe; while thofe who are con-verfant with the hiftory of Hudfon's Bay, and who are thoroughly acquainted with the diftrefs which the natives of the country about it frequently endure, may confider them as no more than the common occurrences of an Indian life, sn which they are frequently driven to the ne-ceflity of eating one another.

Knowing It is the general opinion of the Southern Indians, that when any of their tribe hase been driven to the neceflity of eating human fiefh, they become fo fond of it, that no perfon is ffc in their company. And though it is well known they are never guilty of making this horrid repaft but when driven to it by neceflrty, yet thofe who have made it are not only fliimned, but fo unjverfally detcfted by all who know them, that no Indians iil tent with them, and they are frequently murdered flily. I have fcen feveral of thofe poor wietches who, unfortunately for them, have come under the above defcription, and though they weie perfons fnuch efteemed before hunger had driven them to this ao, were afterwards fo univerfally defpifed and negleftcd, that a fmile never graced their countenances: deep melancholy has been feated on their brows, while the eye moft expreffively fpoke the dictates of the heart, and feemed to fay, "Why do you depife me for my misfortunes? the peii-"od is probably not far diftant, when you may be driven to the likene-" ceftity!"

In the Spring of the year 177J, when I was building Cumberland
Houfe,

Knowing that our conftant loads would not permit us to carry much provifions with us, we agreed to continue a day or two to refrefh ourselves, and to dry a little meat in the fun, as it thereby not only becomes more portable, but is always ready for ufe. On the twenty-fixth, all 26th, that remained of the mulk-ox flefh being properly dried and fit for carriage, we began to proceed on our journey Northward, and on the thirtieth of June arrived at a fmall river, called Ca- 30th. thavvhachaga, which empties itfelf into a large lake called Yath-kyed-whoie, or White Snow Lake. Here we found feveral tents of Northern Indians, who had been fome time employed fpearing deer in their canoes, as they crofled the above mentioned little river. Here aifo vie met D 2 a Nor-

Houfe, an Indian, whofe name was Wapoos, came to the fettlemcnt, at a time when fifteen tents of Indians were on the plantations: they examined him veiy minutely, and found he had come a confideiable way by him-felf, without a gi. n, or ammunition. This made many of them conjecture he had met with, and killed, fome perfoii by the way; and this was the more eafily credited, from the care he teok to conceal a bag of provifions, which he had brought with him, in a lofty pine-tree near the houfe.

Being a ftrangcr, I invited him in, though I faw he had nothing for trade; andduring that interview, Tome of the Indian women examined his bag, and gave it as their opinion that the meat it contained wa- human flefii: inconfequence, it was not without the interference of fome L-; inci-pal Indians, whofe liberality of fcntiment was more extenfive than that in the others, the poor creature favcd his life. Many of the men cleaned and loaded their guns; others had their bows and arrows ready; and even the women took pofieltion of the hatchets, to kill this poor inoffenfive wretch, for no ciime but that of travelling about two hundred miles by himftlf, unaflilted by fire-arms for fupport in his journey.

a Northern Indian Leader, or Captain, called Keelfliies, and a fmall party of his crew, who were bound to Prince of Wales's Fort, with furs and other commodities for trade. When Keel-ihies was made acquainted with the intent of my journey, he readily offered his fervice to bring me any thing from the Fadory that we were likely to land in need of; and though we were then in latitude 63 4 North, and longitude 7 12 Weft from Churchill, yet he promifed to join us again, at a place appointed by my guide, by the fetting in of the Winter. In confequence of this offer, 1 looked over our ammunition and other articles; and finding that a little powder, fhot, tobacco, and a few knives, were likely to be of fervice before the journey could be completed, I determined to fend a letter to the governor of Prince of Wales's Fort, to advife him of my litu-ation, and to defire him to fend by the bearer a certain quantity of the above articles; on which Keelfhies and his crew proceeded on their journey for the Factory the fame day.

Cathawhachaga was the only river we had feen fmce the breaking up of the ice that we could not ford; and as we had not any canoes with us, we were obliged to get ferried acrofs by the flrange Indians. When we arrived on the North fide of this river, where the Indians refided, my guide propofed to flop fome time, to dry and pound fome meat to take with us; to which I readily confented. We alfo fet our fifliing-nets, and caught a confiderable quantity of very fine fifli; fuch as tittemeg, barbie, c.

The number of deer which croited Cathawha-chaga, during our ftay there, was by no means equal to our expectations, and no more than jufl fufecient to fupply our prefent wants; fo that after waiting feveral days in fruitlefs expectation, we began to prepare for moving; and accordingly, on the fixth of July, we fet out, 6th. though we had not at that time as much viclu- als belonging to our company as would furnifti us a fupper. During our ftay here, we had each day got as much fifh or flefh as was fufecient for prefent expenditure5 but, being in hopes of better times, faved none.

Before we left Cathawhachaga, I made feveral obfervations for the latitude, and found it to be 6t, 4 North. I alfo brought up my journal, and filled up my chart to that time. Every thing being now ready for our departure, my guide informed me that in a few days a canoe would be abfolutely neceffary, to enable us to crofs fome unfordable rivers which we fhould meet, and could not avoid. This induced me to purchafe one at the eafy rate of a fmgle knife, the full value of which did not exceed one penny. It mufl be obferved, that the man who fold the canoe had no farther occafion for it, and was glad to take what he could get; but had he been thoroughly acquainted with our neceflities he moft afluredly would have had the confcience to have have alked goods to the amount of ten beaver Ikins at leaft.

This additional piece of luggage obliged me to engage another Indian; and we were lucky enough at that time to meet with a poor forlorn fellow, who was fond of the office, having never been in a much better ftate than that of a beaft of burthen. Thus, provided with a canoe, and a man to carry it, we left Cathawhachaga, as has been obfefved, on the fixth of July, and continued our courfe to the North by Weft, and North North Weft; and that night put up by the lide of a fmall bay of White Snow Lake, where we angled, and caught feveral fine trout, fome of which weighed not lefs than fourteen or fixteen pounds. In the night heavy rain came on, which 9- continued three days; but the ninth proving fine weather, and the fun difplaying his beams very powerfully, we dried our clothes, and proceeded to the Northward. Tovard the evening, however, it began again to rain fo exceffively, that it was with much difficulty we kept our powder and books dry.

On the feventeenth, we faw many mufk-oxen, feveral of which the Indians killed; when we agreed to flay here a day or two, to dry and pound fome of the carcafes to take with us.

To prepare meat in this manner, it requires no farther operation than cutting the lean parts of the animal into thin dices, and drying it in the fun, or by a flow fire, till, after beating it between two flones, U is reduced to a coaifc powder.

syth.

The flefh of any animal, when it is thus prepared, is not only hearty food, but is always ready for ufe, and at the fame time very portable, in moft parts of Hudfon's Bay it is known by the name of Thew-hagon, but amongft the Northern Indians it is called Achees.

Having prepared as much dried flefh as we could tranfport, we proceeded to the Northward j and at our departure left a great quantity of meat behind us, which we could neither eat nor carry away. This was not the firft time we had fo done; and however wafteful it may appear, it is a practice fo common among all the Indian tribes, as to be thought nothing of. On the twenty-fe- 224. cond, we met feveral ftrangers, whom we joined in purfuit of the deer, c. which were at this timic fo plentiful, that we got every day a fuffi-cient number for our fupport, and indeed too frequently killed feveral merely for the tongues, narrow, and fat.

After we had been fome time in company with thofe Indians, I found that my guide feemed to hefitate about proceeding any farther; and that he kept pitching his tent backward and forward, from place to place, after the deer, and the reft of the Indians. On my afking him his reafon for fo doing; he anfwered, that as the year was too far advanced to admit of our arrival at the Coppermine River that Summer, he thought it more advifable to pafs the Winter with fome of the Indians then in company, and alleged that there could could be no fear of our arriving at that river early in the Summer of one thoufand feven hundred and feventy-one. As I could not pretend to contradict him, 1 was entirely reconciled to his propofal; and accordingly we kept moving to the Weftward with the other Indians. In a few days, many others joined us from different quar-3otii. ters; io that by the thirtieth of July we had in all above feventy tents, which did not contain lefs than fix hundred perfons. Indeed our encampment at night had the appearance of a fmall town; and in the morning, when we began tp move, the whole ground (at lead for a large fpace all round) feemed to be alive, with men, won)en, children, and dogs. Though the land was entirely barren, and deftitute of every kind of herbage, except wifti-a capucca and mpfs, yet the deer were fo numerous that the Indians not only killed as many as were fuiiicient for our large number, but often feveral mierely for the fkins, marrow, c. and left the carcafes to rot, or to be devoured by the wolves, foxes, and other beafts ofprey.

In our way to the Vcftward we came to feveral rivers, which, though fmall and of no note, were fo deep as not to be fordable, particularly Doo-baunt Riverf. On thofe occafions only, we

Widi-a-capucca is the name given by the natives to a plant, which is found al! over the country boidering on Hudfon's Bay; and an infufion of it is ufed as tea by all the Europeans fettled in that country.

f- This river, as well as all others dekrving that appellation which I croflcd had recourfe to our canoe, which, though of the 1770. common lize, was too fmall to carry more than r two perfons; one of whom always lies down at full length for fear of making the canoe top-heavy, and the other fits on his heels and paddles. This method of ferrying over rivers, though tedious, is the moft expeditious way thefe poor people can contrive; for they are fometimes obliged to carry their eanoes one hundred and fifty, or two hundred miles, without having occalion to make ufe of them; yet at times they cannot do without them; and were they not very fmall and portable, it would be impoflible for one man to carry them, which they are often obliged to do, not only the diflance above mentioned, but even the whole Summer.

The perfon 1 engaged at Cathawhachaga to car- 6th. ry my canoe proving too weak for the tafk, another of my crew was obliged to exchange loads with him, which feemed perfectly agreeable to all parties; and as we walked but fliort days jour-nies, and deer were very plentiful, all things went on every fmoothly. Nothing material happened till the eig; hth, when we were near lofinsr the 8th, quadrant and all our powder from the following circumftance: the fellow who had been releafed from carrying the canoe proving too weak, as hath been rrofled during this part of my journey, ran to the Eafl and North Eaſt; and both them and the lakes were perfeſlly freſh, and inhabited by filh that are well known never to frequent fait water.

Auouit.

A JOURNEY TO THE been already obferved, had, after the exchange, nothing to carry but my powder and his own trifles; the latter were indeed very inconfidera-ble, not equal in fize and weight to a foldier's knapfack. As I intended to have a little fport with the deer, and knowing his load to be much lighter than mine, I gave him the quadrant and fland to carry, which he took without the leaft heiitation, or feeming ill-will. Having thus eaf-ed myfelf for the prefent of a heavy and cumber-fome part of my load, I fet out early in the morning with fome of the Indian men; and after walking about eight or nine miles, faw, from the top of a high hill, a great number of deer feeding in a neighbouring valley; on which we laid down our loads and erected a flag, as a fignal for the others to pitch their tents there for the night. We then purfued our hunting, which proved very fuccef-ful. At night, however, when we came to the hill where we had left our baggage, I found that only part of the Indians had arrived, and that the man who had been entrufted with my powder and quadrant, had fet off another way, with a fmall party of Indians that had been in our company that morning. The evening being far advanced, we were obhged to defer going in fearch of him till the morning, and as his track could not be eafily difcovered in the Summer, the Southern Indians, as well as myfelf, were very uneafy, fearing we had loll the powder, which was to provide us with food and raiment the remainder of our journey. The very uncourteous behaviour 1770. of the Northern Indians then in company, gave v-nj me little hopes of receiving affiftance from them, any longer than I had wherewithal to reward them for their trouble and expence; for during the whole time I had been with them, not one of them had offered to give me the leaft morfel of victuals, without afking fomething in exchange, which, in general, was three times the value of what they could have got for the fame articles, had they carried them to the Faclory, though feveral hundred miles diftant.

So inconliderate were thofe people, that wherever they met me, they always expe51: ed that I had a great aflbrtment of goods to relieve their neceffities; as if I had brought the Company's warehoufe with me. Some of them wanted guns; all vanted ammunition, iron-work, and tobacco; many were folicitous for medicine; and others prelted me for different articles of clothing: but when they found I had nothing to fpare, except a few nick-nacks and gewgaws, they made no fcruple of pronouncing me a " poor fervant, " noways like the Governor at the Faclory, who, " they faid, they never faw, but he gave them " fomething ufeful. It is fcarcely pofllble to conceive any people fo void of common under-flanding, as to think that the fole intent of my undertaking this fatiguing journey, was to car ry a large affortment of ufeful and heavy implements, to give to all that Hood in need of them; , but inany of them would afli me for what they -v wanted with the fame freedom, and apparently with the fame hopes of fuccefs, as if they had been at one of the Company's Factories. Others, with an air of more generolity, offered me furs to trade with at the fame ftandard as at the Factory; without confidering how unlikely it was that I (houid increafe the enormous weight of my load with articles which could be of no more ufe to me in my prefent fituation than they were to them-felves.

This unaccountable behaviour of the Indians occafioned much ferious reflection on my part-y. as It Ihowed plainly how iittie 1 had to exped if I iliould, by any accident, be reduced to the ne-ceffity of depending upon them for fupport; fo that, though I laid me down to reft, flcep was a flranger to me that night. The following beautiful lines of Dr. Young 1 repeated above an hun-dred tinges:

"Tired N?ure's fweet leflorer, balmy Gleep;

"He, like the world, his ready vifit pays

"Where fuitine fmiles; the wretched he forfakcss

"Swift (1 i. is downy pinions flies fiom woe,

"And lights on lids unfullyd withatear." Nicnr Thoughts.

jj, After paftmg the night in tlds melancholy manner, I got up at day-break, and, with the two Southern Indians, iet out in queft of our defer-ter. Many hours elapfed in fruitlefs fearch after him, as we could not difcover a lino'le track in thf? direction which we were informed he had taken

Au-iuft.

NORTHERN OCEAN.

taken. The day being almoft fpent without the leaft appearance of fuccels, I propoled repairing to the place where 1 had delivered the quadrant to him, in hopes of feeing Tome track in the mofs that might lead to the way the Indians were gone whom our deferter had accompanied. On our arriyal at that place, we found they had ftruck down toward a little river which they had croif-ed the morning before; and there, to our great joy, we found the quadrant and the bag of powder lying on the top of a high ftone, but not a human being was to be feen. On examining the powder, we found that the bag had been opened, and part of it taken out; but, notwithftanding our lofs was very conliderable, we returned with light hearts to the place at which we had been the night before, where we found our baggage fafe, but all the Indians gone: they had, however, been fo confiderate as to fet up marks to direct us what courfe to lleer. By the time we had adjufied our bundles, the day was quite fpent; feeing, however, a fmoke, or rather a iire, in the direction we were ordered to fteer, we bent our way towards it; and a little after ten o'clock at night came up with the rrain body of the Indians; when, after refreihing ourfelves with a plentiful fupper, the firft morfel we had tafted that day, we retired to reft, which I at leaft enjoyed with better fuccefs than the preceding night.

In the morning of the eleventh we proceeded on mh to the Weft, and Weft by South j but on the twelfth twelfth did not move. This gave us an opportunity of endeavouring to afcertain the latitude by a meredian ahitude, when we found the place to be in 6 lo' North nearly. It proving rather cloudy about noon, though exceeding fine weather, I let the quadrant ftand, in order to obtain the latitude more exactly by two altitudes; but, to my great mortification, while I was eating my dinner, a fudden guft of wind blew it down; and as the ground where it ftood was very ftoney, the bubble, the fight-vane, and vernier, were entirely broke to pieces, which rendered the inftru-ment ufelefs. In confequence of this misfortune I refolved to return again to the Fort, though we were then in the latitude of 63" 10 North, and about 10 40 Weft longitude from Churchill River.

CHAP.

Tranfacllons from the Time the Quadrant was broken, till I arrived at the Factory.

Several Jlrange Indians join us from the Northward. They plundered me of all I had; but did not plunder the Southern Indians. My guide plundered. We begin our return to the Factory. Meet with other Indiansi who join our company. Coilesl deer-fkins for clothing. but could not get them dreffed. Suffer? nuch hardjliip from the want of tents and warnt clothing. Moji of the Indians leave us. Meet with Maionabbee, Some account ofhim and his behavi-our to me and the Southern Indians. We remain in his company fome time His obfervations on my tzo unfuccefsful attempts. We leave hifu, and proceed to a place to which he direded us, in order to? nake fnowJhoes and Jledges. Join Matonabbee again and proceed towards the Factory in his company." Ammunition runs Jhort. Myfelf and four Indians fet offpoft for the Factory. Much bewildered in a fnowjiorm; my dog is frozen to death; we lie in a bujh of willows. Proceed on our journey. Great difficulty in crojjing a jumble of rocks, Arrive at the Fort, ihE day after I had the misfortune to break 1770. the quadrant, feveral Indians joined me–v–. from the Northward, fome of whom plundered ifxh.

Auguft.

48 A JOURNEY TO THE imQ, me and my companions of almoh: every ufeful article we had, among which was my gun; and notwithftanding we were then on the point of returning to the Factory, yet, as one of my companions' guns was a little out of order, the lofs was likely to be feverely felt; but it not being in my power to recover it again, we were obliged to reft contented.

Nothing can exceed the cool deliberation of thofe villains; a committee of them entered my tent. The ringleader feated himfelf on my left-hand. They firft begged me to lend them my fidpertogan f to fill a pipe of tobacco. After fmoking two or three pipes, they afked me for feveral articles which I had not, and among others for a pack of cards; but on my anfwering that I had not any of the articles they mentioned, one of them put his hand on my baggage, and afked if it was mine. Before I could anfwer in the affirmative, he and the reft of his companions (fix in number) had all my treafure fpread on the ground. One took one thing, and another another, till at laft nothing was left but the empty bag, which they permitted me to keep. At length

This only confifted of three walking-fticks ftuck into the ground, and a blanket thrown over them.

- Skipertogan is a fmall bag that contains a flint and fteel, alfo a pipe and tobacco, as well as touchwood, c. for making a fire. Some of thefe bags may be called truly elegant; being richly ornamented wiih beads, porcupine-quiils, morfe-hair, c. a work always performed by ihe women; and they are, with much propriety, greatly efteenied by moft Eji-ropeans for the neatnefs of their woikrnaufliip.

length, confiderlng that, though I was going to the Faclory, I fliould want a knife to cut my victuals, an awl to mend my fhoes, and a needle to mend my other clothing, they readily gave me thefe articles, though not without making me underftand that I ought to look upon it as a great favour. Finding them poffefled of fo much ge-nerolity, I ventured to folicit them for my ra. zors; but thinking that one would be fufecient to fhave me during my paffage home, they made no fcruple to keep the other; luckily they chofe the worft. To complete their generofity, they permitted me to take as much foap as I thought would be fufecient to wafli and fhave me during the remainder of my journey to the Factory,

They were more cautious in plundering the Southern Indians, as the relation offuch outrages being committed on them might occafion a war between the two nations; but they had nothing of that kind to dread from the Englifli. However, the Northern Indians had addrefs enough to talk my home-guard Indians out of all they had: fo that before we left them, they were as clean fwept as myfelf, excepting their guns, fome am munition, an old hatchet, an ice-chiffel, and a file to iharpen them.

It may probably be thought ftrange that my guide, who was a Northern Indian, fhould permit his countrymen to commit fuch outrages on thofe under his charge; but being a man of little note, he was fo far from being able to protea

Auguft.

o A JOURNEY TO THE 1770. us, that he was obliged to fubmit to nearly the "" r fame outrage himfeif. On this occaiion he affum-

Auguft.

ed a great air of generofity; but the fact was, he gave freely what it was not in his power to proteft. j Early in the morning of the nineteenth, I fet out on my return, in company with feveral Northern Indians, who were bound to the Factory with furrs and other commodities in trade. This morning the Indian who took my gun, returned it to me, it being of no ufe to him, having no ammunition. The weather for fome time proved fine, and deer were very plentiful; but as the above ravagers had materially lightened my load, by taking every thing from me, except the quadrant, books, c. this part of my journey was the eafieft and moft pleafant of any I had experienced fince my leaving the Fort. In our way we frequently met with other Indians, fo that fcarce-ly a day palted without our feeing feveral fmokes made by other ftrangers. Many of thofe we met joined our party, having furrs and other comm. o-dities for trade., jii The deer's hair being now of a proper length for clothing, it was neceffary, according to the cuftom, to procure as many of their Ikins, while in feafon, as would make a fuit of warm clothing for the Winter: and as each grown perfon requires the prime parts of from eight to eleven of thofe Ikins (in proportion to their fize) to make a complete fuit, it mufl naturally be fuppofed that this this addition to my burthen was very confidera-ble. My load, however cumberfome and heavy, . September.

was yet very bearable; but, after I had earned it feveral weeks, it proved of no fervice; for we had not any women properly belonging to our company, confequently had not any perfon to drefs them; and fo uncivil were the other Indians, that they would neither exchange them for others of an inferior quality already drefled, nor permit their women to drefs them for us, under pretence that they were always employed in the like duty for themfelves and families, which was by no means the cafe; for many of them had fuflicient time to have done every little fervice of that kind that we could have required of them. The truth was, they were too well informed of my poverty to do any afls of generofity, as they well knew I had it not then in my power to re−ward them for their trouble. I never faw a fet of people that poflefled fo little humanity, or that could view the diftreifes of their fellow-creatures with fo little feeling and unconcern; for though they feem to have a great affection for their wives and children, yet they will laugh at and ridicule the diftrefs of every other perfon who is not im-jmediately related to them.

This behaviour of the Indians made our fitua-tion very difagreeable; for as the fall advanced, we began to feel the cold very feverely for want of proper clothing. We fuffered alfo greatly from the inclemency of the weather, as we had no

E 2 tni; 1770. tent to fhelterus. My guide was entirely exempt-jr ed from all thofe inconveniences, having procured a good warm fuit of clothing; and, as one of his wives had long before joined our party, he was provided with a tent, and every other necef- itj,, fry confiftent with their manner of living: but the old fellow was fo far from interefting himfelf in our behalf, that he had, for fome time before, entirely withdrawn from our company; and though he then continued to carry the greateft part of our little remains of ammunidon, yet he did not contribute in the fmalleft degree towards our fupport. As deer, however, were in great plenty, 1 felt little or no inconvenience from his negleft in this refped.

3, th.   Provifions ftill continued very plentiful; which was a fingular piece of good fortune, and the only circumflance which at this time could contribute to our happinefs or fafety; for notwithftand-ing the early feafon of the year, the weather wa? remarkably bad and feverely cold, at leaft it ap. peared fo to us, probably from having no kind ol fkin-clothing. In this forlorn flate we continued our courfe to the South Eaft; and, to add to the gloominefs of our lituation, moft of the Northerr Indians who had been in our company all the firfi part of the fall, were by this time gone a-head, a; we could not keep up vith them for want 01 fnow-flioes.

In the evening of the twentieth, we were join ed from the Weftward by a famous Leader, call d Matonabbee, mentioned in my inftructions; 1770.   who, with his followers, or ffansj, was alfo ffoino; n-"−

O, September.

to Prince of Wales's Fort, with furrs, and other articles for trade. This leader, when a youth, re-fided feveral years at the above Fort, and was not only a perfect mailer of the Southern Indian Ian-, guage, but by being frequently with the Company's fervants, had acquired feveral words of Englifli, and was one of the men who brought the lateft accounts of the Coppermine River; and it was on his information, added to that of one Idot-le-ezey, (who is fmce dead,) that this expedition was fet on foot.

The courteous behaviour of this ftranger ftruck me very fenfibly. As foon as he was acquainted with our diftrefs, he got fuch Ikins as we had with us drefled for the Southern Indians, and furnifh-ed me with a good warm fuit of otter and other Ikins: but, as it was not in his power to provide us with fnow-flioes, (being then on the barren ground,) he dire5ted us to a little river which he knew, and where there was a fmall range of woods, which, though none of the beft, would, he faid, furnifli us with temporary fnow-flioes and fledges, that might materially aflift us during the remaining part of our journey. We fpent feveral nights in company with this Leader, though we advanced towards the Fort at the rate of ten or twelve miles a day; and as provifions abounded, he made a grand feaft for me in the Southern Indian ftile, where there was plenty of good eat-

Odobci.

Offtober.

A JOURNEY TO THE ing, and the whole concluded with finglng and dancing, after the Southern Indian llyle and manner. In this aniufement my home-guard Indians bore no inconfiderable part, as they were both men of fome confequence when at home, and well known to Matonabbee: but among the other Northern Indians, to whom tliey were not known, they were held in no eftimation j which indeed is not to be wondered at, when we confider that the value of a man among thofe people, is always proportioned to his abilities in hunting; and as my two Indians had not exhibited any great ta-lents that way, the Northern Indians fhew-ed them as much refped as they do in common to thofe of very moderate talents among themfelves.

During my converfation Vvith this Leader, he afked me very ferioufly. If I would attempt another journey for the difcovery of the Copper-mines? And on my anfwering in the affirmative, provided I could get better guides than I had hitherto been furnifhed with, he faid he would readily engage in that fervice, provided the gover–nor at the Fort would employ him. In anfwer to this, 1 aflured him his offer would be gladly accepted; and as I had already experienced every hardfliip that was likely to accompany any future trial, I was determined to complete the difcovery, even at the rifque of life itfelf. Matonabbee af-fured me, that by the accounts received from his own countrymen, the Southern Indians, and my-felf, it was very probable I might not experience fo much hardfiiip during the whole journey, as I bad ah-eady felt, though fcarcely advanced one Q(Q third part of the journey.

He attributed all our misfortunes to the mifcon-duct of my guides, and the very plan we purfued, by the defire of the Governor, in not taking any women with us on thisjourney, was. he faid, the principal thing tliat occafioned all our wants: for, faid he, when all the men are heavy laden, " they can neither hunt nor travel to any confider-" able difiance; and in cafe they meet with fuc- cefs in hunting, who is to carry the produce of " their labour? Women, added he, were made " for labour; one of them can carry, or haul, as " much as two men can do. They alfo pitch our " tents, make and mend our clothing, keep us " warm at night; and, in facl, there is no fuch " thing as travelling any confiderable diftance or " for any length of time, in this country, without " their afliflance. " Women, faid he again, " though they do every thing, are maintained at " a trifling expence; for as they always iland cook, the very licking of their lingers in fcarce times, is fufficient for their fubfillence. This, however odd it may appear, is but too true a de-fcription of the fituation oi women in this country; it is at leaft fo in appearance; for the women akvays carry the provilions, and it is more than probable they help themfelves when the men are not prefent.

Early in the morning of the twenty-third, I,3, ftruck out of the road to the Eaftward, with my two companions and two or three Northern Indians, while Matonabbee and his crew continued their courfe to the Factory, promifing to walk fo flow that we might come up with them again; and in two days we arrived at the place to which 3Sth. were directed. We went to work immediately in making fnow-fhoe frames and fledges; but notwithftanding our utmoft endeavours, we could not complete them in lefs than four days. November On the firft of Novcmber we again proceeded on our journey toward the Factory; and on the fixth, came up with Matonabbee and his gang: after which we proceeded on together feveral days; when 1 found my new acquaintance, on all occaiions, the moll fociable, kind, and fenfible Indian I had ever met with. He was a man well known, and, as an Indian, of univerfal knowledge, and generally refpecled.

Deer proved pretty plentiful for fome time, but to my great furprife, when I wanted to give Matonabbee a little ammunition for his own ufe, I found that my guide, Conreaquefe, who had it all under his care, had fo embezzled or otherways expended it, that only ten balls and about three pounds of powder remained; fo that long before ve arrived at the Fort we were obliged to cut up an ice-chiflel into fquare lumps, as a fubftitute for ball. It is, however, rather dangerous firing lumps of iron out of fuch flight barrels as are brought to this part of the world for trade.

Thefe

Thefe, though light and handy, and of courfe well adapted tor the ufs of both Englilli and Indi-, ans in long journies, and of fufficient ilrcngth for "' " leaden fhot or ball, are not ftrong enough for this kind of fhot; and ftrong fowling-pieces would not only be too heavy for the laborious ways of hunting in this country, but their bores being fo much larger, would require more than double the quantity of ammunition that fmall ones do; which., to Indians at leaft, muft be an object of no inconfiderable importance.

I kept company with Matonabbee till the twen- 20th. tieth, at which time the deer began to be fo fcarce that hardly a frefli track could be feen; and as we were then but a fev days walk from the Fort, he advifed me to proceed on wlih all fpeed, while he and his companions followed at leifure. Accordingly, on the twenty-firft, I fet out pod- 21t, hafte, accompanied by one of the home-guard (Southern) Tribe, and three Northern Indians. That night we lay on the South fide of Egg River; but, long before day-break the next morning, the weather being fo bad, with a violent gale of vind from the North Weft, and fuch a drift of fnow, that we could not have a bit of fire: and as no good woods were near to afford us fhelter, we agreed to proceed on our way: efpeciaily as the wind was on our backs, and though the weather was bad near the furface we could frequently fee the moon, and fometimes the ftars, to direct us in our courfe. In this fituation we continued walking

J 7Q, ing the whole day, and it was not till after ten at v-v night that we could find the fmalleft tuft of woods Novembei, j. j. though we Well knew we muft have palled by feveralhummocks of flirubby woods that might have afforded us fome Ihelter, yet the wind blew fo hard, and the fnow drifted fo ex-ceflively thick, that we could not fee ten yards before us the whole day. Between feven and eight in the evening my dog, a valuable brute, was frozen to death; fo that his fledge, which was a very heavy one, I was obliged to haul. Between nine and ten at night we arrived at a fmall creek, on which we walked about three quarters of a mile, when we came to a large tuft of tall willows, luid two or three fets of old tent-poles. Being much jaded, we determined not to proceed any farther that night; fo we went to work, and made the beft defence againft the weather that the fituation of the place and our materials would admit. Our labour confided only in digging a hole in the fnow, and fixing a few deer fkins up to windward of us; but the niofl difficult tafk was that of making a fire. When this was once accomplifhed, the old tent poles amply fuppiied us with fewel. By the time we had finiflied this bufinefs, the weather began to moderate, and the drift greatly to abate; fo that the moon and the Aurora Borealis fhone out with great fplendor, and there appeared every fymptom of the return of fine weather. After eating a plentiful fupper of venifon, therefore, of which we had a lufficient flock to laft us to the Fort, we laid down and got a little fleep. 1770. The next day provinsj fine and clear, thoucrh ex-V; v–J cefllvely fharp, we proceeded on our journey i-early in the morning, and at night lay on the South Eafl lide of Seal River. We fliould have made a much longer day's journey, had we not been greatly embarraffed at fetting out, by ajum-ble of rocks, which we could not avoid without going greatly out of our way. Here I muft ob-ferve, that we were more than fortunate in not attempting to leave the little creek where we had fixed our habitation the preceding night, as the fpot where we lay was not more than two or three miles diftant from this dangerous place; in which, had we fallen in with it in the night, we muft unavoidably have been bewildered, if we had not all periflied; as notwithilanding the advantage of a clear day, and having ufed every pofiible precaution, it was with the utmoft difficulty that we croited it without broken limbs. Indeed it would have been next to an impoffibili-ty to have done it in the night.

The twenty-fourth and twenty-fifth proved fine 24:?,. clear weather, though exce-flively cold; and in the jth. afternoon of the latter, we arrived at Prince of Wales's Fort, after having been abient eight months and twenty-two days, on a fruitlefs, or at leaft an unfuccefsful journey.

CHAP.

Tranfa5lions during our Stay at Prince of Wales's Fort, and the former part of our third Expedition, till our Arrival at Clowey, where we built Canoes, in May 1771.

Preparatiomfor our departure. Refufeto take any of the home-guard Indians with me By fo doing, I offend the Governor, Leave the Fort a third time.-My injlruclions on this expedition. Provijions of all kinds veryfcarce. Arrive at the woods, where we kill fame deer. Arrive at IJland Lake. Ma-ionabbee taken ill. Some remarks thereon. foin the remainder of the hidiansfamilies. Leave Ifland Lake. Defcription thereof. Deer plentifid. Meet aflrange Indian. Alter out courfefrom Wefl North Wefi to Wefi by South. Crofs Cathawhach-aga River, Coffed Lake, Snow-Bird Lake, and Pike Lake. Arrive at a tent offirangers, who are employed in fnaring deer in a pound. Defcription of the pound. Method of proceeding. Remarks thereon. Proceed on our journey. Meet with fever al parties of Indians; by one of whom Ifent a letter to the governor at Prince of Wales's Fort. Arrive at Thleweyazayeth. Employment there. Prsceed to the North North Wefi and North. Arrive at Clowey. One of the Indians wives taken in labour. Re? narks thereon. Cufloms obferved by the Nor-them Indians on thofe occaftons.

NORTHERN OCEAN. 6i

N my arrival at the Fort, I informed the Go- 1770. vernor, of Matonabbee's being fo near. On w-; the twenty-eighth of November he arrived. Not- IITk' withftanding the many difficulties and hardfhips which 1 had undergone during my two unfuc-cefsful attempts, I was fo far from being folicited on this occafion to undertake a third excurfion, that I willingly offered my fervice; which was readily accepted, as my abilities and approved courage, in perfevering under difficulties, were thought noways inferior to the tafk.

1 then determined to engage Matonabbee to be my guide; to which he readily confented, and with a freedom of fpeech and corrednefs of language not commonly met with among Indians, not only pointed out the reafons which had oc-cafioned all

our misfortunes in my two former attempts, but defcribed the plan he intended to purfue; which at the fame time that it was highly fatisfaclory to me, did honour to his penetration and judgment; as it proved him to be a man of extenfive obfervation with refpe6t to times, fea-fons, and places; and well qualified to explain every thing that could contribute either to facilitate or retard the eafe or progrefs of travelling in thofe dreary parts of the world.

Having engaged Matonabbee, therefore, as my guide, I began to make preparations for our departure; but Mr. Norton, the Governor, having been very fully occupied in treding with a large body of Indians, it was the feventh of December December.

before

Ci A JOURNEY TO THE jya7Q before I could obtain from him my difpatches.

-V- It may not be improper to obferve, that he again wanted to force fome of the home-guard Indians (who were his own relations) into our company, merely

Mr. Norton was an Indian; he was born at Prince of Wales's Fort, but had been in England nine years, and confideiing the fmall fum which was expended on his idiication, had made fome progrefs in literature. At his return to HLidfon'sbay he entered into all the abominable vices of his countrymen. He kept for hij. own ufe five or fix of the fineft Indian girls which he could felcct; and notvvithftanding his own uncommon propenfity to the fail fcx, took every means in his power to prevent am: European from having intercourfe with tlie women of the country; for which pur-pofe he proceeded to the moft ridiculous length. To his own fiicnds and country he was fo partial, that he iet more value on, and fhewed more re-fptil to one of their favoutite dogs, than he ever did to his firft officer. Among his miferable and ignorant countrymen he pafled for a proficient in phyfic, and always kept a bos of poifon, toadminifter to thofe who re-fufed him their wives or daughters.

With all thefe bad qualities, no man took more pains to inculcate virtue, motaljty, and continence on others; always painting, in the moftodious colours, the jealous and revengeful difpofition of the Indi. ins, when any attempt was made to violate the cliaftity of their wives or daiigiitcrs. Lectures of th kind from a man of cflabliflied virtue might have had fome Citcft; but wher. they came from one who was known to live in open defiance of every law, human and divine, they were always heard viiih indignation, and confidered as the hypocritical cant of a felfifh debauchee, who vi(hedto engrofs every woman in the country to himfelf.

His apartments were not only convenient but elegant, and always crowded with favourite Indians: at night he locked the doors, and put the keys under his pillow; io that in the morning his dining-room was generally, for the want of neceftary conveniencies, worfe than a iiog-flye. As he advanced in years his jealoufy increafcd, and he aflual! y poifoned two of his women becaufe he thought them partial toother ohjefts more fuitable to their ages. He was a mod notorious fmuggler; but though he put many thoufands into the pockets of the Captains, he il-ldom puta Ihiliing into his own.

An iiflammation in his bowels occaloned his death on the z()th. of December 1773; and though he died in the moft cxcniciatingpain, he retained his jealoufy to the laft; for a few minutes before he expired, hippen-ing to fee an officer laying hold of the hand of o; i cf his woraen who wa j flandins merely with a view that they might engrofs all the credit of taking care of me during the journey: but I had found them of fo little ufe in my two former attempts, that I abfolutely refufed them; and by fo doing, offended Mr. Norton to fuch a degree, that neither time nor abfence could ever afterwards eradicate his dillike of me; fo that at my return he ufed every means in his power to treat mc ill, and to render my life unhappy. However, to deal with candour on this occafion, it muft be acknowledged to his honour, that whatever our private animofities might have been, he did not fuffer them to interfere with public bufi-nefs; and I was fitted out with ammunition, and every other article which Matonabbee thought could be wanted. I was alfo furnifhed, as before, with a fmall affortment of light trading goods, as prefents to the far diftant Indians.

At lad I fucceeded in obtaining my inftrudions, which were as follows:

"Orders wlnSTRUCTionsyor Mr. Samuel " Hearne, going on his 1 bird Expedition to the " North of Churchill River, in quejt of a North " Weji Pajfage, Copper Mines, or any other thi? ig " that may he ferviceahle to the Britijh Nation in

"general, ftandinc; by the fire, he bellowed out, in as loud a voice as his fituation would admit, "God dn you for a b h, if I live IJl knock out your brains." A few minutes after making this elegant apoftrophe, he expired in the greateft agonies that can poflibly be conceived.

This I declare to be the real charafter and manner of life of the late Mr. Mofes Norton.

December,

"general, or the Hifdons Bay Company in par ticular; in tbe year 1770.

"Mr. Samuel Hearne,

"SIR,

"As you have offered your fervice a third time " to go in fearch of the Copper Mine River, c. ' and as Matonabbee, a leading Indian, who has been at thofe parts, is willing to be your guide, we have accordingly engaged him for that fer- vice; but having no other inftrument on the fame conftruclion with the quadrant you had the misfortune to break, we have furnifhedyou " with an Elton's quadrant, being the moft pro- per inftrument we can now procure for mak- ing obfervations on the land.

"The above Leader, Matonabbee, and a few of " his beft men, which he has felecled for that pur- pofe, are to provide for you, affift you in all things, and conduct you to the Copper Mine " River; where you muft be careful to obferve the latitude and longitude, alfo the courfe of " the river, the depth of the water, theiituation " of the Copper Mines, Sec. but your firft in- ftructions, of November lixth, one thoufand fe-ven hundred and lixty-nine, being fufficiently " full, we refer you to every part thereof for " the better regulation of your conduct during this journey.

"As you and your Indian companions are fit- 1770. " ted out with everything: that we think is necef- l'" " fary, (or at leait as many ulerul articles as the nature of travelling in thofe parts will adaiit " of,) you are hereby defired to proceed on your journey as foon as poflible; and your prefenc " guide has promifed to take great care of you, " and conduct you out and home with all conve-" nient fpeed.

"I conclude with my beft wifiies for your " health and happinefs, together with a fuc-" cefsful journey and a quick return in fafety. " ivmen.

"(Signed) Moses Norton, Governor.

"Dated at Prince of Wales's Fort, " 7th December, 1770."

On the feventh of December I fet out on my 7th. third journey; and the weather, confidering the feafon of the year, was for fome days pretty mild. One of Matonabbee's wives being ill, oc-cafioned us to walk fo flow, that it was the thirteenth before we arrived at Seal River; at which time two men and their wives left us, whofe loads, when added to thofe of the remainder of my crew, made a very material difference, efpecially as Matonabbee's wife was fo ill as to be obliged to be hauled on a fledge.

Finding deer and all other game very fcarce, and not knowing how long it might be before vc Gould reach any place where they were in greater plenty, the Indians walked as far each day as their loads and other circumftances would s6th. conveniently permit. On the fixteenth, we arrived at Egg River, where Matonabbee and the reft of my crew had laid up fome provifions and other neceffaries, when on their journey to the Fort. On going to the place where they thought the provifions had been carefully fecured from all kinds of wild beafts, they had the mortification to find that fome of their countrymen, with whom the Governor had firft traded and difpatch-ed from the Fort, had robbed the ftore of every article, as well as of fome of their moft ufeful implements. This lofs was more feverely felt, as there was a total want of every kind of game; and the Indians, not expecting to meet with fo great a difappointment, had not ufed that oeco-iiomy in the expenditure of the oatmeal and other provifions which they had received at the Fort, as they probably would have done, had they not relied firmly on finding a fupply at this place. This difappointment and lofs was borne by the Indians with the greateft fortitude; and I did not hear one of them breathe the left hint of revenge in cafe they fhould ever difcover the offenders: the only effect it had on them was, that of making them put the beft foot foremoft. This was thought fo neceffary, that for fome time we walked every day from morning till night.

The days, however, being fhort, our fledges nno heavy, and fome of the road very bad, our pro- ' . Decern ocr.

grefs feldom exceeded lixteen or eighteen miles a day, and fome days we did not travel fo much.

On the eighteenth, as we were continuing our j courfe to the North Weft, up a fmall creek that empties itfelf into Egg River, we faw the tracks of many deer which had crolted that part a few days before; at that time there was not a frefli track to be feen: fome of the Indians, however, who had lately pafled that way, had killed more than they had occafion for, fo that feveral joints of good meat were found in their old tent-places; which, though only fufficient for one good meal, were very acceptable, as we had been in exceeding ftraitened circumftances for many days.

On the nineteenth, we purfued our courfe in 19th. the North Weft quarter; and, after leaving the above-mentioned creek, traverfed nothing but entire barren ground, with empty bellies, till the twenty-feventh; for though we arrived at fome th, woods on the twenty-fixth, and faw a few deer, four of which the Indians killed, they were at fo great a diftance from the place on which we lay, that it was the twenty-feventh before the meat was brought to the tents. Here the Indians propofed to continue one day, under pretence of repairing their fledges and fnow flioes j but from

December.

6S A JOURNEY TO THE lyo. the little attention they paid to thofe repairs, I was led to think that the want of food was the chief thing that detained them, as they never ceafed eating the whole day. Indeed for many days before we had been in great want, and for the laft three days had not tafted a morfel of any thing, except a pipe of tobacco and a drink of fnow water; and as we walked daily from morning till night, and were all heavy laden, cur ftrength began to fail. I muft confefs that I never fpent fo dull a Chriftmas; and when I recollected the merry feafon which was then palling, and reflecled on the immenfe quantities, and great variety of delicacies which were then expending in every part of Chriftendom, and that with a profufion bordering on wafte, I could not refrain from wifliing myfelf again in Europe, if it had been only to have had an opportunity of alleviating the extreme hunger which I fuftered with the refufe of the table of any one of my acquaintance. My Indians, however, ftill kept in good fpirits; and as we were then acrofs all the barren ground, and faw a few frefli tracks of deer, they began to think that the worft of the road was over for that winter, and flattered me with the expectation of foon meeting with deer and other game in greater plenty than we had done lincc our departure from the Fort. 28th. Early in the morning of the twenty-eighth, we again fet out, and directed our courfe to the

Weftvvard,

Wcflward, through thick fhrubby woods, confift-ing chiefly of ill-lhaped ftunted pines, with fmall dwarf junipers, intermixed here and there, particularly round the margins of ponds and fwamps, with dwarf willow bufhes; and among the rocks and fides of the hills were alfo fome fmall poplars.

On the thirtieth, we arrived at the Eaft lide of Ifland Lake, where the Indians killed two large buck deer; but the rutting feafon was fo lately over, that their flelh was only eatable by thofe who could not procure better food. In the evening, Matonabbee was taken very ill; and from the nature of his complaint, I judged his illnefs to have proceeded from the enormous quantity of meat that he had eat on the twenty-feventh, as he had been indifpofed ever fmce that time. Nothing is more common with thofe Indians, after they have eat as much at a fitting as would ferve fix moderate men, than to find themfelves out of order; but not one of them can bear to hear that it is the effecl of eating too much: in defence of which they fay, that the meaneft of the animal creation knows when hunger it fatisfied, and will leave off accordingly. This, however, is a falfe aifertion, advanced knowingly in fup-port of an abfurd argument; for it is well known by them, as well as all the Southern Indians, that the black bear, who, for fize and the delicacy of its flefli, may juftly be called a refpeclable animal, is fo far from knowing when its hunger is fatisiicdj

December.

-Oth.

A JroltRNty T6 THE fatisfied, that, in the Summer, when thfe berries are ripe, it will gore to fuch a desrree, that it fre-

Dcccmber.,,.

quently, and even daily, vomits up great quantities of new-fwallowed fruit, before it has undergone any change in the ftomach, and immediately renews its repafl with as much eager-nefs as before.

Notwithftanding the Northern Indians are at times fo voracious, yet they bear hunger with a degree of fortitude which, as Mr. Ellis juftly ob-ferves of the Southern Indians, " is much eafier to admire, than to imitate." I have more than once feen the Northern Indians, at the end of three or four days fafting, as merry and jocbfe on the fubjeft, as if they had voluntarily impofed it on themfelves; and would afk each other in the plained terms, and in the merrieft mood, If they had any inclination for an intrigue with a ftrange woman? I muft acknowledge that examples of this kind were of infinite fervice to me, as they tended to keep up my fpirits on thofe occafions vvith a deg: ree of fortitude that would have been impoitible for me to have done had the Indians behaved in a contrary manner, and expreffed any apprehenfion of ftarving. 3sa. Early in the morning of the thirty-firft, we continued our journey, and walked about fourteen miles to the Weftward on Ifland Lake, where we fixed our refidence; but Matonabbee was at this time fo ill as to be obliged to be hauled on a fledge the vhoie day. i'he next morning, however.

ever, he fo far recovered as to be capable of walking; when we proceeded on to the Weft and Weft by North, about fixteen miles farther on the iir fame Lake, till we arrived at two tents, which contained the remainder of the wives and families of my guides, who had been waiting there for the return of their hufbands from the Fort. Here we found only two men, though there were upward of twenty women and children; and as thofe two men had no gun or ammunition, they had no other method of fupporting themfelves and the women, but by catching fifh, and fnaring a few rabbits: the latter were fcarce, but the former were eafily caught in confiderable numbers either with nets or hooks. The fpecies of fifti generally caught in the nets are tittemeg, pike, and barbie; and the only forts caught with hooks are trout, pike, burbut, and a fmall fifh, erroneoufly called by the Englifh tench: the Southern Indians called it the toothed tittemeg, and the Northern Indians call it. faint eah. They are delicate eating; being nearly as firm as a perch, and generally very fat. They feldom exceed a foot in length, and in fhape much refemble a gurnard, except that of having a very long broad fin on the back, like a perch, but this fin is not armed with fimilar fpikes. The fcales are large, and of a footy brown. They are generally moft-eficcmed when broiled or roafted with the fcales on, of courfe the fkin is not eaten.

As the Captain Matonabbee and one man were were indifpofed, we did not move on the fecond of January; but early in the morning of the third fet out, and walked about feven miles to the North Weflward, five of which were on the above mentioned Lake; when the Indians having killed two deer, we put up for the night.

Ifland Lake (near the center) is in latitude 60" 45 North, and 102" 25 Weft longitude, from London; and is, at the part we croffed, about thirty-live miles wide: but from the North Eaft to the South Weft it is much larger, and entirely full of iflands, fo near to each other as to make the whole Lake refemble a jumble of fer-pentine rivers and creeks; and it is celebrated by by the natives as abounding with great plenty of fine fifli during the beginning of the Winter. At different parts of this Lake moft part of the wives and families of thofe Northern Indians who vifit Prince of Wales's Fort in October and November generally refide, and wait for their return; as there is little fear of their being in want of provifions, even without the afliftance of a gun and ammunition, which is a point of real confequence to them. The Lake is plentifully fuppiied with water from feveral fmall rivulets and creeks which run into it at the South Weft end; and it empties itfelf by means of other imall rivers which run to the North Eaft, the principal of which is Nemace-a-feepee-a-filb;, or Little Fifh River. Many of the iflands, as well as the main land round this Lake, abound with dwarf (Jwarf woods, chiefly pines; but in fome parts intermixed with larch and Imall birch trees. The land, like all the reft which lies to the North pf Seal River, is hilly, and full of rocks; and though none of the hills are high, yet as few of the woods grow on their fummits, they in general Ihew their fnowy heads far above the woods which grow in the vallies, or thofe which are fcattered about their lides.

, After leaving Ifland Lake, we continued our old courfe between the Weft and North Weft, and travelled at the eafy rate of eight or nine miles a day. Provifions of all kinds were fcarce till the fixteenth, when the Indians killed twelve deer. This induced us to put up, though early in the day; and finding great plenty of deer in the neighbourhood of our little encampment, it was agreed by all parties to remain a few days, in order to dry and pound fome meat to make it lighter for carriage.

Having, by the twenty-fecond, provided a fuf- ficient ftock of provifton, properly prepared, to carry with us, and repaired our fledges and fnow-flioes, we again purfued our courfe in the North Weft quarter; and in the afternoon fpoke with a ftranger, an Indian, who had one of Matonabbee's wives under his care. He did not remain in our company above an hour, as he onlyfmoked part pf a. few pipes with his friends, and returned to his tent, which could not be far diftant from the place where we lay that night, as the woman and her two children joined us next morning, before we had taken down our tent and made ready for moving. Thofe people were the firft flrangers whom we had met lince we left the Fort, though we had travelled feveral hundred miles; which is a proof that this part of the country is but thinly inhabited. It is a truth well known to the natives, and doubtlefs founded ori experience, that there are many very extenlive tracts of land in thofe parts, which are incapable of affording fupport to any number of the human face even during the fhort time they are palling through them, in the capacity of emigrants, from one place to the other; much lefs are they capable of affording a conflant fupport to thofe who might wifh to make them their fixed refidence at any feafon of the year. It is true, that few rivers or lakes in thofe parts are entirely deftitute of fifli J but the uncertainty of meeting with a fuiecient fupply for any confiderable time together, makes the natives very cautious how they put their whole dependance on that article, as it has too frequently been the means of many hundreds, being ftarved to death, ajd. By the twenty-third, deei were fo plentiful that the Indians feemed to think that, unlefs the feafon, contrary to expectation and general experience, fhould prove unfavourable, there would be no fear of our being in want of provilions during the reft Of the Winter, as dect had always

February.

NORTHERN OCEAN.

ways been known to be in great plenty in the di-reftion which they intended to walk.

On the third of February, we continued our I courfe to the Weft by North and Weft North I Weft, and were fo near the edge of the woods, that the barren ground was in fight to the North- !; ward. As the woods trended away to the Weft, ! we were obliged to alter our courfe to Weft by 11 South, for the fake of keeping among them, as : well as the deer. In the courfe of this day's walk we faw feveral ftrangers, fome of whom remained in our company, while others went on their refpedive ways.

On the fixth, we crofted the main branch of tj Cathawhachaga River; which, at that part, is about three quarters of a mile broad j and after walking three miles farther, came to the fide of Golfed Whoie, or Partridge, Lake; but the day being far fpent, and the weather exceflively cold, we put up for the night.

Early in the morning of the feventh, the wea-, th. ther being ferene and clear, we fet out, and croffed the above mentioned Lake; which at that part is about fourteen miles wide; but from the South South Weft to North North Eaft is much larger. It is impoflible to defcribe the in-tenfenefs of the cold which we experienced this day; and the difpatch we made in crofting the lake is almoft incredible, as it was performed by the greateft part of my crew in lefs than two hours J though fome of the women, who were heavy

A JOURNEY TO THE heavy laden, took a much longer time. Several of the Indians viere much frozen, but none of them more difagreeably fo than one of Matonab-bee's wives, whofe thighs and buttocks were in a manner incrufted with frofi:; and when thawed, feveral blifters arofe, nearly as large as flieeps bladders. The pain the poor woman fuffered on this occafion was greatly aggravated by the laughter and jeering of her companions, who faid that fhe was rightly ferved for belting her clothes fo high. I mull acknowledge that I was not in the number of thofe vho pitied her, as I thought he took too much pains to fhew a clean heel and good leg; her garters being always in fight, which, though by no means confidered here as bordering on indecency, is by far too airy to withftand the rigorous cold of a fevere winter in a high Northern latitude. I doubt not that the laughter of her companions was excited by fimiiar ideas.

When we got on the Weft fide of Partridge Lake we continued our courfe for many days toward the Weft by South and Weft South Weft; when deer were fo plentiful, and the Indians killed fuch vaft numbers, that notwithftanding we frequently remained three, four, or five days in a place, to eat up the fpoils of our hunting, yet at our departure we frequently left great quantities of good meat behind us, which we eould neither eat nor carry with us. This con-duel: is the more excufable among people whofe wandering wandering manner of life and contracted Ideas make every thing appear to them as the effecfl of mere chance. The great uncertainty of their ever vilitlng this or that part a fecond time, induces them to think there is nothing either wrong or improvident in living on the bed the country will afford, as they are paffing through it from place to place; and they feem willing that thofe who come after them fliould take their chance, as they have done.

On the twenty. firft, we crofled The-wholc-ky- o, ft, ed Whole, or Snowbird Lake, which at that part was about twelve or thirteen miles wide, though from North to South it is much larger. As deer were as plentiful as before, we expended much time in kiuing and eating them. This Mato-rabbee aflured me was the bcft way we could employ ourfelves, as the feafon would by no means permit us to proceed in a direct line for the Copper-mine River; but when the Spring advanced, and the deer began to draw out to the barren ground, he would then, he faid, proceed in fuch a manner as to leave no room to doubt of our arrival at the Copper-mine River in proper time.

On the fecond of March, we lay by the fide of Majh "Whooldyahd Whole or Pike Lake, and not far from Doo-baunt Whoie River. On the next jj. day we again began to crofs the above mentioned Lake, but after walking feven miles on it to the Weft South Weft, we arrived at a large tent of

Northern

March.

A JOURNEY TO TFIE

Northern Indians, who had been living there from the beginning of the Winter, and had found a plentiful fubfiftence by catching deer in a pound. This kind of employment is performed in the following manner:

When the Indians defign to impound deer, they look out for one of the paths in which a number of them have trod, and which is obferv-ed to be ftill frequented by them. When thefe paths crofs a lake, a wide river, or a barren plain, they are found to be much the beft for the pur-pofe; and if the path run through a clufter of woods, capable of affording materials for building the pound, it adds conliderably to the commodi-Gufnefs of the fituation. The pound is built by making a ftrong fence with brufhy trees, without obferving any degree of regularity, and the work is continued to any extent, according to the plea-fure of the builders. I have feen fome that were not lefs than a mile round, and am informed that there are others ftill more extenfive. The door, or entrance of the pound, is not larger than a common gate, and the infide is fo crowded with fmall counter-hedges as very much to refemble a maze; in every opening of which they fet a fnare, made with thongs of parchment deer-fkins well twifted together, which are amazingly ftrong. One end of the fnare is ufually made faft to a growing pole; but if no one of a fufficient fize can be found near the place where the fnare is fet, a loofe pole is fub-ftituted in its room, which is alvvays of fuch lize and length that a deer cannot drag it far before it gets entangled among the other woods, which gre all left ftanding except what is found necefla-ry for making the fence, hedges, c.

The pound being thus prepared, a row of fmall brufliwood is ftuck up in the fnow on each fide the door or entrance; and thefe hedge-rows are continued along the open part of the lake, river, or plain, where neither ftick nor ftump befides is to be feen, which makes them the more diftinclly obferved. Thefe poles, or brufli-wood, are generally placed at the diftance of fifteen or twenty yards from each other, and ranged in fuch a manner as to form two fides of a long acute angle, growing gradually wider in proportion to the di fiance they extend from the entrance of the pound, which fometimes is not lefs than two or three miles; while the deer's path is exactly along the middle, between the two rows of brulh-wood.

Indians employed on this fervice always pitch their tent on or near to an eminence that affords a commanding profpecl of the path leading to the pound; and when they fee any deer going that way, men, women, and children walk along the lake or river-fide under cover of the woods, tillthey get behind them, then ftep forth to open view, and proceed towards the pound in the form of a crefcent. The poor timorous deer finding themfelves purfued, and at the fame time taking the two rows of brufhy poles to be two ranks of people ftationed to prevent their paflingon either fide

March.

fidei run ftraight forward in the path till they get into the pound. The Indians then clofe in, and block up the entrance with fome brufhy trees, that have been cut down and lie at hand for that purpofe. The deer being thus enclofed, the women and children walk round the pound, to prevent them from breaking or jumping over the fence, while the men are employed fpearing fuch as are entangled in the fnares, and Ihooting with bows and arrows thofe which remain loofe in the pound.

This method of hunting, if it deferves the name, is fometimes fo fuccefsf-jl, that many families fubfift by it without having occafion to move their tents above once or twice during the courfe of a whole winter; and when the Spring advances, both the deer and Indians draw out to the Eaftward, on the ground which is entirely barren, or at leaft what is fo called in thofe parts, as it neither produces trees or flirubsof any kind, fo that mofs and fome little grafs is all the herbage which is to be found on it. Such an eafy way of procuring a comfortable maintenance in the Winter months, (which is by far the worft time of the year,) is wonderfully well adapted to the fupport of the aged and infirm, but is too apt to occafion an habitual indolence in the young and adlive, who frequently fpend a whole Winter in this indolent manner: and as thofe parts of the country are almoft deftitute of every animal of the furr kind, it cannot be fuppofed that thofe who indulge themfelves in this indolent method of procuring food can be mafters of any thing for trade; whereas thofe who do not get their livelihood at fo eafy a rate, generally procure furrs enough during the Winter to purchafe a fuffici-ent fupply of ammunition, and other European goods, to laft them another year. This is nearly the language of the more induftrious among them, who, of courfe, are of mod importance and value to the Hudfon's Bay Company, as it is from them the furrs are procured which compofe the greateft part of Churchill trade. But in my opinion, there cannot exift a ftronger proof that mankind was not created to enjoy happinefs in this world, than the condud of the miferable beings who inhabit this wretched part of it; as none but the aged and infirm, the women and children, a few of the more indolent and unambitious parr. of them, will fubmit to remain in the parts where food and clothing are procured in this eafy manner, becaufe no animals are produced there whofe furrs are valuable. And what do the more induftrious gain by giving themfelves all this additional trouble? The real wants of thefe people are few, and eafily fupplied; a hatchet, an ice-chiffel, a file, and a knife, are all that is required to enable them, with a little induftry, to procure a comfortable livelihood; and thofe who endeavour to poflefs more, are always the moft unhappy, and may, in fact, be faid to be only flaves and isarriers to the reft, whofe ambition never leads

O them

March.

them to any thing beyond the means of procuring food and clothing, It is true, the carriers pride themfelves much on the refpecl which is fhevvn to them at the Faclory; to obtain which they fre-quently run great rifques of being ftarved to death in their way thither and back; and all that they can pofiibly get there for the furrs they procure after a year's toil, feldom amounts to more than is fufiicient to yield a bare fubfiltence, and a few furrs for the enfuing year's market; while thofe whom they call indolent and mean-fpirited live generally in a (late of plenty, without trouble or rifque; and confequently raufl. be the mod happy, and, in truth, the moft independent alfo. it mutl: be allowed that they are by far the greateft phi-lofophers, as they never give themfelves the trouble to acquire what they can do well enough without. The deer they kill, furnifhes them with food, and a variety of warm and comfortable clothing, either with or without the hair, according as the feafons require; and it mud be very hard indeed, if they cannot get furrs enough in the courfe of two or three years, to purchafe a hatch- et, and iuch other edge-tools as are neceffary for their purpofe. Indeed thofe who take no concern at: all about procuring furrs, have generally an opportunity of providing themfelves with alt their real wants from their more induftrious countrymen, in exchange for provifions, andrea-i dy-dre(I"ed lldnsfor clothing.

It is undoubtedly the duty of every one of the

Com-

Company's fervants to encourage a fpirit of indu-ftry among the natives, and to ufe every means in their power to induce them to procure furrs and other commodities for trade, by affuring them of a ready purchafe and good payment for every thing they bring to the fa(ftory: and I can truly fay, that this has ever been the grand object of my attention. But I muft at the fame time confefs, that fuch conduft is by no means for the real benefit of the poor Indians, it being well known that thofe who have the leaft intercourfe with the Factories, are by far the happieft. As their whole aim is to procure a comfortable fubfiftence, they take the moft prudent methods to accomplifh it; and by always following the lead of the deer, are feldom expofed to the griping hand of famine, o frequently felt by thofe who are called the annual traders. It is true, that there arc few of the Indians, whofe manner of life I have juft defcrib-ed, but have once in their lives at leaft vifited Prince of Waless Fort; and the hardftiips and dangers which moft of them experienced on thofe occafions, have left fuch a lafting impreflion on their minds, that nothing can induce them to repeat their vifits: nor is it, in faft, the interefl of the company that people of this eafy turn, and who require only as much iron-work at a time as can be purchafed with three or four beaver ikins, and that only once in two or three years, fhould be invited to the Factories; becaufe what they beg and fteal while there, is worth, in the way of G 2 trade trade, three times the quantity of furrs which they bring. For this reafon, it is much more for the interell of the Company that the annual traders (hould buy up all thofe fmall quantities of furrs, and bring them in their own name, than that a parcel of beggars fhouid be encouraged to come to the Factory with fcarcely as many furrs as will pay for the victuals they eat while they are on the plantation.

I have often heard it obferved, that the Indians who attend the deer-pounds might, in the courfe of a winter, collect a vaft number of pelts, which would well deferve the attention of thofe who are called carriers or traders; but it is a truth, though unknown to thofe fpeculators, that the deer fkins at that feafon are not only as thin as a bladder, but are alfo full of warbles, which render them of little or no value. Indeed, were they a more marketable commodity than they really are, the remote fituation of thofe pounds from the Company's Factories, muft for ever be an unfur-xnountable barrier to the Indians bringing any of thofe fkins to trade. The fame obfervation may be made of all the other Northern Indians, whofe chief fupport, the whole year round, is venifon; but the want of heavy draught in Winter, and water-carriage in fummer, will not permit them to bring many deer fkins to market, not even thofe that are in feafon, and for which there has always been great encouragement given.

We flopped only one night in company with the Indians Indians whom we met on Pike Lake, and in the 1771. morning of the fourth, proceeded to crofs the-"TT mainder of that Lake j but, though the weather 411. was fine, and though the Lake was not more than twenty-feven miles broad at the place where we croited it, yet the Indians loft fo much time at play, that it was the feventh before we arrived on 7th. the Weft fide of it. During the whole time we were crofiing it, each night we found either points of land, or iqands, to put up in. On the eighth, stb, we lay a little to the Eaft North Eaft of Black Bear Hill, where the Indians killed twodeer, which were the firft we had feen for ten days; but having plenty of dried meat and fat with us, we were by no means in want during any part of that time. On the ninth, we proceeded on our courfe th, to the Weftward, and foon met with as great plenty of deer as we had feen during any part of our journey; which, no doubt, made things go on fmooth and eafy: and as the Spring advanced, the rigour of the winter naturally abated, fo that at times we had fine pleafant weather overhead, though it was never fo warm as to occafion any thaw, unlefs in fuch places as lay expofed to the mid-day fun, and were flieltered from all the cold winds.

On the nineteenth, as we were continuing our igth, courfe to the Weft and Weft by South, we faw the tracks of feveral ftrangers; and on following the main path, we arrived that night at five tents of Northern Indians, who had refided there great part

Maich soth

A JOURNEY TO THE part of the "Winter, fnaring deer in the fame manner as thofe before mentioned. Indeed, it fhould feem that this, as well as fome other places, had been frequented more than once on this occafion; for the wood that had been cut down for fewel, and other ufes, was almoft incredible. Before morning, the weather became fo bad, and the ftorm continued to rage with fuch violence, that we did not move for feveral days; and as fome of the Indians we met with at this place were go-imr to Prince of Wales's Fort in the Summer, I embraced the opportunity of fending by them a Letter to the Chief at that Fort, agreeably to the tenor of my inftruclions. By fumming up my courfes and diftances from my lafl: obfervation,. for the weather at that time would not permit me to obferve, 1 judged myfelf to be in latitude 61 30 North, and about 19 60 of longitude to the Weft of Churchill River. This, and fome accounts of the ufage I received from the natives, with my opinion of the future fuccefs of the journey, formed the contents of my Letter.

Tid. On the twenty-third, the weather became fine and moderate, fo we once more purfued our way, 26th. 2-nd the next day, as well as on the tvventy-fixth, faw feveral more tents of Northern Indians, who were enipk:)yed in the fame manner as thofe we had formerly met; but fome of them having had bad fuccefs, and being relations or acquaintances of part of my crew, joined our company, and proceeded with us to the Weftward. Though the deer did not then keep regular paths, fo as to enable the Indians to catch them in pounds, yet they were to be met with in great abundance in fcattered herds; fo that my companions killed as many as they pleafed with their guns.

We ftili continued our courfe to the Weft and; Weft by South, and on the eighth of April, ar-rived at a fmall Lake, called Thelewey-aza-yeth; but with what propriety it is fo called I cannot difcover, for the meaning of Thelewey-aza-yeth is Little Fifti Hill: probably fo called from a high hill which ftands on a long point near the Weft end of the lake. On an ifland in this Lake we pitched our tents, and the Indians finding deer very numerous, determined to ftay here fome time, in order to dry and pound meat to take with us; for they well knew, by the feafon of the year, that the deer were then drawing out to the barren ground, and as the Indians propofed to walk due North on our leaving the Lake, it was uncertain when we Ihould again meet with any more. As feveral Indians had during the Winter joined our party, our number had now in-creafed to feven tents, which in the whole contained not lefs than feventy perfons.

Agreeably to the Indians' propofals we remained at Thelewey-aza-yeth ten days; during which time my companions were bufily employed (at their intervals from hunting) in preparing fmall ilaves of birch-wood, about one and a quarter inch fquare, and feven or eight feet long. Thefe ferve ferve as tent-poles all the fummer, while on the barren ground; and as the fall advances, are converted into fnow fhoe frames for Winter ufe. Birchrind, together with timbers and other woodwork for building canoes, were alfo another ob-jed of the Indian's attention while at this place; but as the canoes were not to be fet up till our arrival at Clowey, (which was many miles diftant,) all the wood-work was reduced to its proper fize, for the fake of making it light for carriage.

. As to myfelf, I had little to do, except to make a few obfervations for determining the latitude, bringing up my journal, and filling up my chart to the prefent time. I found the latitude of this place 6i 30 North, and its longitude, by my account, 19 Weft of Prince of Wales's Fort. i8th. Having a good ftock of dried provifions, and mod of the neceflary work for canoes all ready, on the eighteenth we moved about nine or ten miles to the North North Weft, and then came to a tent of Northern Indians who were tenting on the North fide of Thelewey-aza River. From thefc Indians Matonabbee purchafed another wife; fo that he had now no lefs than feven, moft of whom would for fize have made good grenadiers. He prided himfelf much in the height and ftrength of his wives, and would frequently fay, few women would carry or haul heavier loads; and though they had, in general, a very mafcu-iine appearance, yet he preferred them to thofe of a more delicate form and moderate ftature.

In a country like this, where a partner in exceltive hard labour is the chief motive for the union, and the fofter endearments of a conjugal life are only confidered as a fecondary objeft, there feems. to be great propriety in fuch a choice; but if all the men were of this way of thinking, what would become of the greater part of the women, who in general are but of low flature, and many of them of a moft delicate make, though not of the ex-acleft proportion, or mofl: beautiful mould? Take them in a body, the women are as deftitute of real beauty as any nation I ever faw, though there are fome few of them, when young, who are tolerable; but the care of a family, added to their conftant hard labour, foon make the moft beautiful among them look old and wrinkled, even before they are thirty; and feveral of the more ordinary ones at that age are perfect antidotes to love and gallantry. This, however, does not render them lefs dear and valuable to their owners, which is a lucky circumftance for thofe women, and a certain proof that there is no fuch thing as any rule or ftandard for beauty. Afk a Northern Indian, what is beauty? he will anfwer, a broad flat face, fmall eyes, high cheek-bones, three or four broad black lines a-crofs each cheek, a low forehead, a large broad chin, a clumfy hook-nofe, a tawny, hide, and breafts hanging down to the belt. Thofe beauties are greatly heightened, or at leaft rendered more valuable, when the poftef-for is capable of dreffing all kinds of ikins, converting verting them into the different parts of their clothing, and able to carry eight or ten ftone in Summer, or haul a much greater weight in Winter. Thefe, and other fimilar accomphfliments, are all that are fought after, or expected, of a Northern Indian woman. As to their temper, it is of little confequence; for the men have a wonderful facility in making the moft ftubborn comply with as much alacrity as could poflibly be ex-petted from thofe of the mildeft and moft obliging turn of mind; fo that the only real difference is, the one obeys through fear, and the other complies cheerfully from a wilhng mind; both knowing that what is commanded muft be done. They are, in fact, all kept at a great diftance, and the rank they hold in the opinion of the men cannot be better exprelted or explained, than by obferv-ing the method of treating or ferving them at meals, which would appear very humiliating, to an European woman, though cuftom makes it fit light on thofe whofe lot it is to bear it. It is ne-ceffary to obferve, that when the men kill any large beaft, the women are always fent to bring it to the tent: when it is brought there, every operation it undergoes, fuch as fplitting, drying, jj pounding, kc. is performed by the women. When any thing is to be prepared for eating, it is the women who cook it; and when it is done, the wives and daughters of the greateft Captains

The flone here mesnt is fourteen pounds.

in the country are never ferved, till all the males, " even thofe who are in the capacity of fervants, "Ihave eaten what they think proper; and in times i of fcarcity it is frequently their lot to be left with-1 out a fingle morfel. It is, however, natural to it ithink they take the liberty of helping themfelves In fecret; but this muft be done with great prudence, as capital embezzlements of provifions in fuch times are looked on as affairs of real confe-quence, and frequently fubjecl them to a very cc fevere beating. If they are pra5lifcd by a woman n- whofe youth and inattention to domeftic concerns p. cannot plead in her favour, they will for ever be ey I blot in her charader, and few men will chufe to lit bave her for a wife.

ot Finding plenty of good birch growing by the f. fide of Theley-aza River, we remained there for a at few days, in order to complete all the wood-work to for the canoes, as well as for every other ufe for lit which we could poflibly want it on the barren le, ground, during our Summer's cruife. On the i) twentieth, Matonabbee fent one of his brothers,, aotjj it and feme others, a-head, with birch-rind and e, wood-work for a canoe, and gave them orders to, gi proceed to a fmall Lake near the barren ground;, called Clowey, where they were defired to make; ii jail poffible hafte in building the canoe, that it, f might be ready on our arrival. p. Having finilhed fuch wood-work as the Indians i; thought vould be neceffary, and having augmented our ftock of dried meat and fat, the twenty- twenty-firft was appointed for moving; but oht of the women having been taken in labour, and it being rather an extraordinary cafe, we were detained more than two days. The inftant, however, the poor woman was delivered, which was not until fhe had fuffered all the pains ufually felt on thofe occafions for near fifty-two hours, the lignal was made for moving when the poor creature took her infant on her back and fet out with the reft of the company; and though another perfon had the humanity to haul her fledge for her, (for one day only,) fhe was obliged to car-ry a confiderable load befide her little charge, and was frequently obliged to wade knee-deep in water and wet fnow. Her very looks, exclufive of her moans, were a fufficient proof of the great painj fhe endured, infomuch that although fhe was a perfon I greatly difliked, her diftrefs at this time fo overcame my prejudice, that I never felt more for any of her fex in my life; indeed her fighs pierced me to the foul, and rendered me very mi. fcrable, as it was not in my power to relieve her.

When a Northern Indian woman is taken in la-i bour, a fmall tent is ere(5ted for her, at fuch a dif-j tance from the other tents that her cries canncjt eaiily be heard, and the other women and youn girls are her conftant vifitants: no male, exce children in arms, ever offers to approach her. It is a circumftance perhaps to be lamented, that thefe people never attempt to affifl each other o thofe occafions, even in the moft critical cafes.

Thii

This is in fome meafure owing to delicacy, but 1771. more probably to an opinion they entertain that v.,-v inature is abundantly fufficient to perform every "p"-thing required, without any external help whatever. When I informed them of the affiftance which European women derive from thefkill and attention of our midwives, they treated it with the utmofl contempt; ironically obferving, " that the many hump-back?, bandy-legs, and other deformities fo frequent among the Englifh, were undoubtedly owing to the great fkill of the perfons who affifted in bringing them into the world, and to the extraordinary care of their nurfes afterward.

A Northern Indian woman after child-birth is eckoned unclean for a month or five weeks; luring which time flie always remains in 1 fmall ent placed at a little diflance from the others, vith only a female acquaintance or two; anddur-ng the whole time the father never fees the child. Their reafon for this practice is, that children vhen firft born are fometimes not very fightly, laving in general large head5, and but little hair, nd are, moreover, often difcoloured by the force)f the labour; fo that were the father to fee them o fuch great difadvantage, he might probably ake a diilike to them, which never afterward ould be removed.

The names of the children are always given to jhem by the parents, or fome perfon near of kin.? hofe of the boys are various, and generally derived g A JOURNEY TO THE rived from fome place, feafon, or animal; the names of the girls are chiefly taken from fome part or property of a Martin; fuch as, the White Martin, the Black Martin, the Summer Martin, the Martin's Head, the Martin's Foot, the Martin's Heart, the Martin's Tail, c.

23a. On the twenty. third, as I hinted above, we be- gan to move forward, and to fhape our courfe nearly North; but the weather was in general fo hot, and fo much fnow had, in confequence, been melted, as made it bad walking in fnow-Ihoes, and fuch exceeding heavy hauling, that it

May. was the third of May before we could arrive at Clowey, though the diftance was not above eighty-five miles from Thelewey-aza-yeth. In our way we croffed part of two fmall Lakes, called Tittameg Take and Scartack Lake; neither of which are of any note, though both abound with, fine fifh.

JVIatonabbee had eiht wives, and they were all called Martins,

CHAP.

Tranfaclions at Clowey, and on our Journey, till our Arrival at the Copper-mine River.

Several Jlrange Indians join us. Indians employed building canoes; dcfcripiion and ufe of them.

More Indians join us to the amount offome hundreds.

Leave Cdowey. Receive intelligence that Keel- hies was near us. Two young men difpatchedfor my letters and goods. Arrive at Fefloew hake; crofs part of it, and make a large fmoke. One of Matonabbees wives elopes. So? ne remarks on the natives. Keeijhies joins us, and delivers my letters, but the goods were all expended. A Northern India?! wijhes to take one of Matonabbee's wives from him; matters compromifed, but had like to have proved fatal to my progrefs. Crofs Pefhevo Lake, when I make proper arrangements for the remainder of my journey. Ma? iy Indians join our party, in order to make war on the Efquimaux at the Copper River. Preparations made for that purpofe while at Clowey. Proceed on our journey to the North. Some remarks on the way. Crofs Cogead Lake 07t the ice. The fun did not fet. Arrive at Conge-cathawhachoga. Find feveral Copper Indians there, Remarks and tranfadions during our flay at Con-gecathawhachaga, Proceed on our journey. Weather very bad. Arrive at the Stoney Mountains. Some account of them. Crofs part of Buffalo Lake g6 A JOURNEY TO THE en the ice. Saw many nwjh-oxen. Defcription of them. Went with fome Indians to view Grizzle-bear Hill. ydn ajirange Northern Indian header called Olye, in company with fome Copper Indians, Their behaviour to me. Arrive at the Coppermine River.

lyyi. "IHE Lake Clowey is not much more than-v- A. twelve miles broad in the wideft part. A

May.

fmall river which runs mto it on the "Weft fide, is faid by the Indians to join the Athapufcow Lake. 3d. On our arrival at Clowey on the third of May, we found that the Captain's brother, and thofe who were fent a-head with him from Theley-aza River, had only got there two days before us; and, on account of the weather, had not made the leaft progrefs in building the canoe, the plan of which they had taken with them. The fame day we got to Clowey feveral other Indians joined us from different quarters, with intent to build their canoes at the fame place. Some of thofe indians had refided within four or five miles, to the South Eaft of Clowey all the Winter; and had procured a plentiful livelihood by fnaring deer, in the manner which has been already defcribed Immediately after our arrival at Clowey, the Indians began to build their canoes, and embraced every convenient opportunity for that purpofe: but as warm and dry weather only is fit for this bufinefs, which was by no means the cafe at pre-fent, it was the eighteenth of May before the canoes noes belonging to my party could be completed. On the nineteenth we began to proceed on our journey; but Matonabbee's canoe meeting with fome damage, which took near a whole day to repair, we were detained till the twentieth. a-th

Thofe veltels, though made of the fame materials with the canoes of the Southern Indians, differ from them both in fhape and conftruflion; they are alfo much fmaller and lighter, and though very flight and fimple in their conftruclion, are neverthelefs the beft that could poliibly be contrived for the ufe of thofe poor people, who are frequently obliged to carry them a hundred, and fometimes a hundred and fifty miles at a time, without having occafion to put them into the water. Indeed, the chief ufe of thefe canoes is to ferry over unfordable rivers; though fometimes, and at a few places, it muft be acknowledged, that they are of great fervice in killing deer, as they enable the Indians to crofs rivers and the narrow parts of lakes; they are alfo ufeful in killing fwans, geefe, ducks, c. in the moulting feafon.

All the tools ufed by an Indian in building his canoe, as well as in making his fnow-fhoes, and every other kind of wood-work, con (id of a hatchet, a knife, a file, and an awl; in the ufe of which they are fo dextrous, that every thing they make is executed with a neatnefs not to be excelled by the moft expert mechanic, afiifted with every tool he could wifh.

In fliape the Northern Indian canoe bears fome H re fern- refemblange to a weaver's fhuttle; being flat-bottomed, with ftraight upright fides, and fbarp at each end; but the ftern is by far the wideft part, as there the baggage is generally laid, and occafionaily a fecond perion, who always lies down at full length in the bottom of the canoe. In this manner they carry one another acrofs rivers and the narrow parts of lakes in thofe little veifels, which feldom exceed twelve or thirteen feet in length, and are from twenty inches to two feet broad in the wideft part. The head, or fore part, is unnecefiarily long, and narrow; and is all covered over with birch-bark, which adds confi-derably to the weight, without contributing to the burthen of the veffel. In general, thefe Indians make ufe of the fingle paddle, though a few have double ones, like the Efquimaux: the latter, however, are feldom ufed, but by thofe who lie in wait to kill deer as they crofs rivers and narrow lakes.

During

See Plate IV. where Fig. A reprcfents the bottom of the canoe, Fig. B being the fore-pai t. Fig. C is the complete frame of one before it is covered with the bark of the birch-tree: it is reprefented on an attificial bank, which the natives raife to build it on. Fig, D is an end view of a fet of ti. Tvbers, bent and lailied in their proper fhapc, and left to dry. Fig. E is the reprefentj. tion of a complete canoe. Fig. F reprefents one of their paddles. Fig. G a fpear with which they kill deer; and Fig. H, their mode of carrying the canoe:

The following references are to the feveral parts of the canoe: Fig. C. I. The ftem. a. The ftern-poh:. 5. Two forked (ticks fupporiing the flem and flern-polt. 4. The gunwales. 5. Small rods placed between the timber and birch-back that covers them, 6. The timbers, 7. The keel-ibn. 8. Large floaes placed there to keep the bottom fteady till the fides are fewed. on.

JM r???

Hi!? r f

During our ftay at Clowcy we were joined by ilpward of two hundred Indians from different quarters, moft of whom built canoes at this place; but as 1 was under the protection of a principal man, no one offered to moleft me, nor can 1 fay they were very clamorous for any thing I had. This was undoubtedly owing to Matonabbee's informing them of my true fituation; which was, that I had not, by any means, fuiecient neceffa-ries for myfelf, much lefs to give away. The few goods which 1 had with me were intended to be referved for the Copper and Dogribbed Indians, who never vilit the Company's Factories. Tobacco was, however, always given away; for every one of any note, who joined us, expefted to be treated with a few pipes, and on fome oc-cacons it was fcarcely poffible to get off without prefenting a few inches to them; which, with the conftant fupplies which I was obliged to fur-nifh my own crew, decreafed that article of my Hock fo faft, that notwithftanding I had yet ad-vanced fo fmall a part of my journey, more than one half of my (lore was expended. Gun-pow-der and fhot alfo were articles commonly alked for by moft of the Indians we met; and in general thefe vere dealt round to them witli a liberal hand by my guide Matonabbee. I muff, however, do him the juftice to acknowledge, that what

The tobaocouf"d in Hudfon's Bay is the Biafil tobacco; which is twilled into the form of a rope, of near an inch diameter, and then wound into a large roll; from which it is taken by mcafures of length, for the nativt-s.

he diftributed was all his own, which he had pur-chafed at the Factory; to my certain knowledge he bartered one hundred and fifty martins' fkins for powder only; befides a great number of beaver, and other furrs, for (hot, ball, iron-work, Snd tobacco, purpofely to give away among his countrymen; as he had certainly as many of thefe articles given to him as were, in his opinion, fuili-cient for our fupport during our journey out and home. May Matonabbee's canoe having been repaired, on the twentieth we left Clowey, and proceeded Northward. That' morning a fmall gang of (tran-gers joined us, who informed my guide, that Captain Keellhies was within a day's walk to the Southward. Keelfhies was the man by whom I had lent a letter to Prince of Wales's Fort, from Cathawhachaga, in the beginning of July one thoufand feven hundred and feventy; but not long after that, having the misfortune to break my quadrant, I was obliged to return to the Fort a fecond time; and though we faw many fmokes, and fpoke with feveral Indians on my return that year, yet he and I milted each other on the barren ground, and I liad not feen or heard of him fmce that time.

As Matonabbee was delirous that 1 fliould receive my letters, and alfo the goods 1 had written for, he difpatched two of his young men to bring them. We continued our journey to the Northward; and the next day faw feveral large fmokes at a great diftance to the Eallward on the barren ground, which were fuppolbd to be made by fome parties of Indians bound to Prince of Wales's Fort with furrs and other commodities for trade.

On the twenty-fecond and twenty third, we proceeded to the North, at the rate of fourteen or fifteen miles a day; and in the evening of the latter, got clear of all the woods, and lay on the bar-ren ground. The flime evening the two young men who were fent for my letters, kc. returned, and told me that Keelfliies had promifed to join us in a few days, and deliver the things to me with his own hand.

The twenty-fourth proved bad and rainy wea-?4th. ther, fo that we only walked about feen miles, when finding a few blafted flumps of trees, we pitched our tents. It was well we did fo, for towards night we had excelfively bad weather, with loud thunder, ftrong lightning, and heavy rain, attended with a very hard gale of wind from the South Weft; toward the next morning, however, the wind veered round to the North Weft, and the weather became intenfely cold and frofly. We walked that day about eight miles to the Northward, when we were obliged to put up, being almoft benumbed with cold. There we found a few dry ftumps, as we had done the day before, which ferved us for fewel.

I have obferved, during my feveral journies in thofe parts, that all the ay to the North of Seal River the edge of the wood is faced with old vi- tlicved csth.

102 A JOURNEY TO THE

The weather on the twenty-fixth was fo bad, "J with fnow and thick drifting fleet that we did not move; but the next morning proving fine and pleafant, we dried our things, and walked about twelve miles to the Northward; moft of the way on the ice of a fmall river which runs into Pefhew Lake. We then faw afmoke to the Southward, which we judged to be made by Keelfhies, fo we put up for the night by the lide of the above-mentioned Lake, where I expected we fhould have waited for his arrival; but, to my great furprize, on the morrow we again fet forward, and walked twenty-two miles to the Northward on Pefhew Lake, and in the afternoon pitched our tents on an ifland, where, by my defire, the Indians made a large fmoke, and propofed to flay a day or two for Claptain Keelfhies.

tnered flumps, aad trees which have been blown down by the wind. They are moftly of the fort which is called herejuniper, but were feldom of any confiderable fize. Thofc blafted trees are. found in fome parts to extend to the diftance of twenty miles from the living woods, and detached patches of them are much farther off; which is a proof that the cold has been encreafing in thofe parts for fome ages. Indeed, fome of the older Northern Indians have aftured me, that they have heard their fathers and grandfathers fay, they remembered the grcateft part of thofe places wheie the trees are now blafled and dead, in a fiourifhing ftate; and that they nere remarkable for abounding with deer. It is a well-known fat, that many deer are fond of frequenting thofe plains where the juniper trees abound near barren grounds, particularly in fine weather during the Winter; but in heavy gales of wind they either take fhelter in the. thick woods, or go out on the open plains. The Indians, who never want a reafon for any thing, fay, that the deer quit the thin flraggiing woods during the Iiigh winds, becaufe the nodding of the trees, when at a confiderable diftance from eachoher, frightens them; but in the midft of a thick forefl, iheconflant ruftlng of the branches lulls them into fecutity, andrendeis ibem an eafy prey to a flcilful hunter.

Probably the fame with Partridge Lake in the Map.

NORTHERN OCEAN. lo In the night, one of Matonabbec's wives and another woman eloped: it was fuppoled they went off to the Eaftward, in order to meet their former hufbands, from whom they had been fometime before taken by force. This aflair made more noife and buftle than I could have fuppof-ed; and Matonabbee fecmed entirely difconcert. ed, and quite inconfolable for the lofs of his wife. She was certainly by far the handfomeft of all his flock, of a moderate fize, and had a fair complexion; fhe apparently poflefted a mild tem. per, and very engaging manners. In fac, fhc feemed to have every good quality that could beexpe(5led in a Northern Indian woman, and that could render her an agreeable companion to an inhabitant of this part of the vorld. She had not, however, appeared happy in her late fituation; and chofc rather to be the fole wife of a fprightly young fellow of no note, fthough very capable of maintaining her,) than to have the feventh or eighth fhare of the affection of the greateft man in the country. I am forry to mention an incident which happened

while we were building tlie canoes at Clowey, and which by no means does honour
to Matonabbee: it is no lefs a crime than that of having actually dabbed the hufband
of the above-mentioned girl in three places; and had it not been for timely affiftance,
would certainly have murdered him, for no other reafon than becaufe the poor man
had fpoken difrefpeclfully of him for having taken his wife away by force. The cool
deliberation

"deliberation with which Matonabbee committed this bloody action, convinced me
it had been a long premeditated defign; for he no fooner heard of the man's arrival,
than he opened one of his wives' bundles, and with the greateft compofure, took out
a new long box-handled knife, went into the man's tent, and, without any preface
whatever, took him by the collar, and began to execute his horrid defign. The poor
man anticipating his danger, fell on his face, and called for af-iiftance; but before
any could be had he received three wounds in the back. Fortunately fen: him, they
all happened on the flioulder-blade, fo that his life was fpared. When Matonabbee
returned to his tent, after commiitting this horrid deed, he fat down as compofedly as
if nothing had happened, called for water to wafh his bloody hands and knife, fmoked
his pipe as ufual, feem-ed to be perfectly at eafe, and afked if l did not think he had
done right?

It has ever been the cuftom among thofe people for the men to wreftle for any
woman to whom they are attached; and, of courfe, the ftrongeft party always carries
off the prize. A weak man, uniefs he be a good hunter and well-beloved, is feldom
permitted to keep a wife that a ftronger man thinks worth his notice: for at any time
when the wives of thofe ftrong wreftlers are heavy-laden either with furrs or provifions,
they make no fcruple of tearing any other man's wife from his bofom, and making her
bear a part of his luggage. This cuftom prevails throughout all their tribes, and caufes
a great fpirit of emulation among their youth, who are upon all occafi-ons, from their
childhood, trying their ftrength and fkill in wreftling. This enables them to pro-ted
their property, and particularly their wives, from the hands of thofe powerful ravifhers;
fome of whom make almoft a livelihood by taking what they pleafe from the weaker
parties, without making them any return. Indeed, it is reprefented as an act of great
generofity, if they condefcend to make an unequal exchange j as, in general, abufe and
infult are the only return for the lofs which is fuftained.

The way in which they tear the women and other property from one another, though
it has the appearance of the greateft brutality, can fcarcely be called fighting. I never
knew any of them receive the leaft hurt in thefe rencontres; the whole buiinefs confifts
in hauling each other about by the hair of the head; they are feldom known either
to llrike or kick one another. It is not uncommon for one of them to cut off his hair
and to greafe his ears, immediately before the conteft begins. This, however, is done
privately; and it is fometimes truly laughable, to fee one of the parties flrutting about
with an air of great importance, and cauing out, "Where is he? Why does he not come
out r" when the other will bolt out with a clean fhorned head and greaf-ed ears, rufl
on his antagonift, feize, him by the hair, and though perhaps a much weaker man,
foon drag him to the ground, while the ftronger is not able to lay hold on him. It
is very frequent on thofe occafions for each party to have fpies, to watch the other's
motions, which puts them more on a footing of equality. For want of hair to pull, they

feize each other about the waift, with legs wide extended, and try their ftrength, by endeavouring to vie who can firft thro wthe other down.

On thefe wreftling occafions the flanders-by never attempt to interfere in the conteft; even one brother offers not to aflift another, unlefs it be with advice, which, as it is always delivered openly on the field during the conteft, may, in fact, be faid to be equally favourable to both parties. It fometimes happens that oneof the wreft-lers is fuperior in flrength to the other; and if a woman be the caufe of the conteft, the veaker is frequently unwilling to yield, notwithftanding he is greatly overpowered. When this happens to be the cafe, the relations and friends, or other bye-ftanders, will fometimes join to perfuade the weaker combatant to give up the conteft, left, by continuing it, he fhould get bruifed and hurt, without the leaft probability of being able to pro-ted: what he is contending for. I obferved that very few of thofe people were diffatisfied with the wives which had fallen to their lot, for whenever any coniiderable number of them were in company, fcarcely a day paflcd without fome overtures being made for contefts of this kind; and it was often very unpleafant to me, to fee the object of the contcft fitting in penfive filence watching her fate, while her hufband and his rival were contending for the prize. I have indeed not only felt pity for thofe poor wretched viflims, but the utmoft indignation, when I have feen them won, perhaps, by a man whom they mortally hated. On thofe occafions their grief and rcluclance to follow their new lord has been fo great, that the bufinefs has often ended in thegreateft brutality; for, in the ftruggle, I have feen the poor girls flripped quite naked, and carried by main force to their, new lodgings. At other times it was plea-fant enough to fee a fine girl led off the field from a huftand fhe difliked, with a tear in one eye and a finger on the other: for cufl: om, or delicacy if you pleafe, has taught them to think it neceffary to whimper a little, let the change be ever fo much to their inclination. I have throughout this account given the women the appellation of girls, which is pretty applicable, as the objects of con-teft are generally young, and without any family: few of the men chufe to be at the trouble of main-taining other people's children, except on particular occafions, which will be taken notice of hereafter.

Some of the old men, who are famous on account of their fuppofed Ikill in conju-ration, have great influence in perfuading the rabble from committing thofe outrages; but the humanity of thefe fages is fcldom known to extend beyond their

Mav.

A JOURNEY TO THE their own families. In defence of them they will, exert their utmoft influence; but when their own relations are guilty of the fame crime, they fel-dom interfere. This partial conducl creates fome fecret, and feveral open enemies; but the generality of their neighbours are deterred, through fear or fuperflition, from executing their revenge, and even from talking difrefpeclfully of them, un-lefs it be behind their backs; which is a vice of which alitfoft every Indian in this country, without exception, is guilty.

Notwithftanding the Northern Indians are fo covetous, and pay fo little regard to private property as to take every advantage of bodily ftrength to rob their neighbours, not only of their goods, but of their wives, yet they are, in other refpecls, the mildeft tribe, or nation, that is to be found on the borders of Hudfon's Bay: for let their affronts or loftes be ever fo great, they never will feek any other revenge than that of wreftling.

As for murder, which is fo common among all the tribes of Southern Indians, it is feldom heard of among them. A murderer is fhunned and de. tcfted by all the tribe, and is obliged to wander up and down, forlorn and forfaken even by his own relations and former friends. In that refpect a murderer may truly be compared to Cain, after he had killed his brother Abel. The cool reception he meets with by all who know him, occa-fions him to grow melancholy, and he never leaves any place but the whole company fay

"There

"There goes the murderer! The women, it is true, fometimes receive an unlucky blow from their hufbands for mifbehaviour, which occafions their death; but this is thought nothing of: and for one man or woman to kill another out of revenge, or through jealoufy, or on any other account, is fo extraordinary, that very few are now xifting who have been guilty of it. At the pre-. fent moment I know not one, befide Matonabbee, who ever made an attempt of that nature; and he is, in every other refpecl, a man of fuch uni-verfal good fenfe, and, as an Indian, of fuch great humanity, that I am at a lofs how to account for his having been guilty of fuch a crime, uniefs it be by his having lived among the Southern Indians fo long, as to become tainted with their blood-thirfty, revengeful, and vindidive difpofition.

Early in the morning of the twenty-ninth, cap- tain Keelfhies joined us. He delivered to me a packet of letters, and a two-quart keg of French brandy; but aflured me, that the powder, fhot,. tobacco, knives, c. which he received at the Fort for me, were all expended. He endeavoured to make fome apology for this, by faying, that fome of his relations died in the Winter, and that hehad, according to their cuftom, throw all his own things away; after which he was obliged to have recourfe to my ammunition and other goods, to fupport himfelf and a numerous family. The very affecting manner in which he related this flory, often crying like a child, was a great proof of his extreme j–j extreme forrow, which he wifhed to perfuade me Kr-u arofe from the recolledlion of his having embez-' zled fo much of my property; but I was of a dif. ferent opinion, and attributed his grief to arife from the remembrance of his deceafed relations. However, as a fmall recompence for my lofs, he prefented we with four ready-dreifed moofe-lkins, which was, he faid, the only retribution he could then make. The moofe-ikins, though not the twentieth part of the value of the goods which he had embezzled, were in reality more acceptable to me, than the ammunition and the other articles would have been, on account of their great ufe as flioe-leather, which at that time was a very fcarce article with us, whereas we had plenty of powder and fliot.

On the fame day that Keelfhies joined us, an Indian man, who had been fome time in our company, infilled on taking one of Matonabbee's wives from him by force, unlefs he complied with his demands, which were, that Matonabbee Ihould give him a certain quantity of ammunition, fome pieces of iron-work, a kettle, and feveral other articles; every one of which, Matonabbee was obliged to deliver, or lofe the woman; for the other man far excelled him in ftrength. Matonabbee was more exafperated on this occafion, as the fame man had fold him the woman no longer ago than the nineteenth of the preceding April. Having expended all the goods he then poffeffed, however, he was determined to make another

NORTHERN OCEAN. m.

another bargain for her; and as flie was what may be called a valuable woman in their eftima-tion; that is, one who was not only tolerably per-fonable, but reckoned very fkilful in manufacturing the different kinds of leather, fkins, and furrs, and at the fame time very clever in the performance of every other domeflic duty required of the fex in this part of the world; Matonabbee was more unwilling to part with her, efpecially as he had fo lately fuffered a lofs of the fame kind.

This difpute, which was after fome hours decided by words and prefents, had like to have proved fatal to my expedition; for Matonabbee, who at that time thought himfelf as great a man as then lived, took this affront fo much to heart, efpecially as it was offered in my prefence, that he almofl determined not to proceed any farther toward the Copper-mine River, and was on the point of ftriking off to the Weftward, with an intent to join the Athapufcow Indians, and continue with them: he being perfectly well acquainted with all their leaders, and moft of the principal Indians of that country, from whom, during a former refidence among them of feveral years, he faid he had met with more civility than he ever did from his own countrymen. As Mato-li abbee feemed refolutely bent on his defign, I had every reafon to think that my third expedition would prove equally unfuccefsful with the two former. I was not, hovever, under the leaft japprehenfion for my own fafety, as he promifed to take me with him, and procure me a paffage to Prince of Wale's Fort, with fome of the Atha-pufcow Indians, who at that time annually vifited the Fadory in the way of trade. After waiting till I thought Matonabbee's paffion had a Httle abated, 1 ufed every argument of which 1 was mafter in favour of his proceeding on the journey; affuring him not only of the future efteem of the prefent Governor of Prince of Wales's Fort, but alfo of that of all his fucceffors as long as he lived; and that even the Hudfon's Bay Company themfelves would be ready to acknowledge his ailiduity and perfeverance, in conducting a bufi-nefs which had fo much the appearance, of proving advantageous to them. After fome conver-fation of this kind, and a good deal of intreaty, he at length confented to proceed, and promifed to make all poflible hafte. Though it was then apth. late in the afternoon, he gave orders for moving, and accordingly we walked about feven miles that night, and put up on another ifland in Pefli-ew Lake. The preceding afternoon the Indians had killed a few deer; but our number was then fo great, that eight or ten deer would fcarcely af-. ford us all a tatte. Thefe deer were the firft we had feen (ince our leaving the neighbourhood of Thelewey-aza-yeth; fo that we had lived all the time on the dried meat which had been prepared before we left that place in April.

The thirtieth proved bad, rainy weather; we walked, however, about ten miles to the Northward, ward, when we arrived on the North fide of Pefli-ew Lake, and put up. Here Matonabbee imme-diatelvtbegan to make every neceffary arrangement for facilitating the executing of ourdefign; and as he had promifed to make all poflible hafte, he thought it expedient to leave mod of his wives and all his children in the care of fome Indians, then in our company, who had his orders to proceed to the Northward at their leifure; and who, at a particular place appointed by him, were to wait our return from the Copper-mine River. Having formed this refolution, Matonabbee fe-lefted two of his young wives who had no children, to accompany us; and in order to make their loads as light as poflible, it was agreed that we fhould not take more ammunition with us than was really necefiary for our fupport, till wc might expect again to join thofe Indians and the women and children. The fame meafures were alfo adopted by all the other Indians of my party; particularly thofe who had a plurality of wives, and a number of children.

As thefe matters took fome time to adjufl, it zi was near nine o'clock in the evening of the thir-ty-firft before we could fet out; and then it was with much difficulty that Matonabbee could pcr-fuade his other wives from following him, with their children and all their lumber; for fuch was their unwillingnefs to be left behind, that he was obliged to ufe his authority before they would onfent confequently they parted in anger j and ve no fooner began our march, than they fet tip a moft woeful cry, and continued to yell moft piteoufly as long as we were within hearing. This mournful fcene had fo little effecl on my party, that they walked away laughing, and as merry as ever. The few who exprefied any regret at their departure from thofe whom they were to leave behind, confined their regard wholly to their children, particularly to the youngeft, fcarcely ever mentioning their mother.

Though it was fo late when we left the women, we walked about ten miles that night before we ilopped. In our way we faw many deer; fevcral of which the Indians kiilcd. To talk of travelling and killing; deer in the middle of the nig-ht, mav at firft view have the appearance of romance; but our wonder will fpeediiy abate, when it is onfidered that we were then to the Northward of 64. of North latitude, and that, in confequence of it, though the Sun did not remain the whole night above the horizon, yet the time it remained below it was fo (hort, and its depreflion even at midnight fo fmall at this feafon of the year, that the light, in clear weather, was quite fuffici-tnt for the purpofc both of walking, and hunting" any kind of game.

It fliould have been obferved, that during our ftay at Clowcy a great number of Indians entered into a combination with thofe of my party to accompany us to the Copper-mine River; and with, no other intent than to murder the Efquimaux, who are underftood by the Copper Indians to frequent that river in confiderable numbers. This fchcme, notwithftanding the trouble and fatigue, as well as danger, with which it muft be obviou-fly attended, was nevcrthelefs fo univcrfally approved by thofe people, that for fome time almoin i every man who joined us propofed to be of the party. Accordingly, each volunteer, as well as thofe who were properly of my party, prepared a target, or fliield, before we left the woods of I iclowey. Thofe targets were compofed of thin Iboards, about three quarters of an inch thick, two jfeet broad, and three feet long; and were intend-! led to ward off the arrows of the Efquimaux. jnotwithftanding thefe preparations, when we came to leave the women and children, as has been already mentioned, only lixty volunteers would go with us; the refl, who were nearly as imany more, though they had all prepared targets, i; ireflectmg that they had a great diftance to walk, and that no advantage could be exp(ed froni ti the expedition, very prudently begged to be ex-f, Cufed, faying, that they could not be fpared for fo. i- long a time from the maintenance of their wives 3g and families; and particularly, as they did not fee any then in our company, who feemed willing uf jto encumber themfelves with fuch a charge. This eti Ifeemed to be a mere evafion, for I am clearly of ic opinion that poverty on one fide, and avarice on iti the other, were the only impediments to their X, oining our party j had they poffefted as many I 2 European

European goods to fquander away among their countrymen as Matonabbee and thofe of my party did, in all probability many might have been found vho would have been glad to have accompanied us. When I was acquainted with the intentions of my companions, and faw the warlike preparations that were carrying on, I endeavoured as much as poffible to perfuade them from putting their inhuman defign into execution; but Co far were my intreaties from having the wiflied-for effect, that it was concluded I was actuated by cowardice; and they told me, with great marks of derifion, that I was afraid of the Efquimaux. As I knew my perfonal fafety depended in a great meafure on the favourable opinion they entertained of me in this refpecl, I was obliged to change my tone, and replied, that I did not care if they rendered the name and race of the Efquimaux extinct; adding at the fame time, that though I was no enemy to the Efquimaux, and did not fee the neceility of attacking them without caufe, yet if I Ihould find it neceltary to do it, for the protection of any one of my company, my own fafety out of the queftion, fo far from being afraid of a poor defencelefs Efquimaux, whom I defpifed more than feared, nothing fhould be wanting on my part to protect all who were with me. This declaration was received with great fatisfaftion; and I never afterwards ventured to interfere with any of their war-plans. Indeed, when I came to confider fcrioufly, I faw evidently that it was the hi died

Mgheft folly for an Individual like me, and in my fituation, to attempt to turn the current of a national prejudice which had fubfiftcd between thole two nations from the earlieft periods, or at leaft as long as they had been acquainted with the exiftence of each other.

Having got rid of all the women, children, dogs, J"! J heavy baggage, and other incumbrances, on the firfl: of June we purfued our journey to the Northward with great fpeed; but the weather was in general fo precarious, and the fnow, fleet, and rain fo frequent, that notwithftanding we embraced every opportunity which offered, it was the fixtecnth of June before we arrived in the latitude of 6' 30, where Matonabbee had propof-ed that the women and children ftiould wait our return from the Copper-mine River.

In our way hither we crofted feveral lakes on the ice; ofwhich Thoy-noy-kyed Lake and Thoy-coy-lyned Lake were the principal. We alfo croffed a few inconfidcrable creeks and rivers, which were only ufeful as they furnifhed a fmall fupply of lih to the natives. The weather, as I have before obfcrved, was in general difagreeable with a great deal of rain and fnow. To make up for that inconvenience, however, the deer were fo plentiful, that the Indians killed not only a fuf-ficient quantity for our daily fupport, but frequently great numbers merely for the fat, marrow and tongues. To induce them to defift from this pradice, I often interefted myfelf, andendea- vourcd, voured, as much as poffible, to convince them in the cleared terms of which I was mailer, of the great impropriety of fuch wafle; particularly at a time of the year when their fkins could not be of any ufe for clothing, and when the anxiety to proceed on our journey would not permit us to ftay long enough in one place to eat up half the fpoils of their hunting. As national cuftoms, however, are not eafily overcome, my remon-ftrances proved ineffectual; and I was always anfwered, that it W3 certainly right to kill plenty, and live on the beft, when and where it was to be got, for that it would be impoilible to do it where every thing was fcarce: and they infilled on it, that killing plenty of deer and other game in one part of the country, could never make them fcarcer in another. Indeed, they were fo accuftomed to kill every thing that came within their reach, that few of them could pafs by a fmall bird's neft, without flaying the young ones, or deftroying the eggs. 20th. From the feventeenth to the twentieth, ue walked between feventy and eighty miles to the North Weitand North North Weft: the srreater part of the way by Cogead Lake; but the Lake being then frozen, we croffed all the creeks and bays of it on the ice.

On the twenty-firft we had bad rainy weather, with fo thick a fog that we could not fee our way: about ten o'clock at night, however, it became fme and clear, and the Sun jqione very bright j indeed 2l(i.

indeed it did not fet all that night, which was a 1771. convincing proof, without any obiervation, that-rp- we were then confiderably to the North of the Ardic Polar Circle.

. As loon as the fine weather began, we fet out Z2d. and walked about feven or eight miles to the Northward, when we came to a branch of Conge-ca-tha-wha-chaga River; on the North fide of which we found feveral Copper Indians, who were allembled, according to annual cuilom, to kill deer as they crofs the river in their little canoes.

The ice being now broken up, we were, for the firll time this Summer, obliged to make ufe of our canoes to ferry acrofs the river: which would have proved very tedious, had it not been for the kindnefs of the Copper Indians, who fent all their canoes to our afiiilance. Though our number was not much lefs than one hundred and fifty, w-e had only three canoes, and thofe being of the common fize, could only carry two perfons each, without baeaije. It is true, when water is fmooth, and a raft of three or four of thole canoes is well fecured by poles lalhed acrofs them, they will carry a much greater weight in proportion, and be much lafer, as there is Scarcely a pofiibihty of their overfetting; and this is the general mode adopted by the people of this country in croffing livers when they have more than one canoe with them.

Having arrived on the North fide of this river, we found that Matonabbse, and feveral others in our company, were perfonally acquainted with moft of the Copper Indians whom we found there. The latter feemed highly pleafed at the interview with our party, and endeavoured, by every means in their power, to convince our company of their readinefs to ferve us to the utmofl; fo that by the time we had got our tents pitched, the ftrangers had provided a large quantity of dried meat and fat, by way of a feaft, to which they invited moft of the principal Indians who accompanied me, as well as Matonabbee and myfelf, who were prefented with fome of the very beft.

It it natural to fuppofe, that immediately after our arrival the Copper Indians would be made acquainted with the nature and intention of our journey. This was no fooner done than they exprefled their entire approbation, and many of them feemed willing and defirous of giving every affiftance; particularly by lending us feveral canoes, which they altured us would be very ufe-ful in the remaining part of our journey, and contribute both to our eafe and difpatch. It muft be obferved, that thefe canoes were not entirely entruded to my crew, but carried by the owners themfelves who accompanied us; as it would have been very uncertain where to have found them at our return from the Copper River.

Agreeably to my inftruclions, I fmoked my calumet of peace with the principal of the Copper Indians, who feemed highly pleafed on the occa-fion J and, from a converfation held on the fub- NORTHERN OCEAN. lai jecl of my journey, I found they were delighted with the hopes of having an European fettlement in thcrr neighbourhood, and feemed to have no idea that any impediment could prevent fuch a fcheme from being carried into execution. Climates and fcafons had no weight with them; nor could they fee where the difliculty lay in gettinj to them; for though they acknowledged that they had never feen the fea at the mouth of the Copper River clear of ice, yet they could fee nothing that (hould hinder a fliip from approaching it; and they innocently enough obferved, that the water was always fo fmooth between the ice and (liore that even fmall boats might get there with great eafe and fafety. How a fhip was to get between the ice and the ftiore, never once occurred to them.

Whether it was from real motives of hofpitall-ty, or from the great advantages which they expected to reap by my difcoveries, I know not. but I muft confefs that their civility far exceeded what I could expect from fo uncivilized a tribe, and I was exceedingly forry that 1 had nothing of value to offer them. However, fuch articles as I had, I diftributed among them, and they were thankfully received by them. Though they have fome European commodities among them, which they purchafe from the Northern Indians, the fame articles from the hands of an Englifhman were more prized. As I was the firft whom they had ever feen, and in all probability might be the laft.

laft, it was curious to fee how they flocked about me, and exprefled as much defire to examine me from top to toe, as an European Naturalift would a non-defcript animal. They, however, found and pronounced me to be a perfect human beinaj, except in the colour of my hair and eyes: the former, they faid, was like the ftained hair of a buffaloe's tail, and the latter, being light, were like thofe of a gull. The whitenefs of my fkin alfo was, in their opinion, no ornament, as they faid it refembled meat which had been fodden in water till all the blood was extracted. On the whole, I was viewed as fo great a curioiity in this part of the world, that during my ftay there, whenever I combed my head, fome or other of them never failed to afk for the hairs that came off, which they carefully wrapped up, faying, "When I fee you again, you fhali again fee your " hair. j,2d. The day after our arrival at Congecathawha- chaga, Matonabbee difpatched his brother, and feveral Copper Indians, to Copper-mine River, with orders to acquaint any Indians they might meet, with the realbn of my vifiting thofe parts, and alfo when they might probably expect us at that river. By the bearers of this meffage 1 fent a prefent of tobacco and fome other things, to induce any flrangers they met to be ready to give us afliftance, either by advice, or in any other way which might be required.

As Matonabbee and the other Indians thought it advisable to leave all the women at this place,: ind proceed to the Copper-mine River without them, it was thought ncceltary to continue here a few diiys, to kill as many deer as would befulh-cient for their fupport during our abfence. And notwithftanding deer were fo plentiful, yet our numbers were fo large, and our daily confumption was fo great, that feveral days elapfed before the men could provide the women with a fufficient quantity; and then they had no other way of preferving it, than by cutting it in thin flices and drying it in the Sun. Meat, when thus prepared, is not only very portable, but palatable; as all the blood and juices are ftill remaining in the meat, it is very nourifliing and wholefome food; and may, with care, be kept a whole year without the leaft danger of fpoiling. It is neceffary, however, to air it frequently during the warm weather, otherwife it is liable to grow mouldy: but as foon as the chill air of the fall begins, it requires no farther trouble till next Summer.

We had not been many days at Congecatha-whachaga before I had reafon to be greatly concerned at the behaviour of feveral of my crew to the Copper Indians. They not only took many of their young women, furrs, and ready-drefled lkins for clothing, but alfo feveral of their bows and arrows, which were the only implements they had to procure food and raiment, for the future fupport of themfclves, their wives, and families. It may probably be thought, that as thefe weapons are of fo fimplc a form, and foe afily con- ftruded.

flrucled, they might foon be replaced, without any other trouble or expence than a little labour 5 but this fuppolition can only hold good in places where proper materials afe eafily procured, which was not the cafe here: if it had, they would not have been an object of plunder. In the midft of a foreft of trees, the wood that would make a Northern Indian a bow and a few arrows, or indeed a bow and arrows ready made, are not of much value; no more than the man's trouble that makes them: but carry that bow and arrows feveral hundred miles from any woods and place where thofe are the only weapons in ufe, their intrinfic value will be found to increafe, in the fame proportion as the materials which are made are lefs attainable.

To do Matonabbee juftice on this occafion, I muft fay that he endeavoured as much as pofiiblc to perfuade his countrymen from taking either furrs, clothing, or bows, from the Copper Indians, without making them fome fatisfaclory return; but if he did not encourage, neither did he endeavour to hinder them from taking as many women as they pieafed. Indeed, the Copper Indian women feem to be much efteem-ed by our Northern traders; for what reafon I know not, as they are in reality the fame people in every refped; and their language differs not fo much as the dialecls of fome of the neareft counties in England do from each other.

See rofliethw? t on the article of Labour.

It is not furprifing that a plurality of wives is cuftomary among thcfe people, as it is fo well adapted to their fituation and manner of life. In my opinion no race of people under the Sun have a greater occafion for fuch an indulgence. Their annual haunts, in queft of furrs, is fo remote from any European fettlement, as to render them the greateft travellers in the known world; and as they have neither horfe nor water carriage, every good hunter is under the neceflity of having feveral perfons to aftift in carrying his furrs to the Company's Fort, as well as carrying back theeuropean goods which he receives in exchange for them. No perfons in this country are fo proper for this work as the women, becaufe they are inured to carry and haul heavy loads from their childhood, and to do all manner of drudgery j fo that thofe men who are capable of providing for three, four, five, fix, or more women, generally find them humble and faithful fervants, af-fe(51: ionate wives, and fond and indulgent mothers to their children. Though cuftom makes this way of life fit apparently eafy on the generality of the women, and though, in general, the whole of their wants feem to be comprized in food and clothing only, yet nature at times gets the better of cuftom, and the fpirit of jealoufy makes its appearance among them: however, as the hufband is always arbitrator, he foon fettles the bufinefs, though perhaps not always to the entire fatisfaclion of the parties.

Much

Much does it redound to the honour of the Northern Indian women when I affirm, that they?. ve the mildeft and moft virtuous females I have ft-zn in any part of North America; though fome think this is more oving to habit, cuftom, and the fear of their hufbands, then from real inclination. It is undoubtedly well known that none can manage a Northern Indian woman fo well as a Northern Indian man; and when any of them have been permitted to remain at the Fort, they have, for the fake of gain, been eafily prevailed on to deviate from that charadler; and a few have, by degrees, become as abandoned as the Southern Indians, who are remarkable throughout all their tribes for being the mod debauched wretches under the Sun. So fxr from laying any reftraint on their fenfual appetites, as long as youth and inclination laft, they give themfelves up to all manner of even inceftuous debauchery; and that in fo beaftly a manner when they are intoxicated, a ftate to which they are peculiarly addicted, that the brute creation are not lefs regardlefs of decency. I knov that fome few Europeans, who have had little opportunity of feeing them, and of enquiring into their manners, have been very lavifh in their praife: but every one who has had much intercourfe with them, and penetration and induftry enough to ftudy their difpofitions, will agree, that no accomphfhments whatever in a man, is fufficient to conciliate thp affections,

NORTHERN OCEAN. or preferve the chaftity of a Southern Indian wo- yy

June.

man.

Notwithftanding this is tlie general charaifler of tlie Southern Indian women, as they are called on the coafts of Hudfon's Bay, and who are the lame tribe with the Canadian Indians, I am happy to have it in my power to infert a. few lines to the memory of one of them, whom I knew from her infancy, and who, I can truly affirm, was directly the reverie of the picture I have drawn.

AIary, the daughter of Mosej Norton, many years Chief at Prince of Wales's Forr, in Hudfon's Bay, though born and brought up in a country of all others the lead favourable to virtue and virtuous principles, pof-ftfled them, and every other good and amiable quality, in the moil eminent degree.

Without the afliilmce of religion, and with no education but what fte received among the diltohite natives of her countiy, (lie would have (hone with fuperior luflre in any other country: for, if an engaging peifon, gentle manners, an eafy freedom, aiifing from a confcioufnefs of innocence, an amiable modedy, and an unrivalled delicacy of fentiment, are graces and virtues which render a woman lovely, none ever had greater pretenfions to general eflcem and regard: while her benevolence, humanity, and fcru-pulous adherence to truth and honefty, would have done honour to the moft enlightened and devout Chridian.

Dutiful, obedient, and affedlionate to her parents; fceady and faithful to her friends; grateful and humble to her benefadors; eafily forgiving and forgetting injuiies; caieful not to offend any, and courteous and kind to all; file was, nevenhelefs, iuficied to perith by the rigours of cold and hunger, amidft her own relations, at a time when the giiping hand of famine was by no means (everely felt by any other member of their company; audit may truly be faid that flie fell a martyr to the principles of virtue. This happened in the Winter of the year 1782, after the French had de-Oroycd Prince of Wales's Fortj at which time Ihe was in the twenty-fe-cond year of her age.

Human nature fhudders at the bare recital of fuch brutality, and reafon ftirinks from the talk of accounting for the decrees of Providence on fuck occafions as this; but they are the drongeft aflurances of a future ftate, lb infinitely fuperior to the prefent, that the enjoyment of every pleafure in this world by the moft woi thlefs and abandoned wretch, or the moft innocent and virtuous woman perlfhing by the moft excruciating of all deaths, re matters equally indifferent. But,

Peace to the afhes, and the virtuous mind. Of her who lived in peace with all mankind;

Learnci jyyj The Northern Indian women are in general fo v-j far from being like thofe I have above defcribed,

J"' that it is very uncommon to hear of their ever been guilty of incontinency, not even thofe who are confined to the fixth or even eighth part of a man.

It is true, that were I to form my opinion of thofe women from the behaviour of fuch as I have been more particularly acquainted with, I fhould have little reafon to fay much in their favour; but impartiality will not permit me to make a few of the worft charaders a ftandard for the general conduct of all of them. Indeed it is but reafonable to think that travellers and interlopers will be always fejvedwith the moft commodious, though perhaps they pay the bell price for what they have.

Learndfrom the heart, unknowing of difguirc, Truth in her thoughts, and candour in her eyes; Stranger alike to envy and to pride. Good fenfe her light, and Nature all her guide; But now removed from all the ills of Hfe,

Here refts the pleafing friend and faithful wife. Waaler.

Her father was, undoubtedly, very blamable for bringing her up in the tender manner which he did, rendering her by that means not only incapable of bearing the fatigues and hardlhips which the reft of her countrywomen think little of, but of providing for herfelf. This is, indeed, too frequent a practice among Europeans in that country, who bring up their children in fo indulgent a manner, that when they retire, and leave their offipring behind, they find themfelves fo helplefs, as to be unable to provide for the few wants to which they arc fubje. The late Mr. Ferdinand Jacobs, many years Chief at York Fort, was the only perfon whom I ever knew that afted in a different manner; though no man could podibly be fonder of his children in other refpeifts, yet as there were fome that he. could not bring to England, he had them brought up entirely among the natives; fo that when he left the country, they fcarcely ever fel; the locsf though they regretted the abfence of a fo. id and indulgent parent.

It may appear ftrange, that while I am extolling the chaftity of the Northern Indian women, I fhould acknowledge that it is a very common cuftom among the men of this country to exchange a night's lodging with each other's wives. But this is fo far from being conlidered as an act which is criminal, that it is cfteemed by them as one of the ftrongeft ties of friendfliip between two families; and in cafe of the death of either man, the other confiders himfelf bound to fupport the children of the deceafed. Thofe people are fo far from viewing this engagement as a mere ceremony, like moft of our Chriftian god-fathers and god-mothers, who, notwithftanding their vows are made in the moft folemn manner, and in the prefence of both God and man, fcarcely ever afterward remember what they have promifed, that there is not an inftance of a Northern Indian having once negleded the duty which he is fuppofed to have taken upon himfelf to perform. Thesouthern Indians, with all their bad qualities, are remarkably humane and charitable to the widows and children of departed friends; and as their fituation and manner of life enable them to do more ads of charity with lefs trouble than falls to the lot of a Northern Indian, few widows or orphans are ever unprovided for among them.

Though thenorthernlndian men make no fcru-ple of having two or three fifters for wives at one time, yet they are very particular in obferving a proper diftance in the confanguinity of thofe they

K admit

June.

130 A JOURNEY TO THE admit to the above-mentioned intercourfe with their wives. The Southern Indians are lefs fcrupulous on thofe occaiions; among them it is not at all uncommon for one brother to make free with another brother's wife or daughter; but this is held in abhorrence by the Northern Indians.

By the time the Indians had killed as many deer as they thought would be fufficient for the fup-port of the women during our abfence, it was the J'v- firft of July; and during this time I had two good obfervations, both by meridional and double altitudes; the mean of which determined the latitude of Congecathawhachaga to be 68 46 North; and its longitude, by account, was 24 2 Weft from Prince of Wales's Fort, or i is 15 Weft of the meridian of London. 4(1. On the fecond, the weather proved very bad, with much fnow and fleet j about nine o'clock

Moft of the Southern Indians, as well the Athapufcow and Neheaway ttibef, are entirely without fcriiple in this refpeft. It is notorioufly known, that many of them cohabit occafionally with their own mothers, and frequently efpoufe their fillers and daughters. I have known feveral of them who, after having lived in that ftate for fome time with their daughters, have given them to their fons, and all parties been perfectly reconciled to it.

In faift, notwithftanding thefeverity of the climate, the licentioufnefsof the inhab-itints cannot be exceeded by any of the Eaftern nations, whofe luxurious manner of life, and genial clime, feem more adapted to excite extraordinary paflions, than the fevere cold of the frigid Zone.

It is true, that few of thofe who live under the immediate protection of the Englifh ever take either their fiflers or daughters for wives, which is probably owing to the fear of incuriing their difpleafure; but it is well known that adsof inceft too often take place among them, though perhaps not fo frequently as among the foreign Indians.

at night, however, it grew more moderate, and 1771. fomewhat clearer, fo that we fet out, and walked-"-

July.

about ten miles to the North by Weft, when we lay down to take a little fleep. At our departure from Congecathawhachaga, fevcral Indians who had entered the war-lift, rather chofe to ftay behind with the women; but their lofs was amply fupplied by Copper Indians, who accompanied us in the double capacity of guides and warriors.

On the third the weather was equally bad with jd. that of the preceding day; we made fhift, however, to walk ten or eleven miles in the fame direction we had done the day before, and at laft were obliged to put up, not being able to fee our way for fnow and thick drift. By putting up, no more is to be underftood than that we got to leeward of a great ftone, or into the crevices of the rocks, where we regaled ourfelves with fuch provifions as we had brought with us, fmoked our pipes, or went to fleep, till the weather permitted us to proceed on our journey.

On the fourth, we had rather better weather, 4th. though conftant light fnow, which made it very difacrreeable under foot. We neverthelefs walk- ed twenty-feven miles to the North Weft, fourteen of which were on what the Indians call the Stony Mountains; and furely no part of the world better deferves that name. On our firfl: approaching thefe mountains, they appeared to be a confufed heap of ftones, utterly inacceffible to the foot of man: but having feme Copper In-K 2 dians dians with us who knew the beft road, we made a tolerable fhift to get on, though not without being obliged frequently to crawl on our hands and knees. Notwithftanding the intricacy of the road, there is a very vifible path the whole way-acrofs thefe mountains, even in the moft difficult parts: and auo on the fmooth rocks, and thofe parts which are capable of receiving an impreffi-on, the path is as plain and well-beaten, as any bye foot-path in England. By the fide of this path there are, in different parts, feveral large, flat, or table ftones, which are covered with ma-iiy thoufands of fmall pebbles. Thefe the Copper Indians fay have been gradually increafed by paffengers going to and from the mines; and on its being obferved to us that it was the univerfal cuftom for every one to add a ftone to the heap, each of us took up a fmall ftone in order to in-creafe the number, for good luck.

Juft as we arrived at the foot of the Stony Mountains, three of the Indians turned back; faying, that from every appearance, the remainder of the journey feemed likely to be attended with more trouble than would counterbalance the pleafure they could promife themfelves by going to war with the Efquimaux.

On the fifth, as the weather was fo bad, with conftant fnow, fleet, and rain, that we could not fee our way, we did not offer to move: but the 4, jh, fixth proving moderate, and quite fair till toward noon, we fet out in the morning, and walked about about eleven miles to the North Weft; when perceiving bad weather at hand, we began to look out for fhelter among the rocks, as we had done the four preceding nights, having neither tents nor tentpoles with us. The next morning fifteen more of the Indians deferted us, being quite fick of the road, and the uncommon bad-nefs of the weather. Indeed, though thefe people are all inured to hardships, yet their complaint on the prefent occafion was not without reafon; for, from our leaving Congecathawhac-haga we had fcarcely a dry garment of any kind, or any thing to fkreen us from the inclemency of the weather, except rocks and caves; the beft of which were but damp and unwholefome lodging. In fome the water was conftantly dropping from the rock that formed the roof, which made our place of retreat little better than the open air; and we had not been able to make one fpark of fire (except what was fufficient to light a pipe) from the time of our leaving the women on the fecond inftant; it is true, in fome places there was a little mofs, but the conftant fleet and rain made it fo wet, as to render it as impoffible to fet fire to it as it would be to a wet fpunge.

We had no fooner entered our places of retreat than we regaled ourfelves with fome raw venifon which the Indians had killed that morning; the fmall ftock of dried provilions we took with us when we left the women being now all expended.

igreeably

Vth.

A JOURNEY TO THE

Agreeably to our expedations, a very fudden and heavy gale of wind came on from the North Weft, attended with fo great a fall of fnow, that the oldeft Indian in company faid, he never faw it exceeded at any tirr. e of the year, much lefs in the middle of Summer. The gale was foon over, and by degrees it became a perfect calm: but the flakes of fnow were fo larg: e as to fur-pafs all credibility, and fell in fuch vaft quantities, that though the fhower only lafted nine hours we were in danger of being fmothered in our caves.

On the feventh, we had a frefh breeze at North Weft, with fome flying fliowers offmall rain, and at the fame time a conftant warm funfliine, which foon diffolved the greateft part of the new-fallen fnow. Early in the mornihg we crawled out of our holes, which were on the North fide of the Stony Mountains, and walked about eighteen or twenty miles to the North Weft by Weft. In our way we crofled part of a large lake on the ice, which was then far from being broken up. This lake I diftinguiflied by the name of Buffalo, or Mufltox Lake, from the number of thofe animals that we found grazing on the margin of it; many of which the Indians killed, but finding them lean, only took fome of the bulls hides for flioe-foals. At night the bad weather returned, with a ftrong gale of wind at North Eaft, and very cold rain and fleet.

This

This was the firft time we had feen any of the mufk-oxen fince we left the Factory. It has been obferved that we faw a great number of them in my firft unfuccefsful attempt, before I had got an hundred miles from the Factory; and indeed I once perceived the tracks of two of thofe animals within nine miles of Prince of Waless Fort. Great numbers of them alfo were met with in my fecond journey to the North: feveral of which my companions killed, particularly on the feven-teenth of July one thoufand feven hundred and feventy. They are alfo found at times in confi-derable numbers near the fea-coaft of Hudfon's Bay, all the way from Knapp's Bay to Wager Water, but are moft plentiful within the Arctic Circle. In thofe high latitudes I have frequently feen many herds of them in the courfe of a day's walk, and fome of thofe herds did not contain lefs than eighty or an hundred head. The number of bulls is very few in proportion to the cows; for it is rare to fee more than two or three full-grown bulls with the largeft herd: and from the number of the males that are found dead, the Indians are of opinion that they kill each other in contending for the females. In the rutting feafon they are fo jealous of the cows, that they run at cither man or beaft who offers to approach them; and have been obferved to run and bellow even at ravens, and other large birds, which chanced to light near themi They delight in the moft ftony and mountainous parts of the barren eround.

ground, and are feldom found at any great diftance Tp from the woods. Though they are a beaft of great magnitude, and apparently of a very unwieldyin-aclive ftruclure, yet they climb the rocks with great eafe and agility, and are nearly as fure-footed as a goat: like it too, they will feed on any thing; though they feem fondeft of grafs, yet in Winter, when that article cannot be had in fufficient quantity, they will eat mofs, or any other herbage they can find, as alfo the tops of willows and the tender branches of the pine tree. They take the bull in Auguft, and bring forth their young the latter end of May, or beginning of June J and they never have more than one at a time.

The mulk-ox, when full grovvn, is as large as the generality, or at lead as the middling fize, of Englifh black cattle; but their legs, though large, are not fo long; nor is their tail longer than that

Mr. Dragge f-ys, in his voyage, vol. ii. p. 260, that the mufk-ox is lower than a deer, but larger as to belly and quarters; which is very far fiom the truth; ihey are of the fize I have here defcribed them, and the Indian always eftimate the flelh of a full-grown cow to be equal in quantity to three deer. I am ferry alio to be obliged to contradict my friend Mr. Graham, who fays that the flelh of this animal is carried on fledges to Prince of Walts's Foit, to the amount of three or four thoufand pounds annually. To the amount of near one thoufand pounds may have been purchafid from the natives in fome particular year. s but it more frequently happens that not an ounce is brought one year out of five. In faft, it is by no means efleemed by the company's fervants, and of courfe no great encouragement is given to introduce it; but i it had been othervvife, their general fituation is fo remote from the fettlement, that it would not be worth the Indians while to haul it to tiie Fort. So that in ia, all that has ever been carried to Prince of Waies's Fort, has mofi: afliirediy been killed out of a herd that has been accidentally found within a moderate diftance of the fettlement; perhaps an hundred miles, which is only thought a ftep by an Indian., of a bear; and, like the tail of that animal, it always bends downward and inward, fo that it is entirely hid by the long hair of the rump and hind quarters: the hunch on their flioulders is not large, being little more in proportion than that of a deer: their hair is in fome parts very-long, particularly on the belly, fides, and hind quarters; but the longeft hair about them, particularly the bulls, is under the throat, extending from the chin to the lower part of the cheft, between the fore-legs; it there hangs down like a horfe's mane inverted, and is full as long, which makes the animal have a moft formidable appearance. It is of the hair from this part that the Efquimaux make their mufletto wigs, and not from the tail, as is afferted by Mr. Ellis; their tails, and the hair which is on them, being too fliort for that purpofe. In Winter they are provided with a thick fine wool, or furr, that grows at the root of the long hair, and hields them from the intenfe cold to which they are expofed during that feafon; but as the Summer advances, this furr loofens from the fkin, and, by frequently rolling themfelves on the ground, it works out to the end of the hair, and in time drops off, leaving little for their Summer clothing except the long hair. This feafon is fo fhort in thofe high latitudes, that the new fleece begins to appear, almoft as foon as the old one drops off; fo that by the time the cold becomes fevere, they are again provided with a Winter-drefs.

Voyage to Hudlbn's Bay, p. it:

The flefli of the mufk-ox noways refembles that of the Weflern buffalo, but is more like that of the moofe or elk; and the fat is of a clear white, nightly tinged with a light azure. The calves and young heifers are good eating; but the flefh of the bulls both fmells and taftes fo ftrong of mulk, as to render it very difagreeable: even the knife that cuts the flefh of an old bull will fmell fo ftrong of mulk, that nothing but fcowring the blade quite bright can remove it, and the handle will retain the fcent for a long time. Though no part of a bull is free from this fmell, yet the parts of generation, in particular the urethra, are by far the moft ftrongly impregnated. The urine itfelf muft contain this fcent in a very great degree; for the fheaths of the bull's penis are corroded with a brown gummy fubllance, which is nearly as high-fcented with mulk as that faid to be produeed by the civet cat; and after having been kept for feveral years, feems not to lofe any of its quality. 8th. On the eighth, the weather was fine and moderate, though not without fome fhowers of rain. Early in the morning we fet out, and walked eighteen miles to the Northward. The Indians killed fome deer; fo we put up by the fide of a fmall creek, that afforded a few willows, with which we made a fire for the firft time fmce our leaving Congecathawhachaga; confequently it was here that we cooked our firfl meal for a whole week. This, as may naturally be fuppofed, was well re- lifhed by all parties, the Indians as well as myfclf. And as the Sun had, in the courfe of the day, dried our clothing, in fpite of the fmall fhowers of rain, we felt ourfelves more comfortable than we had done lince we left the women. The place where we lay that night, is not far from Grizzled Bear Hill; which takes its name from the numbers of thofe animals that are frequently known to refort thither for the purpofe of bringing forth their young in a cave that is found there. The wonderful defcription which the Copper Indians gave of this place exciting the curiofity of fe-veral of my companions as well as myfelf, we went to view it; but on our arrival at it found little worth remarking about it, being no more than a high lump of earth, of a loamy quality, of which kind there are feveral others in the fame neighbourhood, all Handing in the m. iddle of a large marlh, which makes them refemble fo many iflands in a lake. The fides of thefe hills are quite perpendicular; and the height of Grizzled Bear Hill, which is the largefl, is about twenty feet above the level ground that furrounds it. Their fummits are covered with a thick fod of mofs and long grafs, which in fome places projects over the edge; and as the fides are conftantly mouldering away, and wafliing down with every Ihower of rain during the fhort Summer, they muft in time be levelled wdth the marfli in which they are fnuated. At prefent thofe iflands, as I call them, are excellent places of retreat for the birds birds which migrate there to breed; as they can bring forth their young in perfed fafety from every bead except the Quequehatch, which, from the fliarpnefs of its claws and the amazing ftrength of its legs, is capable of afcending the mofl difficult precipices.

On the fide of the hill that I went to furvey, there is a large cave which penetrates a confidera-ble way into the rock, and may probably have been the work of the bears, as we could difco-ver vifible marks that fome of thofe beads had been there that Spring. This, though deemed very curious by fome of my companions, did not appear fo to me, as it neither engaged my attention, nor raifed my furprife, half fo much as the iight of the many hills and dry ridges on the Eaft lide of the marfh, which are turned over like ploughed land by thofe animals, in fearching for ground-fquirrels, and perhaps mice, which con-ftitute a favourite part of their food. It is fur-prifing to fee the extent of their refearches in queft of thofe animals, and ftill more to view the enormous ftones rolled out of their beds by the bears on thofe occalions. At firft I thought thefe long and deep furrows had been effe5ted by lightning; but the natives affured me they never knew any thing of the kind happen in thofe parts, and that it was entirely the work of the bears feeking for their prey.

On the ninth, the weather was moderate and cloudy, with fome flving fhowers of rain. We fet out early in the morning, and walked about forty miles to the North and North by Eaft. In our way we faw plenty of deer and mulk-oxen: feveral of the former the Indians killed, but a fmart ftiower of rain coming on juft as we were going to put up, made the mofs fo vet as to render it impracticable to light a fire. The next day " proving fine and clear, we fet out in the morning, and walked twenty miles to the North by Weft and North North Weft; but about noon the weather became fo hot and fultry as to render walking very difagreeable; we therefore put up on the top of a high hill, and as the mofs was then dry, lighted a fire, and fliould have made a comfortable meal, and been otherwife tolerably happy, had it not been for the mufkettoes, which were uncommonly numerous, and their ftings almoft infufferable. The fame day Matonabbee fent feveral Indians a-head, with orders to proceed to the Copper-mine River as faft as poflible, and acquaint any Indians they might meet, of our approach. By thofe Indians I alfo fent fome fmall prefents, as the fureft means to induce any Grangers they found, to come to our afiiftance.

The eleventh was hot and fultry, like the preceding day. In the morning we walked ten or eleven miles to the North Weft, and then met a Northern Indian Leader, called Oule-eye, and his family, who were, in company with feveral Copper Indians, killing deer with bows and arrows and fpears, as they crofted a little river, by the fide nth.

fide of which we put up, as did alfo the above-mentioned Indians. That afternoon I fmoked my calumet of peace with thefe ftrangers, and found them a quite different fet of people, atleaft in principle, from thofe I had feen at Congeca-thawhachaga: for though they had great plenty of provifions, they neither offered me nor my companions a mouthful, and would, if they had been permitted, have taken the laft garment from off my back, and robbed me of every article I poffeffed. Even my Northern companions could not help taking notice of fuch unaccountable behaviour. Nothing but their poverty proteded them from being plundered by thofe of my crew; and had any of their women been worth notice, they would mofl affuredly have been preff-ed into our fervice. rsth. The twelfth was fo exceedingly hot and fultry, j, that we did not move; but early in the morning of the thirteenth, after my companions had taken what dry provifions they chofe from our unfoci-able ftrangers, we fet out, and walked about fifteen or fixteen miles to the North and North by Eaft, in expedation of arriving at the Coppermine River that day; but when we had reached the top of a long chain of hills, between which we were told the river ran, we found it to be no more than a branch of it which empties itfelf into the main river about forty miles from its influx

This river rur. s nearly North Eafl, and in all probability empties it-ftlf into the Northern Ocean, not far from the Copper River.

flux into the fea. At that time all the Copper Indians were difpatched different ways, fo that there was not one in company, who knew the (horteft cut to the main river. Seeing fome woods to the Weftward, and judging that the current of the rivulet ran that way, we concluded that the main river lay in that direction, and was not very remote from our prefcnt fituation. We therefore directed our courfe by the fide of it, when the Indians met with feveral very fine buck deer, which they deftroyed; and as that part we now traverfed afforded plenty of good fire-wood, we put up, and cooked the moft comfortable meal to which we had fat down for fome months. As fuch favourable opportunities of indulging the appetite happen but feldom, it is a general rule with the Indians which we did not neglect, to exert every art in drefiing our food which the moft refined fkill in Indian cookery has been able to invent, and which confifts chiefly in boiling, broiling, and roafting: but of all the diflies cooked by thofe people, a becaice, as it is called in their language, is certainly the moft delicious, at leaft for a chance, that can be prepared from a deer only, without any other ingredient. It is a kind of haggis, made with the blood, a good quantity of fat flired fmall, fome of the tendereft of the flefh, together with the heart and lungs cut, or more commonly torn into fmall fliivers; all which is put into the ftomach, and roafted, by being fuf-pended before the fire by a ftring. Care muft be taken taken that it does not get too much heat at firft, as the bag would thereby be liable to be burnt, and the contents be let out. When it is fuffici-ently done, it will emit fteam, in the fame manner as a fowl or a joint of meat; which is as much as to fay. Come, eat me now: and if it be taken in time, before the blood and other contents are too much done, it is certainly a moft delicious morfel, even without pepper, fait, or any other feafoning.

After regaling ourfelves in the moft plentiful manner, and taking a few hours reft, (for it was almoft impoffible to lleep for the mulkettoes,) we once more fet forward, directing our courfe to the North Weft by Weft; and after walking about nine or ten miles, arrived at that long wifli= ed-for fpot, the Copper-mine River.

CHAR

Tranfaclions at the Copper-mine River, and till we joined all the women to the South of Cogead Lake.

Some Copper Indians join us. Indians fend three fpies down the river. Begin my furvey.-Spies return and give an account of Jive tents of Efquimaux. lu dians confult the beji method tojieal on thetn in the night, and kill them while ajleep. Crofs the river. Proceedings of the Indians as they advance to-wards the Efquimaux tents. The Indians begin the majfacre while the poor Efquimaux are afieep, and Jlay them all. Much affeded at the fight of one young woman killed clofe to my feet. The behaviour of the Indians on this occafion. Their brutifh treatment of the dead bodies, Seven more tents fee? i on the oppofite fide of the river. The Indians harafs iheni) till they fiy to afooal in the river for fafety. Behaviour of the Indians after killing thofe Efquimaux. Crofs the river, and proceed to the tents on that fide. Plunder their tents, anddeftroy their utenftls. Continue my furvey to the river's mouth, Remarks there. Set out on my return, Arrive at one of the Coppermines. Remarks on it. Many attempts made to induce the Copper Indians to carry their own goods to market. Objiacles to it Villa-ny and cruelty of Keelflnes to feme of thofe poor Indians, Leave the Copper-inme, and ivalk at an L amazing

amazing rate till we join the women by the fide of Cogeadwhoie. Much foot foundered. The appearance very alarming, but foon changes for the better, Proceed to the foulh ward, and join the remainder of the wo7nen and children. Many other Indians arrive with them.

E had fcarcely arrived at the Copper-mine River when four Copper Indians joined J4th. us, and brought with them two canoes. They had feen all the Indians who werefent from us at various times, except Matonabbees brother and three others that were iirft difpatched from Con-gecathawhachaga.

On my arrival here I was not a little furprifcd to find the river differ fo much from the defcrip-tion which the Indians bad given of it at the Factory; for, in (lead of being fo large as to be navigable for fliipping, as it had been reprefented by them, it was at that part fcarcely navigable for an Indian canoe, being no more than one hundred and eighty yards wide, every where full of fhoals, and no lefs than three falls were in fis-htatfirft view. Near the water's edge there is fome wood; but not one tree grows on or near the top of the hills between which the river runs. There appears to have been formerly a much greater quantity than there is at prefent; but the trees feem to have been fet on fire fome years ago, and, in confe-quence, there is at prefent ten fticks lying on the ground, for one green one which is growing be- lide fide them. The whole timber appears to have been, even in its greateft profperity, of fo crooked and dwarfifli a growth as to render it of little ufe for any purpofe but fire-wood.

Soon after our arrival at the river-fide, three Indians were fent off as Ipies, in order to fee if any Efquimaux were inhabiting the river-fide between us and the fea. After walking about three quarters of a mile by the fide of the river, we put up, when moil of the Indians went a hunting, and killed feveral mufk-oxen and fome deer. They were employed all the remainder of the day and night in fplitting and drying the meat by the fire. As we were not then in want of provifions, and as deer and other animals were fo plentiful, that each day's journey might have provided for it-felf, I was at a lofs to account for this unufal oeco-nomy of my companions; but was foon informed, that thofe preparations were made with a view to have victuals enough ready-cooked to ferve us to the river's mouth, without being obliged to kill any in our way, as the report of the guns, and the fmoke of the fires, would be liable to alarm the natives, if any fhould be near at hand, and give them an opportunity of efcaping.

Early in the morning of the fifteenth, we fet ijth, out, when 1 immediately began my furvey, which I continued about ten miles down the river, till heavy rain coming on we were obliged to put upj and the place where we lay that night was the end, or edge of the woods, the whole fpace be.

L 2 tween tween it and the fea being entirely barren hills and wide open marilies. In the courfe of this day's furvey, I found the river as full of fhoals as the part which 1 had fecn before; and in many places it was fo greatly diminifhed in its width, that in our way we pafifed by two more capital falls. j5. h Early in the morning of the fixteenth, the weather being fine and pleafant, I again proceeded with my furvey, and continued it for ten miles farther down the river; but ftill found it the fame as before, being every where full of falls and fhoals. At this time (it being about noon) the three men who had been fent as fpies met us on their return, and informed my companions that five tents of Efquimaux were on the weft fide of the river. The fituation, they faid, was very convenient for furprizing them; and, according to their account, I judged it to be about twelve miles from the place we met the fpies. When the Indians received this intelligence, no farther attendance or attention Vvas paid to my furvey, but their whole thoughts were immediately engaged in planning the beft method of attack, and how they might fteal on the poor Efquimaux the enfuing night, and kill them all while aflcep. To accompllfh this bloody defign more effectually, the Indians thought it neceffary to crois the river as foon as pollible; and, by the account of the fpies, it appeared that no part was more convenient for the purpofe than that where we had met them, it being there very fmooth, and at a confiderablc diftance from any fall. Accordingly, after the Indians had put all their guns, fpears, targets, c. in good order, we croffcd the river, which took up fomc time.

When we arrived on the Weft fide of the river, each painted the front of his target or fliield; fome with the figure of the Sun, others with that of the Moon, feveral with diflcrent kinds of birds and beaftsof prey, and many with the images of imaginary beings, which, according to their lilly notions, are the inhabitants of the different elements, Earth, Sea, Air, c.

On enquiring the reafon of their doing fo, I learned that each man painted his Ihield with the image of that being on which he relied moft for fuccefs in the intended engagement. Some were contented with a fingle reprefentation; while others, doubtful, as I fuppofe, of the quality and power of any iingle being, had their fhields covered to the very margin with a group of hieroglyphics quite unintelligible to every one except the painter. Indeed, from the hurry in which this bulinefs was necefiarily done, the want of every colour but red and black, and the deficiency of Ikill in the artift, moft of thofe paintings had more the appearance of a number of accidental blotches, than " of any thing that is on the earth, or in " the water under the earth;" and though fome few of them conveyed a tolerable idea of the thing intended, yet even thefe were many degrees worfe than our country fignpaintings in England.

When

When this piece of fuperflition was completed, we began to advance towards the Efquimaux tents; but were very careful to avoid crofling any hills, or talking loud, for fear of being feen or overheard by the inhabitants; by which means the diftance was not only much greater than it otherwife would have been, but, for the fake of keeping in the lowcft grounds, we were obliged to walk through entire fwamps of ftiff marly clay, Ibmetimes up to the knees. Our courfe, however, on this occafion, though very ferpentine, was not altogether fo remote from the river as entirely to exclude me from a view of it the whole way: on the contrary, feveral tiroes (according to the iituation of the ground) we advanced fo near it, as to give mea, n opportunity of convincing my-felf that it was as unnavigable as it was in thofe parts which I had furveyed before, and which entirely correfponded with the accounts given of it by the fpies.

It is perhaps worth remarking, that my crew, though an undifciplined rabble, and by no means accullomed to war or command, feemingly acted on this horrid occafion. with the utmofl uniformity of fentiment. here was not among them the ieaft altercation or feparate opinion; all were united in the general caufe, and as ready to follow where Matonabbee led, as he appeared to be ready to lead, according to the advice of an old

Copper Indian, who had joined us on our firft arrival at the river where this bloody bufinefs was iirft propofed.

Never

Never was reciprocity of intereft more generally regarded among a number of people, than it was on theprefent occafion by my crew, for not one was a moment in want of any thing that another could fpare; and if ever the fpirit of difmterefted friendfliip expanded the heart of a Northern Indian, it was here exhibited in the moft extenfive meaning of the word. Property of every kind that could be of general ufe now ceafed to be private, and every one who had any thing which came under that defcription, feemed. proud of an opportunity of giving it, or lending it to thofe who had none, or were moft in want of it.

The number of my crew was fo much greater than that which five tents could contain, and the warlike manner in which they were equipped fo greatly fuperlor to what could be expecled of the poor Efquimaux, that no lefs than a total maita-cre of every one of them was likely to be the cafe, unlefs Providence fhould work a miracle for their deliverance.

The land was fo fituated that we walked under cover of the rocks and hills till we were within two hundred yards of the tents. There we lay in ambufli for fome time, watching the motions of the Efquimaux; and here the Indians would have advifed me to flay till the fight was over, but to this I could by no means confent; for I confidered that when the Efquimaux came to be farprifed, they would try every way to efcape, and if they found me alone, not knowing me from an enemy, they would probably proceed to violence againft me when no perfon was near to afilft. For this reafon I determined to accompany them, telling them at the fame time, that I would not have any hand in the murder they were about to commit, unlefs I found it necefiary for my own fafety. The Indians were not difpleafed at this propofal; one of them immediately fixed me a fpear, and another lent me a broad bayonet for my protection, but at that timel could not be provided with a target; nor did I want to be encumbered with fuch an unneceffary piece of lumber.

While we lay in ambufli, the Indians performed the lafl ceremonies which were thought necef-fary before the engagement. Thefe chiefly confided in painting their faces; fome all black, fome all red, and others with a miixture of the two; and to prevent their hair from blowing into their eyes, it was either tied before and behind, and on both fides, orelfe cut fhort all round. The next thing they confidered was to make themfelves as light as pofiible for running; which they did, by pulling off their flockings, and either cutting off the ileeves of their jackets, or rolling them up clofe to their arm-pits; and though the muflettoes at that time were fo numerous as to furpafs ail credibility, yet fome of the Indians aduaily pulled off their jackets and entered entered the lifts quite naked, except their breech-icloths and fhoes. Fearing I might have occafion to run with the reft, I thought it alfo advifeable to pull off my ftockings and cap, and to tie my hair as clofe up as pofhble.

By the time the Indians had made themfelves thus completely frightful, it was near one o'clock in the morning of the feventeenth; when find- i-jth, ing all the Efquimaux quiet in their tents, they ruflied forth from their ambufcade, and fell on the poor unfufpecling creatures, unperceived till clofe to the very eves of the tents, when they foon began the bloody maffacjre, while I ftood neuter in the rear.

In a few feconds the horrible fcene commenced; it was fliocking beyond defcription; the poor unhappy vidims were furprifed in the midft of their fleep, and had neither time nor power to make any refiftance; men, women, and children, in all upwards of twenty, ran out of their tents ftark naked, and endeavoured to make their efcape; feut the Indians having polteffion of all the land-fide, to no place could they fly for Ihelter. One alternative only remained, that of jumping into the river; but, as none of them attempted it, they all fell a facrifice to Indian barbarity!

The flirieks and groans of the poor expiring wretches were truly dreadful; and my horror was much increafed at feeing a young girl, fee-mingly about eighteen years of age, killed fo near me, that when the firft fpear was ftuck into her fide yyi, fide he fell down at my feet, and twifted round K. my legs, fo that it was with difficulty that I could J"-' difengage myfelf from her dying grafps. As two Indian men purfued this unfortunate victim, I folicited very hard for her life; but the murderers made no reply till they had ftuck both their fpears through her body, and transfixed her to the ground. They then looked me fternly in the face, and began to ridicule me, by afking if I wanted an Kfquimaux wife; and paid not the fmalleft regard to the Ihrieks and agony of the poor wretch, who was twining round their fpears like an eel! Indeed, after receiving much abufive language from them on the occafion, 1 was at length obliged to defire that they would be more expeditious in difpatching their viclim out of her mifery, otherwifel fliould be obliged, out of pity, to aflift in the friendly office of putting an end to the exiftence of a fellow-creature who was fo cruelly wounded. On this requeft being made, one of the Indians haftily drew his fpear from the place where it was fiift lodged, and pierced it through her breaft near the heart. The love of life, however, even in this moft miferable ftate, was fo predominant, that though this might juft-ly be called the moft merciful act that could be done for the poor creature, it feemed to be unwelcome, for though much exhaufted by pain and lofs of blood, file made feveral efforts to ward off the friendly blow. My fituation and the terror cf my mind at beholding this butchery, cannot eafily eafily be conceived, much lefs defcribed; though I fummcd up all the fortitude I was mafter of on the occafion, it was with difficulty that I could refrain from tears; and I am confident that my features muft have feelingly expreffed how fincere-ly I was affecled at the barbarous fcene I then witnefled; even at this hour I cannot refled on the tranfaclions of that horrid day without Ihed-ding tears.

1 he brutifh manner in which thefe favages ufed the bodies they had fo cruelly bereaved of life was fo fliocking, that it would be indecent to defcribe it; particularly their curiofity in examining, and the remarks they made, on the for mation of the women; which, they pretended to fay, differed materially from that of their own. For my own part I muft acknowledge, that however favourable the opportunity for determining that point might have been, yet my thoughts at the time were too much agitated to admit of any fuch remarks; and I firmly believe, that had there actually been as much difference between them as there is faid to be between the Hottentots and thofe of Europe, it would not have been in my power to have marked the diftinclion. I have reafon to think, however, that there is no ground for the affertion; and really

believe that the declaration of the Indians on this occafion, was utterly void of truth, and proceeded only from the implacable hatred they bore to the whole tribe of people of whom 1 am fpeaking.

When 1771.   When the Indians had Completed the murder-'-'- of the poor Efquimaux, feven other tents on the

July.

Eaft fide the river immediately engaged their attention: very luckily, however, our canoes and baggage had been left at a little diftance up the river, fo that they had no way of eroding to get at them.   The river at this part being little more than eighty yards wide, they began firing at them from the Weft fide.   The poor Efquimaux on the oppofite fhore, though all up in arms, did not attempt to abandon their tents; and they were fo unacquainted with the nature of fire-arms, that when the bullets ftruck the ground, they ran in crowds to fee what was fent them, and feemed anxious to examine all the pieces of lead which they found flattened againfl the rocks.   At length one of the Efquimaux men was fliot in the calf of his leg, which put them in great confufion. They all immediately embarked in their little canoes, and paddled to a fhoal in the middle of the river, which being fomewhat more than a gun-fhot from any part of the fhore, put them out of the reach of our barbarians.

When the favages difcovered that the furviv-ing Efquimaux had gained the fhore above mentioned, the Northern Indians began to plunder the tents of the deceafed of all the copper uten-fils they could find; fuch as hatchets, bayonets, knives, c. after which they aflembled on the top of an adjacent high hill, and flanding all in a clufler, fo as to form a folid circle, with their fpears fpears erecl In the air, gave many fliouts of viclo- ry, conllantly clafliing their fpears againft each other, and frequently calling out tima! tima! by way of derifion to the poor furviving Efquimaux, who were landing on the fhoal almoft knee-deep in water.   After parading the hill for fome time, it was agreed to return up the river to the place where we had left our canoes and baggage, which was about half a mile diflant, and then to crofs the river again and plunder the feven tents on.

the Eaft fide. This refolution was immediately put in force; and as ferrying acrofs with only three or four canoes J took a confiderable time, and as we were, from the crookednefs of the river and the form of the land, entirely under cover, feveral of the poor furviving Efquimaux, thinking probably that we were gone about our bulinefs, and meant to trouble them no more, had returned from the Ihoal to their habitations.

When we approached their tents, which we did under cover of the rocks, we found them bufily employed tying up bundles.   Thefe the Indians feized with their ufual ferocity; on which, the

Efquimaux having their canoes lying ready in the water, immediately embarked, and all of them got fafe to the former fhoal, except an old man, who was fo intent on collecting his things, that

Tima in the Efquimaux language is a friendly word fimilar to vihut deer?

J When the fifteen Indians turned back to the Stony Mountains they took, two or three canoes with them; fome of oar crew that were fent-head as niefrlng. rs had not yet returned, which occafioned the number of our canoes to be fo fmall.

that the Indians coming upon him before he could reach his canoe, he fell a facrifice to their fury: I verily believe not lefs than twenty had a hand in his death, as his whole body was like a cullender. It is here necefpary to obferve that the fpies when on the look-out, could not fee thefe feven tents, though clofe under them, as the bank, on which they ftood, ftretched over them.

It ought to have been mentioned in its proper place, that in making our retreat up the river, after killing the Efquimaux on the Weft fide, we faw an old woman fitting by the fide of the water, killing falmon, which lay at the foot of the fall as thick as a fhoal of herrings. Whether from the noifeof the fall, or a natural defect in the old woman's hearing, it is hard to determine, but certain it is, fhe had no knowledge of the tragical fcene which had been fo lately tranfacled at the tents, though fhe was not more than two hundred yards from the place. When we firft perceived her, fhe feemed perfedly at eafe, and was entirely furrounded with the produce of her labour. From her manner of behaviour, and the appearance of her eyes, which were as red as blood, it is more than probable that her fight was not very good; for fhe fcarcely difcerned that the Indians were enemies, till they were within twice the length of their fpears of her. It was in vain that fhe attempted to fly, for the wretches of my crew transfixed her to the ground in a few feconds, and butchered her in the moft favage manner.

manner. There was fcarcely a man among them who had not a thruft at her with hisfpear; and many in doing this, aimed at torture, rather than immediate death, as they not only poked out her eyes, but ilabbed her in many parts very remote from thofe which are vital.

It may appear ftrange, that a perfon fuppofed to be almoft: blind fhould be employed in the bufi-nefs of fifliing, and particularly with any degree of fuccefs; but when the multitude of fifh is taken into the account, the wonder will ceafe. Indeed they were fo numerous at the foot of the fall, that when a light pole, armed with a few fpikes, which was the inftrument the old woman ufed, was put under water, and hauled up with a jerk, it was fcarcely poffible to mifs them. Some of my Indians tried the method, for curiofity, with the old woman's flaff, and feldom got lefs than two at a jerk, fometimes three or four. Thofe fifh, though very fine, and beautifully red, are but fmall, feldom weighing more (as near as I could judge) than fix or feven pounds, and in general much lefs. Their numbers at this place were almoft incredible, perhaps equal to any thing that is related of the falmon in Kamfchatka, or any other part of the world. It does not appear that the Efquimaux have any other method of catching the fifh, unlefs it be by fpears and darts; for no appearance of nets were difcovered either at their tents, or on any part of the fhore. This is the cafe with all the Efquimaux on the Weft fide of Hudfon's Bay; fpearing in Summer, and angling in Winter, are the only methods they have yet devifed to catch fifii, though at times their whole dependance for fupport is on that article.

When

When the Efquimaux who refide near Churchill River travel in Winter, it is always from lake to lake, or from river to river, where they have formed magazines of provifions, and heaps of mofs for firing. As fome of thofc places are at a confiderable diftance from each other, and fome of the lakes of confiderable width, they frequently pitch their tents on the ice, and inftead of having a fire, which the feverity of the climate fo much requires, they cut holes in the ice within their tents, and there fit and angle for fifh; if they meet with any fuccefs, the filli are eaten alive out of the water; and when they are thirfty, water, their ufual beverage, is at hand.

When I firft entered into the employment of the Hudfon's Bay Company, it was as Mate of one of their floops which was employed in trading with the Efquimaux; I had therefore frequent opportunities of obferving the mifetable manner in which thofe people live. In the courfe of our trade with them we frequently purchafed feveral fealfkin bags, which we fuppofed were full of oil; but on opening them have fometimes found great quantities of venifon, feals, and fea-horfe paws, as well as lalmon; and as thefe were of noufe to us, we always returned them to the Indian;;, who eagerly devoured them, though fome of the articles had been perhaps a whole year in that (late; and they feemed to exult greatly in having fo over-reached us in the way of trade, as to have fometimes one third of. their bargain returned.

This rr. ethod o. f preferving their food, though it effeflually guards it from the external air, and from the fiies, does not prevent putrefalion entirely, though it renders its progrefs very flow. Pure train oil is of fuch a quality that it never freezes folid in the coldeft Winters; a happy circum- fiance for thofe people, who are condemned to live in the moft rigorous climate without the afliftance of fire. While thefe magazines laft, they have nothing more to do when hunger aflailsthem, but to open one of the bags, take out a fide of venifon, a few feals, fea-horfe paws, or fome half-rotten falmon, and without any preparation, fit down and make a meal; and the lake or liver by which they pitch their tent, affords them water, which is their conllant drink. Befides the extraordinary food already mentioned, they have feveral other difhes equally ci(gu(ting to an Europeaa palate; I will only mention one, as it was more frequently part of their repaft when I yifite their tents, than any other, except fifh, Thediili I allude

July

NORTHERN OCEAN. ici

When the Indians had plundered the fcven 1771. tents of all the copper utenfils, which feemed the only things worth their notice, they threw all the tents and tent-poles into the river, dcftroyed a vaft quantity of dried flilmon, mulk-oxcn flefli, and other provifions; broke all the ftone kettles; allude to, is made of the raw Tiver of a deer, cut in fmall pieces of about an inch fqiiarc, and mixed up with the contents of the ftomach of the fame animal; and the fartlier digeflion has taken place, the better it isfuited to their tafte. It is impofllbie to defcribe or conceive the pleafure they feem to enjoy when eating fuch unaccountable food: nay, 1 have even feen them eat whofe handfuls of maggots that were produced in meat by flyblows; and it is their conflant cuftom, when their nofes bleed by any accident, to lick their blood into tiieir mouths, and fwallow it. Indeed, if we confider the inhofpitable part of the globe they ate deftined to inhabit, and the great dirtreflcs to wliich they are frequently driven by hunger in confequence of it, we (hall no longer be fui prized at finding they can relilh any thing in common with the mcanefl of the animal creation, but rather admire the wifdom and kindnefsof Providence in forming the palates and powers of all creatures in fuch a manner as is bed adapted to the food, climate, and every other circumflance which may be incident to their refpec-tive fituations.

It is no Icfs true, that tlicfe people, when I firfl knew them, would not cat any of our provifions, n; gar, railin.";, tigs, or even bread; for thoiich fome of them would put a bit of it into their mouihs, they foon fpit it out again with evident marks of diflike; fo that they had no greater relilh for our food than we had for theirs. At prcfent, however, they will eat any part of our provifions, either frefli or falted; and fome of them will drink 3 draft of porter, or a little brandy and water; and they are now fo far civilized, and attached to the Englifli, that 1 am perfuaded any of the company's fcrvants who could habituate themfelves to their diet and manner of life, might now live as fecure under their proteiftion, as under that: of any of the liibes of Indians who border on Hudfon's Bay.

They live in aftate of perfeitt freedqns; no one apparently clairringtlie fuperiority over, or acknowledging the lead fubordination to another except what is due from children to ihtir parents, or fuch of theii kin as take care of them v. hen they are young and incapable of providing for ihen-felves. Thire i;, however, rcafon to; think inaf, when grown up to manhood, they pay for.-. t attention to the advice of the old men, on accoi; nt of their cxpeii. rc?.

and, in fav, did all the mifchicf they poflibly could to diftrefs the poor creatures they could not murder, and who were landing on the flioal before mentioned, obliged to be woeful fpeftators of their great, or perhaps irreparable lofs.

After the Indians had completed this piece of wantonnefs we fat down, and made a good meal of frelh falmon which were as numerous at the place where we now refted, as they were on the XVeft fide of the river. When we had finifhed our meal, which was the firft we had enjoyed for many hours, the Indians told me that they were again ready to aflift me in making an end of my furvey. It was then about five o'clock in the h. morning of the feventeenth, the fea being in fight from the North Weft by Weft to the North Eaft about eight miles diftant. I therefore fet inftant-lv about commencing my furvey, and purfued it to the mouth of the river, which 1 found all the way fo full of flioals and falls that it was not navigable even for a boat, and that it emptied itfelf into the fea over a ridge or bar. The tide was then out; but I judged from the marks which I faw on the edge of the ice, that it Sowed about tuelve or fourteen feet, which will only reach a little way within the river's mouth. The tide being out, the water in the river was perfe6i: ly frefli; bu I am certain of its being the fea, or feme branch of it, by the quantity of whalebone and feal-fldns which the Efquimaux had at their tents, and alfo by the number of feals which I faw on the ice. At the mouth of the river, the fea is full of iflands and fhoals, as far as I could fee with the affiftance of a good pocket telcfcope. The ice was not then broke up, but was melted away for about three quarters of a mile from the main fliore, and to a little diftance round the iflands and fhoals.

By the time I had completed this furvey, it was about one in the morning of the eighteenth; but in thofe high latitudes, and at this feafon of the year, the Sun is always at a good height above the horizon, fo that we had not only day-light, but fun-lhine the whole night: a thick fog and drizzling rain then came on, and finding that neither the river nor fea were likely to be of any ufe, I did not think it worth while to wait for fair weather to determine the latitude exaftly by an obfervation; but by the extraordinary care I took in obferving the courfes and diftances when 1 walked from Congecathawhachaga where 1 had two good obfervations, the latitude may be depended upon within twenty miles at the utmoft. For the fake of form however, after having had fome confultation vdth the Indians, I ereded a mark, and took poffeflion of the coaft, on behalf of the Hudfon's Bay Company.

Having finiflied this bufinefs, we fet out on our return, and walked about twelve miles to the South by Eaft, when we ftopped and took a little ileep, which was the firft time that any of us had clofed our eyes from the fifteenth inftant, and it M 2 was i8th, was now fix o'clock in the morning of the eighteenth. Here the Indians killed a mulk-ox, but the mofs being very wet, we could not make a fire, fo that we were obliged to eat the meat raw, which was intolerable, as it happened to be an old beaft.

Before I proceed farther on my return, it may not be improper to give fome account of the river, and the country adjacent; its productions, and the animals which conftantly inhabit thofe dreary regions, as well as thofe that only migrate thither in Summer, in order to breed and rear their young, unmolefted by man. That I may do this to better purpofe, it will be neceffary to go back to the place where I firft came to the river, which was about forty miles from its mouth.

Befide the ftunted pines already mentioned, there are fome tufts of dwarf willows; plenty of Wifhacumpuckey, (as the Englifh call it, and which they nfe as tea); fome jackafheypuck, which the natives ufe as tobacco; and a few cranberry and heathberry bulhes; but not the leaft appearance of any fruit.

The woods grow gradually thinner and fmaller as you approach the fea; and the laft little tuft of pines that I faw is about thirty miles from the mouth of the river, fo that we meet with nothing between that fpot and the fea-fide but barren hills and marfhes.

The general courfe of the river is about North by Eaft j but in fome places it is very crooked, and Its breadth varies from twenty yards to four or five hundred. The banks are in general a folid rock, both fides of which correfpond fo exaftly with each other, as to leave no doubt that the channel of the river has been caufed by fome terrible convulfion of nature; and the ftream is fup-plied by a variety of little rivulets, that rufii down the fides of the hills, occafioned chiefly by the melting of the fnow. Some of the Indians fay, that this river takes its rife from the North Weft fide of Large White Stone Lake, which is at the diftance of near three hundred miles on a ftraight line; but I can fcarcely think that is the cafe, unlefs there be many intervening lakes, which are fupplicd by the vaft quantity of water that is collected in fo great an extent of hilly and mountainous country: for were it otherwife, I ftiould imagine that the multitude of fmall rivers, which muft empty themfelves into the main ftream in the courfe of fo great a diftance, would have formed a much deeper and ftronger current than I dif-covered, and occafioned an annual deluge at the breaking up of the ice in the Spring, of which there was not the leaft appearance, except at Bloody Fall, where the river was contrafled to the breadth of about twenty yards. It was at the foot of this fall that my Indians killed the Efqui-maux; which was the reafon why I diftinguifhed it by that appellation. From this fall, which is about eight miles from the fea-fide, there are very few hills, and thofe not high. The land between them them is a ftiffloam and clay, which, in fome parts, produces patches of pretty good grafs, and in others tallifh dwarf willows: at the foot of the hills alfo there is plenty of fine fcurvy-grafs.

The Efquimaux at this river are but low in fla-flure, none exceeding the middle fize, and though broad fet, are neither well-made nor flrong bodied. Their complexion is of a dirty copper colour; iom. e of the women, however, are more fair and ruddy. Their drefs much refembles that of the Greenlanders in Davis's Straits, except the women's boots, which are not fliffened out with whalebone, and the tails of their jackets are not more than a foot long.

Their arms and fifhing-tackle are bows and arrows, fpears, lances, darts, c. which exaftly re- femble thofe made ufe of by the Efquimaux in Hudfon's Straits, and which have been well de-fcribed by Crantz; but, for want of good edge-tools, are far inferior to them in workmanfhip. Their arrows are either fhod with a trianglar piece of black flone, like flate, or a piece of copper; but moft commonly the former.

The body of their canoes is on the fame con-ftrucdon as that of the other Efquimaux, and there is no unneceffary prow-projection beyond the body of the veitel; thefe, like their arms and other utenfils, are, for the want of better tools, by no means fo neat as thofe I have feen in Hud-Ibn's Bay and Straits. The double-bladed paddle

See Hift. of Greenland, vol. i. p. i J2156.

die is in univerfal ufe among all the tribes of this people.

Their tents are made of parchment deer-lkins in the hair, and are pitched in a circular form, the fame as thofe of the Efquimaux in Hudfons Bay. Thefe tents are undoubtedly no more than their Summer habitations, for I faw the remains of two miferable hovels, which, from the fituati-on, the ftrudlure, and the vaft quantity of bones, old (hoes, fcraps of fkins, and other rubbifli lying near them, had certainly been fome of their Winter retreats. Thefe houfes were fituated on the South fide of a hill; one half of them were under-ground, and the upper parts clofely fet round with poles, meeting at the top in a conical form, like their fummer-houfes or tents. Thefe tents when inhabited, had undoubtedly been covered with fkins; and in Winter entirely over-fpread with the fnow-drift, which muft have greatly contributed to their warmth. They were fo fmall, that they did not contain more than fix or eight perfons each; and even that number of any other people would have found them but miferable habitations.

Their houfehold furniture chiefly confifts of fione kettles, and wooden troughs of various fizes; alfo diflies, fcoops, andfpoons, made of the buffalo or mufk-ox horns. Their kettles are formed of a pepper and fait coloured ftone; and though the texture appears to be very coarfe, and as porous as a drip-ftone, yet they are perfedly tight, tight, and will found as clear as a china bowl Some of thofe kettles are fo large as to be capable of containing five or fix gallons; and though it is impoltible thefe poor people can perform this arduous work with any other tools than harder ftones, yet they are by far fuperior to any that I had ever feen in Hudfon's Bay; every one of them being ornamented with neat mouldings round the rim, and fome of the large ones with a kind of flute-work at each corner. In fhape they were a long fquare, fomething wider at the top than bottom, like a knife-tray, and flrong handles of the folid ftone were left at each end to lift them up.

Their hatchets are made of a thick lump of copper, about five or fix inches long, and from one and a half to two inches fquare; they are bevill-ed away at one end like a mortice-chiftel. This is lafhed into the end of a piece of wood about twelve or fourteen inches long, in fuch a manner as to acb like an adze: in general they are applied to the wood like a chiltel, and driven in with a heavy club, inftead of a mallet. Neither the weight of the tool nor the fharpnefs of the metal will admit of their being handled either as adze or axe, with any degree of fuccefs.

The men's bayonets and women's knives are alfomade of copper; the former are in fhape like the ace of fpades, with the handle of deers horn a foot long, and the latter exadly refemble thofe defcribed by Crantz. Samples of both thefe implements plements I formerly fent home to James Fitzgerald, Efq. then one of the Hudfon's Bay Committee.

Among all the fpoils of the twelve tents which my companions plundered, only two fmall pieces of iron were found j one of which was about an inch and a half long, and three eighths of an inch broad, made into a woman's knife; the other was barely an inch long, and a quarter of an inch wide. This laft was rivettcd into a piece of ivory, fo as to form a man's knife, known in Hudfon's Bay by the name of Mokeatoggan, and is the only in-ftrument ufed by them in fhaping all their woodwork.

Thofe people had a fine and numerous breed of dogs, with fiiarp erect ears, Iharp nofes, bufhy tails, c. exactly Hke thofc feen among the Ef-quimaux in Hudfon's Bay and Straits. They were all tethered to ftones, to prevent them, as I fup-pofe, from eating the filh that were fpread all over the rocks to dry. I do not recoiled: that my companions killed or hurt one of thofe animals; but after we had left the tents, they often wifh-ed they had taken fome of thofe fine dogs with them.

Though the drefs, canoes, utenfils, and many other articles belonging to thefe people, are very fimilar to thofe of Hudfon's Bay, yet there is one cufloni that prevails among themnamely, that of the men having all the hair of their heads pulled out by the rootswhich pronounces them to

Tulv.

be of a dlfferent tribe from any hitherto feen either on the coaft of Labradore, Hudfon's Bay, or Davis's Straits. The women wore their hair at full length, and exactly in the fame ftile as all the other Efquimaux women do whom I have feen.

When at the fea-fide, (at the mouth of the Copper River,") befides feeing many feals on the ice, I alfo obferved feveral flocks of fea-fowl flying about the fliores; fuch as, gulls black-heads, loons, old wives, haha-wie's, dunter geefe, arctic gulls, and willicks. In the adjacent ponds alfo were fome fwans and geefe in a moulting flate, and in the marflies fome curlews and plover; plenty of hawks-eyes, (i. e. the green plover,) and fome yellow-legs; alfo feveral other fmall birds, that vifit thofe Northern parts in the Spring to breed and moult, and which doubtlefs return Southward as the fall advances. My reafon for this conjedure is founded on a certain knowledge that all thofe birds migrate in Hudfon's Bay; and it is but reafonable to think that they are lefs capable of withftanding the rigour of fuch a long and cold Winter as they muft necefiarily experience in a country which is fo many degrees within the Ardtic Circle, as that is where I now faw them.

That the mufl:-oxen, deer, bears, wolves, wol-varines, foxes, Alpine hares, white owls, ravens, partridges, ground-fquirrels, common fquirrels, ermins, mice, c. are the confi: ant inhabitants of thofe parts, is not to be doubted. In many places, by the fides of the hills, where the fnow lay to a great great depth, the dung of the mufk-oxen and deer was lying in fuch long and continued heaps, as clearly to point out that thofe places had been their much-frequented paths during the preceding Winter. There were alfo many other fimilar appearances on the hills, and other parts, where. the fnow was entirely thawed away, without any print of a foot being vifible in the mofs; which is a certain proof that thefe long ridges of dung muft have been dropped in the Inow as the beafts were paftmg and repaffing over it in the Winter. There are likewife limilar proofs that the Alpine hare and the partridge do not migrate, but remain there the whole year: the latter we found in confiderable flocks among the tufts of willows which grow near the fea.

It is perhaps not generally known, even to the curious, therefore may not be unworthy of obfer-vation,"that the dung of the mufk-ox, though fo large an animal, is not larger, and at the fame time fo near the fhape and colour of that of the Alpine hare, that the difference is not eafily diftinguifh-ed but by the natives, though in general the quantity may lead to a difcovery of the animal to which it belongs.

I did not fee any birds peculiar to thofe parts, except what the Copper Indians call the " Alarm " Bird, or Bird of Warning. In fize and colour it refembles a Cobadekoock, and is of the owl genus. The name is faid to be well adapted to its qualities; for when it perceives any people, or beaft, it directs its way towards them imme- diately, and after hovering over them fome time, flies round them in circles, or goes a-head in the fame direction in which they walk. They repeat their viiits frequently; and if they fee any other moving objects, fly alternately from one party to the other, hover over them for fome time, and make a loud fcreaming noife, like the crying of a child. In this manner they are faid fome-times to follow paltengers a whole day. The Copper Indians put great confidence in thofe birds, and fay they are frequently apprized by them of the approach of ftrangers, and conducted by them to herds of deer and mufk-oxen; which, without their afliftance, in all probability, they never could have found.

The Efquimaux feem not to have imbibed the fame opinion of thofe birds; for if they had, they muft have been apprized of our approach toward their tents, becaufe all the time the Indians lay in ambufh, (before they began the maffacre,) a large flock of thofe birds were continually flying about, and hovering alternately over them and the tents, making a noife fufficient to awaken any man out of the foundeft flsep.

After a lleep of five or fix hours we once more fet oujt, and walked eighteen or nineteen miles to the South South Eaft, when we arrived at one of the copper mines, which lies, from the river's mouth about South South Eaft, diftant about twenty. nire or thirty miles.

This

This mine, if it deferve that appellation, is no more than an entire jumble of rocks and gravel, which has been rent many ways by an earthquake. Through thefe ruins there runs a fmall river; but no part of it, at the time I was there, was more than knee-deep.

The Indians who were the occafion of my undertaking this journey, reprefented this mine to be fo rich and valuable, that if a fa(5lory were built at the river, a fhip might be ballarted with the oar, inftead of ftone; and that with the fame eafe and difpatch as is done with ftones at Churchill River. By their account the hills were entirely compofed of that metal, all in handy lumps, like a heap of pebbles. But their account differed fo much from the truth, that I and almofl. all my companions expended near four hours in fearch of fome of this metal, with fuch poor fuccefs, that among us all, only one piece of any fize could be found. This, however, was remark-ably good, and weighed above four pounds'. I believe the copper has formerly been in much greater plenty; for in many places, both on the furface and in the cavities and crevices of the rocks, the ftones are much tinged with ver-digrife.

It may not be unworthy the notice of the curious, or undeferving a place in my Journal, to remark,

This piece of Copper is now in the poftefnon of the Kujfjn's Bay Company.

remark, that the Indians imagine that every bit of copper they find refembles fome objecl in nature; but by what I faw of the large piece, and fome fmaller ones which were found by my companions, it requires a great fliare of invention to make this out. I found that different people had different ideas on the fubjecf, fcjr the large piece of copper above mentioned had not been found long before it had twenty different names. One faying that it refembled this animal, and another that it reprefented a particular part of another; at laft it was generally allowed to refemble an Alpine hare couchant: for my part, I muft con-fefs that I could not fee it had the leaft refem-blance to any thing to which they compared it. It would be endlefs to enumerate the different parts of a deer, and other animals, which the Indians fay the belt pieces of copper refemble: it may therefore be fufficient to fay, that thelargeft pieces, with the feweft branches and the leaft drofs, are the beft for their ufe; as by the help of fire, and two ftones, they can beat it out to any fhape they wifh.

Before Churchill River was fettled by the Hud-fon's Bay Company, which was not more than fifty years previous to this journey being undertaken, the Northern Indians had no other me-tal but copper among them, except a fmall quantity of iron-work, which a party of them who vifited York Fort about the year one thoufand even hundred and thirteen, or one thoufand fe-

J"iy.

NORTHERN OCEAN. 175 ven hundred and fourteen, purchafed; and a few 177 r. pieces of old iron found at Churchill River, which had undoubtedly been left there by Captain Monk. This being the cafe, numbers of them from all quarters ufed every Summer to refort to thefe hills in fearch of copper; of which they made hatchets, ice-chiifels, bayonets, knives, awls, arrow-heads, c. The many paths that had been beaten by the Indians on thefe occafions, and which are yet, in many places, very perfed-, efpecially on the dry ridges and hills, is furpriling; in the vallies and marfliy grounds, however, they are moftly grown over with herbage, fo as not to be difcerned.

The Copper Indians fet a great value on their native metal even to this day; and prefer it to iron, for almoft every ufe except that of a hatchet,

There is a flrange tradition among thofe people, that the fiifl; perfon who difcovered thofe mines was a woman, and that flie condufted them to the place for feveral years; but as ftie was the only woman in company, fomeof the men took fiich liberties with her as made)ier vow revenge on them; and (he is faid to have been a great conjurer. Accordingly when the men had loaded themfelves with copper, and were going to return, flis refufed to accompany them, and faid ftie would fit on the mine till fhe fjnk into the ground, and that the copper fhould fink with her. The next year, when the mesi went for more copper, they found her funk up to the waift, though ftill alive and the quantity of copper much decreafed; and oa their repeating their vifit the year following, Ihe had quite difappeared, and all the principal part of the mine with her; fo that after that period nothing remained on the furface but a few fmall pieces, and thofe were fcattered at a confiderable diflance from each other. Before that period they fay the copper lay on the furfacc in fuch large heaps, that the Indians had nothing to do but turn it over, and pick fuch pieces as vould beft fuit the different ufes for which they intended it.

J"iy.

A JOURNEY TO THE et, a knife, and an awl: for thefe three neceitary implements, copper makes but a very poor fub-ftitute. When they exchange copper for ironwork with our trading Northern Indians, which is but feldom, the ftandard is an ice-chiffel of copper for an ice-chiffel of iron, or an ice-chiffel and a few arrow-heads of copper, for a half-worn hatchet; but when they barter furrs with our Indians, the eftabiifhed rule is to give ten times the price for every thing they purchafe that is given for them at the Company's Factory. Thus, a hatchet that is bought at the Factory for one beaver-ikin, or one cat-fkin, or three ordinary martins' fkins, is fold to thofe people zt the advanced price of one thoufandr cent.; they alfo pay in proportion, for knives, and every other fmaller piece of iron-work. For a fmall brafs kettle of two pounds, or two pounds and a half weight, they pay lixty martins, or twenty beaver in other kinds of furrs. If the kettles are not bruifed, or iii-ufed in any other refpecft, the Northern

Wha)5 meant by Beaver in other kind of furrs, mud be underfucod as follows: For the eafier trading with the Indians, as well as for the more correftly Ueeping their accounts, the Hudfon's Bay Company have made a full-grown beaver-flcin the ftandard by which they rate all other furrs, according to their refpedive values. Thus in feveral fpecles of furrs, one (kin is valued at the rate of four beaver flcins; fome at three, and others at two; whereas thofe of an inferior qjiality are rather at one; and tliofe of ftill lefs value confidered fo inferior to that of a beaver, that from fix to twenty of their fkins are only valued as equal to one beaver fkin in the way of trade, and do not fetch one-fourth of the price at the London niai-ket. In this manner the term "Made Braver" is to be underftood.

thern traders have the confcience at times to exact fomething more. It is at this extravagant price that all the Copper and Dog-ribbed Indians, who traffic with our yearly traders, fupply them-felves with iron-work. Sec.

From thofe two tribes our Northern Indians ufed formerly to purchafe moft of the furrs they brought to the Company's Factory; for their own country produced very few of thofe articles, and being, at that time, at war with the Southern Indians, they were prevented from penetrating-far enough backwards to meet with many animals of the furr kind; fo that deer-fkins, and fuch furrs as they could extort from the Copper and Dog-ribbed Indians, compofed the whole of their trade; which, on an average of many years, and indeed till very lately, feldom or ever exceeded fix thoufand Made Beaver per annum.

At prefent happy it is for them, and greatly to the advantage of the Company, that they are in perfeft peace, and live in friendlfiip with their Southern neighbours. The good effect of this harmony is already fo viiible, that within a few years the" trade

from that quarter has increafed many thoufands of Made Beaver annually; fbme years even to the amount of eleven thoufand Ikins. Befides the advantaire arifina; to the
N Company
Shice this Journal was written, the Noithern Indiins, by annually vi-filing tlicif Soaihern friends, the Alhapr. icow Indians, have contravslcd the
Company from this increafe, the poor Northern Indians reap innumerable benefits from a fine and plentiful country, with the produce of which they annually load themfelves for trade, without giving the leaft offence to the proper inhabitants.
Several attempts have been made to induce the Copper and Dog-ribbed Indians to vifit the Company's Fort at Churchill River, and for that pur-pofe many prefents have been fent, but they never were attended with any fuccefs. And though fmall-pox, which has carried off nine-tenths of therti, and particularly thofe people who compofed the trade at Churchill Faflory. The few futvivors follow the example of their Southern neighbours, and all trade with the Canadians, who are fettled in the heart of the Athapufcow country: fo that a very few years has proved my (hortfightednefs, and that it would have been much more to the advantage of the Company, as well as have prevented the depopulation of the Northern Indian country, if they had ftill remained at war with the Southern ttibes, and never attempted to better their fituation. At the fame time, it is impoffible to fay what increafe of trade might not, in time, have arifen from a conflant and regular traffic with the different tribes of Copper and Dog-ribbed Indians. But having been totally neglefled for fevcral years, they have now funk into their original barbarifm and extreme indigence; and a war has enfued between the two tribes, for the fake of a few remnants of ironwork which was left among them; and the Dog-ribbed Indians were fo numerous, and fo fuccefsful, as to deflroy almofl the whole race of the Copper Indians.
While I was writing this Note, I was informed by fome Northern Indians, that the few which remain of the Copper tribe have found their waf to one of the Canadian houfes in the Athapufcow Indians country, where they get fupplied with every thing at lefs, or about half the price they were formerly obliged to give; fo that the few fmviving Northern Indians, as well as the Hudion's Bay Company, have now loft every (hadow of any future trade from that quarter, uiiiefs the Company will eflabiilh a fettle-ment with the Athapufcow country, andundcrleil the Canadians.
though feveral of the Copper Indians have vifited 1771, Churchill, in the capacity of fervants to the Nor- "rr thern Indians, and were generally fent back loaded with prefents for their countrymen, yet the Northern Indians always plundered them of the whole foon after they left the Fort. This kind of treatment, added to the many inconveniencies that attend fo long a journey, are great obftacles in their way; otherwife it would be as poffible for them to bring their own goods to market, as for the Northern Indians to go fo far to purchafe them on their own account, and have the fame diftance to bring them as the firft proprietors would have had. But it is a political fcheme of our Northern traders to prevent fuch an intercourfe, as it would greatly leften their confequence and emolument. Superftition, indeed, will, in all probability, be a lafting barrier againfi: thofe people ever having a fettled communication with our Factory; as few of them chufe to travel in countries fo remote from their own, under a pretence that the change of air and provihons (though exactly the fame to which they are accuftomed) are

highly prejudicial to their health; and that not one out of three of thofe who have undertaken the journey, have ever lived to return. The firft of thefe reafons is evidently no more than grofs fuperftition; and though the latter is but too true, it has always been owing to the treachery and cruelty of the Northern Indians, who took them under their protection.

It is but a few years lince, that Captain Keel-fhies, who is frequently mentioned in this Journal, took twelve of thefe people under his charge, all heavy laden with the moft voluable furrs; and long before they arrived at the Fort, he and the reft of his crew had got all the furrs from them, in payment for provifions for their fup-port, and obliged them to carry the furrs on their account.

On their arrival at Prince of Waless Fort, Keelfliies laid claim to great merit for having brought thofe ftrangers, fo richly laden, to the Factory, and affured the Governor that he might, in future, expecl a great increafe in trade from that quarter, through his intereft and afliduity. One of the ftrangers was dubbed with the name of Captain, and treated accordingly, while at the Fort; that is, he was drelted out in the beft manner; and at his departure, both himfelf and all his countrymen were loaded with prefents, in hopes that they would not only repeat the vifit themfelves, but by difplaying fo much generofity, many of their countrymen would be induced to accompany them.

There feems to be great propriety in the conduct of the Governor on this occafion; but however well-intended, it had quite the contrary effect, for Keellhies and the reft of his execrable gang, not content with fharing all the furrs thofe poor people had carried to the Fort, determined

Mr. Moles Norton.

to get alfo all the European goods that had been 177 i. given to them by the Governor. As neither-y Keelfhies nor any of his gang had the courage to kill the Copper Indians, they concerted a deep-laid fcheme for their deftruclion; which u-as to leave them on an ifland. With this view, when they got to the propofed fpot, the Northern Indians took care to have all the baggage belonging to the Copper Indians ferried acrofs to the main, and having ftripped them of fuch parts of their clothing as they thought worthy their notice, went off with all the canoes, leaving them all behind on the ifland, where they perifhed for want. When I was on my journey to the Fort in June one thoufand feven hundred and feventy-two, I faw the bones of thofe poor people, and had the foregoing account from my guide Mato-nabbee; but it was not made known to the Governor for fome years afterward, for fear of prejudicing him againft Keelfliies.

A limilar circumftance had nearly happened to a Copper Indian who accompanied me to the Fort in one thoufand feven hundred and feventy-tvo: after we were all ferried acrofs Seal River, and the poor man's bundle of furrs on the South-fide, he was left alone on the oppofite Ihore; and no one except Matonabbee would go over for him. The wind at that time blew fo hard, that Matonabbee ftripped himfelf quite naked, to be ready for fwimming in cafe the canoe (hould overfet; but he foon brought the Copper Indian fafe over, to the no fmall mortification of the wretch who had the charge of him, and who would gladly have pofifefled the bundle of furrs at the cxpence of the poor man's life.

When the Northern Indians returned for the Factory that year, the above Copper Indian put himfelf under the protection of Matonabbee, who accompanied him as far North as the latitude 64, where they faw fome Copper Indians, among whom was the young man's father, into whofe hands Matonabbee delivered him in good health, with all his goods fafe, and in good order.

Soon after we had left the Copper-mine, there came on a thick fog with rain, and at intervals heavy iliowers of fnow. This kind of weather continued for fome days; and at times it was fo thick, that we were obliged to (iop for feveral hours together, as we were unable to fee our way, and the road was remarkably rocky and intricate. 2id, At three o'clock in the morning of the twenty- fecond, Matonabbee's brother and one of the Copper Indians, who had been firft difpatched a-head from Congecathawhachaga, overtook us. During their abfence they had not difcovered any Indians who could have been ferviceable to my expedition. They had, however, been at the Copper River, and feeing fome marks fet up there to direct them to return, they had made the beft of their way, and had not flept from the time time they left the river till they joined us, though the diftance was not lefs than a hundred miles. When they arrived we were afleep, but we iboa awakened, and began to proceed on our journey. That day we walked forty-two miles; and in cur way paffed Buffalo Lake: at night, we put up about the middle of the Stony Moun= tains. The weather was cxceffively hot and fultry.

On the twenty-third, the weather continued j much the fame as on the preceding day. Early in the morning we fet out, and walked forty-five miles the firll day, during which the Indians killed feveral fine fat buck deer.

About one o'clock in the morning of the twen-ty-fourth, we flopped and took a little refrefli-ment, as we had alfo done about noon the preceding day; but the Indians had been fo long from their wives and families, that they promif-ed not to fleep till they faw them, efpecially as we were then in fight of the hills of Congecatha-whachaga, where we had left the lafl; of them. After refling about an hour, we proceeded on our way, and at fix in the morning arrived at Congecathawhachaga; when, to our great difap-pointment, we found that all our women hd got fet acrofs the river before the Copper Indians left that part; fo that when we arrived, not an Indian was to be found, except an old man and his family, who had arrived in our abfence, and

J4th.

July.

A JOURNEY TO Tfle was waiting at the croffing-place with fome furrs for Ma-tonabbee, who was fo nearly related to the old man as to be his fon-in-law, having one of his daughters for a wife. The old man had another with him, who was alfo offered to the great man, but not accepted.

Our ftay at this place may be faid to have been of very fhort duration; for on feeing a large fmoke to the Southward, we immediately croffed the river, and walked towards it, when we found that the women had indeed been there fome days before, but were gone; and at their departure had fet the mofs on fire, which was then burning, and occafioned the fmoke we had feen. By this time the afternoon was far advanced; we purfued, however, our courfe in the direftion which the women took, for their track we could eafily dif-cover in the mofs. We had not gone far, before we faw another fmoke at a great diftance, for which we ihaped our courfe; and, notwithftand-ing we redoubled our pace, it was eleven o'clock at night before we reached it; when, to our great mortification, we found it to be the place where 23th. the women had flept the night before; having in the morning, at their departure, fet fire to the mofs which was then burning.

The Indians, finding that their wives were fo near as to be within one of their ordinary day's walk, which feldom exceeded ten or twelve miles, determined not to reft till they had joined them.

Accordingly

Accordingly we purfued our courfe, and about j,-j two o'clock in the morning of the twenty-, fifth, come up with fome of the women, who J'"' had then pitched their tents by the fide of Coge-ad Lake.

From our leaving the Copper-mine River tothis time we had travelled fo hard, and taken fo little reft by the way, that my feet and les had fwcll-ed confiderably, and I had become quite ftiff at the ankles. In this fituation I had fo little power to direct my feet when walking, that I frequently knocked them againft the ftones with fuch force, as not only to jar and diforder them, but my legs alfo; and the nails of my toes were bruifed to fuch a degree, that feveral of them fc(-tered and dropped off. To add to this mifliap, the Ikin was, entirely chafed off from the tops of both my feet, and between every toe; fo that the fand and gravel, which I could by no means exclude, irritated the raw parts fo much, that for a whole day before we arrived at the women's tents, I left the print of my feet in blood alm. oft at every ftep I took. Several of the Indians began to complain that their feet alfo were fore; but, on examination, not one of them was the twentieth part in fo bad a ilate as mine.

This being the firfl: time I had been in fuch a lituation, or feen anybody foot-fcundered, I was much alarmed, and under great apprehenfions for the confequences. Though I was but little fatigued fatigued in body, yet the excruciating pain I fuf-fered when walking, had fuch an effed on my fpirits, that if the Indians had continued to travel two or three days longer at that unmerciful rate, I muft unavoidably have been left behind; for my feet were in many places quite honey-comb-ed, by the dirt and gravel eating into the raw flefli.

As foon as we arrived at the women's tents, the firft thing I did, was to wafh and clean my feet in warm water; then I bathed the fwelled parts with fpirits of wine, and dreffed thofe that were raw with Turner's cerate; foon after which I betook myfelf to reft. As we did not move on the following day, I perceived that the fwelling abated, and the raw parts of my feet were not quite fo much inflamed. This change for the better gave me the ftrongeft afturance that reft was the principal thing wanted to effect a fpeedy and complete cure of my painful though in reality very fimple diforder, (foot-foundering,) which I had before confidered to be an affair of the greateft confequence.

Reft, however, though effential to my fpeedy recovery, could not at this time be procured; for as the Indians weredefirous ofjoining the remainder of their wives and families as foon as poffible, they would not ftop even a fmgle day; fo that on the twenty. feventh we again began to move; and though they moved at the rate of eight or nine 7th.

ine miles a day, it was with the utmoft difficulty that I could follow them. Indeed the weather proved remarkably fine and pleafant, and the ground was in general pretty dry, and free from floncs; which contributed greatly to my eafe in walking, and enabled me to keep up with the natives.

On the thirty-firft of July, we arrived at the 31ft place where the wives and families of my companions had been ordered to wait our return from the Copper-mine River. Here we found feveral tents of Indians; but thofe belonging to Mato-nabbee, and fome others of my crew, had not arrived. We faw, however, a large fmoke to the Eaftward, vihich was fuppofed had been made by them, as no other Indians were expeded from that quarter. Accordingly, the next morning, Matonabbce fent fome of his young men in queft 1 of them, and on the fifth, they all joined us; when, contrary to expectation, a great number of other Indians were with them j in all, to the amount of more than forty tents. Among thofe Indians, was the man who Matonabbee fiabbed when we were at Clowey. With the greateft fub-miflion he led his wife to Matonabbee's tent, fet her down by his fide, and retired, without faying a word. Matonabbee took no notice of her, though fhe was bathed in tears; and by degrees, after reclining herfelf on her elbow for fome time, Ihe lay down, and, fobbing, did, feed dinne,eed dinne!

jy,! dinne which is, My hufband, my hufband! On v-v-v- which Matonabbee told her, that if fhe had re Auguft. fpe(5j; ed jiijji 2. S fuch, fhe would not have run away from him; and that flie was at liberty to gc where fhe pleafed. On which fhe got up, with feeming reludance, though mofl afturedly with a light heart, and returned to her former hufband's tent.

CHAP.

Remarks from the Time the Women joined us till our Arrival at the Athapufcow Lake.

Several of the Indians fick. Method ufed by the conjurors to relieve one man, who recovers. Matonabbee and his crew proceed to the South Wei. Mqi of the other Indians feparate, and go their refpeclive ways. Pafs by White Stone Lake, Many deer killed merely for their fkins. Remarks thereon, and on the deer, refpe6lingfeafons and places. Arrive at Point Lake. One of the Indians wives being fick, is left behind to perifh above-ground. Weather very bad, but deer plenty. Stay fome time at Point Lake to dry meat, c. Winterfet in. Superfiitious cufioms obferved by my companions, after they had killed the Ffquimaux at Copper River. A violent gale ofzuind overfets my tent and breaks my quadrant. Some Copper and Dog-ribbed Indians join us. Indians propofe to go to the Athapufcow Country to kill moofe. Leave Point Lake, and arrive at the wood's edge. Arrive at Anawd Lake. Tranfabions there Remarkable inftance of a man being cured of the palfey by the conjurors. Leave Anawd Lake Arrive at the great Athapufcow Lake.

SEVERAL of the Indians being very ill, the conjurers, who are always the doctors, and.- pretend to perform great cures, began to try their "fi"- fkill j- J (kill to effeifi: their recovery. Here it is neceffary Kxj to remark, that they ufe no medicine either for

Augufi. internal or external complaints, but perform all their cures by charms. In ordinary cafes, fucking the part affeded, blowing, and finging to it; haughing, fpitting, and at the fame time uttering a heap of unintelligible jargon, compofe the whole procefs of cure. For fome inward complaints; fuch as, griping in the inteftines, difficulty of making water, Iffc. it is very common to fee thofe jugglers blowing into the anus or into the parts adjacent, till their eyes are almoft ftarting out of their heads: and this operation is performed indifferently on all, without regard either to age or fex. The accumulation of fo large a quantity of wind is at times apt to occafion fome extraordinary emotions, which are not eaiily fuppreifed by a fick perfon; and as there is no vent for it but by the channel through which it was conveyed thither, it fometimes occafions an odd fcene between the dodlor and his patient; which 1 once wantonly called an engagement, but for which I was afterward exceedingly forry, as it highly offended feveral of the Indians; particularly the juggler and the lick perfon, both of whom were men I much efleemed, and, except in that moment of levity, it had ever been no lels my inclination than my intereft to fhew them every refpect that my lituation would admit, I have often admired the great pains thefe jugglers take to deceive their credulous countrymen, while while at the fame time they are indcfatigably in-duftrious and perfevering in their efforts to relieve them. Being naturally not very delicate, they frequently continue their windy procefs lb long, that I have more than once feen the doctor quit his patient with his face and bread in a very dif-agreeable condition. However laughable this may appear to an European, cuflom makes it very indecent, in their opinion, to turn any thing of the kind to ridicule.

When a friend for whom they have a particular regard is, as they fuppofe, danger-oufly ill, belide the above methods, they have recourfe to another very extraordinary piece of fuperftition; which is no lefs than that of pretending to fvvallow hatchets, ice-chiffels, broad bayonets, knives, and the like; out of a fuperftitious notion that undertaking fuch delperate feats will have fome influence in appeafmg death, and procure a relpite for their patient.

On fuch extraordinary occafions a conjuring-houfe is erected, by driving the ends of four long fmall fticks, or poles, into the ground at right. angles, fo as to form a fquare of four, five, fix, or feven feet, as may be required. The tops of the poles are tied together, and all is clofe covered with a tent-cloth or other fkin, exactly in the fliape of a fmall fquare tent, except that there is no vacancy left at the top to admit the light. In the middle of this houfe, or tent, the patient is laid, and is foon followed by the conjurer, or conjurers.

conjurers. Sometimes five- or fix of them give their joint-alliftance; but before they enter, they flrip themfelves quite naked, and as Toon as they get into the houfe, the door being well clofed, they kneel round the fick perfon or perfons, and begin to fucknd blow at the parts effected, and then in a very fhort fpace of time fmg and talk as if converfing with familiar fpirits, which they fay appear to them in the fliape of different beads and birds of prey. When they have had fufficient conference with thofe neceffary agents, orfliadows, as they term them, they afk for the hatchet, bayonet, or the like, which is always prepared by another perfon, with a long ftring fattened to it by the haft, for the convenience of hauling it up again after they have fwallowed it; for they very wifely admit this to be a very neceffary precaution, as hard and compact bodies, fuch as iron and fteel, would be very difficult to digeft, even by the men who are enabled to fwallow them. Befides, as thofe tools are in themfelves very ufe-ful, and not always to be procured, it would be very ungenerous in the conjurers to digeft them, when it is known that barely fwallowing them and hauling them up again is fully fufficient to anfwer every purpofe that is expeded from them. At the time when the forty and odd tents of Indians joined us, one man wasfo dangeroufly ill, that it was thought neceffary the conjurers fliould life fome of thofe wonderful experiments for his recovery one of them therefore immediately, con-

Augalt.

NORTHERN OCEAN.

fented to fwallovv a broad bayonet. Accordingly, a conjuring-houfe was erected in ths manner above defcribed, into which the patient wa conveyed, and he was foon followed by the conjurer, who, after a long preparatory difcourfe, and the neceflary conference with his familiar fpirits, or fhadows, as they call them, advanced to the door and aflsied for the bayonet, which was then ready 6th. prepared, by having a ftring fattened to it, and a ihort piece of wood tied to the other end of the ftring, to prevent him from fwallowing it. I could not help obferving that the length of the bit of wood was not more than the breadth of the bayonet: however, as it anfwered the intended purpofe, it did equally well as if it had been as long as a handfpike.

Though I am not fo credulous as to believe that the conjurer abfolutely fwallowed the bayonet, yet I muft acknowledge that in the twinkling of an eye he conveyed it togod knows where j and the fmall piece of wood, or one exactly like it, was confined clofe to his teeth. He then paraded backward and forward before the conjur-ing-houle for a fliort time, when he feigned to be greatly difordered in his ftomach and bowels; and, after making many wry faces, and groaning moft hideoufly, he put his body into feveral di-ftorted attitudes, very fuitable to the occaiion. He then returned to the door of the conjuring-houfe, and after making many ftrong efforts to vomit, by the help of the ftring he at length, and after tugging at it fome time, produced the bayonet, vvhich apparently he hauled out of his mouth, C; o the no fmall furprize of all prefent. He then looked round with an air of exultation, and ftrutting into the conjuring-houfe, where he renewed his incantations, and continued them without intermillion twenty-four hours. Though I was not clofe to his elbow when he performed the above feat, yet 1 thought myfelf near enough (and 1 can aflure my readers I was all attention) to have detedled him. Indeed I muft confefs that it appeared to me to be a very nice piece of deception, efpecially as it was performed by a man quite naked.

Not long after this flight-of-hand work was over, fome of the Indians afked me what I thought of it; to which I anfwered, that I was too far off fo fee it fo plain as I could wiih; which indeed was no more than the ftricleft truth, be-caufe I was not near enough to detedt the deception. The fick man, however, foon recovered; and in a few days afterwards we left that place and proceeded to the South Weft. On the ninth of Auguft, we once more purfued our journey, and continued our courfe in th South Weft quarter, generally walking about fe-ven or eight miles a day. All the Indians, however, who had been in our company, except twelve tents, ftruck off different ways. As to myfelf, having had feveral days reft, my feet were completely healed, though the fkin remained very tender for fome time.

From

From the nineteenth to the twenty-fifth, we I Hralked by the fide of Thaye-chuck-gyed Whoie, or Large Whiteftone Lake, which is about forty 15th25'th miles long (toiti the North Eaft to the South Weft, but of very unequal breadth. A river from the North Weft fide of this lake is faid to run in a ferpentine manner a long vay to the Weftward; and then tending to the Northward, compofei the main branch of the

Copper-mine River, as has been already mentioned; which may or may not be true. It is certain, however, that there are many rivulets, which empty themfelves into this lake from the South Eaft; but as they are all fmali ftreams, they may probably be no more than what is fufecient to fupply the conftant de-creafe occafioned by the exhalations, which, dur-ing the fliort Summer, fo high a Northern latitude always affords.

Deer were very plentiful the whole way; the Indians killed great numbers of them daily, merely for the fake of their ikins; and at this time of the year their pelts are in good feafon, and the hair of a proper length for clothing.

The great deftruction vhich is made of the deer in thofe parts at this feafon of the year only, is almoft incredible; and as they are never known to have more than one young one at a time, it is wonderful they do not become fcarce: but fo far is this from being the cafe, that the old-eft Northern Indian in all their tribe will affirm that the deer are as plentiful now as they ever have been 5 and though they are remarkably fcarce fome years near Churchill river, yet it is faid, and with great probability of truth, that they are more plentiful in other parts of the country than they were formerly. The fcarcity or abundance of thefe animals in different places at the fame leafon is caufed, in a great meafure, by the winds which prevail for fome tiiiie before; for the deer are fuppofed by the natives to walk always in the direftion from which the wind blows, except when they migrate from Eaft to Weft, or from Weft tor Eaft, in fearch of the oppofitefex, for the purpofe of propagating their fpecies.

It requires the prime part of the fkins of from eight to ten deer to make a complete fuit of warm clothing for a grown perfon during the Winter; all of which fhould, if poflible, be killed in the month of Auguft, or early in September; for after that time the hair is too long, and at the fame time fo loofe in the pelt, that it will drop off with the flighteft injury.

Befide thefe fkins, which muft be in the hair, each perfon requires feveral others to be dreifed into leather, for ftockings and flioes, and light Summer clothing; feveral more are alfo wanted in a parchment ftatc, to make chwla as they call it, or thongs to make netting for their fnow-flioes, fnares for deer, fewing for their fledges, and, in facl, for every other ufe where ftrings or lines of any kind are required: fo that each perfon, on an average, expends, in the courfe gf a year, upwards of twenty deer fkins in clothing and other dome-ftic ufes, exclufive of tent cloths, bags, and many other things which it is impoftible to remember jiind unneceffary to enumerate.

All fkins for the above-mentioned purpofes are, if pollibie, procured between the beginning of Auguft and the middle of Oftober; for when j the rutting feafon is over, and th Winter fets in, jthe deerfkins are not only very thin, but in ge-neral full of worms and warbles; which render them of little ufe, unlefs it be to cut into fine thongs, of which they make fifliing-nets, and nets for the heels and toes of their fnow-fhoes. Indeed the chief ufe that is made of them in Winter is for the purpofe of food; and really when the hair is properly taken off, and aii the warbles are fqueezed out, if they are well-boiled, they are far from being difagreeahle. The Indians, however, never could perfuade me to eat the warbles, of which fome of them are remarkably fond, particularly the children. They are always eaten raw and alive, out of the Ikin; and are faid, by thofe who like them, to be as fine as goofeberries. But the very idea of eating fuch things, exclufive gf their appearance, (many of them being as hrge as the firft joint of the little finger,) was quite fuiscient to give me an unalterable difguft fuch a repaft; and when I acknowledge that iiie warbles out of the deers backs, and the do. medic lice, were the only two things 1 ever faw my companions eat, of which I could not, or did not partake, I truft I fhall not be reckoned over-delicate in my appetite.

The month of October is the rutting feafon with the deer in thofe parts, and after the time of their courtfhip is over, the bucks feparate from the does; the former proceed to the Weftward, to take fhelter in the woods during the Vinter, and the latter keep out in the barren ground the whole year. This, though a general rule, is not without fome exceptions; for I have frequently feen many does in the woods, though they bor no proportion to the number of bucks. This rule, therefore, only (lands good refpecling the deer to the North of Churchill River; for the deer to the Southward live promifcuoufly among the woods, as well as in the plains, and along the banks of rivers, lakes, ts'c. the whole year.

The old buck's horns are very large, with ma-py branches, and always drop off in the m. onth of November, which is about the time they begin to approach the woods. This is undoubtedly wifely ordered by Providence, the better to enable them to efcape from their enemies through the woods; other wife they would become an ea-fy prey to wolves and other beafts, and be liable to get entangled among the trees, even in ranging about in fearch of food. The fame opinion may probably be admitted of the Southern deer, which always refide among the woods; but the Northern deer, though by far the fmallcft in this country, have much the hrgeft horns, and the branches are fo long, and at the fame time fpread ib wide, as to make them more liable to be entangled among the under-woods, than any other fpecies of deer that I have noticed. The young bucks in thofe parts do not fhed their horns fo foon as the old ones: I have frequently feen them killed at or near Chriftmas, and could difcover no appearance of their horns being loofe. The does do not fhed their horns till the Summer; fo that when the buck's horns are ready to drop oft", the horns of the does are all hairy, and fcarcely come to their full growth.

The deer in thofe parts are generally in motion from Eaft to Weft, or from Weft to Eaft, according to the feafon, or the prevailing winds; and that is the principal reafon why the Northern Indians are always fhifting their ftation. From November till May, the bucks continue to the Weftward, among the woods, when their horns begin to fprout; after which they proceed on to the Eaftward, to the barren grounds; and the does that have been on the barren ground all the Winter, are taught by inftincl to advance to the Weftward to meet them, in order to propagate their fpecies. Immediately after the rutting feafon is over, they feparate, as hath been mentioned above. The old vulgar faying, fo generally received among the lower clafs of people in England, concerning the bucks fhedding their yards, or more properly the glands of the penis yearly, whether it be true in England or not, is certainly iiot true in any of the countries bordering on

Hudfon's e A JOURNEY TO THE

Hudfen's Bay. A long refidence among the In-dians has enabled me to confirm this affertion with great confidence, as I have feen deer killed every day throughout the year; and when I have mentioned this circumftance to the Indians, either Northern or Southern, they alw3ys affured me that they never obferved any fuch fymptoms. With equal truth 1 can altert, and that from ocular demonftration, that the animal which is called the Alpine Hare in Hudfon's Bay, adually undergoes fomething fimilar to that which is vulgarly afcribed to the Enghfti deer. I have feen and handled feveral of them, who had been killed juft after they had coupled in the Spring, with the penifes hanging out, dried up, and fhri-velled, like the navel-ftring of young animals; and on examination I always found a paffage through them for the urine to pafs. I have thought proper to give this remark a place in my Journal, becaufe, in all probability, it is not generally known, even to thofe gentlemen who have fnade natural hiftory their chief ftudy j and if their refearches are of any real utility to mankind, it is furely to be regretted that Providence iliould have placed the greateft part of them too remote from want to be obliged to travel for ocular proofs of what they affert in their publications; they are therefore wifely content to flay at home, and enjoy the blefiings with which they arc endowed, relling fatisfied to collect fuch information for their own amufement, and the grati.

gratification of the public, as tliofe who are ne-ceflitated to be travellers are able or willing to give them. It is true, and I am forry it is fo, that I come under the latter defcription; but hope I have not, or fliall not, in the courfe of this Journal, advance any thing that will not ftand the teft of experiment, and the kill of the moft competent judges.

After leaving White Stone Lake, we continued our courfe in the South Weft quarter, feldom walking more than twelve miles a day, and frequently not half that diflance.

On the third of September, we arrived at a September. fmall river belonging to Point Lake, but the wea- 3-ther at this time proved fo boifterous, and there was fo much rain, fnow, and froft, alternately, that we were obliged to wait feveral days before we could crofs it in our canoes; and the water v3ls too deep, and the current too rapid, to attempt fording it. During this interruption, however, our time was not entirely loft, as deer were fo plentiful that the Indians killed numbers of them, as well for the fake of their fkins, as for their flefli, which was at prefent in excellent order, and the Ikins in proper feafon for the fun-dry ufes for which they are deftined.

In the afternoon of the feventh, the weather 7th. became fine and moderate, when we all were ferried acrofs the river; and the next morning gj fhaped our courfe to the South Weft, by the fide of point Lake. After three days journey, which only jyyx. only confifted of about eighteen miles, we came-"v- to a few fmall fcrubby woods, which were the " firft that we had feen from the twenty-fifth of May, except thofe we had perceived at the Copper-mine River.

Que of the Indian's wives, who for fome time had been in a conlumption, had for a few days pail become fo weak as to be incapable of travelling, which, among thofe people, is the moft deplorable flate to which a human being can pofli-bly be brought. "Whether flie had been given over by the doctors, or that it vas for want of friends among them, I cannot tell, but certain it is, that no expedients were taken for her recovery; fo that, without much ceremony, ilie was left unaflifted, to perilli above-ground.

Though this was the firft inftance of the kind I had feen, it is the common, and indeed the con-ftant practice of thofe Indians; for when a grown perfon is fo ill, efpecially in the Summer, as not to be able to walk, and too heavy to be carried, they fay it is better to leave one who is paft recovery, than for the whole family to fit down by them and ilarve to death; well knowing that they cannot be of any fervice to the afhicled. On thofe occaiions, therefore, the friends or relations of the fick generally leave them fome victuals and water; and, if the fituation of the place will afford it, a little firing. AAhen thofe articles are provided, the perfon to be left is acquainted with the road. which the others intend to go; and then, after covering them well up with deer j,-, Ikins, iffc. they take their leave, and walk away-A . Septembei.

crying.

Sometimes perfons thus left, recover; and come up with their friends, or wander about till they meet with other Indians, whom they accompany till they again join their relations. Inftan-ces of this kind are feldom known. The poor woman above mentioned, however, came up with us three feveral times, after having been left in the manner defcribed. At length, poor creature! fhe dropt behind, and no one attempted to go back in fearch of her.

A cuftom apparently fo unnatural is perhaps not to be found among any other of the human race: If properly confidered, however, it may with juftice be afcribed to neceflity and felf-pre-fervation, rather than to the want of humanity and focial feeling, which ought to be the charac-teriftic of men, as the noblell part of the creation. Neceflity, added to national cuftom, contributes principally to make fcenes of this kind lefs lliocking to thofe people, than they muft appear to the more civilized part of mankind.

During the early part of September, the weather was in general cold, with much fleet and fnow; which feemed to promife that the Winter would fet in early. Deer at this time being very plentiful, and the few woods we met with affording tent-poles and firing, the Indians propofed to remain where we were fome time, in order to drefs drefs fkins, and provide our Winter clothing; aifo to make fnow-flioes and temporary fledges, as well as to prepare a large quantity of dried meat and fat to carry with us; for by the accounts of the Indians, they have always experienced a great fcarcity of deer, and every other kind of game, in the direction they propofed we hould go when we left Point Lake.

Toward the middle of the month, the weather became quite mild and open, and continued fo till the end of it; but there was fo much con-ftant and inceifant rain, that it rotted mod of our 2Sth. tents. On the twenty-eighth, however, the wind fettled in the North Weft quarter, when the wea-3cth. jjgj. gi-e fo cold, that by the thirtieth all the ponds, lakes, and other ftanding waters, were frozen over fo hard that we vere enabled to crofs them on the ice without danger.

Among the various fuperftitious cuftoms of thofe people, it is worth remarking, and ought to have been mentioned it its proper place, that immediately after my companions had killed the Efquimaux at the Copper River, they confidered themfelves in a ftate of uncleannefs, which induced them to praclife fome very curious and un-ufual ceremonies. In the firft place, all who vere abfolutely concerned in the murder were prohibited from cooking any kind of viduals, either for themfelves or others. As luckily there were two in company Vvho had not fhed blood, they were employed always as cooks till we joined

Cd the women. This circumftiince was exceed- 1771. indv favourable on mv fide; for had there been "'

"". September.

no perfons of the above defcription in company, that taqc, I was told, would have fallen on me; which would have been no Icfs fatiguing and trou-blefome, than humiliating and vexatious.

When the vidluals were cooked, all the murderers took a kind of red earth, or oker, and painted all the fpace between the nofe and chin, as well as the greater part of their cheeks, almofl: to the ears, before they would tafte a bit, and would not drink out of any other dlfti, or fmoke out of any other pipe, but their own; and none of the Others feemed willing: to drink or fmoke out of theirs.

We had no fooner joined the women, at our return from the expedition, than there feemed to be an univerfal fpirit of emulation among them, vying who fliould firft make a fuit of ornaments for their hufbands, which confifted of bracelets for the wrifts, and a band for the forehead, compof-ed of porcupine quills and moofe-hair, curioufiy wrought on leather.

The cuftom of painting the mouth and part of the cheeks before each meal, and drinking and fmoking out of their own utenfils, was ftriftly and invariable obferved, till the Winter bcg: an to fet in; and during the whole of that time they would never kifs any of their wives or children. They refrained alfo from eating many parts of the deer and other animals, particularly the head, entrails.

o6 A JOURNEY TO THE entrails, and blood; and during their unclean-ncfs, their victuals were never fodden in water, but dried in the fun, eaten quite raw, or broiled, when a fire fit for the purpofe could be procured.

When the time arrived that was to put an end to thefe ceremonies, the men, without a female being prefent, made a fire at fome diftance from the tents, into which they threw all their ornaments, pipe-flems, and difhes, which were foon confumed to afhes; after which a fealt was prepared, confiding of fuch articles as they had long been prohibited from eating; and when all was over, each man was at liberty to eat, drink, and fmoke as he pleafed; and alfo to kifs his wives and children at difcretion, which they feemed to do with more raptures than I had ever known them do it either before or fmce. oaobi. Oclober came in very roughly, attended with heavy falls of fnow, and much drift. On the 6th. fixth at night, a heavy gale of wind from the North Weft put us in great diforder; for though the few woods we paffed had furniflied us with tent-poles and fewel, yet they did not afford us the leaft fhelter whatever. The wind blew with fuch violence, that in fpite of all our endeavours, it overfet feveral of the tents, and mine, among the reft, fliared the difafter, which I cannot fuffi-ciently lament, as the but-ends of the weather tent-poles fell on the quadrant, and though it was in a ftrong wainfcot cafe, two of the bubbles, the

Oaobci-.

NORTHERN OCEAN.

index, and feveral other parts were broken, which rendered it entirely ufelefs. This being the cafe, I did not think. it worth carriage, but broke it to pieces, and gave the brafs-work to the Indians, who cut it into fmall lumps, and made ule of it inftead of ball.

On the twenty-third of October, feveral Cop- jj. per and a few Dog-ribbed Indians came to our tents laden with furrs which they fold to fome of my crew for fuch iron-work as they had to give in exchange. This vifit, I afterwards found, was by appointment of the Copper Indians whom we had feen at Congecathawhachaga, and who, in their way to us, had met the Dog-ribbed Indians, who were alfo glad of fo favourable an opportunity of purchafing fome of thofe valuable articles, though at a very extravagant price: for one of the Indians in my company, though not properly of my party, got no lefs than forty-beaver Ikins, and fixty martins, for one piece of iron which he had flole when he was laft at the Fort.

One of thofe ftrangers had about forty beaver Ikins, with which he intended to pay Matonab-bee an old debt j but one of the other Indians feized

The piece of iron above mentioned was the coulter of a new-fafhioned plough, invented by Captain John Fowler, late Governor at Churchill River, with which he had a large piece of ground ploughed, and afterwards fowed with oats: but the part being nothing but a hot burning fand, like the Spani(h lines at Gibraltar, the fuccefs may eafily be gueft-d; which was; that it did not produce a fingle grain: fcized the whole, notwithftanding he knew it td be in ht Matonabbee's property. This treatment, together with many other infults, which he had received during ray abode with him, made him renew his old refolution of leaving his ovn country, and going to refide with the Athapuf-cow Indians.

As the moft interefting part of my journey was riow over, I did not think it neceffary to interfere in liis private affairs; and therefore did not endeavour to influence him either one way or the other: out of complailance, therefore rather than any thing elfe, I told him, that I thought fuch behaviour very uncourteous, efpecially in a man of his rank and dignity. As to the reafon of his determination, I did not think it worth while to J enquire into it; but, by his difcourfe with the other Indians, I foon underftood that they all intended to make an excurfion into the country o the Athapufcow Indians, in order to kill moofi and beaver. The former of thofe animals are never found in the Northern Indian territories; and the latter are fo fcarce in thofe Northern parts, that during the whole Winter of one thou-fand feven hundred and feventy, I did not fee more than two beaver houfes. Martins are alfo fcarce in thofe parts; for during the above peri od, I do not think that more than fix or eight were killed by all the Indians in my company. This exceedingly fmall nuiiiberj among fo many people, people, may with great truth be attributed to the indolence of the Indians, and the wandering life which they lead, rather than to the great fcarcity of the martins. It is true, that our moving fo frequently from place to place, did at times make it not an objecl: worth while to build traps; but had they taken the advantage of all favourable opportunities, and been poffeffed of half the in-duftry of the Company's fervants in the Bay, they might with great eafe have caught as many hundreds, if not fome thoufands; and when we conlider the extent of ground which we walked over in that time, fuch a number would not have been any proof of the martins being very plentiful.

Except a few martins; wolves, quiquehatches, foxes, and otters, are the chief furrs to be met with in thofe parts, and few of the Northern Indians chufe to kill either the wolf or the quique-hatch, under a notion that they are fomething more than common animals. Indeed, I have known fome of them fo bigotted to this opinion, that having by chance killed a quiquehatch by a gun which had been fet for a fox, they had left it where it was killed, and would not take off its fkin. Notwithftanding this filly notion, which is too frequently to be obferved among thofe people, it generally happens that there are feme in every gang who are lefs fcrupulous, fo that none of thofe furrs are ever left to rot; and even thofe who make a point of not killing the ani-

P mals

Odtobci.

j-yi mals themfelves, are ready to receive their Ikins - from other Indians, and carry them to the Fort

OAober., for trade. 30th. By the thirtieth of October, all our clothing, fnowftioes, and temporary fledges, being corn-November. 1., 1 1 r ift. pleted, we once more began to prepare tor moving; and on the following day fet out, and walked five or fix miles to the Southward.

From the firft to the fifth of November we walked on the ice of a large lake, which, though very confiderable both in length and breadth, is rot difl; inguihed by any general name; on which account I gave it the name of No Name Lake. On the South fide of this lake we found fome wood, which was very acceptable, being the firft: that we had feen fince we left Point Lake. sth. No Name Lake is about fifty miles long from

North to South, and, according to the account of the Indians, is thirty-five miles wide from Eafl; to Weft. It is faid to abound with fine fifli; but the weather at the time we crofled it was fo cold, as to render it impoflible to fit on the ice any length of time to angle. A few exceedingly fine trout, and fome very large pike, however, were caught by my companions.

When we arrived on the South fide of the above lake, we fliaped our courfe to the South Weft; and though the weather was in general very cold, yet as we every night found tufts of wood.

wood, in which we could pitch our tents, we 1771. were enabled to make a better defence againft the; weather, than we had had it in our power to do for fome time paft.

On the tenth of November, we arrived at the "h. edse of the main woods; at which time the Indians began to make proper fledsjes, fome fnow-flioes, c. after which we proceeded again to the South Weft. But deer and all other kinds of game were fo fcarce the whole way, that, except a few partridges, nothing was killed by any in company: we had, neverthelefs, plenty of the provifion which had been prepared at Point Lake.

On the twentieth of the fame month, we ar- aoth. rived at Anawd Whole, or the Indian Lake. In our way we croftcd part of Methy Lake, and walked near eighty miles on a fmall river belonging to it, which empties itfelf into the Great Athapufcow Lake. While we were walking on the above little river, the Indians fet fifhing-nets under the ice every night; but their labour was attended with fo little fuccefs, that all they caught ferved only as a delicacy, or to make a little change in our diet; for the quantity was too trifling to occafion any confiderable faving of our other provifions.

Anawd Lake, though fo fmall as not to exceed twenty miles wide in the broadeft part, is cele-

P 2 braced

Thecourre of this river is reary South Weft.

November 212 A JOURNEY TO 7 HE I-77 I. brated by the natives for abounding with plenty of fifti during the Winter; accordingly the Indians fet all their nets, which were not a few, and met with fuch fuccefs, that in about ten days the roes only were as much as all the women could haul after them.

Tittimeg and barbie, with a few fmall pike, were the only fifli caught at this part j the roes of which, particularly thofe of the tittimeg, are more efteemed by the Northern Indians, to take with them on a journey, than the fifh itfelf; for about two pounds weight of thefe roes, when well bruif-ed, will make near four gallons of broth, as thick as common burgoe; and if properly managed, will be as white as rice, which makes it very pleafing to the eye, and no lefs agreeable to the palate.

The land round this lake is very hilly, though not mountainous, and chiefly confifts of rocks and loofe ftones; there muft, however, be a fmall portion of foil on the furface, as it is in moft parts well clothed with tall poplars, pines, fir, and birch; particularly in the vallies, where the poplars, pine, and birch feem to thrive beft; but the firs were as large, and in as flourifhing a Hate, on the very fummit of the hills, as in any other part.

Rabbits were here fo plentiful, particularly on the South and South Eafl fide of the lake, thajt feveral of the Indians caught twenty or thirty in a night with fnaresj and the wood-partridges were were fo numerous in the fir trees, and fo tame, 1771. that I have known an Indian kill near twenty of-y"

, November.

them in a day with his bow and arrows. The Northern Indians call this fpecies of the partridge Day; and though their flefli is generally very black and bitter, occaiioned by their feeding on the brufh of the fir tree, yet they make a variety, or change of diet, and are thought exceedingly good, particularly by the natives, who, though capable of living fo hard, and at times eating very ungrateful food, are neverthelefs as fond of variety as any people whom I ever faw; and will go as great lengths, according to their circumftan-ces, to gratify their palates, as the greateft epicure in England. As a proof of this aflertion, I have frequently known Matonabbee, and others who could afford it, for the fake of variety only, fend fome of their young men to kill a few partridges at the expence of more ammunition than would have killed deer fufficient to have maintained their families many days j whereas the partridges were always eaten up at one meal: and to heighten the luxury on thefe occafions, the partridges are boiled in a kettle of (heer fat, which it muft be allowed renders them beyond all defcrip-tion finer flavoured than when boiled in water or common broth. I have alfo eat deer-fkins boiled in fat, which were exceedingly good.

As during our flay at Anawd Lake feveral of the Indians, were fickly, the dodors undertook to adminifter relief j particularly to one man, who -j-ji, had been hauled on a fledge by his brother for v,. two months. His diforder was the dead palfey, ovembei. jj-jj affcclcd OHc fide, from the crown of his head to the fole of his foot. Befides this dreadful diforder, he had fome inward complaints, with a total lofs of appetite; fo that he was reduced to a mere fkeleton, and fo weak as to be fcarcely capable of fpeaking. In this deplorable condition, he was laid in the center of a large conjuring-houfe, made much after the manner as that which has been already defcribed. And that nothing might be wanting toward his recovery, the fame man who deceived me in fwallowing a bayonet in the Summer, now offered to fwallow a large piece of board, about the fize of a barrel-ftave, in order to effect his recovery. The piece of board was prepared by another man, and painted according to the direction of the juggler, with a rude reprefentation of fome beaft of prey on one fide, and on the reverfe was painted, according to their rude method, a refemblance of the fky.

Without entering into a long detail of the preparations for this feat, I fhall at once proceed to obferve, that after the conjurer had held the ne-celtary conference with his invifible fpirits, or ihadows, he alked if I was prefent; for he had heard of my faying that I did not fee him fwallow the bayonet fair: and on being anfwered in the afermative, he defired me to come nearer; on which the mob made a lane for me to pafs, and I advanced clofe to him, and found him landing at the conjuring-houfe door as naked as

November.

he was born.

When the piece of board was delivered to him, he propofed at firft only to fhove one-third of it down his throat, and then walk round the company afterward to fhove down another third; and fo proceed till he had fwallowed the whole, except a fmall piece of the end, which was left behind to haul it up again. When he put it to his mouth it apparently flipped down his throat like lightning, and only left about three inches flicking without his lips; after walking backwards and forwards three times, he hauled it up again, and ran into the conjuring-houfe with great precipitation. This he did to all appearance with great eafe and compofure; and notwithftanding I was all attention on the occalion, 1 could not detect the deceit; and as to the reality of its being a piece of wood that he pretended to fwal-low, there is not the leafl reafon to doubt of it, for I had it in my hand, both before and immediately after the ceremony.

To prevent a variety of opinions on this occa-fion, and to leffen the apparent magnitude of the miracle, as well as to give fome colour to my fcepticifm, which might otherwife perhaps appear ridiculous, it is neceflary to obferve, that this feat was performed in a dark and excefiively cold night; and although there was a large fire at fome diflance, which reflected a good light, yet there 1771. there was great room for collufion: for though " the conjurer himfelf was quite naked, there were

November.

feveral of his fraternity well-clothed, who attended him very clofe during the time of his attempting to fwallow the board, as well as at the time of his hauling it up again.

For thefe reafons it is neceflary alfo to obferve, that on the day preceding the performance of this piece of deception, in one of my hunting excur-fions, I accidentally came acrofs the conjurer as he was fitting under a bufli, feveral miles from the tents, where he was bufily employed fhaping a piece of wood exaclly like that part which ftuck out of his mouth after he had pretended to fwallow the remainder of the piece. The ihape of the piece which I faw him making was this,"j which exactly refembled the forked end of the main piece, the fliape of which was this, 1 j t.

So that when his attendants had concealed the main piece, it was eafy for him to ftick the fmall point into his mouth, as it was reduced at the fmall end to a proper fize for the purpofe.

Similar proofs may eafily be urged againfl his fwaliowing the bayonet in the Summer, as no perfon lefs ignorant than themfelves can poflibly place any belief in the reality of thofe feats; yet on the whole, they muft be allowed a confidcra-ble fhare of dexterity in the performance of thofe tricks, and a wonderful deal of perfeverance in what they do for the relief of thofe whom they undertake to cure.

f Not long after the above performance had taken 1771. place, fome of the Indians began to alk me vhat-v- ' . Ill November.

I thought of It. As I could not have any plea for faying that I vtas far off, and at the fame time not caring to affront them by hinting my fufpici-ons of the deceit, I was fome time at a lofs for an anfwer: I urged, however, the impoffibility of a man's fvvallovving a piece of wood, that was not only much longer than his whole back, but nearly twice as broad as he could extend his mouth. On which fome of them laughed at my ignorance, as they were pleafed to call it; and faid, that the ipirits in waiting fwallowed, or otherwife concealed, the ftick, and only left the forked end apparently flicking out of the conjurer's mouth. My guide, Matonabbee, with all his other good fenfe, was fo bigotted to the reality of thofe performances, that he aflured me in the flrongeft terms, he had feen a man, who was them in company, fwailow a child's cradle, with as much eafe as he could fold up a piece of paper, and put it into his mouth; and that when he hauled it up again, not the mark of a tooth, or of any violence, was to be difcovered about it.

This ftory fo far exceeded the feats which I had feen with the bayonet and board, that, for the fake of keeping up the farce, I began to be very inquifitive about the fpirits which appear to them en thofe occafions, and their form; when I was told that they appeared in various fhapes, for al-moft every conjurer had his peculiar attendant; but that the fpirit which attended the man who pretended to fwallow the piece of wood, they faid, generally appeared to him in the fhape of a cloud. This I thought very a-propos to the pre-fent occafion; and I muft confefs that I never had fo thick a cloud thrown before my eyes before or fince; and had it not been by accident, that I faw him make a counterpart to the piece of wood faid to be fwallowed, 1 fiiould have been ftill at a lofs how to account for fo extraordinary a piece of deception, performed by a man who was entirely naked.

As foon as our conjurer had executed the above feat, and entered the conjuring-houfe as already mentioned, five other men and an old woman, all of whom were great profeffors of that art, ftripped themfelves quite naked and followed him, when they foon began to fuck, blow, fing, and dance, round the poor paralytic; and continued fo to do for three days and four nights, without taking the leaft reft or refreftiment, not even fo much as a drop of water. When thefe poor deluding and deluded people came out of the conjuring-houfe, their mouths were fo parched with thirft as to be quite black, and their throats fo fore, that they were fcarceiy able to articulate a fingle word, except thofe that ftand for yes and no in their language.

After fo long an abftinence they were very careful not to eat or drink too much at one time, particularly for the firll day j and indeed fome of them.

them, to appearance, were aim oft as bad as the 1771. poor man they had been endeavouring to relieve. "' But great part of this was feigned; for they lay on their backs with their eyes fixed, as if in the agonies of death, and were treated like young children; one perfon fat conftantly by them, moi-ftening their mouths with fat, and now and then giving them a drop of water. At other times a fmall bit of meat was put into their mouths, or a pipe held for them to fmoke. This farce only lafted for the firft day; after which they feemed to be perfeftly well, except the hoarfenefs, which continued for a confiderable time afterwards. And it is truly wonderful, though the ftricleft truth, that when the poor fick man was taken from the conjuring-houfe, he had not only recovered his appetite to an amazing degree, but was able to move all the fingers and toes of the fide that had been fo long dead. In three weeks he recovered fo far as to be capable of walking, and at the end of fix weeks went a hunting for his family. He was one of the perfons particularly engaged to provide for me during my journey; and after his recovery from this dreadful difor-der, accompanied me back to Prince of Wales's Fort in June one thoufand feven hundred and feventy-two; and fince that time he has frequently vifited the Faclory, though he never had a healthy

His name was Cof-abyagh, the Northern Indian name for the Rock Partridge, jhyi, healthy look afterwards, and at times Teemeci u-v- troubled with a nervous complaint. It may be

November.

added, that he had been formerly of a remarkable lively difpofition; but after his laft illnefs he always appeared thoughtful, fometimes gloomy, and, in fad, the diforder feemed to have changed his whole nature; for before that dreadful paralytic ftroke, he was diftinguiflied for his goodnature and benevolent difpofition; was entirely free from every appearance of avarice; and the whole of his wioies feemed confined within the narrow limits of pofltefling as many goods as were abfolutely neceifary, with his own induftry, to enable him to fupport his family from feafon to feafon; but after this event, he was the moft fradious, quarrelfome, difcontented, and covetous wretch alive.

Though the ordinary trick of thefe conjurers may be eafily deteded, and juftly exploded, being no more than the tricks of common jugglers, yet the apparent good effect of their labours on the fick and difeafed is not fo eafily accounted for. Perhaps the implicit confidence placed in them by the fick may, at times, leave the mind fo perfed:-ly at reft, as to caufe the diforder to take a favourable turn; and a few fuccefsful cafes are quite fufficient to eftabiifh the doctor's character and reputation: But how this confideration could operate in the cafe I have juft mentioned I am at alofs to fay; fuch, however, was the facl, and I leave it to be accounted for by others.

When

When thefe jugglers take a diflike to, and– threaten a (ecret revenge on any perfon, it often v- proves fatal to that perfon; as, from a firm be-Hef that the conjurer has power over his life, he permits the very thoughts of it to prey on his fpirits, till by degrees is brings on a diforder which puts an end to his exillence: and fome- times

As a proof of this, Matonabbee, (who always thought me poftefted of this art,) on his arrival at Prince of Wales's Fort in the Winter of 1778, informed me, that a man whom I had never fcen bnt once, had treated him in fuch a manner that he was afraid of his life; in confequence of which he preflcd me very much to kill him, tiiough 1 was then feveral hundreds of miles diftant. On which, to pleafe this great man to whom I owed fb much, and not expeoing that any harm could poflibly arife from it, I drew a rough iketch of two human figures on a piece of paper, in the attitude of wreftling: in the hand of one of them, I drew the figure of a bayonet pointing to the breaft of the other. This is me, faid I to Matonabbee, pointing to the figure which was holding the bayonet; and the other is your enemy. Oppolite to thofe figures I drew a pine-tree, over which I placed a large human eye, and out of the tree projefted a human hand. This paper 1 gave to Matonabbee, with inftruftions to make it as publicly known as pofuble. Sure enough, the following year, when he came in to trade, he informed me that the man was dead, though at that time he was not lefs than three hundred miles from Prince of Wales's Foit. He afiiired me that the man was in perfed health when he heard of my defign againfl him; but almoft immediately afterwards became quite gloomy, and refufing all kind of fuftenance, in a very few days died. After this I was frequently applied to on the fame account, both by Matonabbee and other leading Indians, but never thought proper to comply with their reqviefts; by which means I not only preferved the credit I gained on the firft attempt, but always kept them in awe, and in fome degree of refpe(n: and obedience to mc. In fact, flrangeas it may appear, it is almofl abfo-liitely neceltary that the chiefs at this place ftould profefs fomcthinga little fupernatural, to be able to deal with thole people. The circum-Oancc here recorded is a fadi well known to Mr. William Jeffetibn, who fucceeded me at Churchill Falory, as well as to all the officers and many of the common men who were at Prince of Wales's Fort at the time.

times a threat of this kind caufes the death of a whole family; and that without any blood being fhed, or the leaft apparent moleftation being offered to any of the parties.

Having dried as many fifh and fifh-roes as we could conveniently take with us, we once more packed up our (lores, and, on the firft day of De-iit. cember, fet out, and continued our courfe to the South Weft, leaving Anawd Lake on the South "Weft. Several of the Indians being out of order, we made but fhort days journies.

From the firft to the thirteenth, we walked along a courfe of fmall lakes, joined to each other by fmall rivers, or creeks, that have communication with Anawd Lake.

In our way we caught daily a few fifli by angling, and faw many beaver houfes; but thefe were generally in fo difficult a fituation, and had fo many ftcnes in the compofition of them, that the Indians killed but few, and that at a great expence of labour and tools.

On the thirteenth, one of the Indians killed two deer, which were the firft that we had feen fince the twentieth of October. So that during a period of near two months, we had lived on the dried meat that we had prepared at Point Lake, and a few fifh; of which the latter was not very confiderable in quantity, except what was caught at Anawd Lake. It is true, we alfo caught a few rabbitsj and at times the wood-partridges were ijtii.

foplentiful, that the Indians killed confiderable ijjy.

numbers of them with their bows and arrows; v but the number of mouths was fo great, that all which was caught from our leaving Point Lake, though if enumerated, they might appear very confiderable, would not have afforded us all a bare fubfiftence; for though 1 and fome others experienced no real want, yet there were many in our company who could fcarcely be faid to live, and would not have exiftcd at all, had it not been for the dry meat we had with us.

When we left the above-mentioned lakes we Ihaped a courfe more to the Southward, and on the twenty-fourth, arrived at the North fide of 24th. the great Athapufcow Lake. In our way we faw many Indian deer, and beaver were very plentiful, many of which the Indians killed; but the days were fo fliort, that the Sun only took a circuit of a few points of the compafs above the horizon, and did not, at its greateft altitude, rife, half-way up the trees. The brilliancy of the Aurora Borealis, however, and of the Stars, even without the afiiftance of the Moon, made fome amends for that deficiency; for it was frequently fo light all night, that I could fee to read a ve-I ry fmall print. The Indians make to difference between night and day when they are hunting of I beaver; but thofe nohurnal lights are always found infuflicient for the purpofe of hunting deer or moofe.

nni. I cio not remember to have met with any tra-wv vellers into high Northern latitudes, who remarked their having heard the Northern Lights make any noife in the air as they vary their colours or polition; which may probably be owing to the want of perfed filence at the time they made their obfervations on thofe meteors. I can pofitively affirm, that in ftill nights I have frequently heard them make a ruftling and crackling noife, like the waving of a large flag in a frefli gale of wind. This is not peculiar to the place of which I am now writing, as I have heard the fame noife very plain at Churchill River; and in all probability it is only for want of attention that it has not been heard in every part of the Northern hemif-phere where they have been known to fhine with any confiderable degree of luftre. It is, however, very probable that thefe lights are fome-times much nearer the earth than they are at others, according to the ftate of the atmofphere, and this may have a great effect on the found: but the truth or falfehood of this conjedure I leave to the determinations of thofe who are better (killed in natural philofophy than I can pretend to be.

Indian deer (the only fpecies found in thofe parts, except the moofe) are fo much larger than thofe which frequent the barren grounds to the North of Churchill River, that a fmall doe is equal in fize to a Northern buck. The hair of the former is of a fandy red during the Winter; and their horns, though much ftronger, are not fo long and branchy as are thofe of the latter kind. Neither is the flefh of thofe deer fo much efteemed by the Northern Indians, as that of the fmaller kind, which inhabit the more Eaftern and Northern parts of the country. Indeed, it muft be allowed to be much coarfer, and of a different flavour; inafmuch as the large Lincolnftiirc mutton differs from grafs lamb. I muft acknowledge, however, that I always thought it very good. This is that fpecies of deer which are found fo plentiful near York Fort and Severn River. They are alfo at times found in confiderable numbers near Churchill River; and I have feen them killed as far North, near the fea-fide, as Seal River: But the fmall Northern Indian deer are feldom known to crofs Churchill River, except in fome very extraordinary cold feafons, and when the Northern winds have prevailed much in the pre-ceding fall; for thofe vifits are always made in the Winter. But though I own that the fiefh of the large Southern deer is very good, I muft at the fame time confefs that the flefti of the fmall Northern deer, whether buck or doe, in their proper feafon, is by far more delicious and the fineft I I have ever eaten, either in this country or any J other; and is of that peculiar quality, that it ne-ver cloys. I can affirm this from my own experience; for, after living on it entirely, as it may be faid, for twelve or eighteen mont4s fuceeffive-

December.

Dtxember.

226 A JOURNEY TO THE i-yi, ly, I fcarcely ever wiflied for a change of foodj though when fifli or fowl came in my way, it was very agreeable.

The beaver being fo plentiful, the attention of my companions Was chiefly engaged on them, as they not only furniflied delicious food, but their fkins proved a valuable acquifition, being a principal article of trade, as well as a ferviceable one for clothing, c.

The fituation of the beaver-houfes is various. Where the beavers are numerous they are found to inhabit lakes, ponds, and rivers, as well as thofe narrow creeks which conned the numerous lakes with which this country abounds; but the two latter are generally chofen by them when the depth of water and other circumftances are fuit able, as they have then the advantage of a current to convey wood and other neceflarics to their habitations, and becaufe, in general, they are more difficult to be taken, than thofe that are built in (landing water.

There is no one particular part of a lake, pond, river, or creek, of which the beavers make choice for building their houfes on, in preference to another; for they fometimes build on points, fometimes in the hollow of a bay, and often on fmall iflands; they always chufe, however, thofe parts that have fuch a depth of water as will refifl the froft in Winter, and prevent it from freezing to the bottom.

The beaver that build their houfes in fmall ri- verf vers or creeks, in which the water is liable to be 1771. drained off when the back fupplies arc dried up-7'

Drccmbet.

by the froft, arc wonderfully taught by inllinft to provide againft that evil, by making a darn quite acrofs the river, at a convenient diftance from their houfes. This I look upon as the molt curious piece of workmanfliip that is performed by the beaver; not fo much for the neatnefs of the work, as for its flrength and real fervice; and at the fame time it difcovers fuch a degree of fdgacity and forefight in the animal, of approaching evils, as is little inferior to that of the human fpecies, and is certainly peculiar to thofe animals.

The beaver-dams differ in fhape according to the nature of the place in which they are built. If the water in the river or creek have but little motion, the dam is almoll llraight; but when the current is more rapid, it is always made with a confiderable curve, convex toward the dream. The materials made ule of in thofe dams are drift-wood, green willows, birch, and poplars, if they can be got; alfo mud and Hones, intermixed in fuch a manner as muff evidently contribute to the flrength of the dam; but in thefe dams there is no other order or method obferved, except that of the work being carried on with a regular fweep, and all the parts being made of equal ftrength.

In places which have been long frequented by beaver undifturbed, their dams, by frequent re-

Q 2 pairing, 1771, pairing, become a folid bank, capable of relifting "CTa great force both of water and ice: and as the

December. o 7 willow, poplar, and birch generally take root and fhoot up, they by degrees form a kind of regular-planted hedge, which I have feen in fome places fo tall, that birds have built their nefls among the branches.

Though the beaver which build their houfes in lakes and other Handing waters, may enjoy a fuffi-cient quantity of their favourite element without the afliftance of a

dam, the trouble of getting wood and other neceffaries to their habitations without the help of a current, muft in fome mea-fure counterbalance the other advantages which are reaped from fuch a lituation; for it muft be obferved, that the beaver which build in rivers and creeks, always cut their wood above their houfes, fo that the current, with little trouble, conveys it to the place required.

The beaver-houfes are built of the fame materials as their dams, and are always proportioned in fize to the number of inhabitants, which feldom exceed four old, and fix or eight young ones; though, by chance, I have feen above double that number.

Thefe houfes, though not altogether unworthy of admiration, fall very Ihort of the general defcription given of them; for inftead of order or regulation being obferved in rearing them, they are of a much ruder ftruclure than their dams,

Thofe

Thofe who have undertaken to defcribe the infide of beaver-houfes, as having feveral apartments appropriated to various ufes; fuch as eating, fleeping, llore-houfes for provifions, and one for their natural occafions, c. muft have been very little acquainted with the fubje5b; or, which is ftill worfe, guilty of attempting to impofe on the credulous, by reprefcnting the greateft falfe-hoods as real facts. Many years conftant refi-dence among the Indians, during which 1 had an opportunity of feeing feveral hundreds of thofe houfes, has enabled me to affirm that every thing of the kind is entirely void of truth; for, not-withftanding the fagacity of thofe animals, it has never been obferved that they aim at any other conveniencies in their houfes, than to have a dry place to lie on; and there they ufually eat their vi(5luals, which they occafionally take out of the water.

It frequently happens, that fome of the large houfes are found to have one or more partitions, if they deferve that appellation; but that is no more than a part of the main building, left by the fagacity of the beaver to fupport the roof. On fuch occafions it is common for thofe different apartments, as fome are pleafed to call them, to have no communication with each other but by water; fo that in fact they may be called double or treble houfes, rather than different apartments of the fame houfe. I have feen a large beaver-houfe built in a fmall ifland, that had near a dozen apart-

December,

December.

230 A JOURNEY TO THE 1771. apartments under one roof: and, two or three j of thefe only excepted, none of them had any communication with each other but by water. As there were beaver enough to inhabit each apartment, it is more than probable that each family knew its own, and always entered at their own door, without having any farther conneclion with their neighbours than a friendly intercourfe; and to join their united labours in erecting their feparace habitations, and building their dams where required. It is difficult to fay whether their intereft on other occafions was anyways reciprocal. The Indians of my party killed twelve old beaver, and twenty-five young and half-grown ones out of the houfe above mentioned; and on examination found that feveral had efcaped their vigilance, aqd could not be taken but at the expence of more trouble than would be fuflicient to take double the number in a lefs difficult lituation.

Travellers who affert that the beaver have two doors to their houfes, one on the land-fide, and the other next the water, feem to be lefs acquainted with thofe animals than others who affign them an elegant fuite of apartments. Such a proceeding would be quite contrary to their manner of life, and at the fame time would render their houfes of no ufe, either to proted them from their enemies,

The difficulty here alluded to, was the numberlefs vaults the beaver had in the fides of the pond, 2nd the immenfe thicknefs of the houfe in fomc parti.

enemies, or guard them againft the extreme cold, 77,. in Winter. '.

The quiquehatches, or wolverceris, are great enemies to the beaver; and if there were a paffage into their houfes on the land-fide, would not leave one of them alive wherever they came.

1 cannot refrain from fmiling, when I read the accounts of different Authors who have written on the oeconomy of thofe animals, as there feems to be a contefl: between them, who fhall moft exceed in ficlion. But the Compiler of the Wonders of Nature and Art feems, in my opinion, to have fucceeded beft in this refped; as he has not only collected all the fictions into which other writers on the fubjecl have run, but has fo greatly improved on them, that little remains to be added to his account of the beaver, befide a vocabulary of their language, a code of their laws, and a Iketch of their religion, to make it the moli: complete natural hiflory of that animal which can poffibly be offered to the public.

There cannot be a greater impofition, or indeed a groffer infult, on common under-ftanding, than the wifli to make us believe the ftories of fome of the works afciibed to the beaver; and though it is not to be fuppofed that the compiler of a general work can be intimately acquainted with every fubject of which it may be neceffary to treat, yet a very moderate (hare of underftanding is furely (ufficient to guard him againft: giving credit to fuch

December.

232 A JOURNEY TO THE j-jjx. fuch marvellous tales, however fmoothly they may be told, or however boldly they may be af-ferted, by the romancing traveller.

To deny that the beaver is poflefled of a very confiderable degree of fagacity, would be as ab-furd in me, as it is in thofe Authors who think they cannot allow them too much. I fhall willingly grant them their full fhare; but it is impof-iible for any one to conceive how, or by what means, a beaver, whofe full height when landing erect does not exceed two feet and a half, or three feet at moft, and whofe fore-paws are not much larger than a half-crown piece, can "drive " flakes as thick as a man's leg into the ground " three or four feet deep." Their " wattling " thofe (lakes with twigs, is equally abfurd; " and their "plaiftering the infide of their houfes " with a compofition of mud and ftraw, and " fwimming with mud and ftones on their tails," are ftill more incredible. The form and iize of the animal, notwithftanding all its fagacity, will not admit of its performing fuch feats; and it would be as impoffible for a beaver to ufe its tail as a trowel, except on the furface of the ground on which it walks, as it would have been for Sir James Thornhill to have painted the dome of St. Paul's cathedral without the affiftance of fcaffold-ing. The joints of their tail will not admit of their turning it over their backs on any occafion whatever, as it has a natural inclination to bend downwards; and it is not without fome confiderable rable exertion that they can keep it from trailing on the ground. This being the cafe, they cannot lit ered: like a fquirrel, which is their common December. pofture: particularly when eating, or when they arc cleaning themfelves, as a cat or fquirrel does, without having their tails bent forward between their legs; and which may not improperly be called their trencher.

So far are the beaver from driving ftakes into the ground when building their houfes, that they lay moft of the wood croitwife, and nearly hori zontal, and without any other order than that of leaving a hollow or cavity in the middle; when any unneceffary branches projed inward, they cut them off with their teeth, and throw them in among the reft, to prevent the mud from falling through the roof. It is a miftaken notion, that the wood-work is firft completed and then plai-ftered; for the whole of their houfes, as well as their dams, are from the foundation one mafs of wood and mud, mixed with ftones, if they can be procured. The mud is always taken from the edge of the bank, or the bottom of the creek or pond, near the door of the houfe; and though their fore-paws are fo fmall, yet it is held clofe up between them, under their throat, that they, I carry both mud and ftones; while they always i drag the wood with their teeth.

All their work is executed in the night; and they are fo expeditious in completing it, that in the courfe of one night I have known them to have

December.

A JOURNEY TO THE have collecled as much mud at their houfes as to have amounted to fome thoufands of their little handfuls; and when any mixture of grafs or ftraw has appeared in it, it has been, moft alturedly, mere chance, owing to the nature of the ground from which they had taken it. As to their de-lignedly making a compofition for that purpofe, it is entirely void of truth.

It is a great piece of policy in thofe animals, to cover, or plaifter, as it is ufually called, the out-lide of their houfes every fall with frefh mud, and as late as poffible in the Autumn, even when the froft becomes pretty fevere 5 as by this means it foon freezes as hard as a ftone, and prevents their common enemy, the quiquehatch, from dif-turbing them during the Winter. And as they are frequently feen to walk over their work, and fometimes to give a flap with their tail, particularly when plunging into the water, this has, with out doubt, given rife to the vulgar opinion that they ufe their tails as a trowel, with which they plaifter their houfes; whereas that flapping of the tail is no more than a cuftom, which they always preferve, even when they become tame and do-meftic, and more particularly fo when they ar ftartled.

Their food chiefly confifts of a large root, fomething refembling a cabbage-ftalk, which grows at the bottom of the lakes and rivers. They eat alfo the bark of trees, particularly that of the poplar, birch, and willow j but the ice pre- preventing them from getting to the land In Win- jy,. ter, they have not any barks to feed upon during v- that feafon, except that of fuch fticks as they cut "" " down in Summer, and throw into the water op-pofite the doors of their houfes; and as they generally eat a great deal, the roots above mentioned conftitute a chief part of their food during the Winter. In fummer they vary their diet, by eating various kinds of herbage, and fuch berries as grow near their haunts during that feafon.

When the ice breaks up in the fpring, the beaver always leave their houfes, and rove about the whole Summer, probably in fearch of a more commodious fituation; but in cafe of not fuc-ceeding in their endeavours, they return again to their old habitations a little before the fail of the leaf, and lay in their Winter ftock of woods. They feldom begin to repair the houfes till the froft commences, and never linifh the outer-coat till the cold is pretty fevere, as hath been already mentioned.

When they fhift their habitations, or when the increafe of their number renders it neceffary to make fome addition to their houfes, or to erecl new ones, they begin felling the wood for thefe purpofes early in the Summer, but feldom begin to build till the middle or latter end of Auguft, and never complete their houfes till the cold weather be fet in.

Not-

December,

A JOURNEY TO THE

Notwithftanding what has been fo repeatedly reported of thofe animals aftembling in great bodies, and jointly ereding large towns, cities, and commonwealths, as they have fometimes been called, I am confident, from many circumftances, that even where the greateft numbers of beaver are fituated in the neighbourhood of each other, their labours are not carried on jointly in the erection of their different habitations, nor have they any reciprocal intereft, except it be fuch as live immediately under the fame roof; and then it extends no farther than to build or keep a dam which is common to feveral houfes. In fuch cafes it is natural to think that every one who receives benefit from fuch dams, fhould affift in erecting it, being fenfible of its utility to all.

Perfons who attempt to take beaver in Winter fhould be thoroughly acquainted with their manner of life, other wife they will have endlefs trouble to effect their purpofe, and probably without fuccefs in the end; becaufe they have always a number of holes in the banks, which ferve them as places of retreat when any injury is offered to their houfes; and in general it is in thofe holes that they are taken.

When the beaver which are fituated in a fmall river or creek are to be taken, the Indians fometimes find it neceffary to ftake the river acrofs, to prevent them from pafling; after which, they endeavour to find out all their holes or places of retreat in the banks. This requires much practice tice and experience to accomplifli, and is performed in the following manner: Every man being furnifhed with an iee-chifel, laflies it to the end of a fmall ftaff about four or five feet long; he then walks along the edge of the banks, and keeps knocking his chifels again ft the ice. Thofe who are well acquainted with that kind of work well know by the found of the ice when they are oppofite to any of the beaver holes or vaults. As foon as they fufped any, they cut a hole through the ice big enough to admit an old beaver; and in this manner proceed till they have found out all their places of retreat, or at leaft as many of them as poflible. While the principal men are thus employed, fome of the underftrap-pers, and the women, are bufy in breaking open the houfe, which at times is no eafy talk; for I have frequently known thefe houfes to be five and fix feet thick; and one in particular, was more than eight feet thick on the crown. When the beaver find that their habitations are invaded, they fly to their holes in the banks for fhelter; and on being perceived by the Indians, which is eafily done, by attending to the motion of the water, they block up the entrance with ftakes of wood, and then haul the beaver out of its hole, either by hand, if they can reach it, or with a large hook made for that purpofe, which is fattened to the end of a long ftick.

In this kind of hunting, every man has the folc right to all the beaver caught by him in the holes

December.

December,

A JOURNEY TO THE or vaults; and as this is a conftant rule, each per-fon takes care to mark fuch as he difcovers, by flicking up the branch of a tree, or fome other diftinguifhing poft, by which he may know them. All that are caught in the houfe alfo are the property of the perfon who finds it.

The fame regulations are obferved, and the fame procefs ufed in taking beaver that are found in lakes and other flanding waters, except it be that of flaking the lake acrofs, which would be both unneceflary and impoflible. Taking beaver-houfes in thefe fituations is generally attended with lefs trouble and more fuccefs than in the former.

The beaver is an animal which cannot keep under water long at a time j fo that when their houfes are broke open, and all their places of retreat difcovered, they have but one choice left, as it may be called, either to be taken in their houfes or their vaults: in general they prefer the latter; for where there is one beaver caught in the houfe, many thoufands are taken in their vaults in the banks. Sometimes they are caught in nets, and in the Summer very frequently in traps. In Winter they are very fat and delicious; but the trouble of rearing their young, the thinnefs of their hair, and their conftantly roving from place to place, with the trouble they have in providing againft the approach of Winter, generally keep them very poor during the fummer feafon, at which time their flefli is but indifferent eating, and their fkins of fo little value, that the Indians 1771. generally finge them, even to the amount of ma- j ny thoufands in one Summer. They have from two to five young, at a time. Mr. Dobbs, in his Account of Hudfon's Bay, enumerates no lefs than eight different kinds of beaver; but it muft be underftood that they are all of one kind and fpecies; his diftinlions arife wholly from the different feafons of the year in which they are killed, and the different ufes to which their fkins are applied which is the fole reafon that they vary fo much in value.

Jofeph Lefranc, or Mr. Dobbs for him, fays, that a good hunter can kill fix hundred beaver in one feafon, and can only carry one hundred to market. If that was really the cafe in Lefranc's time, the canoes muft have been much fmaller than they are at prefent; for it is well known that the generality of the canoes which have vifit-ed the Company's Fadories for the iaft forty or fifty years, are capable of carrying three hundred beaver-ikins with great eafe, exclufive of the Indians luggage, provifions, ts'c.

If ever a particular Indian killed fix hundred beaver in one Winter, (which is rather to be doubted,) it is more than probable that many in his company did not kill twenty, and perhaps feme none at all, fo that by diftributing them among thofe who had bad fuccefs, and others who had no abilities for that kind of hunting, there would

December.

A JOURNEY TO THE would be no neceility of leaving them to rot, or for finging them in the fire, as related by the Author. During my refidence among the Indians I have known fome individuals kill more beaver, and other heavy furrs, in the courfe of a Winter, than their wives could manage; but the overplus was never wantonly deftroyed, but always given to their relations, or to thofe who had been lefs fuccefsful; fo that the whole of the great hunters labours were always brought to the Fadlory. It is indeed too frequently a cuftom among the Southern Indians to finge many otters, as vell as beaver; but this is feldom done, except in Summer, when their Ikins are of fo little value as to be fcarcely worth the duty; on which account it has been always thought impolitic to encourage the natives to kill fuch valuable animals at a time when their fkins are not in feafon.

The white beaver, mentioned by Lefranc, are fo rare, that inftead of being " blown upon by the Company's Factors," as he aflerts, I rather doubt whether one-tenth of them ever faw one during the time of their refidence in this country. In the courfe of twenty years experience in the countries about Hudfon's Bay, though I travelled fix hundred miles to the Weft of the fea-coaft, I never faw but one white beaver-fldn, and it had many reddifli and brown hairs along the ridge of the back, and the fides and belly were of a gloffy filvery filvery white. It was deemed by tlie Indians a 1771. ffreat curiofity; and I offered three times the v ufual price for a icw or them, il they couid be got; but in the courfe of ten years that I remained there afterwards, 1 could not procure another; which is a convincing proof there isnofuch thing as a breed of that kind, and that a variation from the ufual colour is very rare.

Black beaver, and that of a beautiful glofs. are not uncommon: perhaps they are more plentiful at Churchill than at any other Factory in the Bay; but it is rare to get more than twelve or fifteen of their feins in the courfe of one year's trade.

Lcfranc, as an Indian, muft have known better than to have informed Mr. Dobbs that the beaver have from ten to fifteen young at a time; or if he did, he mufl have deceived him wilfully; for the Indians, by killing them in ail ftagcs of geil: ation, have abundant opportunities of afcer-taining the ufual number of their offspring. I have feen fome hundreds of them killed at the feafons favourable for thofe obfervations, and never could difcover more than fix young in one female, and that only in two inltances; for the ufual number, as I have before obferved, is from two to five.

Befides this unerrincr method of afcertainino; the real number of young which any animal has at a time, there is another rule to go by, with

R refpecl

December.

A JOURNEY TO THE refpecl to the beaver, which experience has proved to the Indians never to vary or deceive them, that is by difiection; for on examining the womb of a beaver, even at a time when not with young, there is always found a hardifli round knob for every young he had at the laft litter. This is a circumftance I have been particularly careful to examine, and can aferm it to be true, from real experience.

Moft of the accounts, nay I may fay all the accounts now extant, refpecling the beaver, are taken from the authority of the French who have refided in Canada; but thofe accounts differ fo much from the real ftate and oeconomy of all the beaver to the North of that place, as to leave great room to fufpect the truth of them altogether. In the firft place, the ailertion that they have two doors to their houfes, one on the land-fide, and the other next the water, is, as I have before obferved, quite contrary to facl and common fenfe, as it would render their houfes of no ufe to them, either as places of ftielter from the inclemency of the extreme cold in Winter, or as a retreat from their common enemy the quique-hatch. The only thing that could have made M. Du. Pratz, and other French writers, conjecture that fuch a thing did exift, muft have been from having feen fome old beaver houfes which had been taken by the Indians; for they are always obliged to make a hole in one fide of the houfe houfc before they can drive them out; and it is 1771. more than probable that in lo mild a climate as"

December.

Canada, the Indians do generally make thofe holes on the land-fide, which without doubt gave rile to the fuggeftion.

In refpecl to the beaver dunging in their houfes, as fome perfons affert, it is quite wrong as they always plunge into the water to do it. I am the better enabled to make this aflertion, from having kept feveral of them till they became fo do-mefticated as to anfwer to their name, and follow thofe to whom they were accuftomed, in the fame manner as a dog would do; and they were as much pleafed at being fondled, as any animal I ever law. I had a houfe built for them, and a fmall piece of water before the door, into which they always plunged when they wanted to eafe nature; and their dung being of light a fubftance, immediately rifes and floats on the furface, then feparates and fubfides to the bottom. When the Winter fets in fo as to freeze the water folid, they ftill continue their cuftom of coming out of their houfe, and dunging and making water on the ice; and vihen the weather was fo cold that I was obliged to take them into my houle,

R 2 they

The Northern Indians think that the fagacity of the beaver dire61 them to make that part of their houfe which fronts the Noith much thicker than any other part, with a view of defending theniiblves fioui the cold winds uhich generally blow from that quarter duiing the Winter; and foi this leafon the Northern Indian."- generally bie;; k oucn tliat fijo of the beaver-houlls which exadtiy front the South.

December.

244 A JOURNEY TO THE jjmi they always went into a large tub of water which I fet for that purpofe: fo that they made not the leaft dirt, though they were kept in my own fitting-room, where they were the conftant companions of the Indian women and children, and were fo fond of their company, that when the Indians were abfent for any confiderable time, the beaver difcovered great figns of uneafinefs, and on their return fhewed equal marks of plea-fure, by fondling on them, crawling into their laps, laying on their backs, fitting erefi: like a iquirrel, and behaving to them like children who fee their parents but feldom. In general, during the Winter they lived on the fame food as the women did, and were remarkably fond of rice and plum-pudding: they would eat partridges and frefti venifon very freely, but I never tried them with fifli, though I have heard they will at times prey on them. In fact, there are few of the granivorous animals that may not be brought to be carnivorous. It is well known that our do-meftic poultry will eat animal food: thoufands of sreefe that come to London market are fattened. en tallow-craps; and our horfes in Hudfon'sbay would not only eat all kinds of animal food, but alfo drink freely of the wafh, or pot-liquor, intended for the hogs. And we are affured by the moft authentic Authors, that in Iceland, not only black cattle, but alfo the flieep, are almoft entirely fed on filh and fifh. bones during the Winter feafon.

fcafon. Even in the liles of Orkney, and that in Summer, the flieep attend the ebbing of the tide,, as regular as the Efquimaux curlew, and go down to the fiiore which the tide has left, to feed on the fea-weed. This, however, is through nccel-fity, for even the famous Ifland of Pomona will not afford them an exiftcnce above high-water-mark.

With refpecl to the inferior, or flave-beaver, of which fome Authors fpeak, it is, in my opinion, very difficult for thofe who are befl acquainted with the ceconomy of this animal to determine whether there are any that deferve that appellation or not. It fometimes happens, that a beaver is caught, which has but a very indifferent coat, and which has broad patches on the back, and fhoulders almofl wholly without hair. This is the only foundation for alferting that there is an inferior, or flave-beaver, among them. And when one of the above defcription is taken, it is perhaps too haftily inferred that the hair is worn off from thofe parts by carrying heavy loads: whereas it is moil probable that it is caufed by a diforder that attacks them fomewhat iimilar to the mange; for were that falling off of the hair occafioned by performing extra labour, it is natural to think that inftances of it would be more frequent than they are; as it is rare to fee one of them

This belag the largcft of the Orkney Iflands, is called by the Inhabitants the Main Land.

them in the courfe of feven or ten years. I have feen a whole houfe of thofe animals that had nothing: on the furface of their bodies but the fine foft down; all the long hairs having molted off. This and every other deviation from the general run is undoubtedly owing to fome particular dif-order.

CHAP.

Tranfaclions and Remarks from our Arrival on the South Side of the Athapufcow Lake, till our Arrival at Prince of Wales's Fort on Churchill River.

Crofs the Athapufcow Lake. Defcripfwn of it and its produdiom, as far as could be difcovered in Winter when the fnow was on the ground. FijJy found in the lake. Defcription of the hujfalo; of the moofe or elk and the method of drejfing their fkins, find a ivoman alone that had not feen a human face for more than fcven months Her account how fhe came to be in thatfttuation; and her curious method of procuring a livelihood. Many of my Indians wrefllcd for her. Arrive at the Great Athapufcow River. Walk along the fide of the River for feveral days, and thenfirike off to the Eaft-ward. Difficulty in getting through the woods in 7nany places. Meet with fome flrange Northern Indians on their return from the Fort. Meet more fir angers, whom my companions plundered, and from whom they took one of their young women. Curious manner of life which thofe ftrangers lead, and the reafon they gave for roving fo far from their ufual refidencc. Leave the fine level country of the At ha-pufcows, and arrive at the Stony Hills of the Noj-ihern Indian Country. Meet fome flrange Northern Indians, one of whom carried a letter for me to

Prince

Prince of Wales's Fort, in March one ihoufand even hundred and feventy-one and now gave? ne an-fiver to it, dated twentieth of June following.- Indians begin preparing wood-work and birch-rind for canos. The equincdial gale very fevere. Indian method of running the moofe deer down by fpeed of foot.-Arrival at 1 heeleyaa River.-.-See fo? ne firangers.-The bruialiiy of my companions. A tremendous gale and fnow-drft. Meet with morejlrangers; remarks on it. Leave all the elderly people and children, and proceed direclly to the Fort. Stop to build canoes, and then advance, Several of the Indians die through hunger, and many others are obliged to decline the journey for want (f ammunition. A violent fierm and inundation, that forced us to the top of a high hill, where we fftffered great dijirefs for? nore than two days. Kill fever al deer. The Indians method cf pre-ferving the ficjh without the ajffiance of fait. See fever al Indians that were going to linnpfs Bay. Game of all kinds remarkably plentiful. Arrive at the Fadory.

FTER expending force days in hunting beaver, we proceeded to crofs the Athapuf-cow Lake; but as we had loft much time in hunting deer and beaver, which vere very plentiful on feme cf the iflands, it was the ninth of 9th. January before we arrived on the South fide.

This lake from the bed information which I could get from the natives, is about one hundred

A"5"n3: aitiecjmiljp- Itiit. d f. c o'v: i. aik; Aw SMf-JIifjaJiixxmi, and twenty leagues long from Eaft to Weft, and twenty wide from North to South. The point where we croffed it is faid to be the narrovveft. It is full of iflands; moft of which are clothed with fine tall poplars, birch, and pines, and are well flocked with Indian deer. On fome of the large iflands we alfo found feveral beaver; but this muft be underilood only of fuch iflands as had large ponds in them; f(; r not one beaver-houfe was to be ictn on the margin of any of them.

The lake is flored with great quantities of very fine fi(h; particularly between the iflands, which in fome parts are fo clofe to each other as to form very narrow channels, like little rivers, in which I found (when angling for fifli a confideiable current fetting to the Kaftward.

The iifh that are common in this lake, as well as in mod of the other lakes in this country, are pike, trout, perch, barbie, tittameg, and methy; the two laft are names given by the natives to two Ipecies of fifh which are found only in ihis country. Befidcs thefe, we alfo caught another kind of fifh, which is faid by the Northern Indians to be peculiar to this lake; at leaft none of the fame kind have been met with in any other. The body of this fifii much refembieu a pike in hape; but the fcales, which are very large and ftiff, are of a beautifully bright filver colour: the mouth is large, and fituated like that of a pike; but when open, much refembles thatof afturgeonj and though not provided with any teeth, takes a bait as ravenoully as a pike or a trout. The fizes we caught were from two feet long to four feet. Their flefh, though delicately white, is very foft, and has fo rank a tafte, that many of the Indians, except they are in abfolute want, will not eat it. The northern Indians call this fifh Shees. The trout in this lake are of the largeft fize I ever faw: fome that were caught by my companions could not, I think, be lefs than thirty-five or forty pounds weight. Pike are alfo of an incredible lize in this extenfive water; here they are feldom molefted, and have multitudes of fmaller fifli to prey upon. If I fay that I have feen fome of thefe fifh that were upwards of forty pounds weight, I am fure I do not exceed the truth.

Immediately on our arrival on the South fide of the Athapufcow Lake, the fcene was agreeably altered, from an entire jumble of rocks and hills, for fuch is all the land on the North fide, to a fine level country, in which there was not a hill to be feen, or a ftone to be found: fo that fuch of my companions as had not brafs kettles, loaded their fledges with fi: ones from fome of the laft iflands, to boil their victuals with in their birch-rind kettles, which will not admit of being expof-ed to the fire. They therefore heat flones and drop them into the water in the kettle to make it boil.

Buffalo, moofe, and beaver were very plentiful; and we could difcover, in many parts through which which we pafled, the tracks of martins, foxes, quiquehatches, and other animals of the furr kind; lb that they were by no means fcarce: but my companions never gave themfelves the leaft trouble to catch any of the three laft mentioned animals; for the buffalo, moofe, and beaver engaged all their attention; perhaps principally fo on account of the excellency of their flefli; whereas the flefh of the fox and quiquehatch are never eaten by thofe people, except when they are in the greateft diflrefs, and then merely to fave life, their reafons for this Ihall be given in a fubfequent part of my Journal.

The buffalo in thofe parts, I think, are in general much larger than the Engiifli black cattle; particularly the bulls, which, though they may not in reality be taller than the largeft fize of the Englifh oxen, yet to me always appeared to be much larger. In fad, they are fo heavy, that when fix or eight Indians are in company at the fkinning of a large bull, they never attempt to turn it over while entire, but when the upper fide is fkinned, they cut off the leg and flioulder, rip up the belly, take out all the inteftines, cut off the head, and make it as light as pollible, before they turn it to Ikin the under fide. The fkih is in fome places of an incredible thicknefs, particularly about the neck, where it often exceeds an inch. The horns are fhort, black, and almoft llraight, but very thick at the roots or bafe.

The head of an old bull is of a great iize and weight indeed: fome which I have feen were (o large, that I could not without difficulty lift them from the ground; but the heads of the cows are much fmaller. Their tails are, in general, about a foot long, though fome appear to be exclufive of the long brufh of hair at the end, longer. The hair on the tails of the bulls is generally of a fme gioffy black; but the brufti at the end of the cows' tails is always of a rufty brown, probably owing to being ftained with their urine.

The hair of the body is foft and curled, fome-what approaching to wool; it is generally of a fandy brown, and of an equal length and thick-nefs all over the body: but on the head and neck it is much longer than it is on any other part.

The Indians, after reducing all the parts of the fkin to an equal thicknefs by fcraping, drefs them in the hair for clothing; when they are light, loft, warm, and durable. They alfo drefs fome ofthofe fkins into leather without the hair, of which they make tents and fhoes j but the grain It is remarked by Mr. Cate(by,: n his defcription of this animal, that no man can lift one of their heads. Thofe I faw in the Athapufcow country arefuch as I have defcribed; and I am afmred by the Company's fer-vants, as well as the Indians who live near Hudfon's Houfe, that the buf-falos there are much fmaller; fa that the fpecies Mr. Catefby faw, or wrote of, mufl; have been much larger, or have had very large heads; for it is well known that a man of any tolerable flrength can lift two and a half, or three hundred pounds weight. I think that the heads of his biiffalos are too heavy for the bodies, as the bodies of thofe I faw in (he Athapufcow country appear to have been of equal weight with his.

is remaikably open and fpungy, by no means equal in goodnefs to that of the fkin ot the moofe: nor am I certain that the curriers or tanners in Europe could manufacture thefe fkins in fuch a manner as to render them of any confiderable value; for, to appearance, they are of the fame quality which the fkins of the mulk-ox, which are held in fo little eftimation in England, that when a number of them was fent home from Churchill Factory, the Company iilued out orders the year following, that unlefs they could be pur-chafed from the Indians at the rate of four fkins for one beaver, they would not anfver the expence of fending home; a great proof of their being of very little value.

The buffalos chiefly delight in wide open plains, which in thofe parts produce very long coarfe grafs, or rather a kind of fmall flags and rufhes, upon which they feed; but when purfued they always take to the woods. They are of fuch an amazing flrength, that when they fly through the woods from a purfuer, they frequently brufh down trees as thick as a man's arm; and be the fnow ever fo deep, fuch is their ftrength and agility that they are enabled to plunge-through it fafler than the fwifteft Indian can run in fnou (hoes. To this I have been an eye-wit-nefs many times, and once had the vanity to think that I could have kept pace with them; but though I was at that time celebrated for being particularly fleet of foot in fnovv-fhoes, I foon found found that I was no match for the buffalos, not- withftanding they were then plunging through fuch deep fnow, that their bellies made a trench in it as large as if many heavy facks had been hauled through it. Of all the large beafts in thofe parts the buffalo is eafieft to kill, and the moofe are the moft difficult; neither are the deer very cafy to come at, except in windy weather: indeed it requires much practice, and a great deal of patience, to flay any of them, as they will by no means fuffer, a direct approach, unlefs the hunter be entirely flieltered by woods or willows. The flefh of the buffalo is exceedingly good eating; and fo entirely free from any difagreeable fmell or tafle, that it refembles beef as nearly as poffible: the flefh of the cows, when fome time gone with calf, is efleemed the finefl; and the young calves, cut out of their bellies, are reckoned a great delicacy indeed. The hunch on their backs, or more properly on their fhoulders, is not a large fiefhy lump, as fome fuppofe, but is occaiioned by the bones that form the withers being continued to a greater length than in mofl other animals. The flefh which furrounds this part being fo equally intermixed with fat and lean, is reckoned among the nicefi bits. The weight, however, is by no means equal to what has been commonly reported. The tongue is alfo very delicate; and what is moft extraordinary, when the beails are in the pooreft ftate, which happens regularly at certain feafons, their tongues are then very fat and fine; fome fay, fatter than when they are in 172. the beft order; the truth of which, I will not– confirm. They are fo efteemed here, however, J"" that many of them are brought down to the Company's Factory at York as prefents, and are efteemed a great luxury, probably for no other reafon but that they are far-fetched; for they are by no means fo large, and I think them not fo fine, as a neat's tongue in England.

The moofe deer is alfo a large beaft, often exceeding the largefthorfe both in height and bulk; but the length of the legs, the bulk of the body, the fhortnefs of the neck, and the uncommon length of the head and ears, without any appearance of a tail, make them have a very aukward appearance. The males far exceed the females in fize, and differ from them in colour. The hair of the male, which is long, hollow, and foft, like that of a deer, is at the points nearly black, but a little way under the furface it is of an afti-colour, and at the roots perfedly white. The hair of the female is of a fandy brown, and in fome parts, particularly under the throat, the belly, and the flank, is nearly white at the fur-face, and mofl delicately fo at the root.

Their legs are fo long, and their necks fo fliort, that they cannot graze on level ground like other animals, but are obliged to brouze on the tops of large plants and the leaves of trees duriijcr the Summer; and in Winter they always feed on the tops of willows, and the fmall branches of thq birch.

A JOUxr. NSY TO THK birch-tree; on which account they are nfver found during that feafon but in fuch places as can afford them a plentiful fupply of their favourite food: and though they have no fore-teeth in the upper-jaw, yet 1 have often feen willows and fmall birch-trees cropped by them, in the fame manner as if they had been cut by a gardener's (heers, though fome of them were not fmalier than common pipe-ftems; they feem particularly partial to the red willovv.

In Summer they are generally found to frequent the banks of rivers and lakes, probably with no other view than to have the benefit of getting into the water, to avoid the innumerable multitudes of mulkettos and other flies that pefter them exceedingly during that feafon. There is alfo a variety of water-plants, of which the moofe are very fond, and which are adapted to their necellities in a peculiar manner during the Sum-mer feafon, as they can eafily brouze on them when nearly emerged in water, to avoid the torment of the flies.

The head of the moofe is, as I have obferved, remarkably long and large, not very unuke that' of a horfe; but the nofe and noftrils are at leaft twice as large. The ears are about a foot long, and large; and they always fliand ered:. Their faculty of hearing is fuppofed to be more acute than either their fight or fcent; which makes it very difficult to kill them, efpecially as the Indians in thofe parts have no other method (f doing it but by creeping after them, among the; 1 ees and bufhes, till they get within gun-fliot; taking care always to keep to leeward of the nioofe, for fear of being overheard. In Summer, when they frequent the margins of rivers and lakes, they are often killed by the Indians in the water, while they are croffing rivers, or fwim. ming from the main to iflands, Izc. When purfu, ed in this manner, they are the molt inoflenfive of all animals, never making any refiftance; and the young ones are fo fimple, that I remember to have feen an Indian paddle his canoe up to one of them, and take it by the poll without the lead oppofition: the poor harmlefs animal feeming at the fame time as contented along lide the canoe, as iffwimmingby the lide of its dam, and looking up in our faces with the fame fearlefs innocence that a houfe-lamb would, making ufe of its fore-foot almofl: every inftant to clear its eyes of mufliettoes, which at that time were remarkably numerous.

II have alfo feen women and boys kill the old moofein this Situation, by knocking them on the head with a hatchet; and in the Summer of one thoufand feven hundred and feventy-five, when I was on my paftage from Cumberland Houfe to j York Fort, two boys killed a fine buck moofe in the water, by forcing a flick up its fundament j for they had neither gun, bow, nor arrows with them. The common deer are far more dangerous to approach in canoes, as they kick up their hind

S legs legs with fuch violence as to endanger any birch-rind canoe that comes within their reach; for which reafon all the Indians who kill deer upon the water are provided with a long flick that will reach far beyond the head of the canoe.

The moofe are alfo the ealiefl to tame and do-mefticate of any of the deer kind. I have repeatedly feen them at Churchill as tame as Iheep, and even more fo; for they would follow their keeper any diftance from home, and at his call return with him, without the leaft trouble, or ever offering to deviate from the pathf.

The flefh of the moofe is very good, though the grain is but coarfe, and it is much tougher than any other kind of venifon. The nofeis moft excellent, as is alfo the tongue, though by no means fo fat and delicate as that of the common deer. It is perhaps worth remarking, that the livers of

The itioofe foririerly Cent to liis Majcfly was from that place. A young male was alfo put on boaicl thefhip, but it died on thepaflage, otherwife it is probable they might have piopagated in this country.

I Since the above was written, the fame Indian that brought all the above-mentioned young moofe to the Faiflory liad, in the year 1777, two Others, fo tame, that when on his pafiage to Prir. ce of Wales's Fort in a canne, the moofe always followed him. long the bank of the tiver; and at night, or on any other occafion when the Indains landed, the young moofe generally came and fondled on them, in the fame manner as the mofldo-mefiic animal would have done, and never offered to flray ftom the tents. Unfortunately, in crofling a deep bay in one of the lakes, on a fine day,) all the Indians that weie not interefted in the fafe-landing of thofe engaging creatures, paddled from point to point; and the man that owned them not caring to go fo far about by himfelf, accompanied the others, in hopes they would follow him round asufual; but at night the young mooedid not arrive; and as the howling of fome wolves was heard in that quarter, it was fuppofed they had been devoured by them, as they weic never afterward feen.

the moofe are never found, not even at any time of the year; and, Hke the other deer, they have no gall. The fat of the intcftines is hard, like fuet; but all the external fat is foft, like that of a breaft of mutton, and when put into a bladder, is as fine as marrou In this they differ from all the other fpecies of deer, of which the external fat is as hard as that of the kidnies.

The moofe in all their actions and attitudes appear very uncouth, and when dif-turbed, never run, only make a kind of trot, which the length of their legs enables them to do with great fwift-ncfs, and apparently with much eafe; but were the country they inhabit free from under-wood, and dry under-foot, fo that horfemen and dogs might follow them, they would become an eafy prey, as they are both tender-footed and fliort-wlnded: But of this more hereafter.

The lldns of the moofe, when drefted by the natives, make excellent tent-covers and fhoe-lea-ther; and in fa6t every other part of their clothing. Thefe, like the fkins of the buflalo, are of very unequal thicknefs. Some of the Indian women, who are acquainted with the manufacture of them, will, by means of fcraping, render them. as even as a piece of thick cloth, and when well dielted they are very foft; but not being drelt-

Mr. Du Prnz, in his defcription of this animal, fays, it is never found farther North than Cape Breton and Nova Scotia: but I have feen thcin in great numbers in the Athapufcovv Country, which cannot be much ilftiortof 60" Novth latitude.

ed in oil, they always grow hard after being wet, unlets great care be taken to keep rubbing them January. j., drying. The fame may be faid of all the Indian-drcffcd leather, except that of the wewaikilh, which will wafli as well as fhammoy-leather, and always preferve its foftnefs. The female raoqfe never have any horns, but the males have them of a prodigious fize an4 weight, and very different in fliape from thofe of the common deer. The extremity of each horn is palmated to the fize of a common fliovel, from which a few fliort branches fhoot out; and the fliaft of the horn is frequently as large as a com-, mon man's wrift. They fhed them annually like the common deer. The horns of the moofe are frequently found to exceed fixty pounds weight; and their texture, though of a large fize and of fuch rapid growth, is much harder than any other fpecies of deer-horns in thofe parts.

Though, the fiefh of the moofe is efteemed by moll Indians both for its flavour and fubllance, yet the Northern Indians of my crew did not reckon either it or the flefh of the buffalo fub-flantial food. This 1 fiiould think entirely proceeded from prejudice, efpeciaily with refpecf to the moofe; but the flefli of the bufialo, though fo fine to the eye, and pleafing to the tafte, is fo light and eafy of digeftion, as not to be deemed fubftantial food by any Indian in this country, either Northern or Southern. The moofe have from one to three young at a time, and generally bring bring them forth in the latter end of April, or 1772. beffinnine; of May. "T o ij Jamiary.

Sooii after our arrival no the South-fide of Athapufcow Lake, Matonabbee propofed continuing our courfe in the South Weft quarter, in hopes of meeting fome of the Athapufcow Indians; becaufe 1 wiflied, if poltible, to purchafe a tent, and other ready-drcffed fldns from them; as a fupply of thofe articles vould at this time have been of material fervice to us, being in great want both of tents and Ihoe-leather: and though my companions were daily killing either moofe or bufialo, the weather was fo exceffively cold, as to render drefiing their fkins not only very trouble-fome, but almoft impraclicable, efpeciaily to the generality of the Northern Indians, who are not veil acquainted with the manufacture of that kind of leather.

To drefs thofe fkins accordins; to the Indian method, a lather is made of the brains and fome of the fofteft fat or marrow of the animal, in which the fkin is well foaked, when it is taken out, and not only dried by the heat of a fire, but hung up in the fmoke for feveral days-, it is then taken down, and well foaked and wafhed in warm svater, till the grain of the fkin is perfectly open, and has imbibed a fufficient quantity of water, afcer Vvhich it is taken out and wrung as dry as poftible, and then dried by the heat of a flow fire j care being taken to rub and ftretch it as long as ny mciflure remains in the fkin. By this fimple method method, and by fcraping them afterwards, fome of the moofe fkins are made veiy delicate both to the eye and the touch. jj(j On the eleventh of January, as fome of my companions were hunting, they faw the track of a iilrange fnow-fhoe, which they followed; and at a confiderable diftance came to a little hut, where they difcovered a young woman fitting alone. As they found that fhe underilood their language, they brought her with them to the tents. On examination, ihe proved to be one of the Weftern Dogribbed Indians, who had been taken prifoner by the Athapufcow Indians in the Summer of one thoufand feven hundred and feventy; and in the lollowincr Summer, when the Indians that took her prifoner were near this part, flie had eloped from them, with an intent to return to her own country; but the diftance being fo great, and having after (he was taken prifoner, been carried in a canoe the whole way, the turnings and windings of the rivers and lakes were fo numerous, that die forgot the track; fo fhe built the hut in which we found her, to proteft her from the weather during the Winter, and here fhe had refided from the firft fetting in of the fall.

From her account of the moons paft fince her. elopement, it appeared that ihe had been near feven months without feeing a human face; during all which time fhe had fupported herfelf very well by fnaring partridges, rabbits, and fquir-reis; fhe had alfo killed two or three beaver, and (ome porcupines. That fhe did not feem to have been been in want is evident, as fhe had a fmall flock of provifions by her when fhe was difcovered; and was in good health and condition, and I think one of the fineft women, of a real Indian, that I have feen in any part of North America.

The methods praclifed by this poor creature to procure a livelihood were truly admirable, and are great proofs that neceflity is the real mother of invention. When the few dcer-finews that fhe had an opportunity of taking with her were all expended in making fnares, and fewing her clothing, Ihe had nothing to fupply their place but the fmews of the rabbits legs and feet; thefe Ihe twifled together for that purpofe with great dexterity and fuccefs. The rabbits, Idc. which flie caught in thofe fnares, not only furniilied her with a comfortable fubfiftence, but of the fldns fhe made a fuit of neat and warm clothinsr for the Winter. It is fcarcely poflible to conceive that a perfon in her forlorn fituation could be fo compofed a to be capable of contriving or executing any thing that was not abfolutely necef-fary to her exiftence; but there were fufficient proofs that fhe had extended her care much far, ther, as all her clothing, befide being calculated for real fervice, fhewed great tafte, and exhibited no little variety of ornament. The materials, though rude, were very curioufly wrought, and fo judicioufly placed, as to make the whole of

Tanuar 264 A JOURNEY TO THE 1772. Iier garb have a very pleafirig, though rather romantic appearance.

Her leifure hours from hunting had been employed in twilling the inner rind or bark ot willows into fmall lines, like net-twine, of which fhe had fome hundred fathoms by her; viith this fhe intended to make a fidiing-net as foon as the Spring advanced. It is of the inner bark of willows, twifted in this manner, that the Dog-ribbed Indians make their fiihing-nets; and they are much perferable to thofe made by the Northern Indians.

Five or fix inches of an iron hoop, made into a knife, and the fliank of an arrow-head of iron, which ferved her as. an awl, were all the metals.; this poor woman had with her when fhe eloped; and with thefe implements fhe had made herfclf complete fnow-lhoes, and feveral other ufe-lul articles.

Her method of m. aking a fire was equally fin-g-ular and curious, havinq: no other materials for that purpofe than two hard fulphurous ftones. Thefe, by long friction and hard knocking, produced a few fparks, which at length communicated to feme touchvood; but as this method

The Northern Inaians mak? their fioiir. g-nets with fjr. all thongs cut from raw deer-fldns; which when dry appear very good, but after being foaked in water fdme time, grow fo foft and flipper, that when large fifll ftrike the net, the hitches are very apt to flip and! et them efcape. Be-fide this inconvenience, they are very liable to rot, iinlefs they be fre-mtentiy taken out of the water and dhd.

was attended with great trouble, and not always with fuccefs, flie did not fuffcr her lire to go out all the Winter. Hence we may conclude that fhe had no idea of producing fire by friclion, in the manner practiced by the Efquimaux, and many other uncivilized nations; becaufe if (he had, the above-mentioned precaution would have beenun-neceflary.

The Angularity of the circumftance, the come-linefs of her perlon, and her approved accomplifh-ments, occafioned a ftrong conteft between feve-ral of the Indians of my party, who fhould have her for a wife; and the poor girl was actually won and loft at wreflling by near half a fcore different men the fame evening. My guide, Mate-nabbcc who at that time had no lefs than feven wives, all women grown, befides a young girl of eleven or twelve years old, would have put in for the prize alfo, had not one of his wives made him afhamed of it, by telling him that he had already more wives than he could properly attend. This piece of fatire, however true, proved fatal to the poor girl who dared to make fo open a declaration; for the great man, Matonabbee, who would willingly have been thought equal to eight or ten men in every refpecl, took it as fuch an affront, that he fell on her with both hands and feet, and bruifed her to fuch a degree, that after lingering fome time fhe died.

When the Athapufcow Indians took the above Pogribbed Indian woman prifoner, they according

January.

A JOURNEY TO THE ing to the univerfal cuftom of thofe favages, fur-prifed her and her party in the night, and killed every foul in the tent, except herfelf and three other young women. Among thofe whom they killed, were her father, mother, and hufband. Her young child, four or five months old, Ihe concealed in a bundle of clothingr, and took with her undifcovered in the night; but when fhe arrived at the place where the Athapufcow Indians had left their wives, (which was not far diftant,) they began to examine her bundle, and finding the child, one of the women took it from her, an4 killed it on the fpot.

This laft piece of barbarity gave her fuch a difguft to thofe Indians, that notwithf-tanding the man who took care of her treated her in every refpecl as his wife, and was, fhe faid, remarkably kind to, and even fond of her; fo far was fhe from being able to reconcile herfelf to any of the tribe, that Ile rather chofe to expofe herfelf to mifery and want, than live in eafe and affluence among perfons who had fo cruelly murdered her infant. The poor woman's relation of this lliockinsr It is too common a cafe with moft of the tribes of Southern Indians for the women to cleliie their hufbands or friends, when going to war; to bring them a flave, that they may have the pleafure of killing it; and ibme of thete inhuman women will accompany their litifbands, and murder the women and children as faft as their hufbands do the men;

When I was at Cumberland Houfe, (an inland fettlement that I efta-blifbed for the Hudfbn's Bay Company in the year 1774,) I was particularly acquainted with a very young lady of this extraordinary turn; who v. l. en I defircd fonie Indians thit vveie going to war to bring me a young flave.

lliocking flory, which flie delivered in a very af-feding manner, only excited laughter among the fiivages of my party.

In a converfation with this woman foon afterward, (lie told us, that her country lies fo far to the Weftward, that flie had never feen iron, or any other kind of metal, till Ihe was taken prifo-ner. All of her tribe, fhe obferved, made their hatchets and ice-chifels of deer's horns, and their knives of Hones and bones; that their arrows were fliod with a kind of flate, bones, and deer's horns; and the inflruments which they employed to make their wood-work were nothing but beaver's teeth. Though they had frequently heard of the ufeful materials which the nations or tribes to the Eaft of them were fupplied with from the Englifli, fo far were they from drawing nearer, to be in the way of trading for ironwork, Iffc. that they were obliged to retreat farther back, to avoid the Athapufcow Indians, who made furprifing fiaughter among them, both in Winter and Summer.

On the fixteenth, as we were continuing our,6th.

courfe flave, which I intended to have brought upas a domenic, Mifs was equally defirous that one might be brought to her, for the cruel purpofe of murdering it. It is fcarcely pofllble to exprefs my aftoniltiment, en hearing fuch an extraordinary requeft made by a young creature fcaicely fixteen years old; however, as foon as I recovered from my furpiife, I ordered her to leave the fettlcment, which (he did, with thofe who were going to war; and it is therefore probable (he might not be difappointed in her reqncft. The next year I was ordered to the command of prince of Wales's Fortj ad therefore never faw her afterward.

courfe in the South Weft quarter, we arrived at the grand Athapufcow River, which at that part is about two miles wide, and empties itfelf into the srreat lake of the fame name we had fo lately croired, and which has been already de-fcribed. i

The woods about this river, particularly the pines and poplars, are the talleft and ftouteft I have feen in any part of North America. The birch alfo grows to a confiderable fize, and fome fpecies of the willov are likewife tall: but none of them have any trunk, like thofe in England.

The bank of the river in moft parts is very high, and in fome places not lefs than a hundred feet above the ordinary furface of the water. As the foil is of a loamy quality, it is very fubjecl to moulder or wafli away by heavy rains, even during the fhort Summer allotted to this part of the globe. The breaking up of the ice in the Spring is annually attended with a great deluge, when, lam told, it is not uncommon to fee whole points of land wafhed away by the inundations; and as the wood grows dole to the edge of the banks, vaft quantities of it are hurried down the ilream by the irreliftible force of the water and ice, and conveyed into the great lake already mentioned; on the ihores and iflands of which, there lies the greateft quantity of drift wood I ever faw. Some of this wood is large enough to make mafts for the largeft fiiips that are built. The banks of the river in general are fo fteep as to be inacceflible to either either man or beaft, except in feme flacks, or gulleys, that have been wore down by heavy rains, backwaters, or deluges; and even thofe flacks are, for the moft part, very diilicult to af-cend, on account of the number of large trees which lie in the way.

There are feveral low iflands in this river, which are much frequented by the moofe, for the fake of the fine willows they produce, which furnilh them with a plentiful fupply of their favourite food during the Winter. Some of thofe iflands are alfo frequently by a number of rabbits; but as larger game could be procured in great plenty, thofe fm. all animals were not deemed worthy our notice at prefent.

Befidethe grand river already mentioned, there are feveral others of lefs note, which empty them-felves into the great Athapufcow Lake: There are alfo feveral fmall rivers and creeks on the North Eaft fide of the Lake that carry off the fu-perfluous waters, fome of which, after a variety of windings through the barren grounds to the North of Churchill River, are lofl; in the marflies and low grounds, while others, by means of many fmau channels and rivulets, are difcharged into other rivers and lakes, and at laft, doubtlefs, find their way into Hudfon's Bay. Thefe rivers, though numberiefs, are au fo fuh of flioals and ftones, as not to be navigable for an Indian canoe to any confiderable diftance; and if they were, it would be of little or no ufe to the natives, as none of them lead within feveral hundred miles of Churchill River.

Agreeably to Matonabbee's propofal, we continued our courfe up the Athapufcow River for many days, and though we paffed feveral parts which we well knew to have been the former Winter-haunts of the Athapufcow Indians, yet we could not fee the leaft trace of any of them having been there that feafon. In the preceding Summer, when they were in thofe parts, they had fet fire to the woods; and though many months had elapfed from that time till our arrival there, and notwithftanding the fnow was then very deep, the mofs was ftiil burning in many places, which at firft deceived us very much, as we took it for the fmoke of ftrange tents; but after going much out of our way, and fearching very diligently, we could not difcover the leaft track of a ftranger.

Thus difappointed in our expectations of meeting the Southern Indians, it was refolved (in Council, as it may be called) to expend as much time in hunting buffalo, moofe, and beaver as we could, fo that we might be able to reach Prince of Wales's Fort a little before the ufual time of the fhips arrival from England. Accordingly, after having walked upvvafds of forty miles by the 27tb. fide of Athapufcow River, on the twenty-feventh of January we ftruck oif to the Eaftward, and left the River at that part where it begins to tend due South.

In confequence of this determination of the In- 1772.

dians, we continued our courfe to tlie Eaftward;- but as game or all kmds was very plcntirul, we made but fhort days journies, and often remained two or three days in one place, to eat up the fpoils or produce of the chace. The woods through which we were to pafs were in many places fo thick, that it was neceffary to cut a path before the women could pafs with their fledges j and in other places fo much of the woods had formerly been fet on fire and burnt, that we were frequently obliged to walk farther than we other-wife fliould have done, before we could find green brufh enough to floor our tents.

Froni the fifteenth to the twenty-fourth of Fe- Fchru?. rr. bruary, we walked along a fmall river that emp- 5'24h ties itfelf into the Lake Clowey, near the part where we built canoes in May one thoufand tvvi hundred and feventy-one. This little river is that which we mentioned in the former part of this Journal, as having communication with the Atha-pufcow Lake: but, from appearances, it is of no . confequence whence it takes its rife, or where it empties itfelf, as one half of it is nearly dry three-fourths of the year. The intervening ponds, however, having fufficient depth of water, are, we may fuppofe, favourable fituations for beaver, ! as many of their houfes are to be found in thofe parts.

i On the twenty-fourth, a fl: range Northern In- 24th.

dian leader, called Thlew-fa-nell-ie, and feveral of

February.

272 A JOURNEY TO THE j,2. s followers, joined us from the Eaftvvard. This leader prefented Matonabbee and myfelf with a foot of tobacco each, and a two-quart keg of brandy, which he intended as a prefent for the" Southern Indians; but being informed by my companions, that there was riot the leaft probability of meeting any, he did not think it worth any farther carriage. The tobacco was indeed ve ry acceptable, as our ftock of that article had been expended fome time. Having been fo long without tailing fpirituous- liquors, I would not partake of the brandy, but left it entirely to the Indians, to whom, as they were numerous, it was fcarce-ly a tafte for each. Few of the Northern Indians are fond of fpirits, efpccially thofe vho keep at a diftance from the Fort: fome who are near, and who ufually ftioot geefe for us in the Spring, will drink it at free coft as faft as the Southern Indians, but few of them are ever fo imprudent as to' buy it.

The little river lately mentioned, as well as the adjacent lakes and ponds, being well-llocked with beaver, and the land abounding with moofe and buffalo, we were induced to make but flow pro-grefs in our journey. Many days were fpent in hunting, feafting, and drying a large quantity of fiefh to take with us, particularly that of the buffalo; for my companions knew by experience, that a few days walk to the Eailward of our prefent fituation would bring us to a part where we ifiould flot fee any of thofe animals.

The ftrangers who had joined us on the twenty-fourth iiitbrmed us, that all were well at Prince of Wales's Fort when tliey left it lail:; which according to their account of the Moons paft fmce, muft have been about the filth of November one thoufand feven hundred and feventy-one. Thcfe ftrangers only remained in our company one night before the Leader and part of his crew left us, and proceeded on their journey to the North Weftward; but a few of them having procured fome furrs in the early part of the Winter, joined our party, with an intent to accompany us to the Fadory.

Having a good fcock of dried meat, fat, 'sfc. prepared in the beft manner for carriage, on the twenty-eighth we Ihaped our courfe in the South Eaft quarter, and proceeded at a much greater rate than we had lately done, as little or no time was now loll in hunting. The next day we faw the tracks of fome ftrangers; and though I did not perceive any of them myfelf, fome of my companions were at the trouble of fearching for them, and finding them to be poor inoffenlivc people, plundered them not only of the few furrs which they had, but took alfo one of their young women from them.

Every additional acl of violence committed by my companions on the poor and diflrefled, ferv-ed to increafe my indignation and diflike; this laft acl, however, dif-pleafed me more than all rl their former actions, becaufe it was committed an a fet of harmlefs creatures, whofe general manner of life renders them the moll fecluded from fociety of any of the human race.

Matonabbee afiured me, that for more than a generation paft one family only, as it may be called, (and to which the young men belonged who were plundered by my companions,) have taken up their Winter abode in thofe woods, which are iituated fo far on the barren ground as to be quite out of the track of any other Indians. From the beft accounts that I could colleft, the latitude of this place muft be about 631, or 63 at leaft; the longitude is very uncertain. From my own experience 1 can affirm, that it is fome hundreds of miles both from the fea-fide and the main woods to the Weftward. Few of the trading Northern Indians have vifited this place; but thofe who have, give a pleaiing defcription of it, all agreeing that it is iituated on the banks of a river which has communication with feveral fine lakes. As the current fets to the North Eaft-ward, it empties Itfelf, in all probability, into fome part of Hudfon's Bay; and, from the latitude, no part feems more likely for this communication, than Baker's Lake, at the head of Che-fterfield's inlet. This, however, is mere conjecture; nor is it of any confequence, as navigation on any of the rivers in thofe parts is not only impracticable, but would be alfo unprofitable, as they do not lead into a country that produces any thing hiiif for trade, or that contains any inhabitants worth vifiting.

The accounts given of this place, and the man- """y-ner of life of its inhabitants, would, if related at. full length, fill a volume: let it fuffice to obferve, "that the fituation is faid to be remarkably favourable for every kind of game that the barren ground produces at the different feafons of the year; but the continuance of the game with them is in general uncertain, except that of fifii and partridges. That being the cafe, the few who compofe this little commonwealth, are, by long cuflom and the conftant example of their forefathers, poffcoed of a provident turn of mindj with a degree of frugality unknown to every other tribe of Indians in this country except the Efquimaux.

Deer is faid to viiit this part of the country in aftonifhing numbers, both in Spring and Autumn, of which circumllances the inhabitant avail themfelves, by killing and drying as much of their 9e(h as poffible, particularly in the fall of the year; fo that they feldom are in want of a good Winter3 flock.

Geefe, ducks, and fwans vifit here in great plenty during their migrations both in the Spring and Fall, and by much art, joined to an infur-mountable patience, are caught in confiderable numbers in fnares, and, without doubt, make

T 2 a very

To fnarc fwans, gecfe, or ducks, ia the water, it requiies no other pracel's 1772. a very pleafing change in the food. It is aifo res. FTbtuir' ported, "though I confefs I doubt the truth of it,) that procefs that to make a number of lieds, or fences, projetft into the water, at right angles, from the banks of a river, lake, or pond; for it is obferv-ed that thole birds genciaily fwim near the margin, for the benefit ot feeding on the grafs, c. Thofe fences are continued for fome dirtance from the fhore, and feparated two or three yards from each other, fo that openings are left fufficiently large to let the birds fwim through. In each of thofe openings a fnare is hung and fattened to a (lake, which the bird when intangled cannot drag from the bottom; and to prevent the fnare from being wafted out of its proper place by ihe wind, it is fecured co the flakes which form tfie opening, with tender gtafs, whicii is eafily broken.

This method, though it has the appearance of being very fimple, is ne-verihelefs attended with much trouble, particularly when we confider the fmallnefs of their canoes, and the great inconveniency they laboui under in performing works of this kind in the water. Many of the flakes ufed on thofe occafions are of a confiderable length and fize, and the fmall branches which form the principal part cf "he ht-dges, are not arranged without much cau ion, for fear of overfetting the canoes, particularly where the water is deep, as it is in fome of the lakes; and in many of the rivers the current is very fwift, which renders this bufinefs equally troublefomc When the lakes and rivers'are fhallow, the natives are frequently at the pains to make fences from ftrore to ihore.

To fnare thofe birds in their nefts requires a confiderable degree of art and, as the natives fay, a-great dealof ckanlinefs; for they have obferved, that when fnares have been fet by thofe whole hands were not clean, the birds would not go into the nefl.

Even the goofc, though fo firrple a bird, is notoiioufly known to fotfake, fcer eggs, if hty were breathed on by the Indians.

The fmallt. fpccies of birds which make their nefl on the ground, are by; no means fo dtlicate, of courfe lefs care is neceflaiy to fnare them. It has-been obferved that all birds which build in the ground go into their nefl at one pirtic;; lar file, and out of it on the oppofite. The Indians, tho-roughlv convinced of this, always fet the fnares on the fide on which the bird enters the nefl; and if caic be taken in fetting them feldom failof fciaing iheir objel. For fmall birds, fuch as laiks, and many others of equal fize, the Indians only ufe two or three haiis out of their head; but for larger birds, particularly fwans, gecfe, and ducks, they make fnares of deer-finews, twifted like packthread, nd occafioaally cf a fmall thong cut from a parchment dser-ikin.

NORTHERN OCEAN, that a remarkable fpecies of partridges as large as Endifli fowls, are found in that part of the country only. Thofe, as well as the common partidges, it is fliid, are killed in confiderable numbers, with fnares, as well as with bows and arrows.

The river and lakes near the little foreft where the family above mentioned had fixed their abodej abound with fine fifli, particularly trout and barbie, which are eafily caught; the former with hooks, and the latter in nets. In facl, 1 have not feen or heard of any part of this country which feems to polfefs half the advantages requifite for a conflant refidence, that are afcribed to this little fpot. The defcendents, however, of the prefent inhabitants muft in time evacuate it for want of wood, which is of fo flow a growth in thofe regions, that what is ufed in one year, exclufive of what is cut down and carried away by theef-quimaux, muft coft many years to replace.

It may probably be thought ftrange that any part of a community, apparently fo commodiou- fly fituated, and happy within themfclves, fliould be found at fo great a diftance from the reft of their tribe, and indeed nothing but necefiity could poflibly have urged them to undertake a journey of fo many hundred miles as they have done; but no fituation is without its incortve-niences, and as their woods contain no birch-trees of fuilicient fize, or perhaps none of any fize.

Februarv.

278 A JOURNEY TO THE 1772. ize, this party had come fo far to the Weftward to procure birch-rind for making two canoes, and feme of the fungus that grows on

the outfide of the birch-tree, which is ufed by all the Indians in thofe parts for tinder. There are two forts of thefe fungufes which grow on the birch-trees one is hard, the ufeful part of which much re-fembles rhubarb; the other is foft and fmooth like velvet on the outfide, and when laid on hot aflies for fome time, and well beaten between two flones, is fomething like fpunk. The former is called by the Northern Indians Jolt-thee, and is known all over the country bordering on Hud-fons Bay by the name of Pefogan, it being fo called by the Southern Indians. The latter is only

The Indians, both Northern and Southern, have found by experience, that by boiling the pefogan in water for a confideiable time, the texture is fomuch improved, that when thoroughly dried, fome parts of it will be nearly as foft as fpunge.

Some of thoft fungufes are as large as a man's head; the outfide, which is very hard and black, and much indented with deep cracks, being of no ufe, is always chopped oit with a hatchet. Befides the two forts of touchwood already mentioned, there is another kind of it in thofe parts, that I think isinfinitely preferable to either. This is found in old decayed poplars, and lies in flakes pf various fizes and thicknefs; fome is not thicker than (hamoy leather, others are as thick as a (hoe-fole. This, like the fungus of the birch-tree, is always moift when taken from the tree, but when dry, i. is very fo t and flexible, and takes fire readily from the fpark of a fteel; but it is much improved by being kept dry in a bag that has contained gunpowder. It is rather furprizing that the Indians, whofe ipode of life I have been defcribing, have never acquired the method of making fire by fridtion, like the Efquimaiix. It is alfo equally fiirptizing they do not make ufe of the fkin-canoes. Probably deer-flcins cannot be ijianufadtured to withfiand the water; for it is well known that the Efqui-iraux ufe always feal-fkins for that purpofe, though they are in the habit Oi killing great numbers of deer.

only ufed by the Northern tribes, and is called 1772. by them Clalte-ad-dee.

By the firft of March we began to leave the fine level country of the Athapufcows, and again to approach the flony mountains or hills which bound the Northern Indian country. Moofe and beaver ftill continued to be plentiful; but no buffaloes could be feen after the twenty-ninth of February.

As we were continuing our courfe to the Eaft South Eaft, on the fourteenth we difcovered the ntb. tracks of more ftrangers, and the next day came up with them. Among thofe Indians was the man who had carried a letter for me in March one thoufand feven hundred and feventy-one, to the Chief at Prince of Wales's Fort, and to which he had brought an anfwer, dated the twenty-firft of June. When this Indian received the letter from me, it was very uncertain what route we fliould take in our return from the Copper River, and, in all probability, he himfelf had not then determined on what fpot he would pafs the prefent winter; confequently our meeting each other was merely accidental.

Thefe Indians having obtained a few furrs in the courfe of the Winter, joined our party, which now confifted of twenty tents, containing in the whole about two hundred perfons; and indeed our company had not been much lefs during the lyhofe winter.

From

From the ftrangers who laft joined us we re-?; ceived fome ready-dreffed moofe-ikins for tenting and (hoe leather; alfo fome other (Idns for clothing, for all of which the Chief at the Fadory was to pay on our arrival.

I cannot fufhciently lament the lofs of my quadrant, as the want of it muft render the courfe of my journey from Point Lake, where it was broken, very uncertain; and my warch Hopping while 1 was at the Athapufcow Lake, has contributed greatly to the misfortune, as i am now deprived of every means of eftimating the diftances which we walked wiih any degree of accuracy, particularly in thick weather, when the Sun could not be feeuo ih. ls Indians were employed at all convenient times in procuring birch-rind and making wood work ready for building canoes; aifb in preparing fmall flaffs of birch-wood, to take with them on the barren ground, to ferve as tent-poles all, the Summer; and which, as hath been already obferved, they convert into fnow-fhoe frames when the Winter fets in. Here it may be proper to obferve, that none of thofe incidental avocations interfere with, or retard the Indians in their journey; for they always take the advantage of every opportunity which offers, as they pafs along, and when they fee a tree fit for their purpofe, cut it down, and either ftrip off the bark, if that be what they want, or fplit the trunk in pieces; and after hewing it roughly with their hatchet, carry it to the tent, where in the evenings, or in the morning before they fet out, they reduce it with their knives to the fiiape and fize which is required.

Providons being plentiful, and the weather fine, we advanced a little each day; and on the nineteenth took up our lodgings by the lide of,9th. Wholdyeah-chuckd Whoie, or Large Pike Lake. In our way we croffed another fmall lake, where we caught fome trout by angling, and killed a few deer and one moofe.

On the twentieth we croffed Large Pike Lake, 20th. which at that part was not more than feven miles wide; but from North North Weft to the South South Eaft is much longer. The next day we arrived at Bedodid Lake, which in general is not more than three miles wide, and in feveral places much lefs; but it is upviard of forty miles long, which gives it the appearance of a river. It is faid by the Indians to be (hut up on all fides, and entirely furrounded with high land, which produces vaft quantity of fir trees, but none of them grow to a great height in thofe parts: their branches, however, fpread wider than thofe of firs of three times their height and thicknefs do in Europe; fo that they refemble an apple-tree in ihape, m. ore than any fpecies of the pine. They iccm rich in tar, as the wood of them will burn like a candle, and emit as flrong a fmell, and as much black fmoke, as the ftaves of an old tar-barrel J barrel; for which reafon no Indians chufe to burn it in their tents, or even out of doors, for the piarpofe of cooking their victuals.

The thaws began now to be very confiderable, and the under-woods were fo thick in thefe parts as to render travelling through them very difficult; we therefore took the advantage of walking on the ice of the above-mentioned Lake, which lay nearly in the direction of our courfe j but after proceeding about twenty-two miles on it, the Lake turned more toward the North, on which account we were obliged to leave it, ftrik-ing oflpto the Eaftward; and after walking fourteen miles farther, we arrived at Noo-flietht Whole, or the Hilmfland Lake, fo called from a very high ifland which ftands in it.

From the twenty-eighth to the thirty-firft of March, we had fo hard a gale of wind from the South, as to render walking on lakes or open plains quite impoffible, and the violence witl which the trees were blown down made walking in the woods fomewhat dangerous; but though feverai had narrow efcapes, no accident happened.

From the middle to the latter end of March, Ap, u. and in the beginning of April, though the thaw was not general, yet in the middle of the day it was very confiderable: it commonly froze hard in the nights; and the young men took the advantage of the mornings, when the fnow was Jiard crufled over, and ran down many raoofe; irt.

NORTHERN OCEAN, fbr in thofe fituations a man with a good pair of fnow-flioes will fcarcely make any imprefllon on the fnow, while the moofe, and even the deer, will break through it at every ftep up to the bel-ly. Notwithftanding this, however, it is very feldom that the Indians attempt to run deer down. The moofe are fo tender-footed, and fo fliort-wmdsd, that a good runner will generally tire them in lefs than a day, and very frequently in fix or eight hours; though I have known fome of the Indians continue the chace for two days, before they could come up with, and kill the game. On thofe occafions the Indians, in general, only take with them a knife or bayonet, and a little bag containing a fet of fire-tackle, and are as lightly clothed as poffible; fome of them will carry a bow and two or three arrows, but I never knew any of them take a gun unlefs fuch as had been blown or burfted, and the barrels cut quite fliort, which, when reduced to the leaft poffible lize to be capable of doing any fervice, muft be too great a weight for a man to run with HI his hand for ih many hours together.

When the poor moofe are incapable of making farther fpeed, they ftand and keep their purfuers at bay with their head and fore-feet; in the ufe of which they are very dexterous, efpecially the latter; fo that the Indians who have neither a bow nor arrows, nor a fliort gun, with them, are ge-nerally obliged to lafli their knives or bayonets to the end of a long flick, and ftab the moofe at a diftance.

a diflance. For want of this neceftary precaution, feme of the boys and fool-hardy young men, who have attempted to ru(h in upon them, have frequently received fuch unlucky blows from their fore-feet, as to render their recover very doubtful.

The flefh of the moofe, thus killed, is far from being well-tafted, and 1 fhould think mufl be very unwholefome, from being over-heated; as by running fo many hours together, the animal mufl: have been in a violent fever; the fleh being foft and clammy, muft have a very difa-greeable tafte, neither refembling fiih, ilefli, nor fowl.

The Southern Indians ufe dogs for this kind of bunting, which makes it eafier and more expeditious; but the Northern tribes having no dogs trained to that exercife, are under the neceltity of doing it themfelves. On the feventh we croited a part of Thee-lee- aza River: at which time the fmall Northern deer were remarkably plentiful, but the moofe began to be very fcarce, as none were killed after the third.

Though I was a fwift runner in thofe days, I never accompanied the Indians in one of thofe chaces, but have heard many of them fay, that after a long one, the mooje, when killed, did rot produce more thafi a quart of blood, the remainder being all fettled in the flefli; which, in that ftate, muft be ten times worfe tafted, than the fpleen or milt of a bacon hog.

On the twelfth, we faw feveral fwans. flying to the Northward; tliey were the firft birds of paffage we had feen that Spring, except a icw fnow-birds, which always precede the migrating birds, and confequently are with much propriety called the harbingers of Spring. The fwans al-fo precede all the other fpecies of water-fowl, and migrate fo early in the ieafon, that they find no open water but at the falls of rivers, where they are readily met, and fometimes fiiot, in confide-rable numbers.

On the fourteenth, we arrived at another part 14th of Theelee-aza River, and pitched our tents not far from fome families of ftrange Northern Indians, who had been there fome time fnaring deer, and who were all fo poor as not to have one gun amons: them.

The villains belonging to my crew were fo far from adminiftering to their relief, that they robbed them of almoft every ufeful article in their poflefiion; and to complete their cruelty, the men joined themfelves in parties of fix, eight, or ten in a gang, and dragged feveral of their young women to a little diilance from their tents, where they not only ravifhed them, but otherwife ill-treated them, and that in fo barbarous a manner, as to endanger the lives of one or two of them. Humanity on this, as well as on feveral other iimilar occafions during my refidcnce among thofe wretches, prompted me to upbraid them with with their barbarity; but fo far were my remon. ftrances from having the delired effedl, that they afterwards made no fcruple of telling me in the plaineft terms that if any female relation of mine had been there, Ihe fliould have been ferved in the fame manner.

Deer being plentiful, we remained at this place ten days, in order to dry and prepare a quantity of the flefh and fat to carry with us; as this was the laft time the Indians expected to fee fuch plenty until they met them again on the barren ground. During our ftay here, the Indians completed the wood-work for their canoes, and procured all their Summer tent-poles, c; and while we were employed in this neceffary bufmefs, the thaw was fo great that the bare ground began to appear in many places, and the ice in the rivers, where the water was (hallow and the current rapid, began to break up; fo that we were in daily exped: ation of feeing geefe, ducks and other birds of paffage.

On the twenty-fifth, the weather, being cool and favourable for travelling, we once more fet out, and that day walked twenty miles to the Eaftward; as fome of the women had not joined us, we did not move on the two following days.

On the twenty-eighth, having once more muf-tered all our forces, early in the morning we fet out, and the next day paffed by Thleweyaza Yeth, 25th.

asth,.

the place at which we had prepared wood-work for canoes in the Spring one thoufand fcven hundred and feventy-one.

As the mornin? of the firft of May was ex- ay ceedingly fine and pleafant, with a light air from the South, and a great thaw, we walked eight or nine miles to the Eaft by North, when a heavy fall of fnow came on, which was followed, or indeed more properly accompanied, by a hard gale of wind from the north Weft. At tie time the bad weather began, we were on the top of a high barren hill, a confiderable diftance from any woods; judging it to be no more than a fquall, we fat down, in expectation of its foori paffing by. As the night, however, advanced, the gale increafed to fuch a degree, that it was impoflible for a man to ftand upright; fo that we were obliged to lie down, without any other defence againft the weather, than putting our fledges and other lumber to windward of us, which in reality was of no real fervice, as it only harboured a great drift of fnow, with which in fome places we were covered to the depth of two or three feet; and as the night was not very cold, I found myfelf, and many others who were with me, long before morning in a puddle of water, occafioned by the heat of our bodies melting the fnow.

The fecond proved fine pleafant weather, with ti. warm funfhine. In the morning, having dried

A JOURNEY TO THE ail our clothing, we proceeded on our journey. In the afternoon we arrived at the part at which my guide intended we fhould build our canoes j but having had Ibme difference with his countrymen, he altered his nniind, and determined to proceed to the Eaftward, as long as the feafon would permit, before he attempted to perform that duty. 3d. Accordingly, on the third, we purfued our way, and as that and the following day were very cold, which made us walk brilkly, we were enabled to make good days' journies; but the fifth was fo hot and fultry, that wc only walked about thirteen miles in our old courfe to the Eaft by North, and then halted about three-quarters of a mile to the South of Black Bear Hill; a place which I had feen in the Spring of one thoufand feven hundred and feventy-one.

On the fixth, the weather was equally hot with the preceding day; in the morning, however, we moved on eleven miles to the Eaft, and then met fcveral ftrange Indians, who informed us that a few others, who had a tolerable cargo of furrs, and were going to the Fadory that Summer, were not far diftant.

On receiving this intelligence, my guide, Ma-tonabbee, fent a meflenger to delire their company. This was foon complied with, as it is an univerfal practice with the Indian Leaders, both Northern and Southern, when going to the company's Factory, to ufe their influence and inte- reft reft in convafling for companions; as they find by experience that a large gang gains them much refpecl. Indeed, the generality of Europeans who reiide in thofe parts, being utterly unacquainted with the manners and cuftoms of the In-dians, have conceived fo high an opinion of thofe Leaders, and their authority, as to imagine that all who accompany them on thofe occafions are entirely devoted to their fervice and command all the year; but this is fo far from being the cafe, that the authority of thofe great men, when abfent from the Company's Fadory, never extends beyond their own family, and the trifling refpect which is (hown them by their countrymen during their refidence at the Factory, proceeds only from motives of interell.

The Leaders have a very difagreeable talk to perform on thofe occafions; for they are not only obliged to be the mouth-piece, but the beggars for all their friends and relations for whom they have a regard, as well as for thofe whom at other times they have reafon to fear. Thofe unwelcome commiflions, which are impofed on them by their followers, joined to their own defire of being thought men of great confequence and in-tereft with the Englifli, make them very trou–blefome. And if a Governor deny them any thing which they afk, though it be only to give away to the moft worthlefs of their gang, they immediately turn fulky and impertinent to the higheft degree j and however rational they may ; j5 A JOURNEY TO THE

Yn'n. Other times, are immediately divefted of w J every degree of reafon, and raife their demands ' to fo exorbitant a pitch, that after they have re- ceived to the amount of five times the value of all the furrs they themfelves have brought, they never ceafe begging during their ftay at the Factory; and, after all, few of them go away thoroughly fatisfied.

After

As a pmof of this aitartion I take the liberty, thovgb a little foreign to the narrative of my journey, to infert one inflance, out of many hun Jr. eds of the kind that happen at the difierdt Faflories in Hudfon's Bay, but perhaps np where fo frequently as at Churchill. In Oifober 177, my oid guide, Matonabbee, came at the head cf a large gang of Northern Indians, to tiade at Prince of Wales's Fort; at vhich time I had the honour to command it. When the ufual ceremonies had peffed, I drefied hijm out as a Captain of the firft rank, and alio clothed his fix wives from top to toe: after which, that is to fay, during his ftay at the Faflory, which vas ten nays, he begged feven lieutenants' coats fifteen cotnmon coafs, eighteen hats, eighteen fliiits, eight guns, one hundred ad forty povnds weight of gunpowder, with (hot, ball, and flints in proportion; together with many hatchets, icechiffels, files, bayonets, knives, and a great quantity of tobacco, cloth, blankets, combs, Isokingi-glaffes, ftockings, handkerchiefs, c. befides numljetlefs finall articles, fuch as awls, needles, pait, fleels, c. in all to the amount of upwards of feven hundred beaver in the way of trade, to give awayamong his followers. This wasexclufiwe of his pwn prefent, which confifted of a variety of goods to the vlue of fpu;- Jvufl. dred beaver more. But the moft extraordinary of hisdernandswas twelve. pounds of powder, twenty-tight pounds of ftot and ball, four pounds of tobacco, fcxne articles of clothing, and feve-ral pieces of iron. voic Ct to give to two men who had hauled his tent and othr luipber the preceding Winter. This demand was lb very unreafonable, that I made fome fcruple, or at icft hefitated to comply with it, hinting that he was the person who ont to ftisfy thoc; men for thei;-fefyices; but I was foon V fwered, That he did npt expeft to have been deniedfach a trifle as that noasi and for the future he would cany his goods where he could get his own price for them. On my alking him where that was. he replisd, in a very infolent tone, "To the Canadian Traders." I was glad to comply with his demands; and I here infert the anecdote, as a fpecimen of an Indian's confcience.

May,

NORTHERN OCEAN. 291

After flopping four days at this place, Mato- 1772. nabbee, and all the Indians who were to acconi- pany me to the Fort, agreed to leave the elderly people and young children here, in the care of fome Indians who were capable of providing for them, and who had orders to proceed to a place called Cathawhachaga, on the barren grounds, and there wait the return of their relations from the Factory. Matters of this kind being fettled, apparently to the entire fatisfalion of all parties, we rcfumed our journey on the eleventh of May, jj, and that at a much brifker pace than we could probably have done when ail the old people and young children were with us. In the afternoon of the fame day we met fome other Northern Indians, who were alfo going to the Fort with furrs; thofe joined our party, and at night we all pitched our tents by the fide of a river that empties itfelf into Doo-baunt Lake. This day all of us threw away our fnow-fhoes, as the ground was fo bare in mod places as not to require any fuch alliftance; but fledges were occa-iionally ferviceable for fome time, particularly when we walked on the ice of rivers or lakes.

The weather on the twelfth was fo exceedingly hot and fultry, and the water fo deep on the top of the ice of the above-mentioned river, as to render walking on it not only very troublefome, but dangerous; fo after advancing about five miles we pitched our tents, and the warm weather being hkeiy to continue, th Indians immedi-

U 2 ately

May.

A JOURNEY TO THE ately began to build their canoes, which were completed with fuch expedition, that in theafter- istii, noon of the eighteenth we again fet forward on our journey, but the day being pretty far fpent, we only walked about four miles, and put up for the night.

9ti- The morning of the nineteenth was fme plea-fant weather; and as all the water was drained off from the top of the ice, it rendered walking on it both fafeand eafy; accordingly we fet out pretty early, and that day walked upwards of twenty miles to the Eaft North Eaft on the above-mentioned river. The next day proved fo cold, that after v. alking about fifteen miles, we were obliged to put up; for having left Doo-baunt River, we were frequently obliged to wade above the knees through fwamps of mud, water, and wet fnow; which froze to our ftockings and fhoes in fuch a thick cruft, as not only rendered walking very laborious, but at the fame time fub-jecled us to the danger of having our legs and feet frozen.

2, ft. The weather on the twenty-firft was more fe-vere than on the preceding day; but the fwamps and ponds being by that time frozen over, it was tolerable walking: we proceeded therefore on our journey, but the wind blew fo frefii, that we had not walked fixteen miles, before we found that thofe who carried the canoes could not pof-fibly keep lip with us, fo that we put up for this'night. In the courfe of this day's journey we croflted the North Weft Bay of Wholdyahd 1772. Lake; which, at that part, is called by the Nor- gt" thern Indians A Naw-nee thad Whoie. Ihis day feveral of the Indians turned back, not being able to proceed for want of provifions. Game of all kinds indeed were fo fcarce, that, except a few geefe, nothing had been killed by any of our party, from our leaving the women and children on the eleventh inftant, nor had we feen one deer the whole way.

The twenty-fecond proved more moderate, azd. when all our party having joined, we again advanced to the North Eaft, and after walking about hirteen miles, the Indians killed four deer. Our. umber, however, had now fo increafed, that)ur fmall Northern deer w-ould fcarcely afford us all a fingle meal.

The next day we continued our journey, ge- j nerally walking in the North Eaft quarter; and on the twenty-fifth, crofted the North bay of ii-They-hole-kyed Whoie, or Snow-bird Lake; and at night got clear of all woods, and lay on the barren ground. The fame day feveral of the Indians ftruck off another way, not being able to proceed to the Fort for want of ammunition. As we had for fome days paft made good jour-nies, and at the fame time were all heavy-laden, and in great diftrefs for provifions, fome of my companions were fo weak as to be obliged to leave their bundles of furrs; and many others

All the fiirrs thus left were properly fecured in caves and crcviii s ot others were fo reduced as to be no longer capable of proceeding with us, having neither guns nor ammunition; fo that their whole dependence for fupport was on the fifh they might be able to catch; and though fifh was pretty plentiful in moft of the rivers and lakes hereabout, yet they were not always to be depended on for fuch an immediate fupply of food as thofe poor people required.

Thouffh I had at this time a fufficient ftock of ammunition to ferve me and all my proper companions to the Fort, yet feif-prefervation being the firft law of Nature, it was thought advifable to referve the greateft part of it for our own ufej efpecially as geefe and other fmaller birds were the only game now to be met with, and which, in times of fcarcity, bears hard on the articles of powder and fhot. Indeed moft of the Indians who actually accompanied me the whole way to the Fadory had fome little ammunition remaining, which enabled them to travel in times of real fcarcity better than thofe whom we left behind; and though we affifted many of them, yet feveral of their women died for want. It is a melancholy truth, and a difgrace to the little humanity of which thofe people are poffeffed, to think, that in times of want the poor women always the rocks, fo as to withftand any attempt that might be made on them by hearts of prey, and were well ihielded from the weather; 6 that, in all probability, few of them were loih

May.

NORTHERN OCEAN.

always come offfhort; and when real diflrefs approaches, many of thenn are per-mitted to llarve, when the males are amply provided for.

The twenty-fixth was fine and pleafant. In the a-mornincr we let out as ufual, and after walkinsr about five miles, the Indians killed three deer j a our numbers were greatly leitened, thefe ferv-ed us for two or three meals, at a fmall expence of ammunition.

In continuing our courfe to the Eaftward, we-cfoffed Cathawhachaga River, on the thirtieth of May, on the ice, which broke up foon after the laft perfon had crofted it. We had not been long on the Eaft fide of the river before we perceived bad weather near at hand, and began to make every preparation for it which our fituation would admit; and that was but very indifferent, being on entire barren ground. It is true, we had complete fets of Summer tent-poles, and fuch tent-cloths as are generally ufcd by the Northern Indians in that feafon; thefe were arranged in the bell: manner, and in fuch places as were moft likely to afford us fhelter from the threatening ftorm. The raiu foon began to defcend in fuch torrents as to make the river overflow to fuch a degree as foon to convert our firft place of retreat into an open fea, and oblige us in the middle of the night to af-femble at the top of an adjacent hill, where the violence of the wind would not permit us to piich a tent; fo that the only fhelter we could obtain was to take the tenkloth about our ihouldcrs

May.

296 A JOURNEY TO THE and lit with our backs to the wind; and in this fituation we were obliged to remain without the leaft refreftment, till the morning of the Tnne third of Junc: in the courfe of which time the 3- wind fhifted all round the compafs, but the bad weather ftill continued, fo that we were con-ftantly obliged to fhift our pofition as the wind changed.

The weather now became more moderate, though there was flill a frefh gale from the North Weft, with hard froft and frequent fhowers of " fnow. Early in the morning, however, we proceeded on our journey, but the wet and cold I had experienced the two preceding days fo benumbed my lower extremities, as to render walking for fome time very troublefome. In the courfe of this day's journey we faw great numbers of geefe flying to the Southward, a few of which we killed; but thefe were very difpropor-tionate to the number of mouths we had to feed, and to make up for our long fafting. 8th. From that time to the eighth we killed every day as many geefe as were fufficient to perferve life; but on that day we perceived plenty of deer, fve of which the Indians killed, which put us all into good fpirits, and the number of deer we- then faw afforded great hopes of more plentiful times during the remainder of our journey. It. is almoft needlefs to add, that people in our di-ilreffed fituation expended a little time i. n eating, and flicing fome of the iiefh ready for drying; but the drying it occafioned no delay, as we fa-ftened it on the tops of the women's bundles, and dried it by the fun and wind while we were walking; and, ftrange as it may appear, meat thus prepared is not only very fubllantial food, but pleafant to the tafte, and generally much efteemed by the natives. For my own part I muft acknowledge, that it was not only agreeable to my palate, but after eating a meal of it, I have always found that I could travel longer without victuals, than after any other kind of food. All the dried meat prepared by the Southern Indians is performed by expofmg it to the heat of a large fire, which foon exhaufts all the fine juices from it, and when fufficiently dry to prevent putrefaction, is no more to be compared with that cured by the Northern Indians in the Sun, or by the heat of a very flow fire, than meat that has been boiled down for the fake of the foup, is to that which is only fufficiently boiled for eating: the latter has all the juices remaining, which, being eafily diffolved by the heat and moifture of the flomach, proves aftrong and nourifliing food; whereas the former being entirely deprived of thofe qualities, can by no means have an equal claim to that charafter. Mofl of the Europeans, however, are fonder of it than they are of that cured by the Northern Indians. The fame may be faid to the lean parts of the beail, which are firfl dried, and then reduced into a kind of powder. That done by the Northern

A JOUPKEY TO TEfe thern Indians is entirely free froki fmoke, and quite foft and mellow in the mouth; whereas that which is prepared by the Southern tribes is generally as bitter as foot with fmoke, and is as hard as the fcraps of horn, c. which are burnt to make hardening for the cutlers. I never knew, that any European was fo fond of this as they, are of that made by the Northera Indians.

On the ninth, as we were continuing our courfe to the Factory, which then lay in the South Eaft quarter, we faw feveral fmokes to the North Eaft, and the fame day fpoke with many Northern Indians, who were going to Knapp's Bay to meet the Churchill floop. Several of thofe Indians had furrs with them, but having fome time before taken up goods on truft at Prince of Wales's Fort, were taking that method to delay the payment of them. Defrauds of this kind have been pra6lifed by many of thofe people with great fuccefs, ever fmce the furr-trade has been eftabliflied with the Northern Indians at Knapp's Bay; by which means debts to a confiderable amount are annually loft to the Company, as well as their Governor in the Bay.

Being defirous of improving every opportunity that the line weather afforded, we did not lofe much time in converfation with thofe Indians, but proceeded on our couife to the South Eaft, while they continued theirs to the North Eaft.

For many days after leaving thofe people, we had the good fortune to meet with plenty of pro-vifions; and as the weather was for a long time remarkably fine and pleafant, our circumftances were altered fo much for the better, that every thing feemed to contribute to our happinefs, as if defirous to make fome amends for the fevere hunger, cold, and exceflive hardfliips that we had fuffered long before, and which had reduced us to the greatcft mifery and want.

Deer was fo plentiful great part of the way, that the Indians killed as many as were wanted, without going out of their road; and every lake and river to which we came feemed willing to give us a change of diet, by affording us plenty of the fineft fifti, which we caught either with hooks or nets. Gecfe, partridges, gulls, and many other fowls, which are excellent eating, were alfo in fuch plenty, that it only required ammunition, in fkilful hands, to have procured as many of them as we could defire.

The only inconvenience we now felt was from frequent (bowers of heavy rain; but the intervals between thefe Ihowers being very warm, and the Sun Ihining bright, that difficulty was eaiiiy overcome, efpecially as the belly was plentifully fupplied with excellent victuals. Indeed the very thoughts of being once more arrived fo near home, made me capable of encountering every difficulty, even if it had been hunger itfelf in the moft formidable fhape.

joo A JOURNEY TO THE 1772. On the eighteenth we arrived at Egg River, "-from which place, at the folicitation of my guide

June. r.

lath. Matonabbee, I fent a letter poft-hafte to the Chief at Prince of Wales's Fort, adviling him of my being fo far advanced on my return. The weather at this time was very bad and rainy, which caufed us to lofe near a whole day; but upon the fine weather returning, we again proceeded at our ufual rate of eighteen or twenty miles a day, fometimes more or lefs, according as the road, the weather, and other circumftances, would admit.

Deer now began to be not quite fo plentiful as they had been, though we met with enough for prefent ufe, which was all we wanted, each per-fon having as much dried meat as he could con- veniently carry, befides his furrs and other necef-fary baggage.

2gj, Early in the morning of the twenty-fixth we arrived at Seal River; but the wind blowing right up it, made fo great a fea, that we were obliged

Mr. Jeremie is very fncorrea in his account of the fituation of this River, and its courfe. It is not eafy to guefs, whether the Copper or Dog-ribbed Indians be the nation he calls Platfcotez de Chiens: if it be the forirei-, he is much miflaken; for they have abundance of beaver, and other animals of the furr kind, in their country: and if the latter, he is equally wrong to affeit that they have copper-mines in their country; for neither copper nor any other kind of metal is in ufe among them,

Mr, Jeren-iie was not too moded when he faid, (fee Dobb's Account of Hudfon's bay, p. 19.) "he could not fay any thing pofitivcly ingoing farther

June.

obliged to wait near ten hours before we could 1772. venture to crofs it in our little canoes. In the after- farther" North;" for in my opinion he never was To far North or Weflas he pretends, othervifc he would have been more corres in his defcr. pti-on of thole parts.

The Strait he mentions is undoubtedly no other tliaii what is now called Chefter-field's Inlet, which, in fome late and cold feafons, it not dear of ice the whole Summer: for I will affirm, that no Indian, either Northern or Southern, ever faw cither Wager Water or Repiilfe Bay, except, the two men who accompanied Captain Middleton; and though thofe men were feleifted from fome hundiedsfor their univerlal knowledge of thofe parts, yet they knew nothing of the coafl fo far North as Marble Jfland.

As a farther proof, that no Indians, except the Efquimaux, ever fre-. quent fuch high latitudes, unlefs at a great didance from the fca, I muft here mention, that fo late as the year 1763, when Captain Chriftopher went to furvcy Cheferfi=ld's Inlet, though he was furnilhed with the moft intelligent and experienced Northern Indians that could be found, they did not know an inch of the land to the North of Whale Cove.

Mr. Jer; mie is alb as much miflaken in what he fays concerning Chaichill River, as he was in the direifiion of Seal River; for he fays that no woods were found but in fome iflands which lie about ten or twelve miles up the river. At the time he wrote, which was long before a fet-tlemcnt was made there, wood was in great plenty on both fides the river; and that within five miles of where Prince of Wales's Fort now flands. But as: o the iflands of which he fpeaks, if they ever exiftedj they have of late years mofl afluredly difappeared; for fince the Company have had a fettlement on that liver, no one ever faw an iilanj in it that produced timber, or wood of any dcfcription, within forty miles of the Fort. But the great number of flumps now remaining, from which, in all probability, the trees have been cut for firing, are fufficient to prove that when Churchill River was firfl- fettled, wood was then in great plenty; but in the courfe of feventy-fix years refidence in one place, it is natural to fuppofe it was much thinned near the Settlement. Indted for fome years pad common feel is fo fcarce near that Factory, that it is the chief employment of molt of the fervants for upward of feven months in the year, to procure as much wood as will fupply the fires for a Winter, and a. little timber for neceflary repairs.

afternoon the weather grew more moderate, fo that we were enabled to ferry over the river; after which we refumed our journey, and at night pitched our tents in fome tufts of willows in fight of the woods of Po-co-thee-kis-co River, at which we arrived early in the morning of the twenty-eighth; but the wind again blowing very hard in the North Eaft quarter, it was the after-9th. noon of the twenty-ninth before we could attempt to crofs it.

Juft at the time we were crofling the South branch of Po-co-thee-kis-co River, the Indians that vere fent from Egg River with a letter to the Chief at Churchill, joined us on their return, and brought a little tobacco and fome other articles which I had defired. Though it was late in the afternoon before we had all croffed the river, yet we walked that evening till after ten o'clock, and then put up on one of the Goofe-hunting Iflands, as they are generally called, about ten miles from the Faftory. The next morning I arrived in good health at Prince of Wales's Fort, after having been abfent eighteen months and twenty-three days on this laft expedition; but from my iirft fetting out with Captain Chawchinaha, it was two years feven months and twenty-four days.

Though my difcoveries are not likely to prove of any material advantage to the Nation at large, or indeed to the Hudfon's Bay Company, yet I have the pleafure to think that I have fully complied

June.

A JOURNEY TO THE plied with the orders of my Mafters, and that it 1772. has put a final end to all difputes, concerning a North Weft Paffage through Hudfons Bay. It will alfo wipe off, in fome meafure, the ill-grounded and unjuft afperfions of Dobbs, Ellis, Robfon, and the American Traveller; who have all taken much pains to condemn the conduct of the Hud-fon's Bay Company, as being averfe from difcove-rics, and frpm enlarging their trade.

CHAP.

A lhort Defcription of the Northern Indians, alfo a farther Account of their Country, Manufactures, Cuftoms, Iffc.

An account of the perforis and tempers of the Norther, Indians. They pojfefs a great deal of art and cunning. Are very guilty of fraud when in their power, and generally exa6l more for their furrs than any other tribe of Indians. Always diffatisfied yet have their good qualities. The men in general jea bus of their wives. Their marriages. Girls always betrothed when children and their reafonsfor it. Great care and confinement of young girls from the age of eight or nine years old. Divorces common among thofe people. The wo7nen are lefs prolific than in warmer countries. Remarkable piece of fuperftition obfervsd by the women at particular periods. Their art in making it an excufefor a temporary feparation from their hufbands on any Utile quarrel. Reckoned very unclean on thofe occafi-ons. The Northern Indians frequently for the want of firing, are obliged to eat their meat raw.-Some through necejfity obliged to boil it in veffels made of the rind of the birch-tree. A remarkable difh among thofe people. The young animals always cut out of their dams eaten, and accounted a great delicacy. The parts of generation of all animals eat by the men and hoys. Manner of pajjtng their tune, and method of killing deer in Summer ivith bows and arrows Their tents, dogs, Jledges, he. Snowfooes. Their partiality to domejlic vermin. Vtmoft extent of the Northern hidian country. Face cf the country. Species of fijh. A peculiar kind of mofs ufeful for the fupport of man. Northern Indian method of catching ffly, either with hooks or nets, Ceremony obferved when two parties of thofe people meet. Diverfions in common ufe. Afingular diforder which attacks fame of thofe people. Their fuperftition with refped to the death of their friends. Ceremony obferved on thofe occafi ons. Their ideas ofthefirjl inhabitantsoj the world. No formof religion among them. Remarks on that circumjlance. The extreme mifery to which old o. ge is expo fed. Their opinion of the Aurora Borealis, kc. So? ie account of?Iatonabbee, and his fervi-ces to his country, as well as to the Hudfon's Bay company.

S to the perfons of the Northern Indians, they are in general above the middle fizc; well-proportioned, ftrong, and rcbuft, but not corpulent. They do not pofitefs that activity oi-body, and livelinefs of difpofition, which are fo-commonly met with among the other tribes of Indians who inhabit the Weft coaft of Hudfon's Bay.

Their complexion is fomewhat of the copper caft, inclining rather toward a dingy brown; and their hair, Hke all the other tribes in India, is black, ftrong, and ftraight. Few of the men have any beard j this feldom makes its appearance till they are arrived at middle-age, and then is by no means equal in quantity to what is ob-ferved on the faces of the generality of Europeans J the little they have, however, is exceedingly flrong and briftly. Some of them take but little pains to eradicate their beards, though it is confidered as very unbecoming; and thofe who do, have no other method than that of pulling it out by the roots between their fingers and the edge of a blunt knife. Neither fex have any hair under their armpits, and very little on any other part of the body, particularly the women; but on the place where Nature plants the hair, I never knew them attempt to eradicate it.

Their features are peculiar, and different from any other tribe in thofe parts; for they have very low foreheads, fmall eyes, high cheek-bones, Roman nofes, full cheeks, and in general long broad chins. Though few of either fex are exempt from this national fet of features, yet Nature feems to be more flrid in her obfervance of it among the females, as they feldom vary fo much as the men. Their Ikins are foft, fmooth, and poliqied; and when they are drefted in clean clothing, I have feen fcvcrai of the Southern Iiuiian n-. en who were near fix feet high, preferve a fingle lock of their hair, that, when let down, would trail on the ground as they walked. This, howeverjjis but feldom feen; an4, fome have fufpefted it to be falfe: but I have examined the hair of feveral of thtm and found it to le real, , clothing, they are as free from an offenfive fmell as any of the human race.

Every tribe of Northern Indians, as well as the Copper and Dog-ribbed Indians, have three or four parallel black ftrokes marked on each cheek; which is performed by entering an awl or needle under the fkin, and, on drawing it out again, immediately rubbing powdered charcoal intoth wound.

Their difpolitions are in general morofe and covetous, and they feem to be entirely unacquainted even with the name of gratitude. They are for ever pleading poverty, even among them-felves; and when they vifit the Factory, there i not one of them who has not a thoufand wants.

When any real diftrelted objects prefent thcm-fclves at the Company's Factory, they are always relieved with viduals, clothes, medicines, and every other necefiary, gratis; and in return, they inftruct every one of their countrymen how to behave, in order to obtain the fame charity. Thus it is very common to fee both men and wom. en come to the Fort half-naked, when either the fevere cold in Winter, or the extreme troublefomenefs of the flies in Summer, make it nc-ceftary for every part to be covered. On thof? occafinns they are feldom at a lofs for a plaufible iftory, which they relate as the occafion of theic diftrefs, (whether real or pretended,) and never . fail to interlard their hiflory with plenty of fighs, groans, and tears, fometimes affecting to be lame, and even blind, in order to excite pity. Indeed, I know of no people that have more command of their pallions on fuch occafions; and in thofe re-fpeds the women exceed the men, as I can affirm with truth I have feen fome of them with one fide of the face bathed in tears, while the other has exhibited a fignificant fmile. Falfe pretences fbr obtaining charity are fo common among thofe people, and fo often detected, that the Governor is frequently obliged to turn a deaf ear to many who apply for relief; for if he did not, he might give away the whole of the Company's i goods, and by degrees all the Northern tribe would make a trade of begging, inftead of bringing furrs, to purchafe what they want. It may truly be faid, that they poflefs a confiderable degree of deceit, and are very complete adepts in the art of flattery, which they never fpare as long as they find that it conduces to their inte-reft, but not a moment longer. They take care always to feem attached to a new Governor, and flatter his pride, by telling him that they i look up to him as the father of their tribe, onjl whom they can fafely place their dependance; and they never fail to depreciate the generolityii of his predeceltor, however extenfive that mighf have been, however humane or difinterefted his conduct; and if afperfing the old, and flattering the new Governor, has not the delired effect in al reafonable time, they reprefent him as the word of j characters, and tell him to his face that he is on(of the moft cruel of men; that he has no feeling for the diftreltes of their tribe, and that many-have pcriihed for want of proper affiftance, (which, if it be true, is only owing to want of humanity among themfelves,) and then they boaft of having received ten times the favours and prefents from his predeceftor. It is remarkable that thofe are moft lavifli in their praifes, who have never either deferved or received any favours from him. In time, however, this language alfo ceafes, and they are perfectly reconciled to the man whom rhey would willingly have made a fool, and fay, " he " is no child, and not to be deceived by them.

They differ fo much from the reft of mankind, that harfli uncourteous ufage feems to agree bet-ter with the generality of them, particularly the lower clafs, than mild treatment; for if the leaft refpecl be fhown them, it makes them intolerably infolent; and though fome of their leaders may be exempt from this imputation, yet there are but few even of them who have fenfe enough to fet a proper value on the favours and indulgences which are granted to them while they remain at the Companys Factories, or elfewhere within their territories. Experience has convinced me, that by keeping a Northern Indian at a diftance, he may be made ferviceable both to himfelf and the Company; but by giving him the leaft indulgence at the Factory, he will grow indolent, inactive, and troublefome, and only contrive cofitrive methods to tax the gcnerolity of an Eu ropcan.

The greateft part of thefe people never fail to defraud Europeans whenever it is in their power, and take every method to over-reach them in the way of trade. They will difguile their perfans and change their names, in order to defraud them of their lawful debts, which they are fometimes permitted to contract at the Company's Factory; and all debts that arc outftanding at the fuccefiion of a new Governor are entirely loft, as they always declare, and bring plenty of witneltes to prove, that they were paid long before, but that their names had been forgotten to be ftruck out of the book.

Notwithftanding all thofe bad qualities, they are the mildeft tribe of Indians that trade at any of the Company's fettlementsj and as the great-eft part of them are never heated with liquor, are always in their fenfe?, and never proceed to riot, or any violence beyond bad language.

The men are in general very jealous of their wives, and I make no doubt but the fame fpirit reigns among the women; but they are kept fo much in awe of their hufbands, that the liberty of thinking is the greateft privilege they enjoy. The prefence of a Northern Indian man ftrikes a peculiar avc into his wives, as he always altumes the fame authority over them that the mafter ci i a fam. ily in Europe ufually does over his dome-iic lervants.

Their

Their marriages are not attended with any ceremony; all matches are made by the parents, or next of kin. On thofe occafions the women feem to have no choice, but implicitly obey the will of their parents, who always endeavour to marry their daughters to thofe that feem moft likely to be capable of maintaining them, let their age, per-fon, or difpofition be ever fo defpicable.

The girls are always betrothed when children, but never to thofe of equal age, which is doubt-lefs found policy with people in their fituation, where the exiftence of a family depends entirely on the abilities and induftry of a fmgle man. Children, as they juftly obferve, are fo liable to alter in their manners and difpofition, that it is impoflible to judge from the adions of early youth what abilities they may poftefs when they arrive at puberty. For this reafon the girls are often fo difproportionably matched for age, that it is very common to fee men of thirty-live or forty years old have young girls of no more than ten or twelve, and fometimes much younger. From the early age of eight or nine years, they are pro-hibited by cuftom from joining in the moft innocent amufements with children of the oppofite fex; fo that when fitting in their tents, or even when travelling, they are watched and guarded with fuch an unremitting attention as cannot be exceeded by the moft rigid difcipline of an Englifli boarding-fchool. Cuftom, however, and conftant example, make fuch uncommon reftraint and confine- confinement fit light and eafy even on children, whofe tender ages feem better adopted to innocent and cheerful amufements, than to be cooped up by the fide of old women, and conftantly employed in fcraping ikins, mending fhoes, and learning other domeftic duties neceffary in the care of a family.

Notwithftanding thofe uncomm. on reftraints on the young girls, the conduct of their parents is by no means uniform or confiftent with this plan; as they fet no bounds to their converfati-on, but talk before them, and even to them, on the m. ofl indelicate fubjecls. As their ears are accuiiomed to fuch laneuaq-e from their earlieft youth, this has by no means the fame efie5J: on them, it would have on girls born and educated in a civilized country, where every care is taken to prevent their morals from being contaminated by obfcene converfiition. The Southern Indians are ftili lefs delicate in converfation, in the pre-ience of their children.

The women among the Northern Indians are in general more backward than the Southern Indian women; and though it is well known that neither tribe lofe any time, thofe early connections are feldom produftive of children for fome years.

Divorces are pretty common among the Northern Indians; fometimes for incontinency, but more frcvquently for want of what they deem necefiary accomplifhments, or for bad behaviour.

This

This ceremony, in either cafe, conlifts of neither more nor lefs than a good drubbing, and turning the woman out of doors; telling her to go to her paramour, or relations, according to the nature of her crime.

Providence is very kind in caufing thefe people to be lefs prolific than the inhabitants of civilized nations; it is very uncommon to fee one woman have more than five or fix children; and thefe are always born at fuch a diflance from one another, that the youngeft is generally two or three years old before another is brought into the world. Their eafy births, and the ceremonies which take place on thofe occalions, have already been mentioned; 1 fhall therefore only obferve here, that they make no ufe of cradles, like the Southern Indians, but only tie a lump of mofs between their legs, and always carry their children at their backs, next the Ikin, till they are able to walk. Though their method of treating young children is in this refpecl the moft uncouth and awkward I ever faw, there are few among them that can be called deformed, and not one in fifty who is not bow-legged.

There are certain periods at which they never permit the women to abide in the fame tent with their hulbands. At fuch times thev are obliged to make a fmall hovel for themfelves at fome dif-tance from the other tents. As this is an uni-verfal cuftom among all the tribes, it is alfo a piece of policy with the women, upon aiiy difference with with their hufbands, to make that an excufe for a temporary reparation, when, without any ceremony, they creep out (as is their ufual cuftom on thofe occafions) under the eves of that fide of the tent at which they happen to be fitting; for at thofe times they are not permitted to go in or out through the door. This cuftom is fo generally prevalent among the women, that I have frequently known fome of the fulky dames leave their hufoands and tent for four or five days at a time, and repeat the farce twice or thrice in a month, while the poor men have never fufpecled the deceit, or if they have, delicacy on their part has not permitted them to enquire into the matter. I have known Matonabbee's handfome wife, who eloped from him in May one thoufand feven hundred and feventy-one, live thun-nardy, as they call it, (that is alone,) for feveral weeks together, under this pretence; but as a proof he had fome fufpicion, (he was always carefully watched, to prevent her from giving her company to any other man. The Southern Indians arc alfo very delicate in this point; for though they do not force their wives to build a feparate tent, they never lie under the fame clothes during this period. It is, however, equally true, that the young girls, when thofe fymptoms make their firft appearance, generally go a Httle diftance from the other tents for four or five days, and at their return wear a kind of veil or curtain, made of beads, for fome time after, as a mark of modefty; as they are then confidered marriageable, and of courfe are called women, though fome at thofe periods are not more than thirteen, while others at the ae of fifteen or lixteen have been reckon-ed as children, though apparently arrived at nearly their full growth.

On thofe occafions a remarkable piece of fuper-ilitlon prevails among them j women in this fitu-ation are never permitted to walk on the ice of rivers or lakes, or near the part where the men are hunting beaver, or where a fifliing-net is fet, for fear of averting their fuccefs. They are alfo prohibited at thofe times from partaking of the head of any animal, and even from walking in, or crofting the track where the head of a deer, moofe, beaver, and many other animals, have lately been carried, cither on a fledge or on the back. To be guilty of a violation of this cuftom is confidered as of the greateſl importance; be-caufe they firmly believe that it would be a means of preventing the hunter from having an equal fuccefs in his future excurfions.

Thofe poor people live in fuch an inhofpitable part of the globe, that for want of firing they are frequently obliged to eat their viftuals quite raw, particularly in the Summer feafon, while on the barren ground; but early cuftom and frequent neceffity make this practice fo familiar to them, that fo far from finding any inconvenience arife from it, or having the leaft diflike to it, they frequently do it by choice, and particularly in the article article of fifli; for when they do make a pretence of dreffing it, they feldom warm it through. I have frequently made one of a party who has fat round a freih-killed deer, and aflifted in picking the bones quite clean, when I thought that the raw brains and many other parts were exceedingly good; and, however ftrange it may appear, I muft beftow the fame epithet on half-raw fifli: even to this day I give the preference to trout, falmon, and the brown tittemeg, when they are not warm at the bone.

The extreme poverty of thofe Indians in general will not permit one half of them to purchafe brafs kettles from the Company; fo that they are flill under the neceflity of continuing their original mode of boiling their victuals in large upright veltels made of birch-rind. As thofe veflels will not admit of being expofed to the fire, the Indians, to fupply the defed, heat ftones red-hot and put them into the water, which foon occafions it to boil J and by having a conftant fucceffion of hot ftones, they may continue the procefs as long as it is neceffary. This method of cooking, though very expeditious, is attended with one great evil; the victuals which are thus prepared are full of fand: for the ftones thus heated, and then immerged in the water, are not only liable to Oliver to pieces, but many of them being of a coarfe gritty nature, fall to a mafs of gravel in the kettle, which cannot be prevented from mixing with the vicliuals which are boiled in it. Be- iides fides this, they have feveral other methods of preparing their food, fuch as roafting it by a firing, broiling it, Iffc, but thefe need on farther defcription.

The moft remarkable difh among them, as well as all the other tribes of Indians in thofe parts, both Northern and Southern, is blood mixed with the half-digefted food which is found in the deer's ftomach or paunch, and boiled up with a fufficient quantity of water, to make it of the confluence of peafe-pottage. Some fat and fcraps of tender flefh are alfo fhred fmall and boiled with it. To render this dilh more palatable, they have a method of mixing the blood with the contents of the ftomach in the paunch itfelf, and hanging it up in the heat and fmoke of the fire for feveral days; which puts the whole mafs into a ftate of fermentation, and gives it fuch an agreeable acid tafte, that were it not for prejudice, it might be eaten by thofe who have the niceft palates. It is true, fome people with delicate ftomachs would not be eafily perfuaded to partake of this difh, efpecially if they faw it dreffed; for moft of the fat which is boiled in it is firft chewed by the men and boys, in order to break the globules that contain the fat; by which means it all boils out, and mixes with the broth: whereas, if it were permitted to remainas it came from the knife, it would ftill be in lumps, like fuet. To do juftice, however, to their cleanlinefs in this particular, I muft pbferve, that they are very care-careful that neither old people with bad teeth, nor young children, have any hand in preparing this difh. At firft, I muft acknowledge that I was rather fhy in partaking of this mefs, but when I was fufficiently convinced of the truth of the above remark, I no longer made any fcruple, but always thought it exceedingly good.

The ftomach of no other large animal beflde the deer is eaten by any of the Indians that border on Hudfon's Bay. In Winter, when the deer feed on fine white mofs, the contents of the ftomach is fo much efteemed by them, that I have often feen them fit round a deer where it was killed, and eat it warm out of the paunch. In Summer the deer feed more coarfely, and therefore this difh, if it deferve that appellation, is then not fo much in favour.

The young calves, fawns, beaver, c. taken out of the bellies of their mothers, are reckoned moft delicate food; and I am not the only European who heartily joins in pronouncing them the great-eft dainties that can be eaten. Many gentlemen who have ferved with me at Churchill, as well as at York Fort, and the inland fettlements, will readily agree with me in aflerting, that no one who ever got the better of prejudice fo far as to tafte of thofe young animals, but has immediately become exceflively fond of them; and the fame may be faid of young geefe, ducks, r. in the ftiell. In fact, it is almoft become a proverb in the Northern fettlements, that whoever wifties wifhes to know what is good, muft live with the Indians.

The parts of generation belonging to any bead they kill, both male and female, are always eaten by the men and boys; and though thofe parts, particularly in the males, are generally very tough, they are not, on any account, to be cut with an edge-tool, but torn to pieces with the teeth; and when any part of them proves too tough to be maflicated, it is thrown into the fire and burnt. For the Indians believe firmly, that if a dog fliould eat any part of them, it would have the fame effect on their fuccefs in hunting, that a woman croflIng their hunting-track at an improper period would have. The fame ill-fuccefs is fuppofed alfo to attend them if a woman eat any of thofe parts.

They are alfo remarkably fond of the womb of the buffalo, elk, deer, lfc, which they eagerly devour without wafhing, or any other procels but barely ftroking out the contents. This, in fome of the larger animals, and efpecially when they are fome time gone with young, needs, no defcription to make it fufficiently difgufting; and yet I have known fome in the Company's fervice remarkably fond of the difli, though I am not one of the number. The womb of the beaver and deer is well enough, but that of the moofe and buffalo is very rank, and truly difgufting.

I he Indian method of preparing this unaccountable difh is by throwing

Our Northern Indians who trade at the Fa(? to. ry, as well as all the Copper tribe, pafs their whole fummer on the barren ground, where they generally find plenty of deer; and in fome of the rivers and lakes, a great abundance of fine fifli.

Their bows and arrows, though their original weapons, are, fince the introduction of fire-arms among them, become of little ufe, except in kill-in5 deer as they walk or. run through a narrow pafs the filthy bagacrofs a pole directly over the fire, the fmoke of which, they fay, much improves it, by taking off the original flavour; and when any of it is to be cooked, a large flake, like as much tripe, is cut of! and boiled. for a few minutes; but the many large nodes with which the iufide of the womb is ftudded, make it abominable. Thefe nodes are as incapable of being diverted of moifture as the fkin of a live eel; but when boiled, much refemble, both in fiiape and colour, the yolk of an egg, and are fo called by the natives, and as eagerly devoured by them.

The tripe of the buffalo is exceedingly good, and the Indian method of cooking it infinitely fuperior to that praiifed in Europe. When opportunity will permit, they wa(h it tolerably clean in cold water, ftripoff all the honey-comb, and only boil it about half, or three-quarters of an hour: in that time it is fufficiently done for eating; and though lathcr tougher than what is prepared in England, yet is exceedingly pleafant to the tafle, and muft be much more nourifliing than tripe that has been foked and fcrubbed in many hot waters, and then boiled for ten or twelve hours.

The lefler flomach, or, as fame call it, the many-folds, either of buffalo, mooie, or deer, areufually eat raw, and are very good; but that of the moofe, unlefs great care be taken in wafning it, is rather bitter, owing to the nature of their food.

The kidneys of both moofe and buffab are ufually eat raw by the Southern Indians; for no fooner is one of thofe beafls killed, than the hunter rips up its belly, thrufts in his arm, fnatches out the kidneys, and eats them warm, before the animal is quite dead. They alfo at times put their mouths to the wound the ball has made, and fuck the biood; which they fay quenches thirft, and is very nourilhing.

pafs prepared for their reception, where fevcral Indians lie concealed for that purpofe. This method of hunting is only practicable in Summer, and on the barren ground, where they have an extenfive profpecl, and can fee the herds of deer at a great diftance, as well as difcover the nature of the country, and make every neceitary arrangement for driving them through the narrow defiles. This method of hunting is performed in the following manner:

When the Indians fee a herd of deer, and intend to hunt them with bows and arrows, they ob-ferve which way the wind blows, and always get to leeward, for fear of being fmelled by the deer. The next thing to which they attend, is to fearch for a convenient place to conceal thofe who are appointed to flioot. This being done, a large bundle of fticks, like large ramrods, (which they carry with them the whole Summer for the purpofe,) are ranged in two ranks, fo as to forn the two fides of a very acute angle, and the flicks placed at the diftance of fifteen or twenty yards from each other. When thofe neceffary arrangements are completed, the women and boys fepa-rate into two parties, and go round on both fides, till they form a crefcent at the back of the deer, which are drove right forward; and as each of the (licks has a fmall flag, or more properly a pendant, faftened to it, which is eafily waved to and fro by the wind, and a lump of mofs fluck on each of their tops, the poor timo-Y rous""

rou3 deer, probably taking them for ranks of people, generally run ftraight forward between the two ranges of flicks, till they get among the Indians, who lie concealed in fmall circular fences, made with loofe ftones, mofs, tsfc. When the deer approach very near, the Indians who arc thus concealed ftart up and fhoot; but as the deer generally pafs along at full fpeed, few Indians have time to fhoot more than one or two arrows, unlefs the herd be very large.

This method of hunting is not always attended with equal fuccefs; for fometimes after the Indians have been at the trouble of making places of-fhelter, and arranging the flag-flicks, Ifc. the deer will make off another way, before the women and children can furround them. At other times I have feen eleven or twelve of them kilkd with one volley of arrows; and if any gun-men attend on thofe occalions, they are always placed behind the other Indians, in order to pick up the deer that efcape the bow-men. By thefe means I have feen upwards of twenty fine deer killed at one broadfide, as it may be termed.

Though the Northern Indians may be faid to kill a great number of deer in this manner during the Summer, yet they have fo far lofl the art of fhooting with bows and arrows, that I never knew any of them who could take thofe weapons only, and kill either deer, moofe, or buffalo, in the common, wandering, and promifcuous method of hunting. The Southern Indians, though they they have been longer ufed to fire-arms, are far more expert with the bow and arrow, their original weapons.

The tents made ufe of by thofe Indians, both in Summer and Winter, are generally compofcd of dcer-fkins in the hair; and for convenience of carriage, are always made in fmall pieces, feldom exceeding five buck-fkins in one piece. Thefe tents, as alfo their kettles, and fome other lumber, are always carried by dogs, which are train-ed to that fervice, and are very docile and tracta-ble. Thofe animals are of various fizes and colours, but all of the fox and wolf breed, withfliarp nofes, full bufliy tails, and Iharp ears (landing erecl. They are of great courage when attacked, and bite fo fliarp, that the fmalleft cur among them will keep feveral of our largeft Englifli dogs at bay, if he can get up in a corner. Thele dogs are equally willing to haul in a fledge, but as few of the men will be at the trouble of making fledges for them, the poor women are oblig-ied to content themfelves with leffening the bulk of their load, more than the weight, by making the dogs carry thefe articles only, which are always laflied on their backs, much after the fame manner as packs are, or ufed formerly to be, on. pack-horfes.

A In the fall of the year, and as the "Winter advances, thofe people few the fkins of the deers legs together in the fhape of long portnanteaus, which, when hauled on the fnaw s the hair lies, are as flippery as an otter, and ferve them as temporary fledges while on the barren ground; but when they arrive at any woods, they then make proper fledges, with thin boards of the larch-tree, generally known in Hudfon's Bay by the name of Juniper.

Thofe fledges are of various fizes, according to the ftrength of the perfons who are to haul them: fome I have feen were not lefs than twelve or fourteen feet long, and fifteen or fixteen inches wide, but in general they do not exceed eight or nine feet in length, and twelve or fourteen inches in breadth.

The boards of which thofe fledges are compof-ed are not more than a quarter of an inch thick, and feldom exceed five or fix inches in width; as broader would be very unhandy for the Indians to work, who have no other tools than an ordinary knife, turned up a little at the point, from which it acquires the name of Bafe-hoth among the Northern Indians, but among the Southern tribes it is called Mo-co-toggan. The boards are fewed together with thongs of parchment deer-fliin, and feveral crofs bars of wood are fewed on the upper fide, which ferves both to ftrengthen the fledge and fccure the ground-laflijng, to which the load is always fattened by other fmaller thongs, or fi: ripes of leather. The head or fore-part of the fledge is turned up fo as to form a femi-circle, of at leafi: fifteen or twenty in ches diameter. This prevents the carriage from diving into light fnow, and enables it to Aide over the inequalities and hard drifts of fnow which are conftantly met with on the open plains and barren grounds. The trace or draught-line to thofe fledges is a double firing, or flip of leather, made fall to the head; and the bight is put acrofs theflioul-ders of the perfon who hauls the fledge, fo as to reft againft the breaft. This contrivance, though fo fimple, cannot be improved by themoft ingenious collar-maker in the world.

Their fnow-flioes differ from all others made ufe of in thofe parts; for though they are of the galley kind, that is, fliarp-pointed before, yet they are always to be worn on one foot, and cannot be fliifted from fide to fide, like other fnow-flioes; for this reafon the inner-fide of the frames are almoft ftraight, and the outer-fide has a very large fweep. The frames are generally made of birch-wood, and the netting is compof- ed of thongs of deer-flin; but their mode of filling that compartment where the foot refts, is quite different from that ufed among the Sou-i thern Indians.

Their clothing, which chiefly confifts of deer ins in the hair, makes them very fubjed: to be loufy; but that is fo far from being thought a difgrace, that the beft among them amufe them-fclves with catching and eating thefe vermin j of which they are fo fond, that the produce of a k)ufy head or garment affords them not only pleafing amufement, but a delicious repaft. My old guide, Matonabbee, was fo remarkably fond of thofe little vermin, that he frequently fet five

or fix of his ftrapping wives to work to loufe their hairy deer-fkin fhifts, the produce of which being always very confiderable, he eagerly received with both hands, and licked them in as faft, and with as good a grace, as any European epicure would the mites in a cheefe. He often affured me that fuch amufement was not only very pleafing, but that the objects of the fearch were very good; for which 1 gave him credit, telling him at the fame time, that though I endeavoured to habituate myfelf to every other part of their diet, yet as I was but a fojourner among them, I had no inclination to accuflom myfelf to fuch dainties as I could not procure in that part of the world vhere I was moft inclined to refide.

The Southern Indians and Efquimaux are equally fond of thofe vermin, which are fo de-tellable in the eyes of an European; nay, the latter have many other dainties of a fimilar kind for befide making ufe of train-oil as a cordial and as fauce to their meat, I have frequently feeni them eat a whole handful of maggots that were produced in meat by fly-blows. It is their coni ftant culiom to eat the filth that comes from the. nofe i and when their nofes bleed by accident, I they always lick the blood into their mouths, and 1 wallow it.

The track of land inhabited by the Northern i Indians is very extenfive, reaching from the fifty-innth to the fixty-eighth degree of North lati- tude; tudc; and from Eaft to Weft is upward of five hundred miles wide. It is bounded by Churchill River on the South; the Athapufcow Indians Country on the Weft; the Dog-ribbed and Copper Indians Country on the North; and by Hud-fon's Bay on the Eaft. The land throughout that whole track of country is fcarcely any thing but one folid mafs of rocks and ftcnes, and in moft parts very hilly, particularly to the Weft-ward, among the woods. The furface, it is very true, is in moft places covered with a thin fod of mofs, intermixed with the roots of the Wee-fa-ca-pucca, cranberries, and a few other infignificant fhrubs and herbage; but under it there is in general a total want of foil, capable of producing any thing except what is peculiar to the climate. Some of the marfhes, indeed, produce feveral kinds of grafs, the growth of which is amazingly rapid; but this is dealt out with fo fparing a hand as to be barely fufficient to ferve the geefe, fwans, and other birds of paflage, during their migrations in the Spring, and Fall, while they remain in a moulting ftate

The many lakes and rivers with which this part of the country abounds, though they do not fur-nifh the natives with water-carriage, are yet of infinite advantage to them; as they afford great numbers of fifli, both in Summer and Winter. The only fpecies caught in thofe parts are trout, tittameg, (or tickomeg,) tench, two forts of barbie, (called by the Southern Indians Na-may-pith,) burbot.

burbot, pike, and a few perch. The four former are caught in all parts of this country, as Viell the woody as the barren; but the three latter are only caught to the Weftward, in fuch lakes and rivers as are fituated among the woods; and though fome of thofe rivers lead to the barren ground, yet the three laft mentioned fpecies of fi(h are fel-dom caught beyond the edge of the woods, not even in the Summer feafon.

There is a black, hard, crumply mofs, that grows on the rocks and large ftones in thofe parts, which is of infinite fervice to the natives, as it fometimes furniflies theni with a temporary fubfiflence, when no animal food can be procured. This mofs, when boiled, turns to a gummy confidence, and is more clammy in the mouth than fago; it may, by adding either mofs or water, be made to almofl any confiftence. It is fo palatable, that all who tafte it generally grow fond of it. It is remarkably good and pleafing when ufed to thicken any kind of broth, but it is generally mofi: efteemed when boiled in lifh-liquor.

The only method praclifed by thofe people to catch fifh either in Winter or Sum-mer, is by angling and fetting nets; both of which methods is attended with much fuperftition, ceremony, and unneceflary trouble; but 1 will endeavour to defcribe tiiem in as plain and brief a manner as poifible.

When they make a new fifhing-net, which is always always compofed of fmall thongs cut from raw deer-fkins, they take a number of bird bills and feet, and tie them, a little apart from each other, to the head and foot rope of the net, and at the four corners generally fallen fome of the toes and jaws of the otters and jackafhes. The birds feet and bills made choice of on fuch occafions are generally thofe of the laughing goofe, wavey, (or white goofe,) gulls, loons, and black-heads; and unlefs fome or all of thefe be faftened to the net, they will not attempt to put it into the water, as they firmly believe it would not catch a fmgle lifli.

A net thus accoutred is fit for fettino whene-ver occalion requires, and opportunity offers; but the firft filh of whatever fpecies caught in it, are not to be fodden in the water, but broiled whole on the fire, and the ilelh carefully taken from the bones without diflocating one joint; after which the bones are laid on the fire at full length and burnt. A iiricl obfer vance of thefe rules is fup-pofed to be of the utmoft importance in promoting the future fuccefs of the new net; and a neglect of them would render it not worth a farthing.

When they fifli in rivers, or narrow channels that

They frequently fell new nets, which have rot been wet more than once or twice, becaufe they have not been fuccefsful. Thofe nets, when foked in water, are eafily opened, and then make mofl: excellent heel and tae netting for fnovv-lhoes. In general it is far fuperior to the netting cut by the Southern Indian women, and is not larger than common net-twine.

that join two lakes together, they could frequently, by tying two, three, or more nets together, fpread over the whole breadth of the channel, and intercept every lizable fifli that pafled; but inftead of that, they fcatter the nets at a confide-rable diftance from each other, from a fuperftiti. ous notion, that were they kept clofe together, one net would be jealous of its neighbour, and by that means not one of them would catch a fmgle fifh.

The methods ufed, and ftridly obferved, when angling, are equally abfurd as thofe I have mentioned; for when they bait a hook, a compofition of four, five, or fix articles, by way of charm, is concealed under the bait, which is always fewed round the hook. In fad:, the only bait ufed by thofe people is in their opinion a compofition of charms, inclofed within a bit of fifh fkin, fo as in fome meafure to refemble a fmall fifh. The things ufed by way of charm, are bits of beavers tails and fat, otter's vents and teeth, mulk-rats guts and tails, loon's vents, fquirrel's teflicles, the crudled milk taken out of the flomach of fucking fawns and calves, human hair, and num-berlefs other articles equally abfurd.

Every mafter of a family, and indeed almoft every other perfon, particularly the men, have a fmall bundle of fuch tralh, which they always carry with them, both in Summer and Winter; and without fome of thofe articles to put under their bait, few of them could be prevailed upon to put a hook into the water, being fully per-fuaded that-they may as well fit in the tent, as attempt to angle without fuch afliftance. They have alfo a notion that fifh of the fame fpecies inhabiting different parts of the country, are fond of different things; fo that almoll every lake and river they arrive at, obliges tl. em to alter the compofition of the charm. The fame rule is obferved on broiling the firft fruits of a new hook that is ufed for a new net; an old hook that has already been fuccefsful in catching large fifh is efteemcd of more value, than a handful of new ones which have never been tried.

Deer alfo, as well as fifh, are very numerous in many parts of this country; partic-ularly to the North of the fixtieth degree of latitude. Alpine hares are in fome parts of the barren ground pretty plentiful, where alfo fome herds of muik-oxen are to be met with; and to the Weflward, among the woods, there are fome rabbits and partridges. With all thofe feeming fources of plenty, however, one half of the inhabitants, and perhaps the other half alfo, are frequently in danger of being flarved to death, owing partly to their want of ceconomy; and moft of thefe fcenes of diflrefs happen during their journies to and from Prince of Wales's Fort, the only place at which they trade.

When Northern Indians are at the Factory, they are very liable to fleal any thing they think think will be ferviceable; particularly iron hoops, fmall bolts, fpikes, carpenters tools, and, in fliort, all fmall pieces of iron-work which they can turn to advantage, either for their own ufe, or for the purpofe of trading with fuch of their countrymen as feldom vifit the Company's Settlement: among themfelves, however, the crime of theft is feldom heard of.

When two parties of thofe Indians meet, the ceremonies which pafs between them are quite different from thofe made ufe of in Europe on iimilar occafions; for when they advance within twenty or thirty yards of each other, they make a full halt, and in general fit or lie down on the ground, and do not fpeak for fome minutes. At length one of them, generally an elderly man, if any be in company, breaks filence, by acquainting the other party with every misfortune that has befallen him and his companions from the lafl time they had feen or heard of each other; and alfo of all deaths and other calamities that have befallen any other Indians during the fame period, at leafl as many particulars as have come to his knowledge.

When the firfl has finifhed his oration, another aged orator, (if there be any) belonging to the other party relates, in like manner, all the bad news that has come to his knowledge; and both parties never fail to plead poverty and famine on all occafions. If thofe orations contain any news that in the leaft afiect the other party, it is not long long before fome of them begin to figh and fob, and foon after break out into a loud cry, which is generally accompanied by moft of the grown perfons of both fexes; and fometimes it is common to fee them all, men, women, and children, in one univerfal howl. The young girls, in particular, are often very obliging on thofe oc-cafions; for I never remember to have feen a crying match (as I called it) but the greateft part of the company aftifted, although fome of them had no other reafon for it, but that of feeing their companions do the fame. When the firft tranfports of grief fubfide, they advance by degrees, and both parties mix with each other, the men always affociating with the men, and the women with the women. If they have any tobacco among them, the pipes are pafted round pretty freely, and the converfation foon becomes general. As they are on their firft meeting acquainted with all the bad news, they have by this time nothing left but good, which in general has fo far the predominance over the former, that in lefs than half an hour nothing but fmiles and cheerfulnefs are to be feen in every face; and if they be not really in want, fmall prefents of pro-vicons, ammunition, and other articles, often take place; fometimes merely as a gift, but more frequently by way of trying whether they cannot get a greater prefent.

They have but few diverfions; the chief is (hooting fhooting at a mark with bow and arrows; and another out-door game, called Holl, which in fome meafure refembles playing with coits; only it is done with fhort clubs, fharp at one end. They alfo amufe themfelves at times with dancing, which is always performed in the night. It is remarkable that thofe people, though a diftincl nation, have never adopted any mode of dancing of their own, or any fongs to which they can dance j fo that when any thing of this kind is attempted, which is but feldom, they always endeavour to imitate either the Dog-ribbed or Southern Indians, but more commonly the former, as few of them are fufeciently acquainted either with the Southern Indian language, or their manner of dancing. The Dog-ribbed method is not very difficult to learn, as it only confifts in lifting the feet alternately from the ground in a very quick fucceffion, and as high as poffible, without moving the body, which fhould be kept quite ftill and motionlefs; the hands at the fame time being clofed, and held clofe to the breaft, and the head inclining forward. This diverfion is always performed quite naked, except the breech-cloth, and at times that is alfo thrown off; and the dancers, who feldom exceed three or four at a time, always Hand clofe to the mufic. The mufic may, by ftraining a point, be called both vocal and inftrumental, though both are fufficiently humble. The former is no more than than a frequent repetition of the words hee, hee, hee, ho, ho, ho, Iffc. which, by a more or lefs frequent repetition, dwelling longer on one word and fhorter on another, and railing and lowering the voice, produce fomething like a tune, and has the defired effect. This is always accompanied by a drum or tabor; and fometimes a kind of rattle is added, made with a piece of dried buffalo fkin, in fhape exadly like an oil-flafk, into which they put a few Ihot or pebbles, which, when fhook about, produces mufic little inferior to the drum, though not fo loud.

This mode of dancing naked is performed on-ly by the men; for when the women are ordered to dance, they always exhibit without the tent, to mufic which is played within it; and though their method of dancing is perfe(5l: ly decent, yet it has ftiil lefs meaning and aflion than that of the men: fx)r a whole heap of them crowd together in a ftraight line, and juft fhuffle them-felves a little from right to left, and back again in the fame line, without lifting their feet from the ground; and when the mufic flops, they all give a little bend of the body and knee, fomewhat like an awkward curtfy, and pronounce, in a little fhrill tone, h-e-e, h-o-o-oe. Befide thefe diverlions, they have another lim-ple in-door game, which is that of taking a bit of wood, a button, or any other fmall thing, and after ihifting it from hand to hand feveral times, afking afking their antagonift, which hand it is iri? When playing at this game, which only admits of two perfons, each of them have ten, fifteen or twenty fmall chips of wood, like matches; and when one of the players gueffes right, he takes one of his antagonift's fticks, and lays it to his own; and he that firft gets all the flicks from the other in that manner is faid to win the game, which is generally for a fingle load of powder and fhot, an arrow, orfome other thing of incon-fiderable value.

The women never mix in any of their diverli-ons, not even in dancing; for when that is required of them, they always exhibit without the tent, as has been already obferved; nor are they allowed to be prefent at a feaft. Indeed, the whole courfe of their lives is one continued fcene of drudgery, viz. carrying and hauling heavy loads, dreffing fkins for clothing, curing theici provifions, and praclifing other neceflary dome-flic duties which are required in a family, without enjoying the lead diverfion of any kind, on relaxation, on any occafion whatever; and excepi in the execution of thofe homely duties, in whicti they are always inflructed from their infancy! their fenfes feem almofl as dull and frigid as th(, zone they inhabit. There are indeed fome ex I ceptions to be met with among them, and I fup pofe it only requires indulgence and precept t(j make fome of them as lofty and infolent as any: womer women in the world. Though they wear their hair at full length, and never tie it up, Hke the Southern Indians; and though not one in fifty of them is ever poftefled of a comb, yet by a wonderful dexterity of the fingers, and a good deal of patience, they make fliift to ftroke it out fo as not to leave two hairs entangled; but when their heads are infefted with vermin, from which very few of either fex are free, they mutually afiift each other in keeping them under.

A fcorbutic diforder, refembling the worfl: flage of the itch, confumptions, and fluxes, are their chief diforders. The firft of thefe, though very troublefome, is never known to prove fatal, un-lefs it be accompanied with fome inward complaint; but the two latter, with a few accidents, carries off great numbers of both fexes and all ages: indeed few of them live to any great age, probably owing to the great fatigue they undergo from their youth up, in procuring a fubfi-ftence for themfelves and their offspring.

Though the fcorbutic diforder above mentioned does appear to be infectious, it is rare to fee one have it without the whole tent's crew being more or lefs aflfecled with it; but this is by no means a proof of its being contagious; I rather attribute it to the effects of fome bad water, or; the unwholefomcnefs of fome fifli they may catch in particular places, in the courfe of their wandering manner of life. Were it otherwife, 2 fingle family would in a fliort time communi- cate it to the whole tribe; but, on the contrary, the difeafe is never known to fpread. In the younger fort it always attacks the hands and feet, not even fparing the palms and foles. Thofe of riper years generally have it about the wrifts, in-fleps, and pofteriors; and in the latter particu larly, the blotches, or boils as they majuilly be called are often as large as the top of a man's thumb. This diforder moft frequently makes its appearance in the Summer, while the Indians are out in the barren ground; and though it is by no means reckoned dangerous, yet it is fo ob-fdnate, as not to yield to any medicine that has ever been applied to it while at the

Company's Factory. And as the natives themfelves never make ufe of any medicines of their own preparing. Nature alone works the cure, which is never performed in lefs than twelve or eighteen months; and fome of them are troubled with this difagree-able and loathfome diforder for years before they are perfectly cured, and then a dark livid mark remains on thofe parts of the fldn which have been affected, for many years afterwards, and in fome during life.

"When any of the principal Northern Indians-die, it is generally believed that they are conjured to death, eirher by fome of their own countrymen, by fome of the Southern Indians, or by fome of the Efquimaux: too frequently the fuf-picion falls on the latter tribe, which is the grand leafon of their never being at peace with thofe poor poor and diftrefled people. For fome time paft, however, thofe Efquimaux who trade with our floops at Knapp's Bay, Navel's Bay, and Whale Cove, are in perfect peace and friendfhip with the Northern Indians; which is entirely owing to the protection they have for feveral years pafl received from the Chiefs at the Company's Fort at Churchill River. But thofe of that tribe who

Z 2 live In the Summer of i 756, a paity of Nos-thern Incians lay in wait at Knapp's Bay till the floop had failed out of the harbour, when they fell on the poor Efquimaux, and killed every foul. Mr. John Bean, then Mailer of the floop, and fince Matter of the Trinity yacht, with all his crew, heard the guns very plain; but did not know the m aning or reafon of it till the Summer following, when he found the fhocking remains of more than foity Efquimaux, who had been murdcted in that cowardly manner; and for n other reafon but becaufe two principal Northern Indians had died in the preceding Winter.

No ETquimaux were feen at Knapp's Bay for feveral years after; and thofe who trade there at prefent have undoubtedly been drawn from the Northward, fince the above unhappy tranfaiflion; for the convenience of being nearer the woods, as well as being in the way of trading with the floop that calls there annually. It is to be hoped that the meafures taken by the Governors at Prince of Wales's Fort of late years, will efreftiially prevent any fuch calamities happening in future, and by degrees be the means of bringing about a lafting, friendly, and reciprocal intereft between the two nations.

Not with (landing the pacific and friendly terms which basin to dawn between thofe two tribes at Knapp's Bay, Navel's Bay, and Whale Cove, farther North hoflilities continue, and moft barbarous murders are perpetrated: and the only proteflion the Efquimaux have fiom the furv of their enemies, is their remote fituation in the Winter, and tht-ir refiding chiefly on iflandv and peninfulas in Summer, which renders them lefsliable to be fuiprifed during that feafon. But even this fecluded life docs not prevent the Northern Indians from harafling them greatlv, and at times they are fo clofely purfued as to be obliged to leave mofl of their goods, and utenfils to be deftroycd by their enemy; whicfh muft be a great lofs, as thefe cannot be replaced but at the expence of much time and labour; atid the want of them in the main time mull cieate much diflrefs both to them- live fo far to the North, as not to have any in-tercourfe with our veflels, very often fall a facri-fice to the fury and fuperftition of the Northern Indians; who are by no means a bold or warlike people; nor can I think from experience, that they are particularly guilty of committing acts of wanton cruelty on any other part of the human race befide the i:. fquimaux. Their hearts, however, th'trafelvesand their families, as they can feldom procure any part of their livelihood without the affiflance of a confiderable apparatus.

In 1756, the Efquimaux at Knapp's Bay fent two of their youths to Prince of Wales's Fort in the floop, and the Summer following they were darried back to their friends, loaded with ptefents, and much plealed with the treatment they received while at the Fort. In 1767, they again fent one from Knapp's Bay and one from Whale Cove; and though during their Hay at the Fort they made a confiderable progrels both in the Southern Indian and the Englifh languages, yet thofe intercourfes have not been any ways advantageous to the Company, by increafmgthe trade from that quarter. In fat, the only fatisfaftion they have found forthe great xpence they have from time to time incirred, by introducing thofe Grangers, is, that through the good conduct of their upper fervants at Churchill River, they have at length fo far humanized the hearts of thofe two tribes, that at prefent they can meet each other in a friendly manner j whereas, a few years fince, whenever they met, each party premeditated the deftrutftion of the other; and what made their war more fhocking, vias, they never gave quarter: fo that the ftrongell party always killed the weakeft, without fparing either man, womrn, or child.

It is but a few years ago that the floop's crew who annually carried them all their wants, durft not venture on (hore among the Efquimaux unarmed, for fear of being murdered; but latterly they are fo civilized, that the Company's fervants vifit their tents with the greateft freedom and fafety, are always welcome, and defired to partake of fuch provifions as they have: and knowing now our averlion from train-oil, they take every means in their power to convince our people that the viduals prepared for them is entirely free from it. But the fmell of their tents, cook-iug-utenfrls, and other furniture, is fcarcely lefs offenfive than Greenland Dock, However I have eaten both fifli and venifon cooked by them in Co cleanly a manner, that 1 have reliffecd them veiy much, and partaken of them with a good appetite.

ever,-are In general founfufccptible of tendernefs, that they can view the decpelt diftrefs in thofe who are not immediately related to them, without the lead emotion; not even half io much as the generality of mankind feel for the fufferings of the meaneft of the brutq creation. I have been prefent when one of them, imitating the groans, diftorted features, and contracted pofition, of a man who had died in the moft excruciating pain, put the whole company, except myfelf, intp the moft violent lit of laughter.

The Northern Indians never bury their dead, but always leave the bodies where they die, fo that they are fuppofed to be devoured by beafts and birds of prey; for which reafon they will not eat foxes, wolves, ravens, c. unlefs it be through, mere neceflity.

The death of a near relation affects them fo fen-fibly, that they rend all their cloths from their backs, and go naked, till fome perfons lefs ffli(-ed relieve them. After the deth of a father, mother, huiband, wife, fon, or brother, they mourn, as it may be called, for a whole year, which they meafure by the moons and feafons. Thofe mournful periods are not diftinguilhed by any particular drefs, except that of cutting ofith? hair; and the cer. mony confillis in almoft perpetually crying. Even when walking, as well as at all other intervals from fleep, eating, and conver-fation, they make an odd howling noife, often repeating the relationfliip of the deceafed. But as this is in a great meafure mere form and cuf-tom, fome of them have a method of foftening the harfhnefs of the notes, and bringing them out in a more mufical tone than that in which they ling their fongs. When they refle(5t feriouflyon the lofs of a good friend, however, it has fuch an effect on them for the prefent, that they give an uncommon ioofe to their grief. At thofe times they feem to fympathife (through cuftom) with each other's afflicIions fo much, that I have often feen feveral fcores of them crying in concert, when at the fame time not above half a dozen of them had any more reafon for fo doing than I had, unlefs it was to preferve the old cuftom, and keep the others in countenance. The women are remarkably obliging on fuch occafions; and as no reftricIion is laid on them, they may with truth be faid to cry with ail their might and main; but in common converfation they are obliged to be very moderate.

They have a tradition among them, that the firft: perfon upon earth was a woman, who, after having been fome time alone, in her refearches for berries, which was then her only food, found an animal like a do, which followed her to the cave where flie lived, and foon grew fond and domeftic. This dog, they fay, had the art of transforming itfelf into the fliape of a handfome young man, which it frequently did at night, but as the day approached, always refumed its former ftiape f fo that the woman looked on all that paff- v on thofe occafions as dreams and delufions. i hefc traniormalions were loon productive of the confequcnccs vvliich at prefent generally follow fuch intimate connexions between the two ilxes, and the mother of the world began to advance in her pregnancy.

Not long after this happened, a man of fuch a furprifing height that his head reached up to the clouds, came to level the land, which at that time was a very rude mafs; and after he had done this, by the help of his walking-ltick he marked out all the lakes, ponds, and rivers, and immediately cauicd them to be filled with water. He-then took the dog, and tore it to pieces j the guts he threw into the lakes and rivers, commanding them to become the different kinds of fifli; the fiefli he difperfed over the land, commanding it to become different kinds of beafts and land-animals; the ikin he alfo tore in fmall pieces, and threw it into the air, commanding it to become all kinds of birds; after which he gave the wo-n: ian and her offspring full power to kill, eat, and never fpare, for that he had commanded them to multiply for her ufe in abundance. After this injunction, he returned to the place whence he came, and has not been heard of fince.

Religion has not as yet begun to dawn among the Northern Indians; for though their conjurors do indeed fing fongs, and make long fpeech-es, to fome beafts and birds of prey, as alfo to imaginary beings, which they fay ailift them in performing performing cures on the fick. yet they, as well as their credulous neighbours, are utterly defti-tute of every idea of practical religion. It is true, fome of them will reprimand their youth for talking difrefpcclfully ci particular beafts and birds; but it is done uith fo little energy, as to be often retorted back in derifion. Is either is this, nor their cullom of not killing wolves and. quiquehatches, univerlally obierved, and thofe who do it can only be viewed with more pity and contempt than the others; for I always found it arofe merely from rh, greater degree of confidence which they had in the fupernatural power of their conjurors, which induced them to believe, that talking lightly or difrefpeclfully of any thing they feemed to approve, would materially aftedt their health and happinefs in this world: and I never found any of them that had the leaft idea of futurity, Matunabbee, without one exception, was a man of as clear ideas in other matters as any that I ever faw. he was not only a perfect mailer of the Southern Indian language, and their belief, but could tell a better itory of our Saviour's birth and life, than one half of thofe who call themfelves Chriitians; yet he always declared to me, that neither he, nor any of his countrymen, had an idea of a future flate. Though he had been taught to look on things of this kind as ufelefs, his own good fenfe had taught him to be an advocate for univerial toleration; and I have leen him feveral times afiilt: at fome of the moft facred rites performed by the Southern Indians, apparently with as much zeal, a; if he had. given as much credit to them as they did: and with the fame liberality of fentiment he would, I am perfuaded have aflired at the altar of a Chri. ftian church, or in a Jewifti fynagogue; not with a view to reap any advantage himfelf, but merely, as he obfervcd, to aflill others who believed in fuch ceremonies.

Beins: thus deflitute of all relifrlous controul, thefe people have, to ufe Maton-abbee's own words, " nothing to do but confult their own intereft, " incunations, and pallions; and to pafs through " this world with as much eafe and contentment as poffible, without any hopes of reward, or painful fear of puniihment in the next." In this rtare of mind they are, when in profperity, the happieft of mortals; for nothing but perfonal or family calamities can difturb their tranquillity, while misfortunes of the lefler kind fit light on them. Like mod other uncivilized people, they bear bodily pain with great fortitude, though in that refpect I cannot think them equal to the Southern Indians.

Old age is the greateft calamity that can befal a Northern Indian; for when he is pad labour, he is neglected, and treated with great difrcfped, even by his own children. l hey not only lerve him laft at meals, but generally give him the coarfeft and worft of the victuals: and fuch of the ikins as they do not chufe to wear, are made up in the clumfiefl manner into clothing for theif aged parents; vho, as they had, in all probability, treated their fathers and mothers with the fame negled, in their turns, fubmitted patiently to their lot, even without a murmur, knowing it to be the common misfortune attendant an old age; fo that they may be faid to wait patiently for the melancholy hour when, being no longer capable of walking, they are to be left alone, to ftarve and perifli for want. This, however, ihocking and unnatural it may appear, is never-thelefs fo common, that, among thofe people, one half at leaft of the aged perfons of both fexes ab-folutely die in this miferable condition.

The Northern Indians call the Aurora Borealis, Ed-thin; that is, Deer: and when that meteor is very bright, they fay that deer is plentiful in that part of the atmofphere; but they have never yet extended their ideas fo far as to entertain hopes of tafting thpfe celeftial animals.

Befide this filly notion, they are very fuperfti-tious with refpecl to the exiftence of feveral kinds of fairies, called by them Nant-e-na, whom they frequently fay they fee, and who are fuppofed by them

Their ideas in this refpeft are founded on a principle one would not imagine. Expetience has llien them, that when a hairy deer-fkin is biifkly ftroked with the hand in a iai k night, it will emit many fparks of tledlrical fire, as the back of a cat will. The idea which the Southern Indians have of this meteor is equally romantic, though more pleafing, as they believe it to be the fpirits of their departed friends dancing in the clouds; and when the Aurora Borealis is remarkably blight, at which time they vary mofl in colour, form, and filuation, they fay, their deceafed Xriends arc very merry.

them to inhabit tlie different elements of earth, fea, and air, according to their (everal qualities. To one or other of thofe fairies tliey ufualiy attribute any change in their circumilances, either for the better or worfe 5 and as they are led into this way of thinking entirely by the art of the conjurors, there is no fuch thing as any general mode of belief; for thoie jugglers differ fo much from each other in their accounts of thefe beings, that thofe who believe any thing they fay, have little to do but change their opinions according to the will and caprice of the conjuror, who is al-moll daily relating fome new whim, or extraordinary event, which, he fays, has been revealed to him in a dream, or by fome of his favourite fairies, when on a hunting excurfion.

Some

Some Account cf Matonabbee, and of the eminent Services which he rendered to his Country as well as to the Hudfon's Bay Company.

Matonabbee was the fon of a Northern Indian by a flave woman, who was formerly bought from fome Southern Indians who came to Prince! of Wales's Fort with furrs, lfc. This match wasi made by Mr. Richard Norton, then Governor, who detained them at and near the Fort, for the fame purpofe as he did thofe Indians called Home guard. As to Matonabbee's real age, it is im-poflible to be particular; for the natives of thofci parts being utterly unacquainted with, letters, or the ufe of hieroglyphics, though their memories are not lefs retentive than thofe of other nations, cannot preferve and tranfmit to pofterity the ex-aft time when any particular event happens. Indeed, the utmoll extent of their chronology reaches no farther, than to fay. My fon, or my daugh-i ter, was born in fuch a Governor's time, and) fuch an event happened during fuch a perfon's life-time (though, perhaps, he or fhe has been dead many years). However, according to appearance, and fome corroborating circumflances, Matonabbee was born about the year one thou- fand feven hundred and thirty-fix, or one thou-fand feven hundred and thirty-feven; and his father dying while he was young, the Governod tooia took the boy, and, according to the Indian cuf-toiii, adopted him ashisfon.

Soon after the death of Matonabbee's father, Mr. Norton went to England, and as the boy did not experience from his fucccllor the fame regard and attention which he had been accuftomed to receive form Mr. Norton, he was foon taken from the Factory by fome of his fathers relations, and continued with the Northern Indians till Mr. Ferdinand Jacobs fucceeded to the command of Pi ince of Wales's Fort, in the year one thoufand ft en hundred and fifty-two; when out of re-e: ard to old Mr. Norton, (who was then dead,) Mr. Jacobs took the firft opportunity that oftered to detain Matonabbee at the Factory, where he was for feveral years employed in the hunting-fervice with fome of the Company's fervants, particularly with the late Mr. Mofes Norton, (fon of the late Governor,) and Mr. Magnus Johnftonf.

In the courfe of his long (lay at and near the Fort, it is no wonder that he fliould have become perfed mailer of the Southern Indian language, and made fome progrefs in the Enghfh. It was during this period, that he gained a knowledge of the Chrillian faith; and he always declared, that it was too deep and intricate for his compre-benfion. Though he was a perfect bigot with refpect

Afterwards Governor.

I Mailer of the Churchill floop.

refpeft to the arts and tricks of Indian jugglers yet he could by no means be imprefled with a belief of any part of our religion, nor of the religion of the Southern Indians, who have as firm a belief in a future ftate as any people under the-j Sun. He had fo much natural good fenfe and liberality of fentiment, however, as not to think that he had a right to ridicule any particular feci on account of their religious opinions. On the contrary, he declared, that he held them all equally in efteem, but was determined, as he came into the world, fo he would go out of it, without profeffing any religion at all Notwithftanding his aversion from relisrion, I have met with few Chriftians who poffelted more good moral qualities, or fewer bad ones.

It is impoflible for any man to have been more punctual in the performance of a promife than he was; his fcrupulous adherence to truth and ho-nefty would have done honour to the mod enlightened and devout Chriftian, while his benevolence and univerfal humanity to all the human race, according to his abilities and manner of life, I mud here obferve, that when we went to war with the Efqui-maux at the Copper River in July 1771, it was by no means his propofai: on the contrary, he was forced into it by his countrymen. For I have heard him fay, that when he firft vifited that river, in company with I-dot-le-aza, they met with feveral Efquimaux; and To fur from killing them, were very friendly to them, and made them fraall prefents of fuch articles as they could beft fpare, and that would be-of molt ufe to them. It is more than probable that the two bits of iion foucd among the plunder life, could not be exceeded by the moft illuftrl-ous perfonage now on record; and to add to his other good qualities, he was the only Indian i it I ever faw, except one, who was not guilty of backbiting and flandering his neighbours.

In ftature, Matonabbce was above the common fize, being nearly fix feet high; and, except that his neck was rather (though not much) too (hort, he was one of the fined and bell proportioned men tliat I ever faw. In complexion he was dark, like the other Northern Indians, but his face was not disfigured by that ridiculous cuftom of marking the cheeks with three or four black lines. His features were ragular and agreeable, and yet fo ftrongly marked and expreflive, that they formed a completeindex of his mind; which, as he never intended to deceive or diflemble, he never wioied to conceal. In converfation he was eafy, lively, and agreeable, but exceedingly mo-deft; and at table, the noblenefs and elegance of his manners might have been admired by the firft perfonages in the world j for to the vivacity of a

Frenchman, (ler while I was there, were part of thofe prefents. There were alfo a few long beads found among thofe people, but quite different from any that tlie Hndfon's Bay Company had ever fent to the Bay; fo that the only probable-xay they could have come by them, muft have been by an inter, courfe withlbme of their tribe, who had dealings with the Danes in Davis's Straits. U is very probable, however, they might have paded through many hands hclorc they reached this remote place. Had they bad an immedi. ite intercourfc with the Efquimaux in Davis's Straits, it is natural to fuppofe that iron would not have been fo fcarce among them as it feemed to be; indeed the diftance is too great to admit of it.

I have feen two Northern Indians who meafuied fix feet three inches; and one, fix feet four inches.

Frenchman, and the fincerity of an Englifhman, he added the gravity and noblenefs of a Turk; all fo happily blended, as to render his company and converfation univerfally pleafmg to thofe who underltoodeither the Northerner Southern Indian languages, the only languages in which he could converfe.

He was remarkably fond of Spanifli wines, though he never drank to excefs; and as he would not partake of fpirituous liquors, however fine in quality or plainly mixed, he was always mafter of himfelf. As no man is exempt from frailties, it is natural to fuppofe that as a man he had his fhare; but the greateft with which 1 can charge him, is jealoufy, and that fometimes carried him beyond the bounds of humanity.

In his early youth he difcovered talents equal to the greateft talk that could poffibly be expected from an Indian. Accordingly Mr. Jacobs, then Governor at Prince of Wales's Fort, engaged him, when but a youth, as an Ambaffador and Mediator between the Northern Indians and the Athapufcow Tribe, who till then had aha ays been at war with each other. In the courfe of this embalty Matonabbee not only difcovered the moft brilliant and folid parts, but ftiewed an extenfive knowledge of every advantage that could arife to both nations from a total fupprefli-on of hoftilities; and at times he difplayed fuch inftances of perfonal courage and magnanimity, as are rarely to be found among perfons of fupe-rior condition and rank.

He had not penetrated far into the country of the Athapufcow Indians, before he came to feve-ral tents with inhabitants; and there, to his great furprife, he found Captain Keelfhies, (a perfon frequently mentioned in this Journal,) who was then a prifoner, with all his family and fome of his friends, the fate of whom was then undetermined; but through the means of Matonabbee, though young enough to have been his fon, Keel-ihies and a few others were releafed, with the lofs of his effects and all his wives, which were fix in number. Matonabbee not only kept his ground after Keelfhies and his fmall party had been permitted to return, but made his way into the very heart of the Athapufcow country, in order to have a perfonal conference with all or moft of the principal inhabitants. The farther he advanced, the more occafion he had for intrepidity. At one time he came to five tents of thofe favages, which in the whole contained fix-teen men, befides their wives, childern, and fer-vants, while he himfelf was entirely-alone, except one wife and a fervant boy. The Southern Indians, ever treacherous, and apparently the more kind when they are premeditating mifchief, fecm-ed to give him a hearty welcome, accepted the lenders of peace and reconciliation with apparent

A a fatisfadion,

The fame perfon was at Piince of Wales's Fort when the French ariiv edonthe Sth of Auguft 1782, andfaw them demolifh the Fort.

fatisfadion, and, as a mark of their approbation, each tent in rotation made a feaft, or entertainment, the fame night, and invited him to partake; at the laft of which they had concerted a fcheme to murder him. He was, however, fo perfedl a mafter of the Southern Indian language, that he foon difcovered their defign, and told them, he was not come in a hoftile manner, but if they attempted any thing of the kind he was determined to fell his life as dear as poffible. On hearing this, fome of them ordered that his fer-vant, gun, and fnow-flioes, (for it was winter,) lliould be brought into the tent and fecured; but he fprung from his feat, feized his gun and fnow-fhoes, and went out of the tent, telling them, if they had an intention to moleft him, that was the proper place where he could fee his enemy, and be under no apprehenfions of being Ihot cowardly through the back. " I am fare " (faid he) of killing two or three of you, and if " you chufe to purchafe my life at that price, " now is the time; but if otherwife, let me de-" part without any farther moleftation. They then told him he was at liberty to go, on condition of leaving his fervant; but to this he would not confent. He then rufhed into the tent and took his fervant by force from two men; when finding there was no appearance of farther danger, he fet out on his return to the frontiers of his own country, and from thence to the Factory.

The year following he again vifited the Atha-pufcow country, accompanied by a confiderable number of chofen men of his own nation, who were fo far fuperior to fuch fmall parties of the Southern Indians as they had met, that they commanded refped wherever they came; and having traverfed the whole country, and converf-ed with all the principal men, peace and friend-fliip were apparently re-eftablifhed. Accordingly, when the Spring advanced the Northern Indians began to difperfe, and draw out to the Eaft-ward on the barren ground; but Matonabbee, and a few others, chofe to pafs the Summer in the Athapufcow country. As foon as the Southern Indians were acquainted with this defign, and found the number of thenorthern Indians fo reduced, a fuperior number of them dogged and harafled them the whole Summer, with a view to furprife and kill them when afleep; and with that view twice actually approached fo near their tents as fifty yards. But Matonabbee told them, as he had done when alone, that though there were but few of them, they were all determined to fell their lives as dear as poitible: on vhich the Southern Indians, without making any reply, retired; for no Indians in this country have the courage to face their enemies when they find them apprized of their approach, and on their guard to receive them.

Notwithftandino; all thefe difcourao-ements and great dangers, Matonabbee per-levcred with cou-

A a 2 rage rage and refolution to vilit the Athapufcow Indians for feveral years fucceffively; and at length, by an uniform difplay of his pacific difpofition, and by rendering a long train of good offices to tliofe Indians, in return for their treachery and perfidy, he was fo happy as to be the fole inftru-ment of not only bringing about a lafting peace, but alfo of eftablifliing a trade and reciprocal in-tereft between the two nations.

After having performed this great work, he was prevailed upon to vifit the Copper-mine River, in company with a famous leader, called I-dat-le-aza; and it was from the report of thofe two men, that a journey to that part was propof-ed to the Hudfons Bay Company by the late Mr. Mofes Norton, in one thoufand feven hundred and fixty-nine. In one thoufand feven hundred and feventy he was engaged as the principal guide on that expedition; which he performed with greater punctuality, and more to my fatisfaclion, than perhaps any other Indian in all that country would have done. At his return to the Fort in one thoufand feven hundred and feventy-two, he was made head of all the Northern Indian nation; and continued to render great fervices to the Company during his life, by bringing a greater quantity of furrs to their Factory at Churchill River, than any other Indian ever did, or ever will do. His laft vifit to Prince of Wales's Fort was in the Spring of one thoufand feven hundred and eighty-two, and he intended to have repeated repeated it in the Winter following; but when he heard that the French had deftroyed the Fort, and carried off all the Company's fervants, he never afterwards reared his head, but took an opportunity, when no one fufpedted his intenti-on, to hang himfelf. This is the more to be wondered at, as he is the only Northern Indian who, that I ever heard, put an end to his own exiftence. The death of this man was a great! ofs to the Hudfon's Bay Company, and was attended with a moft melancholy fcene; no lefs than the death of fix of his wives, and four chil dren, all of whom were ftarved to death the fame Winter, in one thoufand feven hundred and eighty-three.

CHAP.

An Account of the principal adrupeds found in the
Northern Parts ofhudfon's Bay. The Buffalo,

Moofe, Mujk-ox, Deer and Beaver. A capital Mijiake cleared up refpeeing the We-was-kijlo.

Animals with Canine Teeth. The Wolf

Foxes of various colours Lynx, or Wild Cat Polar, or White Bear Black Bear Brown Bear Wolvereneotter Jackajh Wejack Skunk- Pine Martin Ermine, or Stote.

Animals with cutting Teeth.-The Mufk Beaver Porcupine Varying Hare American Hare Common Squirrel Ground Squirrel Mice of various Kinds, and the Cafior Beaver.

The Pinnated adrupeds with finlike Feet, found in Hudfon's Bay, are but three in number, viz. the Warlus, or Sea-Horfe, Seal, and Sea-Unicorn,

The Species of Fifh found in the Salt Water of Hudfon's Bay are alfofew in number; being the Black Whale White Whale Salmon and Kepling,

Shellfifh, and empty Shells off ever al kinds, found on the Sea Coafl near Churchill River.

Frogs of various ft7. es and colours; alfo a great variety of Grubbs, and other Infeds, akuays found in a frozen flate during Winter, but when expofedto the heat of ajl. w fire arefoun re-animated.

An Account offome of the principal Birds found in the Northernparts of Hud-fon'sbay; as well thofe that only 7nigrate there in Summer as thofe that are known to brave the coldefi Winters: Eagles of various kinds Hawks of various Jizes and plu? nage White or Stjowy Owl Grey or moiled Owl Cob-a-dee- cooch Raven Cinerious Crow Wood Pecker Ruffed Groufe Pheafint Wood Partridge Willow Partridge Rock Partridge Pigeon Red- breafted Thrufj Grojheak Snow Bunting

White-crowned Bimting Lapland Finch two forts Lark Titmeufe Swallow Martin Hopping Crane Brown Crane Bitron Carlow, two forts jfack Snipe Red Godwart Plover Black Guile met Northern Diver Black-throated Diver Red-throated Diver White Gull-Grey Gull Black-headpellican- Goofander–Swans of two fpedescommon Grey Goofe Canada Goofewhite or Snow Goofeblue Goofehornedwavylaugh ing Goofebarren Goofebrent Goofedunter Goofe–Bean Goofe.

The Species of Water-Fowl ufually called Duck, that refort to thofe Paris annually are in great va-riety; but thofe that are mofl efteemed are, the Mallard Duck Long-tailed Duck, Wigeon, and Teal,

Of the Vegetable Produdions as far North as Church ill River, particularly the mofl ufefid; fuch as the

Berry-bearing Bujhes, he. Goofeberrycrau berry Heathberry Dewaier-berryblack Cur rans'-Juniper-berrypartridge berry Sirawber- ryeye-berry Blue-Berryy-and a fmallf-peeies of Hips.

Burridgecoltsfoot Sorrel Dandelion Wijh-a-capucca fackafhey-puck Mofs of vari-ous forts Grafs of fever al kinds and Vetches

The Trees found fo far North near the Sea, con-fji only of Pines Juniper Small Poplar-Bujh willows and Creeping Birch.

BEFORE I conclude this work, it may not be improper to give a fliort account of the principal Animals that frequent the high Northern latitudes, though moft of them are found alfo far to the Southward, and confequently in much milder climates. The buffalo, muflc-ox, deer, and the moofe, have been already defcribed in this Journal. I Ihall therefore only make a few remarks on the latter, in order to rectify a mif-take, which, from wrong information, has crept into Mr. Pennant's Arctic Zoology. In page 21 of that elegant work, he claffes the Moofe with the We-was-ki(h, though it certainly has not any affinity to it.

The We-was-kifh, or as fome (though improperly) call it, the Wafkeffe, is quite a different animal from the moofe, being by no means fo large in fize. The horns of the We-waskifh are fome-thing fimilar to thofe of the common deer, but are not palmated in any part. They fland more upright, have fewer branches, and want the brow-antler. The head of this animal is fo far from being ueing like that of the Moofe, that the nofe i-. fliarp, like the nofe of a fheep: indeed, the whole external appearance of the head is not very unlike that of an afs. The hair is ufually of a fandy red; and they are frequently called by the Englifh who vifit the interior parts of the country, red deer. Their flefti is tolerable eating; but the fat is as hard as tallow, and if eaten as hot as poflible, will yet chill in fo fliort a time, that it clogs the teeth, and fticks to the roof of the mouth, in fbch a manner as to render it very difagree-able. In the Spring of one thoufand feven hundred and feventy-five, 1 had thirteen fledge-loads of this meat brought to Cumberland Houfe in one day, and alfo two of the heads of this animal un-ikinned, but the horns were chopped off; a proof of their wearing them the whole Winter. They are the moft ftupid of all the deer kind, and frequently make a fhrill whittling, and quivering noife, not very unhke the braying of an afs, which direds the hunter to the very fpot where they arc. They generally keep in large herds, and when they find plenty of paflure, remain a long time in one place. Thofe deer are feldom an object of chace with the Indians bordering on Bafquiau, except when moofe and other game fail. Their ikins, when drefled, very much re-femble that of the moofe, though they are much thinner, and have this peculiar quality, that they will wafli as well as fliamoy leather; whereas all the other leathers and pelts drefled by the Indians, if they get wet, turn quite hard, unlefs great care be taken to keep conftantly rubbing them while drying.

The perfon who informed Mr. Pennant that the we-was-kifli and the moofe are the fame animal, never fawone of them; and the only reafon he had to fuppofe it, was the great refemblance of their fldns: yet it is rather ftrange, that fo indefatigable a collector of Natural Hillory as the late Mr. Andrew Graham, fhould have omitted making particular enquiry about them: for any foreign Indian, particularly thofe that refide near Bafquiau, could eafily have convinced him to the contrary.

Animals with Canine Teeth.

Wolves. Wolves are frequently met with in the countries Weft of Hudfon's Bay, both on the barren grounds and among the woods, but they are not numerous; it is very uncommon to fee more than three or four of them in a herd. Thofe that keep to the Weftward, among the woods, are generally of the ufual colour, but the greateft part of thofe that are killed by the Efquimaux are perfectly white. All the wolves in Hudfon's Bay are very fhy of the human race, yet when (harp fet, they frequently follow the Indians for feveral days, but always keep at a diftance. They are great enemies to the Indian dogs, and frequently frequently kill and eat thofe that are heavy loaded, and cannot keep up with the main body. The Northern Indians have formed ftrange ideas of this animal, as they think it does not eat its viduals raw; but by a lingular and wonderful fagacity, peculiar to itfelf, has a method of cooking them without fire. The females are much fwifter than the males; for which reafon the Indians, both Northern and Southern, are of opinion that they kill the greateft part of the game. This cannot, however, always be the cafe; for to the North of Churchill they, in general, live a forlorn life all the Winter, and are feldom (een in pairs till the Spring, when they begin to couple; and generally keep in pairs all the Summer. They always burrow under. ground to bring forth their yonng; and though it is natural to fuppofe them very fierce at thole times, yet I have frequently feen the Indians go to their dens, and take out the young ones and play with them. I never knew a Northern Indian hurt one of them: on the contrary, they always put them carefully into the den again; and I have fome-times feen them paint the faces of the young Wolves with vcrmillion, or red ochre.

The Arctic Foxes are in fome years remarka-Foxes of bly plentiful, but generally moft fo on the barren J",).."" ground, near the fea-coaft. Notwithftanding what has been faid of this animal only vifiting the fettlements once in five or feven years, I can affirm there is not one year in twenty that they arc not cauirht va 110113 CO-caught in greater or Icfs numbers at Churchill; and I have known that for three years running,, not lefs than from two hundred to four hundred have been caught each year within thirty miles of the Fort. They always come from the North along the coaft, and generally make their appearance at Churchill about the middle of Odober, but their Ikins are feldom in feafon till November J during that time they are never molefted, but permitted to feed round the Fort, till by degrees they become almoft domeftic. The great numbers of thofe animals that vifit Churchill River in fome years do not all come in a body, as it would be impoflible for the fourth part of them to find fubfiftence by the way; but when they come near the Fort, the carcaites of dead whales lying along the fhores, and the fldn and other offal, after boiling the oil, afford them a plentiful repaft, and prove the means of keeping them about the Fort till, by frequent reinforcements from the Northward, their numbers are fo far in-creafed as almoft to exceeded credibility.

When their fkins are in feafon, a number of traps and guns are fet, and the greateft part of I them are caught in one month, though fome few are found during the whole Winter. I have frequently known near forty killed in one night within half a mile of Prince of Wales's Fort; but this feldom happens after the firft or fecond night. When Churchill River is frozen over near the mouth, the greateft part of the furviving white

Foxes

Foxes crofs the river, and direct their courfe to the Southward, and in fome years affemble in confiderable numbers at York Fort and Severn River. Whether they are all killed, or what becomes of thofe which efcape, is very uncertain; but it is well known that none of them ever migrate again to the Northward. Befides taking a trap fo freely, they are otherwife fo fimple, that I have feen them fhot off-hand while feeding, the fame as fparrows in a heap of chaff, fometimes two or three at a fhot. This fport is always moft fuccefsful in moon-light nights; for in the daytime they generally keep in their holes among the rocks, and under the hollow ice at high-water-mark.

Thefe animals will prey on each other as readily as on any other animals they find dead in a trap, or wounded by gun; which renders them fo deftrudive, that I have known upvards of one hundred and twenty Foxes of different colours eaten, and deftroyed in their traps by their comrades in the courfe of one Winter, within half a mile of the Fort.

The Naturalifts feem ftill at a lofs to know their breeding-places, which are doubtlefs in every part of the coaft they frequent. Several of them breed near Churchill, and I have feen them in confiderable numbers all along the Weft coaft of Hudfon's Bay, particularly at Cape Efquimaux, Navel's Bay, and Whale Cove, alfo on Marble ifland J fo that wuth fome degree of confidence we ma- ainrm, that they breed on every part of the coaft they inhabit during the Summer feafon. Ihey generally have from three to five young at a litter; morel never faw with one old one. When young they are all over almoft of a footy black, but as the fall advances, the belly, fides, and tail turn to a light afh-colour; the back, legs, fome part of the face, and the tip of the tail, changes to a lead colour; but when the Winter fets in they become perfectly white: the ridge of the back and the tip of the tail are the lafl places that change to that colour; and there are few of them which have not a few dark hairs at the tip of the tail all the Winter. If taken young, they are eafily domellicated in fome degree, but I never faw one that was fond of being carefted; and they are always impatient of confinement.,. White Foxes, when killed at any confidera-

The White

Fo2c. ble diflance from the fea coafl, (where they cannot poftibly get any thing to prey upon, except rabbits, mice, and partridges,) are far from being difagreeable eating. And on Marble Ifland I have fhot them when they were equal in flavour to a rabbit; probably owing to their feeding entirely on eggs and young birds; but near Churchill River they are as rank as train-oil.

The Lynx, or Wild Cat, is very fcarce to

The Lynx, r,

Of Wildcat, the North of Churchill; but is exaclly the fame as thofe which are found in great plenty to the South Weft. I have obferved the tracks of this animal at Churchill, and feen them killed, and have have eaten of their flefli in the neighbourhood of York

Fort. The flefli is white, and nearly as good as that of a rabbit. They arc I think, much larger than that which is defcribed in the Arctic Zoology; they never approach near the fettle-ments in Hudfons Bay, and are very deftruflive to rabbits; they feldom leave a place which is frequented by rabbits till they have nearly killed them all.

The Polar or White Bear, though common-ne p. on the fea-coaft, is feldom found in its Winter gjJ'''''' retreats by any of our Northern Indians, except near Churchill River; nor do 1 fuppofe that the Efquimaux fee or kill any of them more frequently during that feafon; for in the courfe of many years refidence at Churchill River, I fcarce-ly ever faw a Winter flin brought from the Northward by the floop. Probably the Efqi-maux, if they kill any, may referve the fliins for their own ufe; for at that feafon their hair is very long, with a thick bed of wool at the bottom, and they are remarkably clean and white. The Winter is the only feafon that fo oily a (km as the Bear's can poflibly be cleaned and dreffed by thofe people, without greafing the hair, which is very unpleafant to them; for though they eat train-oil, isfc. yet they are as careful as pollible to keep their clothes from being greafed with it. To drefs one of thofe greafy ikms in Winter, as foon as taken from the beaft, it is fl: retched out on a fmooth patch of fnow, and there flaked down.

down, where it foon freezes as hard as a board: while in that ftate, the women fcrape off all the fat, till they come to the very roots of the hair. It is fometimes permitted to remain in that pofiti-on for a confiderable time; and when taken from the fnow, is hung up in the open air. The more intenfe the froft, the greater is its drying quality; and by being wafted about by the wind, with a little fcraping, it in time becomes perfectly fupple, and both pelt and hair beautifully white. Drying deer, beaver, and otter (kins, in this manner render their pelts very white, but not fupple; probably owing to the clofe texture and thicknefs of their Ikins; whereas the fkin of the bear, though fo large an animal, is remarkably thin and fpungy.

Black It is rather fingular that the Polar Bears are feldom found on the land during the Winter, on which account it is fuppofed they go out on the ice, and keep near the edge of the water during that feafon, while the females that are pregnant feek ftielter at the ftirts of the woods, and dig themfelvesdensin the deepeft drifts of Inow they can find, where they re-main in a ftate of inactivity, and without food, from the latter end of December or January, till the latter end of March; at which lime they leave their dens, and bend their courfe towards the fea with their cubs; which, in general, are two in number. Notwithftanding the great magnitude of thofe animals when full grown, yet their young are not larger than rabbits, and when they leave their dens, in March. I have frequently feen them not larger than a white fox, and their fteps on the fnow not bigger than a crown-piece, when thofe of their dam meafure near fifteen inches long and nine inches broad. They propagate when young, or at leaft before they are half-grown; for I have killed young females not larger than a London calf, with milk in their teats; whereas fome of the full grown ones are heavier than the largeft of our common oxen. Indeed I was once at the killing of one, when one of its hind feet being cut off at the ankle, weighed fifty-four pounds. The males have a bone in theirMV, as a dog has.

Black Beis are not very numerous to the The Black-North Weft of Churchill. The manner of hfe is the fame of the reft of the fpecies, though the face of the country they inhabit, differs widely from the more mild climates. In Summer they proul about in fearch of berries, c. and as the Winter approaches, retire to their dens, which are always under-ground; and generally, if not always, on the fide of a fmall hillock. The Bears that inhabit the Southern parts of America are faid to take up their winter abode in hollow trees; but I never faw any trees in my Northern travels, that could afford any fuchlhelter.

The places of retreat of thofe Bears that burrow under-ground are eafily difcovered in Winter, by the rime that hangs about the mouth of the den j for let the fnow be ever fo deep, the

B b heat has, and of couite unite in copulation; but the time of their cqurtfhip is I believe, not exacfily known: probably it may be in July or Auguft, for at thofe times I have often been at the killing them, when the males were fb attached to their miflreftss, that after the female was killed, the male would put his two foie-paws over, and fuffcr himfelf to be fiiot before he would quit her. I have frequently feen and killed thofe animals near twelve leagues from the land; but as the Fail of the year advances, they are taught by in(iinl to feek the fhore. Though fuch a tremendous animal, they are very fhy of coming near a man; but when clofely purfued in the water, they frequently attack the boat, feize the oars, and wreft them from tlic hands of the flrongeft man, fceming defirous to go on board; but the people on tliofe occafions are always provided with firearms and hatchets, to prevent fuch an unwelcome vifit. The fle(h of this animal, when killed in Winter, (if not too old,) is far from being unplea-fant eating; and the young cubs, in the Spring, are rather delicate than othetwifc. The teats of the females are only two in number, and are placed between the fore-legs. The bed Drawing of this Animal I have feen, is that done by Mr. Webber, among the Plates of Cook's laft Voyage.

heat and breath ot the animal prevents the mouth of the den from being entirely doled up. Ihey generally retire to their Winter quarters before the fnow is of any confiderable depth, and never come abroad again (unlefs difturbed) till the thaws are confiderable, which in thofe high latitudes is feldom till the latter end of March or the beginning of April; fo that the few Black Bears that inhabit thofe cold regions may be faid to fubfifl for four months at leaft without food. I have been prefent at the killing two of them in Winter; and the Northern Indian method is limi-lar to that faid to be in ufe among the Kamtfchat-kans; for they always blocked up the mouth of the den with logs of wood, then broke open the top of it, and killed the animal either with a fpear or a gun; but the latter method is reck-pned both cowardly and wafteful, as it is not poftible for the Bear either to make its efcape, or to do the Indians the leaft injury. Sometimes they put a fnare about the Bear's neck, and draw up his head clofe to the hole, and kill him with a hatchet. Though thofe animals are but fcarce to the North of Churchill, yet they are fo-nume-rous between York Fort and Cumberland Houfe, that in one thoufand feven hundred and feventy-four I faw eleven killed in the courfe of one day's journey, but their flefli was abominable. This was in the month of June, long before any fruit was ripe, for the want of which they then fed entirely on water infects, which in fome of the lakes lakes we croffed that day were in aftonifhing multitudes.

The method by which the Bears catch thofe infects is by fwimming with their mouths open, in the fame manner as the whales do, when feeding on the fea-fpider.

There was not one of the Bears killed that day, which had not its ftomacu as full of thofe infedls (only) as ever a hog's was with grains, and when cut open, the flench from them was intolerable. I have, however, eaten of fome killed at that early feafon which were very good; but they were found among the woods, far from the places where thofe infed: s haunt, and had fed on grafs and other herbage. After the middle of July, when the berries begin to ripenj they are excellent eating, and fo continue till January or February following; but late in the Spring they are, by long fafting, very poor and dry eating.

The Southern Indians kill great numbers of thofe Bears at all feafons of the year; but no encouragement can prevent them from lingeing al-

The infects here fpoken of are of two kinds; the one is nearly black, its (kin hard like a beetle, and not very nnlike a grafshopper, and darts through the water with great eafe, and with fome degree of velocity. The other fort is brown, has wings, and is as foft as the common cieg-fly. The latter are the mod numerous; and in fome of the lakes fuch quantities of them are forced into the bays in gales of wind, and there prefted together in fuch multitudes, that they are killed, and remain there a great nui-fance; for I have feveral times, in my inland voyages from York Fort, found it fcarcely polliblc to land in fome of thofe bays for the intolerable ftench of thofe infects, which in fome places were lying in putrid mafles to the depth of two or three feet. It is more than probable, that the Bear, pccafionally feed on thefe deadinfefts.

mofi: every one that is in good condition: fo that the few fkins they do fave and bring to the market, are only of thofe which are fopoor that their flelliis not worth eating. In faci, the fkinning of a Bear Ipoiu the meat thereof, as much as it would do to fkin a young porker, or a roaftlng pig. The fame may be faid of fwans fthe Ikins of which the Company have lately made an article of trade;; othervvife thoufands of their fldns might be brought to market annually, by the In dians that trade with the Hudfon's Bay Company's fervants at the different fettlements about the Bay. The Brown Brown Bears are, I behevc, never found in "" the North-Indian territories: but I faw the fkin of an enormous grizzled Bear at the tents of the Efquimaux at the Copper River; and many of them are faid to breed not very remote from that part. Thewoive- The WolVERENE is comnion in the Northern regions, as far North as the Copper River, and perhaps farther. They are equally the inhabitants of woods and barren grounds; for the Efquimaux to the North of Churchill kill many of them when their fkins are in excellent feafon: a proof of their It is common for the Southern Indians to tame and domefticate the young cubs; and they are frequently taken fo young that they cannot eat. On thofe occafions the Indians oblige their wives who have milk in their breafts tofuckle them. And one of the Company's fervants, whofe name is Ifaac Batt, willing to be as great a brute as his Indian companions, abfc-liitely forced one of his wives, who had recently loft her infant, to fuckle a yciung Bear.

rene their being capable of braving the feverefl: cold. They are very How in their pace, but their wonderful fagacity, ilrength, and acute fent, make ample amends for that defect; for they are fel-dom killed at any feafon when they do not prove very fa;: a great proof of their being excellent providers. With refpecl to the iiercenefs of this animal which fome affert, 1 can fay little, but I 1 know them to be bcafts of great courage and refolution, for I once faw one of them take pof-feflion of a deer that an

Indian had killed, and though the Indian advanced within twenty yards, he would not relinquifh his claim to it, but fuf-fered himfelf to be (liot Handing on the deer. I once faw a fimilar inftance of a lynx, or wild cat, which alfo fuffered itfelf, to be killed before it would rehnquilh the prize. The wolverenes have alfo frequently been feen to take a deer from a wolf before the latter had time to begin his repaft after killing it. Indeed their amazing flrength, and the length and fliarpnefs of their claws, render them capable of making a ftrong reliftance againft any other animal in thofe parts, the Bear not excepted. As a proof of their amazing Ilrength, there was one at Churchill fome years fince, that overfet the greatell part of a large pile of wood, (containing a whole Winter's firing, that meafured upwards of feventy yards round,) to get at fome provifions that had been hid there by the Company's fervants, when going to the Factory to fpend the Chriftmas holidays.

days. The facl was, this animal had been lurking about in the neighbourhood of their tent (which was about eight miles from the Factory) for fome weeks, and had committed many depredations on the game caught in their traps and fnares, as well as eaten many foxes that were killed by guns fet for that purpofe: but the Wolverene was too cunning to take either trap or gun himfelf The people knowing the mifchievous-difpolition of thofe animals, took (as they thought) the moft effeclual method to fecure the remains of their provifions, which they did not chufe to carry home, and accordingly tied it up in bundles and placed it on the top of the wopd-pile, (about two miles from their tent,) little thinking the Wolverene would find it out; but to their great furprize, when they returned ta their tent after the holidays, they found the pile of wood in the ftate already mentioned, though fome of the trees that compofed it were as much as two men could carry. The only reafon the people could give for the animal doing fo much mifchief was, that in his attempting to carry off the booty, fome of the fmall parcels of provifions had fallen down into the heart of the pile, and fooner than lofe half his prize, he purfued the above method till he had accomplilhed his ends. The bags of flour, oatmeal, and peafe, though of no ufe to him, he tore all to pieces, and fcattered the contents about on the fnow; but every bit of animal food, confiding of beef, pork, bacon, venifon.

venifon, fait geefe, partridges, 't. to a confide-rable amount, he carried away. Thefe animal are great enemies to the Beaver, but the manner of life of the latter prevents them from falling into their clutches fo frequently as many other animals; they commit vaft depredations on the foxes during the Summer, while the young ones are fmall; their quick fcent directs them to their dens, and if the entrance be too fmall, their flrength enables them to widen it, and go in and kill the mother and all her cubs. In fact, they are the moft deftruclive animals in this country.

Otteks are pretty plentiful in the rivers to the The otwr. North of Churchill, as far as latitude 62; farther North I do not recollecl to have feen any. In Winter they generally frequent thofe parts of rivers where there are falls or rapids, which do not freeze in the coldeft Winters; becaufe in fuch (ituations they are moft likely to find plenty of fifh, and the open water gives them a free ad-mifiion to the fhore, where they fometimes go to eat the fiqi they have caught; but moft commonly lit on the ice, or get on a great ftone in the river. They are frequently feen in the very depth of Winter at a conftderable diftance from

Mr. Graham fays they take their lodging in the clefts of locks, or ia hollow trees. 1 he former I acknowledge, hut I believe that neither Mr. Graham noi any of the Company's fervants ever faw an inftance of the latter. In faft, dining all my travels in the incerior parts of Hudfon's Bay, I never faw a hollow tree that was capable of affording fhtlter to any larger animal than martins, jackafhe?, or uejacks; much leii the juiqa-hatch or Bear, as fome have afierted.

any known open water, both in woods and on open plains, as well as on the ice of large lakes; but it is not known what has led them to fuch places: perhaps merely for amufement, for they are not knovn to kill any game on the land during that feafon. If purfued when among the woods in Winter, (where the fnow is always light and deep,) they immediately dive, and make conliderable way under it, but are eafily traced by the motion of the fnow above them, and foon overtaken. The Indians kill numbers of them with clubs, by tracing them in the fnow; but fome of the old ones are fo fierce when cloe purfued, that they turn and fly at their purfuer, and their bite is fo fevere that it is much dreaded by the Indians. Befides this method of killing them, the Indians have another, which is equally fuccefsful; namely, by concealing themfelves within a reafonable gun-fhot of the Otters ufual landing-places, and waiting their coming out of the water. This method is more generally prac-tifedin moon-light nights. They alfo flioot many of them as they are fporting in the water, and Ibme few are caught in traps.

The Otters in this, as well as every other part of the bay, vary in fize and colour, according to age and feafon. In Summer, when the hair is very Ihort, they are almoft black, but as the Winter advances, they turn to a beautiful dark auburn, except a fmall fpot under the chin, which is of a filver gray. This colour they retain all the Winter; ter; but late in the Spring (though long before they fhed their coiit) they turn to a dull rufty brown; fo that a perfon who is acquainted with thofe changes can tell to a great nicety, by looking at the Ikins, fwlien offered for fale,; the very time they were killed, and pay for them according to their value. The number of their young is various, from three to live or fix. They unite in copulation the fame as a dog, and fo do every other animal that has a bone in the penis. I will here enumerate all of that defcription that I know of in thofe parts, ih-z. bears of all forts, wolves, wolvereens, foxes, martins, otters we-jacks, jackafties, Ikunks, and ermines.

Jackash. This animal is certainly no other The Tack-than the lefler Otter of Canada, as its colour, " iize, and manner of life entirely correfpond with the defcription of that animal in Mr. Pennant's Arctic Zoology. They, like the larger Otter, are frequently found in Winter feveral miles from any water, and are often caught in traps built for martins. They are fuppofed to prey on mice and partridges, the fame as the martin; but when by the fide of rivers or creeks, they generally feed on fifli. They vary fo much in fize and colour, that it was very eafy for Mr. Pennant to have miftaken the fpecimen fent home for another animal. They are the eafieft to tame and domefti- cate

The Otter is very fond of play; and one of their favourite paftimes is, to get on a high ridge of fnow, bend their fore-feet backward, ar. d fiide down the fide of it, fometimes to the diflance of twenty yards.

cate of any animal I know, except a large fpecies of field-mice, called the Hair-tailed Moufe; for in a very fhort time they are fo fond, that it is fcarce-ly poffible to keep them from climbing up one's legs and body, and they never feel themfelves happier than when fitting on the (houlder; but when angry, or frightened, (like the llcunk,) they emit a very difagreeable fmell. They fleep very much in the day, but prowl about and feed in the night; they are very fierce when at their meals, not fuffering thofe to whom they are moft attached to take it from them. I have kept feveral of them., but their over-fondnefs made them trou-blefome, as they were always in the way; and their fo frequently emitting a difagreeable fmell, rendered them quite difgulling. The We- Though the We JACK and Skunk are never Skunk." found in the Northern Indian country, yet I cannot help obferving that the foetid fmell of the latter has not been much exaggerated by any Author. When I was at Cumberland Houfe, in the Fall of one thoufand feven hundred and feventy-four, fome Indians that were tenting on

Mr. Graham afterts that this animal frequents the banks of creeks, and feeds on fifh; but thefe are by no means their ufual haunts. I have, however, no doubt, but when they find fifli on the land, that they may eat it, like other carnivorous animals; but they are as fiiy of taking the water as a domeftic cat. They climb trees, and catch partridges, mice, and rabbits, with as much eafe as a martin. They are eafily tamed and domefticated, are very fond of tea-leaves, have a pleafantmuflcy fmell, and, aj-e very playful, the plantation killed two of thofe animals, and made a feaft of them; when the fpot where they were finged and gutted was fo impregnated with that naufeous fmell which they emit, that after a whole Winter had clapfed, and the fnow had thawed away in the Spring, the fmell was flill intolerable. I am told, however, that the flefh is by no means tainted with the fmell, if care be taken in gutting, and taking out the bag that contains this furprifmg effluvia, and which they have the power of emitting at pleafure; but I rather doubt their being capable of cjeding their urine fo far as is reported; I do not think it is their urine which contains that peftilential effluvia, for if that was the cafe, all the country where they frequent would be fo fcented with it, that neither man nor beaft could live there with any degree of comfort.

The Common Pine Martin is found in moftyje Pins
Martin.
parts of this country, and though very fcarce in what is abfolutely called the Northern Indian territory, yet by the Indians ftroliing toward the borders of the Southern Indian country, are killed in great numbers, and annually traded for at Churchill Factory.

The Ermine, or Stote, is common in thofe The Er-parts, but generally more plentiful on the barren stote. ground, and open plains or marflies, than in the woods; probably owing to the mice being more numerous in the former fituations than in the latter.

latter. In Summer they are of a tawney brown, but in "Winter of a delicate white all over, except the tip of the tail, which is of a gloffy black. They are, for their iize, the ftrongeft and moft courageous animal I know: as they not only kill partridges, but even attack rabbits with great fuccefs. They fometimes take up their abode in the out-oifices and provilion-flieds belonging to the Factories; and though they commit feme de-predations, make ample amends by killing great numbers of mice, which are very numerous and deftruclive at moft of the fettlements in the Bay. I have taken much pains to tame and domefticate this beautiful animal, but never could fucceed; for the longer I kept it the more reftlefs and impatient it became.

Animals with Cutfmg Teeth.

Themuflc The Musk Rat, or Musquash; or, asnatura-' lifts call it, the Musk Beaver; is common in thofe parts; generally frequenting ponds and deep fwamps that do not freeze dry in Winter. The manner of life of this fpecies of animals is peculiar, and refembles that of the Beaver, as they are in fome refpects provident, and build houfes to flielter themfelves from the inclemency of the cold in Winter; but inftead of making thofe houfes on the banks of ponds or fwamps, like the Beaver, they generally build them on the ice as foon as it is fkinned over, and at a confide-r ible diftance from the fliore; always taking care to keep a hole open in the ice to admit them to dive for their food, which chiefly confifts of the roots of grafs: in the Southern parts of the country they feed much on a well known root, call Ca-Linus Arofiiatiais. The materials made ufe of in building their houfes arc mud and grafs, which they fetch up from the bottom. It fometimes h. ippens in very cold Winters, that the holes in their houfes freeze over, in fpite of all their efforts to keep them open. When that is the cafe, and they have no provifions left in the houfe, the ilrongeft preys on the weakeft, till by degrees only one is left out of a whole lodge. I have fcen feveral inftances fufficient to confirm the truth of this aifertion; for when their houfes were broke open, the fkeletons of feven or eight have been found, and only one entire animal. Though they occafionally eat lih and other animal food, yet in general they feed very clean, and when fat are good eating, particularly when nicely fmged, fcalded, and boiled. They are eafily tamed, and foon grow fond; are very cleanly and playful, and fmell exceedingly pleafant of mufk; but their refemblance to a Rat is fo great. that few are partial to them. Indeed the only difference between them and a common Rat, ex-clufive of their fuperior fize, is, that their hind-feet are large and webbed, and the tail, inflead of being round, is flat and fcaly.

Though

Though I have before faid, that the Mufk Beaver generally build their houfes on the ice, it is not always the cafe; for in the Southern parts of the couniry, particularly about Cumberland Houfe, 1 have feen, in fome of the deep fvvamps that were over-run with ruflies and long grafs, many fmall iflands that have been raifed by the induftry of tho(e animals; on the tops of which they had built their houfes, like the beaver, fome of which were very large. The tops of thofe houles are favourite breeding places for the geefe, which bring forth their young brood there, without the fear of being molefted by foxes, or any other deilruclive animal, except the Eagle., Fo cupinES are fo fcarce to the North of

The Porcu-

Pe. Churchill River, and I do not recollect to have feen moretha. n fix during almoft three years reli-dence among the Northern Indians. Mr. Pennant obferves in his Arclic Zoology, that they always have two at a time; one brought forth alive and the other ftill-born; but I never faw an inftance of this kind, though in different parts of the country I have feen them killed in all flashes of pregnancy. Ihe flefh of the porcupine is very delicious, and fo much efteemed by the Indians, that they think it the greatefl: luxury hat their country affords. The quills are in great

This information was given to Mr. Pennant from the authority of Mr. Graham; but the before-mentioned account of feeing them killed in all flages of pregnancy, when no fymptoms of that kind appeared, will I hope, be fuiscient to cle: r up that miftake.

great requeft among the women; who make them into a variety of ornaments, fuch as fhot-bags, belts, garters, bracelets, Is'c. Their mode of copulation is fingular, for their quills will not permit them to perform that office in the ufual mode, like other quadrupeds. To remedy this inconvenience, they fometimes lie on their fides, and meet in that manner; but the ufual mode is for the male to lie on his back, and the female to walk over him, (beginning at his head,) till the arts of generation come in contact. They are the moft forlorn animal I know; for in thofe parts of Hudfon's Bay where they are moft numerous, it is not common to fee more than one in a place. They are fo remarkably flow and ftupid, that our Indians going with packets from Fort to Fort often fee them in the trees, but not having occafion for them at that time, leave them till their return; and fhould their abfence be a week or ten days, they are fure to find them within a mile of the place where they had feeii them before.

Foxes of various colours are not fcarce in thofe Foxes of,.,. v - 1 1. various Co-parts; but the natives iivmg iuch a wandermg lours.

life, feldom kill many. It is rather ftrange that no other fpecies of Fox, except the white, are found at any diftance from the woods on the barren ground; for fo long as the trade has been 6ftabliflied with the Efquimaux to the North of

Churchill, I do not recoiled: that Foxes of any t)ther colour than white were ever received from them.

Hares, g A JOURNEY TO THE

Varying TIic Varying Hares afC numerous to the

North of Churchill River, and extend as far as latitude 72", probably farther. They delight moil in rocky and iiony places, near the borders of woods; though many of them brave the cold-eft Winters on entire barren ground. In Sum-mer they are nearly the colour of our Englifli wild rabbit; but in Winter affume a moft delicate white all over, except the tips of the ears, which are bhck. They are, when full grown and in good condition, very large, many of them weighing fourteen or fifteen pounds; and if not too old, are good eating. In Winter they feed on long rye-grafs and the tops of dwarf willows, but in Summer eat berries, and different forts of fmall herbage. They are frequently killed on the South-fide of Churchill River, and feveral have been known to breed near the fettlement at that place. They muft multiply very faft, for when we evacuated Prince of Wales's Fort in one thou-fand feven hundred and eighty-two, it was rare to fee one of them within twenty or thirty miles of that place; but at our return, in one thoufand feven hundred and eighty-three, we found them in fuch numbers, that it was common for one man to kill two or three in a day within half a mile of the new fettlement. But partly perhaps, from fo many being killed, and partly from the furvivors being fo frequently diaurbed, they have fliifted'their fituation, and are at prefent as fcarce near the fettlement as ever. The Northern Indians Indians purfue a finguhr methovi of (liootlng thofe Hares; finding by long experience that thefe animals will not bear a direct approach, when the Indians fee a hare iitting, they walk round it in circles, always drawing nearer at every revolution, till by degrees they get within gun-fliot. The middle of the day, if it be clear weather, is the beft time to kill them in this manner; for before and after noon, the Sun's altitude being fo fmall, makes a man's fliadow fo long on the fnow, as to frighten the Hare before he can approach near enough to kill it. The fame may be faid of deer when on open plains, who are frequently more frightened at the long ihadow than at the man himfelf.

The American Hares, or, as they are calledj:. in Hudfon's Bay, Rabbits, are not plentiful in the Eaftern parts of the Northern Indian country, not even in thofe parts that are fituated among the woods; but to the Weftward, bordering on the Southern Indian country, they are in fome places pretty numerous, though by no means equal to what has been reported of them at York Fort, and forne other fettlementsin the Bay.

The furr of thofe animals, when killed in the beft part of the feafon, was for many years entirely neglected by the furriers; for fome lime paft the Company have ordered as many of their ikins to be fent home as can be procured j they are but of fmall value.

The flcfh of thofe Hares is generally more C c efteemed

The Am;-: an Haie.

eftecmcd than that of the former. They are in feafon all the Winter; and though they generally feed on the brufli of pine and fir, during that feafon, yet many of the Northern Indians eat the contents of the ftomach. They are feldom fought after in Summer, as in that feafon they are not efteemed good eating; but as the Fall advances they are, by feeding on berries, Is'c. moft excellent. In Spring they fhed their Winter coat, and during the Summer are nearly the colour of the Englifli wild rabbit, but as the Winter advances they becoftie nearly white. In thick weather they are eafily (hot with the gun; but the moft ufual method of killing them is by fnares, fet nearly in the manner defcribed by Dragge in the Firft Volume of his North Weft Paffacre.

The Com- The ComMON Squirrels are plentiful in the jnon quir- y paits of this country, and are caught by the natives in confiderable numbers with fnares, while the boys kill many of them with blunt-headed arrows. The method of fnaring them is rather curious, though very fimple, as it confifts of nothing more than fetting a number of fnares all round the body of the tree in which they are feen, and arranging them in fuch a manner that it is fcarcely poffible for the fquirrels to defcend without being entangled in one of them. This is generally the amulement of the boys. Though fmali, and feldom fat, yet they are good eating.

The beauty and delicacy of this animal induced me to attempt taming and domefti-cating fome of them.

them, but without fuccefs; for though feveral of them were fo familiar as to take any thing out of my hand, and fit on the table where I was writing, and play with the pens, c. yet they never would bear to be handled, and were very mifchicvous; gnawing the chair-bottoms, window-curtains, faflies, is'c. to pieces. They are an. article of trade in the Company's ftandard, but the greateft part of their fkins, being killed in Summer, are of very little value.

The Ground Squirrels are never found inthecround the woody parts of North Amer-ica, but are very "'" plentiful on the barren ground, to the North of Churchill River, as far as the latitude 71, and probably much farther. In iize they are equal to the American Grey Squirrel, though more beautiful in colour. They generally burrow among the rocks and under great ftones, but fometimes on the fides of fandy ridges; and are fo provident in laying up a Winter's (lock during the Summer, that they are feldom feen on the furfacfe of the fnow in Winter. They generally feed on the tufts of grafs, the tender tops of dwarf willows, c. and are for the moft part exceedingly fat, and good eating. They arc eafily tamed, and foon grow fond; by degrees they will bear handling as well as a cat; are exceeding cleanly, very playful, and by no means fo reitlefs and impatient of confinement as the Common Squirrel.

Mice are in great plenty and variety in all Mice of va arts of Hudfon's Bay; the marflies being inha-""" C c 2 bited ,; j88 A JOURNEY TO THE bited by one fpecies, and the dry ridges by another. The Shrew Mou. fe is frequently found in Beaver houfes during Winter, where they not only find a warm habitation, but alfo pick up a comfortable livelihood from the fcraps left by the Beaver. Mofl of the other fpecies build or make nefts of dry grafs, of fuch a fize and thicknefs, that when covered with how, they mull be fuf-ficiently warm. They all feed on grafs in general, but will alfo eat animal food when they can get it. The Hair-tailed Moufe is the largeft in the Northern parts of the Bay, being little inferior in lize to a common rat. They always burrow under ftones, on dry ridges; are very inoffenlive, and fo eafily tamed, that if taken when full-grown, fome of them will in a day or two be perfectly reconciled, and are fo fond of being handled, that they will creep about your neck, or into your bofom. In Summer they are grey, and in Winter change to white, but are by no means fo beautiful as a white ermine. At that feafon they are infefted with multitudes of fmall lice, not a lixth part fo large as the mites in a cheefe; in fact, they are fo fmail, that at firft fight they only appear like reddifli-brown dull, but on clofer examination are all perceived in motion. In one large and beautiful animal of this kind, caught in the depth of Winter, I found thofe little vermin fo numerous about It, that almoft every hair was covered with them as thick as ropes wit hi onions, and when they approached near the ends of the hair they may be faid to change the moufe from white to a faint brown. At that time I had an excellent microfcope, and endeavoured to ex-r. mine them, and to alcertain their form, but the weather was fo exceedingly cold, that the glaffes became damp with the moifture of my breath before 1 could get a fingle fight. Ihe hind-feet of thcfe Mice are exactly like thofe of a Bear, and the fore-feet are armed with a horny fubftance, (that I never faw in any other fpecies of the Moufe,) which is wonderfully adapted for Icraping away the ground where they wifli to take up their abode. They are plentiful on fome of the ftony ridges near Churchill Fa5tory, but never approach the houfe, or any of the out-offices. From appearances they are very local, and feldom ftray far from their habitations even in fummer, and in Winter they are feldom feen on the furface of the fnow; a great proof of their being provident in Summer to lay by a flock for that feafon.

Pinnated Suadrueds.

With refpecl to the Pinnated Quadrupeds with fin-like feet, there are but few fpecies in Hud-fon's Bay. The Walrus, or Sea-Horfe, and Seals, are the only ones that I know.

The Walrus arc numerous about Merry andthewai-Jones's Iflands, but more fo on a fmall ifland called Sea-Horfe Ifland, that lies in the fair way going ing to Whale Cove. In July one thoufand feven hundred and fixty-feven, when on my voyage to the North of Churchill River, in paffing Sea-Horfe Ifland, we faw fuch numbers of thofe animals lying on the ftiore, that when fome fwivel guns loaded with ball were fired among them, the whole beach feemed to be in motion. The great-eft part of them plunged into the water, and many of them fwam round the veffel within mufket-fhot. Every one on board exerted their fkill in killing them, but it was attended with fo httle fuccefs, that the few which were killed funk to he bottom, and thofe which were mortally wounded made oflf out of our reach.

With what propriety thofe animals are called Horfes, I cannot fee; for there is not the leail refemblance in any one part. Their bodies, fins, Zffc. are exactly like thofe of an enormous Seal, and the head is not very unlike that animal, ex-. cept that the nofe is much broader, to give room for the two large tufks that proje from the upper jaw. Thofe tufks, and their red fparkling eyes, make them have a very fierce and formidable appearance.

They are generally found in confiderable numbers, which indicate their love of fociety; and; their affeclion for each other is very apparent, as they always flock round thofe that are wounded, and when they fink, accompany them to the bottom, but foon rife to the furface, and make a hideous roaring, and of all amphibious animals, they they are at times the leaft fenfible of danger from man that I know.

They often attack fmall boats merely through wantonnefs, and not only put the people in great confufion, but fubjecl them to great danger j for they always aim at flaving the boat with their tufks, or endeavour to get in, but are never known to hurt the people. In the year one thoufand feven hundred and fixty-fix fomeof the Hoop's crew, who annually fail to the North to trade with the Efquimaux, were attacked by a great number of thofe animals; and notwith-ftanding their utmoft endeavours to keep them off, one more daring than the reft, though a fmall one, got in over the ftern, and after fitting and looking at the people fome time, he again plunged into the water to his companions. At that inftant another, of an enormous fize, was getting in over the bow; and every other means proving ineffeclual to prevent fuch an unwelcome vifit, the bowman took up a gun, loaded with goofe fhot, put the muzzle into the Horfe's mouth, and fliot him dead; he immediately funk, and was followed by all his companions. The people then made the beft of their way to the veffelg and juft arrived before the Sea-Horfes were ready to make their fecond attack, which in all probability might have been worfe than the firft, as they feem-ed much enraged at the lofs of their companion. Thofe animals are of various fizes, according to age and other circumftances j fome are not larger larger than an old Seal but there are thofe among them that are not lefs than two ton weight.

The fkin and teeth are the moft valuable parts to the natives; for the far is hard and grifly, and the flei coarfe, black, and cough.

Thofe animals are feldom found on the contiv nent which borders on Hudfon's Bay, or far up, in bays, rivers, or inlets, but ufually frequent fmall iflands, and fea-girt fhoals, at fome dillance from the main land; but as thofe places are frozen over for many miles during Winter, it is natural to think they keep at the edge of the water among the driving ice during that feafon. They are (uppofcd to feed chiefly on marine plants, and perhaps on fhell-fifh, for their excrement is exceedingly offenlive. Seals. Seals of various fizes and colours are com- mon in moft parts of Hudfon's Bay, but moft numerous to the North. Some of thofe animals are beautifully fpeckled, black and white; others are of a dirty grey. The former are generally fmall, but fome of the latter arrive at an amazing lize, and their fkins are of great ufe to the Efquimaux; as it is of them they cover their canoes, make all their bo(n-! egs and fhoes, befides many other parts of their clothing. The Seal-fldns are alio of great ule to thole people as a fubftitute for cafks, to preferve oil, c. for Winter ufej they are alfo blown full of wihd and dried, and then ufed as buoys on the whale-fifhery. The flefh and fat of the Seal is alfo more efteemed by the Efcjui- maux maux than thofe of any other marine animal, fal-mon not excepted.

Belidcs thcfc, the Sea-Unicorn is known toseaunu frequent Hudfon's Bay and Straits, but I never hw one of them. Their horns are frequently pur-chafei from our friendly Efquimaux, who probably gel them in the way of barter from thofe tribes that refide more to the North; but I never could be informed by the natives whether their Ikins are like thofe of the Whale, or hairy like thofe of the Seal; I fuppofe the former.

Species of Fiji).

The Fifli that inhabit the fait water of Hudfons Bay are but few: the Black Whale, White Whale, Salmon, and a fmall fifh called Kepling, are the only fpecies of fea-fifh in thofe parts.

The Black Whale is fometimes found as far Black
Vhale
South as Churchill River, and I was prefent at the killing of three there; but this was in the courfe of twenty years. To the Northward, particularly near Marble Ifland, they are more plentiful; but notwithftanding the Company carried on a fifliery In the Fall of the year i 768, a fine rock cod was Jiove on fhore in a iigh gale of wind, and was eaten at the Gavernor's table; Meflrs. William Wales and Jofcph Dymond, who went out to obferve the tranfit of Venus which happened on the 3d of June 1769, partook of it; but I never heard of one being caught with a hook, nor ever law an entire fiih of that de-icription in thofe parts: their jaw-bones are, however, frequently found on the fhores.

fioiery in that quarter, from the year one thou-fand feven hundred and fixty-five till one thou-fand feven hundred and feventy-two, they were fo far from making it anfwer their expeclations, that they funk upwards of twenty thoufand pounds; which is the lefs to be wondered at, when we coniider the great inconveniencies and expences they laboured under in fuch an undertaking. For as it was impollible to profecute it from England, all the people employed on that fervice were obliged to refide at their fettlement all the year at extravagant wages, exclufive of their maintenance. The harpooners had no lefs than fifty pounds per annum ftanding wages, and none of the crew lefs than from fifteen to twenty-five pounds; which, together with the Captains falaries, wear and tear of their veftels, and other contingent expences, made it appear on calculation, that if there were a certainty of loading the veftels every year, the Company could not clear themfelves. On the contrary, during the feven years they perfevered in that undertaking, only four Black Whales were taken near Marble Ifland; and, except one, they were fo fmall, that they would not have been deemed payable fifli in the Greenland fervice. But the Hudfon's Bay Com-pany, with a liberality that does honour to them, though I have heard that no Whale caught by our Gteenland (hips is called a Pay-fi(h; that is, that no cinolument arifes to the haqdoener that flrikes it; uniefs thelong? ft blade of the bone, iifually called Whale-bone, mea-fiires fix feet; whereas thofe kiucd in Hudfon's Bay feldom meafured more than four feet and an half.

though perfeclly acquainted with the rules obferv-ed in the Greenland fervice, gave the fame premium for a fucking fifli, as for one of the greateft magnitude.

White Whales are very plentiful in thofe white parts, particularly from Chefterfield's Inlet to York Fort, or Hay's River, on the Weft fide of the Bay; and from Cape Smith to Slude River on the Eaft fide. On the Weft coaft they are generally found in the greateft numbers at the mouths of the principal rivers; fuch as Seal River, Churchill, Port Nelfon, and Hay's Rivers. But the Eaft fide of the Bay not being fo well known. Whale River is the only part they are known to frequent in very confiderable numbers. Some years ago the Company had a fettlement at this river, called Richmond Fort; but all their endeavours to eftablifli a profitable fifliery here prov-ed ineftectual, and the few Indians who reforted to it with furrs proving very inadequate to the expences, the Company determined to evacuate it. Accordingly, after keeping up this fettlement for upward of twelve years, and finking many thoufands of pounds, they ordered it to be burnt, for the more eafily getting the fpikes and other iron-work. This was in the year one thoufand feven hundred and fifty-eight.

At the old eftablifhed Factories on the Weft fide of the Bay, the Company have been more fiiccefsful in the White Whale fifhery, particular-ly at Churchill, were fuch of the Company's fer-vants as cannot be employed during that feafon to more benefit for the Company, are fent on that duty, and in fonie fuccefsful years they fend home from eight to thirteen tons of fine oil. To encourage a fpirit of induftry among thofe employed on this fervice, the Company allows agra-tuity, not only to the harpooners, but to every man that fails in the boats; and this gratuiry is fo ample as to infpire them with emulation, as they well know that the more they kill, the greater will be their emolument. Salmon. Salmon are in fome feafons very numerous on the North Weft fide of Hudfon's Bay, particularly at Knapp's Bay and Whale Cove. At the latter I once found them fo plentiful, that had we been provided with a fufficient number of nets, cafks, and fait, we might foon have loaded the veflel with them. But this is feldom the cafe, for in fome years they are fo fcarce, that it is with difecuky a few meals of them can be procured during our flay at thofe harbours. They are in fome years fo plentiful near Churchill River, that I have known upward of two hundred fine fifli taken out of four fmali nets in one tide within a quarter of a mile of the Fort; but in other years they are fo fcarce, that barely that number have been taken in upward of twenty nets during the whole feafon, which generally begins the latter end of June, and ends about the middle or latter end of Auguft.

Befide the fifh already mentioned, I know of no other that inhabits the fait water except the

Kepling,

Kepijno

Kepling, which is a fmall fifli about tlie fize of a fmelt, but moft excellent eating. In fonie years they refort to the fliores near Churchill River in fuch multitudes to fpavvn, and fuch numbers of them are left dry among the rocks, as at times to be quite offenfive. In other feafons they are fo fcarce, that hardly a meal can be procured.

The fame remark may be made on almoft every fpeciesof game, which conftitutes the greateft part of the fare of the people refiding in thofe parts. For inftance, in fome years, hundreds of deer may eafily be killed within a mile of York Fort; and in others, there is not one to be feen within twenty or thirty miles. One day thou-fands and tens of thoufands of geefe are feen, but the next they all raife flight, and go to the North to breed. Salmon, as I have lately obferved, is fo plentiful in fome years at Churchill River, that it might be procured in any quantity; at others fo fcarce as to be thought a great delicacy.

In fact, after twenty years refidence in this country, I am perfuaded that whoever relies much on the produce of the different feafons, will frequently be deceived, and occafionally expofe himfelf and men to great want.

To remedy this evil, it is moft prudent for thofe in command to avail themfelves of plentiful feafons, and cure a fufficient quantity of the leaft periftiable food, particularly geefe.

Shell

Shell Fijh,

Shell FUh, Shell Fish of a variety of kinds are alfo found in fome parts of Hudfon's Bay. Mufcles in par-ticular are in great abundance on the rocky ftiores near Churchill River, and what is vulgarly called the Periwincle are very plentiful on the rocks which dry at low-water. Small Crabs and Star-fifli are frequently thrown on the fhore by the furf in heavy gales of wind; and the empty ftiells of Wilks, fmall Scallops, Cockles, and many other kinds, are to be found on the beaches in great plenty. The fame may be faid of the interior parts of the country, where the banks of the lakes and rivers abound with empty Ibells of various kinds; but the fifh themfelves have never been difcovered by the natives.

Frogs Grubs, and other Inftis,

Frogs of various colours are numerous in thofe "' parts as far North as the latitude b i. They always frequent the margins of lakes, ponds, rivers, andfwamps: and as the Winter approaches, they burrow under the mofs, at a confiderable diftance from the water, where they remain in a frozen ftate till the Spring. I have frequently feen them them dug up with the mofs, (when pitching tents in Winter,) frozen as hard as ice; in which flate the legs are as eafily broken ofl as a pipe-ftem, without giving the leall fenfation to the animal; but by wrapping them up in warm Ikins, and expofing them to a flow fire, they foon recover life, and the mutilated animal gains its ufual adivity; but if they are permitted to freeze again, they are paft all recovery, and are never more known to come to life. The fame may be faid of the various fpecies of Spiders and all the sprs and Grub kind, which are very numerous in thofe" parts. I have feen thoufands of them dug up with the mofs, when we were pitching our tents in the Winter; all of which were invariably en-clofed in a thick web, which Nature teaches then: i to fpin on thofe occalions; yet they were apparently all frozen as hard as ice. The Spiders, if let fall from any height on a hard fubftance, would rebound like a grey pea; and all the Grub kind are fo hard frozen as to be as eafily broken as a piece of ice of the fame fize; yet when ex-pofed to a flow heat, even in the depth of Winter, they will foon come to life, and in a fliort time recover their ufual motions.

Birds,

The feathered creation that refort to thofe parts in the different feafons are numerous, but fuch

Eagles.

A JOURNEY TO THE as brave the fevere Winter are but few in number, and ftiall be particularly noticed in their proper places.

Eagles of feveral forts are found in the country bordering on Hudfon's Bay during the Summer; but none, except the common brown Fifli-ino- Eagle, ever frequent the Northern parts. They always make their appearance in thofe dreary regions about the latter end of March or beginning of April, and build their nefts in lofty trees, in the crevices of inacceffible rocks near the banks of rivers. They lay but two eggs, (which are white,) and frequently bring but one voung. They generally feed on fifti, which they catch as they are fwimming near the furface; but they are very deftruclive to the mufk rat and hares, as alfo to geefe and ducks, when in a moulting flate, and frequently kill young beaver. Their nefts are very large, frequently fix feet in diameter; and before their young can fly, are fo provident, that the Indians frequently take a moft excellent meal of fifh, fleoi, and fowl from their larder. Though they bring forth their young fo early as the latter end of May, or the beginning of June, yet they never fly till September j a little after which they migrate to the Southward. They are the moft ravenous of any bird I know; for when kept in confinement or in a tame ftate as it may be called, I have known two of them eat more than a buihel of fifli in a day. They are never known to breed on the barren grounds grounds to the North of Churchill River, though many of the lakes and rivers in thofe parts abound with variety of filh. This is probably owing to the want of trees or high rocks to build in. The Northern Indians are very partial to the quill-fcathers of the Eagle, as well as to thofe of the hawk, to wing or plume their arrows with, out of a fuperftitious notion that they have a. greater effect than if winged with the feather-s of geefe, cranes, crows, or other birds, that in fact would do equally as well. The flefli of the Eagle is ufually eaten by moft of the Indians, but is always black, hard, and fifhy; even the young ones, when in a callow ftate, though the flefii is delicate white, are fo rank as to render them very unpleafant to fome perfons, except in times of neceffity.

Hawks of various fizes and plumage frequent Hawks of the different parts of the country round Hudfons Bay during Summer. Some of thofe Hawks are fo large as to weigh three pounds, and others fo fmall as not to exceed five or fix ounces. But the weight of thofe, as well as every other fpe-cies of Birds, is no ftandard for the Naturaliil to go by; for at different feafons, and when in want of food, they are often fcarcely half the weight they are when fat and in good order. Notwithftanding the variety of Hawks that re-fort to thofe parts in Summer, I know but one fpecies that brave the intenfe cold of the long Winters to the North of Churchill River 5 and

P d that that is what Mr. Pennant calls the Sacre Falcon. They, like the other large fpecies of Hawks, prey much on the white groufe or partridge, and alfo on the American hare, ufually called here Rabbits. They are always found to frequent thofe parts where partridges are plentiful, and are de-tefted by the fportfmen, as they generally drive all the game off the ground near their tents; but, in return, they often drive thither frefti flocks of fome hundreds. Notvvithftanding this, they fo frequently baulk thofe who are employed on the hunting fervice, that the Governors generally give a reward of a quart of brandy for each of their heads. Their flefh is always eaten by the Indians, and fometimes by the Englifli; but it. is always black, hard, and tough, and Ibmetimes has a bitter tafte.

The Indians are fond of taming thofe birds and frequently keep them the whole Summer; but as the Winter approaches they generally take flight, and provide for themfelves. When at Cumberland Houfe I had one of them, of which my people were remarkably fond; and as it never wanted for food, would in all probability have remained with us all the Winter, had it not been killed by an Indian who did not know it to be tame. White or The beautiful fpecies of W htte or Snowy Owl Snovvyowi j ommon in all parts of Hudfons Bay, as far North as the Copper-mine River. Thefe birds,- when flying or fitting, appear very large, but whea licilledj killed, feldom weigh more than three and a half, or four pounds, and fometimes fcarcely half that weight. They generally feed on mice and partridges, and are at times known to kill rabbits. They are, like the hawk, very troublefome to the fportfmen; and, contrary to any other bird that I know, have a gret propenfity to follow the report of a gun, and frequently follow the hunters (as they are ufually called in Hudfon's Bay) the whole day. On thofe occafions they ufually perch on high trees, and watch till a bird is killed, when they ikim down and carry it off before the hunter can get near it; but in return, the hunters, when they fee them on the watch, frequently decoy them within gan-fhot, by throwing up a dead bird, which the Owl feldom refufes to accept; but the fportfman being fully provided for this vifit, and on his guard, generally fhoots them before they can carry off the partridge. They are, however, fo great a hindrance to thofe employed on the hunting fervice, that the fame pre mium is given for one of their heads as for that of a hawk.

In Winter they are frequently very fat, their iflefli delicately white, and generally efteemed good eating, both by Englifli and Indians, Thofe Owls always make their nefts on the ground, generally lay from three to four eggs, but feldom hatch more than two; and in the extreme North the young ones do not fly till September. They never migrate, but brave the coldeft Winters,

Dd 2 even even on the barren ground, far remote from any woods; and in tnoie fituations perch on high rocks and ftones, and watch for their prey. Greyer- ipccies of Gp. ey or MotTLED Owl are by

M. uied UQ reans fo numerous as the former, are fome-thing inferior in fize, and always frequent the woods. They never go in fearch of their prey in the day time, but perch on the tops of lofty pines, and are eafily approached and fhot. Their food js generally known to be mice and fmall birds yet their fielh is delicately white, and nearly as good as a barn-door fowl; of courfe it is much efteemed both by the Englifh and Indians. This fpecies of Owl is called by the Southern Indians Ho-ho, and the former Wap-a-kee-thow. Cob-a-dee- Befidcs thoic two fpecics of Owls, there is another that remains in liudfon's Bay all the year, and is called by the Indians Cob-a-dee-cooch. It h fo iar inferior in fize to the two former, that it fcldom weighs half a pound; is of a mottled brown, the feathers long, and of a moft delicate foft and (ilky quality. In general this fpecies feed on mice, and birds they find dead; and ire fo impudent at times, that they light on a partridge when killed by the hunter, but not being able to carry it off, are often obliged to relinquifh the prize. Like the White Owl, at times though but feldom, they follow the report of a gun, and by fo frequently fkimming round the fporrfmen, frighten the game nearly as much as the hawk. They feldom go far from the woods, build in trees, and lay from two to four eggs. They are never fat, and their flefh is eaten only by the Indians.

Ravens of a moft beautiful gloity black, riclily R='-tinged with purple and violet colour, arc the conftant inhabitants of Iludfon's Bay; but are fo far inferior in fize to the Englifli Raven, that they are ufually called Crows. They build their nefts in lofry pine-trees, and generally lay four fpeckled eggs; they bring forth their young fo early as the latter end of May, or the beginning of June. In Summer many of them frequent the barren grounds, feverai hundred miles from any woods; probably invited there by the multitudes of deer and mufl-oxen that are killed by the Northern Indians during that feafon, merely for thir fkins, and who leave their flefh to rot, or be devoured by beafts or birds of prey. At thofe times they are very fat, and the flefh of the young ones is delicately white, and good eating. Buc in Winter they are, through neceflity, obliged to feed on a black mofs that grows on the pine-trees, alio on deer's dung, and excrements of other animals. It is true, they kill fome mice, vhich. they find in the furface of the fnow, and catch many wounded partridges and hares; in fome parts of the country they are a great nuifance to the hunter, by eating the game that is either caught in fnares or traps. With all this ailiftance, they are in general fo poor during the fevere cold in Winter, as to excite wonder how they poflibly can exift.

Their

Their faculty of fcent muft be very acute; for in the coldeft days in Winter, when every kind of effluvia is almoft inftantaneoufly deftroyed by the froft, 1 have frequently known buffaloes and other beafts killed where not one of thofe birds ere feen; but in a few hours fcores of them would gather about the fpot to pick up the dung, blood, and other offal. An unarmed man may approach them very near when feeding, but they are fhy of thofe that have a gun; a great proof that they fmell the gunpowder. They are, however, frequently hot by guns fet for foxes; and fometimes caught in traps built for martins. Though, on the whole, they may be called a ftiy bird, yet their neceffities in Winter are fo great, that, like the White Owl, they frequently follow the report of a gun, keep prudent ly at adiftance from the fportfman, and frequently carry off many wounded birds. Their quills make moft excellent pens for drawing, or for ladies to write with. The Cinereous Crow, or, as it is called bv the

Cinereous -fow. Southern Indians, Whifk-e-jonifh, by the Englifli Whifkey-jack, and by the Northern Indians Gee-za, but as fome pronounce it, and that with more propriety, Jee-za, though claffed among the Crows, is in reality fo fmall, as feldom to weigh three ounces; the plumage grey, the feathers very long, foft, and liky, andin general entirely un-webbed, and in fome parts much refembles hair. This bird is very familiar, and fond of frequenting ing habitations, either houfes or tents; and fo much given to pilfering, that no kind of provi-fions k can come at, either freoi or ildt, is fafe from its depredation. It 15 io bold as to come into tents, and fit on the edge of the kettle when hanging over the fire, and (leal visuals out of the diflies. It is very troublefome to the hunters, both Englifh and Indian, frequently following them a whole day; it will perch on a tree while the hunter is baiting his martin-traps, and as foon as his back is turned go and eat the baits. It is a kind of mockbird, and of courfe has a variety of notes; it is eafily tamed, but never lives long in confinement. It is well known to be a provident bird, laying up great quantities of berries in Summer for a Winter ftock;

but its natural propenfity to pilfer at all feafons makes it much detefted both by the Engliih and Indians. It builds its neft in trees, exadly like that of the blackbird and thrufh; lays four blue eggs, but feldom brings rfore than three young ones.

1 know of only one fort of Wood-pecker that Wood-frequents the remote Northern parts of Hudlon's Bay; and this is difiinguiflied by Mr. Pennant by the name of the Golden Winged Bird; but to the South Weft that beautiful fpecies of Wood-pecker with a fcarlet crown is very frequent. The manner of life of this fpecies is nearly alike, always building their nefts in holes in trees, and feeding on worms and infeds. They generally have have from four to fix young at a time. They are faid to be very deflruclive to fruit-trees that are raifed in gardens in the more Southern parts of America; but the want of thofe luxuries in Hudfon's Bay renders them very harmlefs and inoffenfive birds. The red feathers of the larger fort, which frequent the interior and Southern parts of the Bay, are much valued by fome of the Indians, vho ornament their pipe-ftems with them, and at times ufe them as ornaments to their children's clothing. Neither of the two fpecies here mentioned ever migrate, but are eonftant inhabitants of the different climates in which they are found. Grocfe. There are feveral fpecies of Grouse in the different parts of Hudfon's Bay; but two of the largeft, and one of them the moft beautiful, never reach fo far North as the latitude 59: but as I have feen them in great plenty near Cumberland Houfe, I (hall take the liberty to defcribe them. Theriiftcd The RufFED Grouse. This is the moft beau-Groufc.-fj q 11 jj. j. g claffed under that name.

They are of a delicate brown, prettily variegated with black and white: tail large and long, like that of a hawk, which is ufually of an orange-colour, beautifully barred with black, chocolate, ana white; and the tail is frequently expanded like a fan. To add to their beauty, they have a ruff of glolty black feathers, richly tinged with purple round the neck, which they can erecl at pleafure: this they frequently do, but more particularly ticularly fo when they fpread their long tail, which gives them a noble appearance. In fize they exceed a partridge, but are inferior to a pheafant. In Winter they are ufually found perched on the branches of the pine-trees; and in that feafon are fo tame as to be eafily approached, and of courfe readily (hot.

They always make their nefts on the ground, generally at the root of a tree, and lay to tlie number of twelve or fourteen eggs. In fome of the Southern parts of America feveral attempts have been made to tarne thofe beautiful birds,. by taking their eggs and hatching them under do-meflic hens, but it was never crowned with fuc-cefs; for when but a few days old, they always make their efcape into the woods, where they probably pick up a fubfiftence. Their flefli is delicately white and firm, and though they are feldom fat, they are always good eating, and are generally efteemed beft when larded and roahed, or nicely boiled with a bit of bacon.

There is fomething very remarkable in thofe birds, and I believe peculiar to them-felves, which is that of clapping their wings with fuch a force, that at half a mile diftance it refembles thunder. I have frequently heard them make that noife near Cumberland Houfe in the month of May, but it was always before Sun-rife, and a little after Sun-fet. It is faid by Mr. Barton and Le Hontan, that they never clap in this manner but in the Spring and Fall, and I muft acknowledge that ed Groufe, 410 A JOURNEY TO THE that I never heard them in Winter, though 1 have killed many of them in that feafon. The Indians informed me they never make that noife but when feeding, which is very probable; for it is notorioufly known that all the fpecies of Groufe feed very early in the mornings, and late in the afternoons. This (pedes is called by fome of the Indians bordering on Hudfon's Bay, Pus-pus-kee, and by others Pus-pus-cue. Sharp-tail- Sharp-tailed Grouse, or as they are called in Hudfon's Bay, Pheafant. Thofe birds are always found in the Southern parts of the Bay, arc very plentiful in the interior parts of the country, and in fome Winters a few of them are fliot at York Fort, but never reach fo far North as Churchill. In colour they are not very unlike that of the Fnglifh hen pheafant; but the tail is fliort and pointed, like that of the common duck; and there is no perceivable difference in plumage between the male and female. When full-grown, and in good condition, they frequently weigh two pounds, and though the flelh is dark, yet it is juicy, and always efteemed good eating, particularly when larded and roafted. In Summer they feed on berries, and in Winter on the tops of the dwarf birch, and the buds of the poplar. In the Fall they are tolerably tame, but in the fevere cold more Ihy; frequently perch on the tops of the higheft poplars, out of moderate gun-fliot, and will not fuffera near approach. They fometimes, when diilurbed in this fituati- on, dive into the fnow; but the fportfman is equally baulked in his expectations, as they force their way fo faft under it as to raife flight many yards diftant from the place they entered, and very frequently in a difierent direflion to that from which the fportfman expects. They, like the other fpecies of groufe, make their nefts on the ground, and lay from ten to thirteen eggs. Like the Ruffed Groufe, they are not to be tamed, as many trials have been made at York Fort, but without fuccefs j for though they never made their efcape, yet they always died, probably for the want of proper food; for the hens that hatched them were equally fond of them, as they could poflibly have been had they been the produce of their own eggs This fpecies of Groufe is called by the Southern Indians Aw-kis-cow.

The Wood Partridges have acquired that wood Par-name in Hudfon's Bay from their alvays fre- " quenting the forefts of pines and fir; and in Winter feeding on the brufh of thofe trees, though they are fondeft of the latter. This fpecies of Groufe is inferior in iize and beauty to the Ruffed, yet may be called a handfome bird; the plumage being of a handfome brown, elegantly fpotted with white and black. The tail is long, and tipped with orar;;?; e; and the legs are warmly-covered withfhort feathers, but the teet are naked. They are generally in the extreme with re- fpect

Thu I aftert from my own experience when at Cumberland Houfe.

fpect to fhynefs; fometimes not fuffering a man to come within two gun-lhots, and at others fo s taiiie that the fportfman may. kill five or fix out of one tree without fhifting his ftation. They are feen in fome years in conliderable numbers near York Fort. They are very fcarce at Churchill, though numerous in the interior parts, particularly on the borders of the Athapufcow Indians country, where I have feen my Indian companions kill many of them with blunt-headed arrows. In Winter their flelh id black, hard and bitter, probably owing to the relinous quality of their food during that feafon; but this is not ob-ferved in the rabbits, though they feed exa5tly in the fame manner in Winter: on the contrary, their flefti is efteemed more delicate than that of the Englifh rabbit. The Southern Indians call this fpecies of Partridge, Mifticka-pethow; and the Northern Indians call it. Day. Willow The Willow Partridges have a flrong black

Paitndge. j with fcarlct cyc-brows, very large and beautiful in the male, but lefs confpieuous-in the female. In Summer they are brown, elegantly barred and mottled with orange, white, and black; and at that feafon the males are very-proud and handfome, but the females are lefs beautiful, being of one univerfal brown As the Fall advances they change to a delicate white, except fourteen black feathers in the tail, which are alfo tipped with white; and their legs and feet, quite down to the nails, are warmly covered with with feathers. In the latter end of September and beginning of October they gather in flocks of fome hundreds, and proceed from the open plains and barren grounds, (where they ufually breed,) to tlie woods and brufh-willows, where they hord together in a ftate of focicty, till dif-perfc-d by their common enemies, the hawks, or hunters. They are by far the moft numerous of any of the groufe fpecies that are found in Hud-fon's Bay; and in fome places when permitted to remain undifturbed for a confiderable time, their number is frequently fo great, as almoft to exceed credibility. I fhall by no means exceed truth, if I affert that I have feen upward of four hundred in one flock near Churchill River; but the p-reateft number I ever faw was on the North lide of Port Nelfon River, when returning withapack-ct in March one thoufand feven hundred and fixty-eight: at that time 1 faw thoufands flying to the North, and the whole furface of the fnow feemed to be in motion by thofe that were feeding on the tops of the fliort willows. Sir Thomas Button mentions, that when he wintered in Port Nelfon River in one thoufand fix hundred and twelve, his crew killed eighteen hundred dozen of thofe birds, which I have no reafon to doubt; and Mr. Jeremie, formerly Governor at York Fort, when that place was in the poflellion of the French, and then called Fort Bourbon, aflerts, that he and fcventy-nine others eat no lefs lefs than ninety thoufand partridges and twenty-five thoufand hares in the courfe of one Winter; which, conlidering the quantity of venifon, geefe, ducks, V. enumerated in his account, that were killed that year, makes the number fo great, that it is fcarcely poffible to conceive what eighty men could do with them; for on calculation, ninety thoufand partridges and twenty-five thoufand hares divided by eighty, amounts to no lefs than one thoufand one hundred and twenty-five partridges, and three hundred and twelve hares per man. his is by far too great a quantity, particularly when it is confidered that neither partridges nor hares are in feafon, or can be procured in any numbers, more than kvea months in the year. Forty thoufand partridges and five thoufand hares would, I think, be much nearer the truth, and will be found, on calculation, to be ample provifion for eighty men for fe-ven months, exclufive of any change. The common weight of thofe birds is from eighteen to twenty-two ounces when firft killed; there are fome fev that are nearly that weight when fit for the fpit, but they are fo fcarce as by no means to ferve as a ftandard; and as they always hord with the common fize, there is no room to fufpecl them of another fpecies. As all thofe over-grown partridges are notorioufly known to be males, it is more than probable that they are imperfe51:, and grow large and fat like capons; and every one that has had an opportunity of tafting tafting thofe large partridges, will readily allow that they excel the common fort as much in flavour as they do in fize. It is remarked in thofe birds, as well as the Rock Partridge, that they are provided with additional clothing, as it may be called; for every feather, from the largeft to the fmalleft, except the quills and tail, are all double. The under-feather is foft and downy, fliooting from the fhaft of the larger;

and is wonderfully adapted to their iituation, as they not only brave the coldeft Winters, but the fpccies now under confideration always burrow under the fnow at nights, and at day light come forth to feed. In Winter they are always found to frequent the banks of rivers and creeks, the fides of lakes and ponds, and the plains which abound with dwarf willows; for it is on the buds and tops of that tree they always feed during the Winter. In fummer they eat berries and fmall herbage. Their food in Winter being fo dry and harfli, makes it neccffary for them to fwal-low a confiderable quantity of gravel to promote digeftion; but the great depth of fnow renders it very fcarce during that feafon. The Indians having confidered this point, invented the method now in ufe among the Englifh, of catching them in nets by means of that fimple allurement, a heap of gravel. The nets for this purpofe are from eight to twelve feet fquare, and are ftretch-ed in a frame of wood, and ufually fet on the ice of rivers, creeks, ponds, and lakes, about one hundred hindred yards from the willows, but in fome fituations not half that diftance. Under the center of the net a heap of inow is thrown up to the fize of one or two bafhels and when well packed is covered wirh gravel. To fet the nets, when thus prepared, requires nb other trouble than lifting up one fide of the frame, and fupport-ing if with two fniali props, about four feet long: a line is faftened to thofe props, and ihe other end being conveyed to the neighbouring willows, is always fo contrived that a man can get to it without being feen by the birds under the net. When every thing is thus prepared, the hunters ha; ve nothing to do but go into the adjacent willows and woods, and when they ftart game, endeavour to drive them into the net, which at times is no hard tafk, as they frequently run before them like chickens; and fometimes require no driving, for as foon as they fee the black heap of gravel on the white fnow they fly ftraight towards it. The hunter then goes to the end of the line to watch their motions, and when he fees there are as many about the gravel as the net can cover, or as many as are likely to go under at that time, with a fudden pull he hauls down the ilakes, and the net falls horizontally on the fnow, and enclofes the grcateft part of the birds that are under it. The hunter then runs to the yiet as foon as poflible, and kills all the birds by biting them at the back of the head. He then fets up the net, takes away all the dead game, and repeats repeats the operation as often as he pleafes, or as long as the birds are in good humour. By this fimple contrivance I have known upwards of three hundred partridges caught in one morning by three perfons; and a much greater number might have been procured had it been thought neceflary. Early in the morning, juft at break of day, and early in the afternoon, is the beft time for this fport. It is common to get from tliirty to feventy at one hawl; and in the Winter of one thoufand feven hundred and eighty-fix, Mr. Prince, then Mafter of a floop at Churchill River, actually caught two hundred and four at two hawls. They are by no means equally plentiful every year; for in fome Winters I have known them fo fcarce, that it was impoffible to catch any in nets, and all that could be procured with the gun would hardly afford one day's allowance per week to the men during the feafon; but in the Winter one thoufand feven hundred and eighty-five, they were fo plentiful near Churchill, and fuch numbers were brought to the Factory, that I gave upward of two thoufand to the hogs. In the latter end of March, or the beginning of April, thofe birds begin to change, from white to their beautiful Summer plumage, and the firlt brown feathers make their appearance on the neck, and by degrees fpread over the whole bo-

Mr. Dragge olferves, in his North Wtfl Paflage, that vhen the partridges begin to change colour, the firft Lrown fctbers appeal in the rump; tsidges.

418 A JOURNEY TO THE dy; but their Summer drefs is feldom complete till July. The feathers of thofe birds make excellent beds, and as they are the perquifite of the hunters, are ufually fold to the Captains and Mates of the Companys' Ihips, at the eafy rate of three pence per pound. Rock Par- Rock Partridges. TMs fpccies of Groufc are in Winter of the fame colour as the former, but inferior in lize; being in general not more than two-thirds of the weight. They have a black line from the bill to the eye, and differ in nature and manner from the Willow Partridge. They never frequent the woods or willows, but brave the fevereft cold on the open plains. They always feed on the buds and tops of the dwarf birch, and after this repaft, generally fit on the high ridges of fnow, with their heads to windward. They are never caught in nets, like the illow Partridge; for when in want of gravel, their bills are of fuch an amazing flrength, that they pick a fufecient quantity out of the rocks. Belide, being fo much inferior in fize to the former fpecies, their flefh is by no means fo good, being black, hard, and bitter. They are in general, but this is fo far from being a general mle, tliat an experi-iiced Htidfonian muft fmilc at the idea. That Mr. Dragge never faw an inftance of this kind I will not fay, but when Nature deviates fo far from its ufual courfe, it is undoubtedly owing to fome accident; and nothing is more likely than that the feathers of the bird Mr. Dragge had examined, had been, truck off by a haw; and as the ufual feafon for changing their plumage was near, the Summer feathers fupplied thtir place; for out of the many hundreds of thoufund? that I have leen killed, 1 never faw or heard of a fimilar infince.

ral, like the V7ood Partridge, either exceeding wild or very tame j and vhen in the latter humour, I have known one man kill one hundred and twenty in a few hours; for as they ufually keep in large flocks, the fportfman can frequently kill fix or eight at a fliot. Thefe, like the Willow Partridge, change their plumage in Summer to a beautiful fpeckled brown; and at that feafon are fo hardy, that, unlefs fliot in the head or vitals, they will fly away with the greatefl quantity of hot of any bird I know. They difcover great fondnefs for their young; for during the time of incubation, they will frequently fuffer themfelves to be taken by hand off their eggs. Pigeons of a fmall fize, not larger than a thrufli, are in fome Summers found as far North as Churchill River. The bill is of a flefti-colour, legs red, and the greateft part of the plumage of a light lilac or blufli. In the interior parts of the country they fly in large flocks, and perch on the

E e 2   poplar

Beficles tlie birds already mentioned, hich form a condant difh at our tables in Hudfon's Bay, during their refpedtive feafons, Mr. Jerome allerts, that during t! ie time he was Governor at York Fort, the buhard was common. But fmce that Fort was delivered up to the Englifh at the peace of Utrecht in 1713, none of the Company's lervants have ever feen one of thofe biids: nor does it appear b all the Jouinals now in the poficflio. i of the Hudfon's Bay Company, that any Cu: h bird was ever fcen in the moft Southern parts of the Bay, much lefs at Yoik Fort, which is in the latitude 57 North; fo that a capital error, or a svilful deiign to millead, niuft have taken, place. Indeed, his account of the country immediately where he refided, and the productions of it, are fo erroneoufly flaced aj to deferve no notice. His colleague, De le Potiies, arterts the sxihenc of the budard in thofe parts, and with an equal regard to troth.

Rfd-btea. T edthiufh.

420 A JOURNEY TO THE poplar trees in fuch numbers that I have feeo twelve of them killed at one fhot. They ufually feed on poplar buds, and are good eating, though feldom fat. They build their nefts in trees, the fame as the Wood Pigeons do; never lay but two eggs, and are very fcarce near the fea-coaft in the Northern parts of Hudfon's Bay.

The Red-breasted Thrushes, commonly called in Hudfon's Bay the Red Birds, but by fome the Black Birds, on account of their note, and by others the American Fieldfares ufually make their appearance at Churchill River about the middle of May, build their nefts of mud, like the Englllh Thrufli, and lay four beautiful blue eggs. They have a very loud and pleafing note, which they generally exercife moft in the mornings and evenings, when perched on fome lofty tree near their neft; but when the young can fly they are filent, and migrate to the South early in the Fall. They are by no means numerous, and are generally feen in pairs; they are never fought after as an article df food, but when killed by the Indian boys, are efteemed good eating, though they always feed on worms and infects.

Grosbeak. Thefe gay birds vifit Churchill River in fome years fo early as the latter end of March, but are by no means plentiful; they are always feen in pairs, and generally feed on the buds of the poplar and willow. The male is in moft parts of its plumage of a beautiful crimfon, but the female of a dull dirty green. In form they

Oioilea. k.

Bunting.

NORTHERN OCEAN. 421 they much refemble the Englifli bullfinch, but are near double their fize. They build their nctis in trees, fometimes not far from the ground; lay four white eggs, and always hatch them in June. They are faid to have a pleafing note in Spring, though I never heard it, and are known to retire to the South early in the Fall. The Englifli re-fiding in Hudfon3 Bay generally call this bird the American Red Bird.

Snow Buntings, univerfally known in Hud-fon's Bay by the name of the Snow Birds, and in the Ifles of Orkney by the name of Snow Flakes, from their vifiting thofe parts in fuch numbers as to devour the grain as foon as fown, in fome years are fo deftruclive as to oblige the farmer to fow his fields a fecond, and occafionally a third time. Thefe birds make their appearance at the Northern fettlements in the Bay aboiit the latter end of May, or beginning of April, when they are very fat, and not inferior in flavour to an ortolan. On their firft arrival they generally feed on grafs-feeds, and are fond of frequenting dunghills. At that time they are eafily caught in great numbers under a net baited with groats or oatmeal; but as the Summer advances, they feed much on worms, and are then not fo much efteemed. They fometimes fly in fuch large flocks, that I have killed upwards of twenty at one fhot, and have known others who have killed double that number. In the Spring their plumage is prettily variegated, black and white; but their Summer drefs may be called elegant, though not gay. They live long in confinement, have naturally a pleafing note, and when in company with Canary birds foon imitate their fong. I have kept many of them in cages in the fame room with Canary birds, and always found they funs: in Winter as well as in Summer: but even in confinement they change their plumage according to the feafon, the fame as in a wild ftate. This fpecies of bird feem fond of the coldefl regions, for as the Spring advances they fly fo far North that their breeding-places are not known to the inhabitants of Hudfon's Bay. In Autumn they return to the South in large flocks, and are frequently Ihot in confiderable numbers merely as a delicacy; at that feafon, however, they are by no means fo good as when they firft make their appearance in Spring.

White. CROWNED Bunting. This fpecies is inferior in fize to the former, and feldom make their appearance till June. They breed in moft parts of the Bay, always make their nefts on the ground, at the root of a dwarf willow or a goofe-berry-bufli. During the time their young are in a callow ftate they have a delightful note, but as ibon as they are fledged they become filent, and retire to the South early in September, j. apiand Lapland Finch. This bird is common on Hudfon's Bay, and never migrates Southward in the coldeft Winters. During that feafon it generally frequents the juniper plains, and feeds on the fmall

White-unung.

Finch.

fmall buds of that tree, alfo on grafsfeeds; but at the approach of Summer it flies IHll farther North to breed. A variety of this bird is alfo common, and is beautifully marked with a red forehead and breaft. It is moft common in the Spring, and frequently caught in nets fet for the Snow Bunting; and when kept in cages has a pleafing note, but feldom lives long in confinement, though it generally dies very fat.

Larks of a pretty variegated colour frequent larks. thofe parts in Summer, and always make their appearance in May; build their nefts on the ground, ufually by the fide of a ftone at the root of a fmall bufli, lay four fpeckled eggs, and bring forth their young in June. At their firft arrival, and till the young can fly, the male is in full fong; and, like the fl?. y. lark, foars to a great height, and generally defcends in a perpendicular direction near their neft. Their note is loud and agreeable, but confifts of little variety, and as foon as the young can fly they become fllent, and retire to the Southward early in the Fall. They are impatient of confinement, never fing in that ftate, and feldom live long.

The Titmouse is ufually called in Hudfon's"""'-Bay, Blackcap. This diminutive bird braves the coldeft Winter, and during that feafon feeds on the feeds of long rye-grafs, but in Summer on infedts and berries. The Southern Indians call this bird Kifs-kifs-hefliis, from a twittering noife they make, which much refembles that word in found.

Swallows

Swallows. Swallows vifit thefe parts in confiderable numbers in Summer, and are very domeftic; building their nefts in neceffaries, ftables, and other out-offices that are much frequented. They feldom make their appearance at Churchill River till June, and retire South early in Auguft. They, like the European Swallow, gather in large flocks on the day of their departure, make feve-ral revolutions round the breeding-places, and then take their leave till the next year. 1 do not recollecl to have feen any of thole birds to the North of Seal River.

Martins, Martins alfo vifit Hudfon's Bay in great numbers, but feldom fofar North as Churchill River. They ufually make their nefts in holes form. ed in the fteep banks of rivers-, and, like the Svval-Ipw, lay four or five fpeckled eggs; and retire Southward in Auguft. At the Northern fettle-ments they are by no means fo domeftic as the Swallow.

Hooping Crane, This bird vifits Hudfon's Bay in the Spring, though not in great numbers. They are generally feen only in pairs, and that not very often. It is a bird of confiderable fize, often equal to that of a good turkey, and the great length of the bill, neck, and legs, makes it meafure, from the bill to the toes, near fix feet in common, and fome much more. Its plumage is of a pure white, except the quill-feathers, which are black; the crown is covered with a red fkin, thinly bcfet with black briftles, and the legs are large

Hooping Cidne.

large and black. It ufually frequents open fwamps, the fides of rivers, and the margins of lakes and ponds, feeds on frogs and fmall fifli, and efteemed good eating. The wing-bones of this bird are fo long and large, that I have known them made into flutes with tolerable fuccefs. It feldom has more than two young, and retires Southward early in the fall.

The Brown Crane. This fpecies is far infe-""

Ciane.

rior in fize to the former, being feldom three feet and a half in length, and on an average not weighing fevcn pounds. Their haunts and manner of life are nearly the fame as that of the Hooping Crane, and they never have more than two young, and thofe feldom fly till September. They are found farther North than the former, for I have killed feveral of them on Marble Ifland, and have feen them on the Continent as high as the latitude 65'. They are generally efteemed good eating, and, from the form of the body when fit for the fpit, they acquire the name of the North Weft Turkey. There is a circumftance refpecl-ing this bird that is very peculiar; which is, that the gizzard is larger than that of a fwan, and remarkably fo in the young birds. Tlie Brown Cranes are frequently feen in hot calm days to foar to an amazing height, always flying in circles, till by degrees they are almoft out of light, yet their note is fo loud, that the fportfman, before he fees their lituation, often fancies they are very near him. They viftt Hudfon's Bay in far greater greater numbers than the former, and are very good eating. Bitterns. BitTERNS are common at York Fort in Summer, but are feldom found fo far North as Churchill River. I have feen two fpecies of this bird; fome having affi-coloured legs, others with beautiful grafs-green legs, and very gay plumage. They always frequent marfhes and fwamps, alfo the banks of rivers that abound with reeds and long grafs. They generally feed on infects that are bred in the water, and probably on fmall frogs; and though feldom fat, they are generally good eating. They are by no means numerous even at York Fort, nor in fa in the moft Southern parts of the Bay that I have vifited.

Curlews. There are two fpecies of this bird which frequent the coafts of Hudfon's Bay in great numbers during Summer, and breed in all parts of it as far North as the latitude 72"; the largeft of this fpecies is diftinguifhed by that great Naturalift Mr. Pennant, by the name of the Ef-quimaux Curlew. They always keep near the fea coaft;

attend the ebbing of the tide, and are frequently found at low-water-mark in great numbers, where they feed on marine infecls, which they find by the fides of ftones in great plenty; but at high-water they retire to the dry ridges and wait the receding of the tide. They fly as Heady as a woodcock, anfwer to a whittle that refembles their note; lay long on their wings, and are a moft excellent fl: iot, and at times are delicious V'

Curlew.

delicious eating. The other fpecies of Curlew are in colour and fhape exactly like the former, though inferior in fize, and differ in their manner of life, as they never frequent the waters-edge, but always keep among tlie rocks and dry ridges, and feed on berries and fmall infecls. The flefh of this bird is generally more eftecmed than that of the former, but they are by no means fo numerous. This fpecies of Curlew are feldom found farther North than Egg River.

Jack Snipes. Thofe birds vifit Hudfon's Bay S"?"-in Summer in confiderable numbers, but are feldom feen to the North of Whale Cove. They do not arrive till the ice of the rivers is broke up, and they retire to the South early in the Fall. During their flay, they always frequent marflies near the fea coaft, and the fhores of great rivers. In manner and flight they exactly referable the European Jack Snipe j and when on the wing, fly at fuch a diftance from each other, that it is but feldom the beft fportfman can get more than one or two at a fhot. Their flefh is by no means fo delicate as that of the Englifh Snipe.

Red GodWAits, ufually called at the Northern Rd ood-fettlements in Hudfon's Bay, Plovers. Thole birds vifit the fhores of that part in very large flocks, and ufually frequent the marfhes and the margins of ponds. They alfo frequently attend the tide, like the Efquimaux Curlews; fly down to low. water-mark, and feed on a fmall fiili, not much unlike a fhrimp j but as the tide flows, they they retire to the marfhes. They fly in fuch large flocks, and fo clofe to each other, that I have often killed upwards of twelve at one fliot; and Mr. Atkinfon, long refident at York Fort, adlually killed feventy-two at one ftiot; but that was when the birds were fitting. Near Churchill River they are feldom fat, though tolerably fleflry, and are generally good eating. They ufu-ally weigh from ten to thirteen ounces; the female is always larger than the male, and differs in colour, being of a much lighter brown. They retire to the South long before the froft commences; yet I have feen this bird as far North as the latitude 71 50. Spotted Spotted Godwait, known in Hudfons Bay

Godwait. y jg name of Yellow Legs. This bird alfo vi-fits that country in confider-able numbers, but more fo in the interior parts; and ufually frequents the flat muddy banks of rivers. In fum-mer it is generally very poor, but late in the Fall is, as it may be called, one lump of fat. This bird, with many others of the migratory tribe, I favv in confiderable numbers as far North as the latitude yi 54; and at York Fort I have known them fhot fo late as the latter end of October: at which time they are in the greatefi; perfection, and mofl: delicious eating, more particularly fo when put into a bit of pafte, and boiled like an apple-dumpling; for in fact they are generally too fat at that feafon to be eaten cither roafted or boiled.

Hebridal

Hebridal Sandpipers, but more commonly Hebridai known in Hudfon's Bay by the Name of Whale " '"" Birds, on account of their feeding on the carcafes of thofe animals which frequently lie on the fliores, alfo on maggots that are produced in them by fly-blows. Thefe birds frequent thofe parts in confiderable numbers, and always keep near the margin of the fea. They may, in fad, be called beautiful birds, though not gay in their plumage; they are ufually very fat, but even when firft killed they fmell and tafte fo much like train-oil as to render them by no means pleafing to the palate, yet they are frequently eaten by the Company's fervants. As the Summer advances they fly fo far North of Churchill River, that their breeding-places are not known, though they remain at that part till the beginning of July, and return early in the Fall. They are by no means large birds, as they feldom weigh four ounces. The bill is black, plumage prettily variegated black and white, and the legs and feet are of a beautiful orange colour.

Plovers, commonly called Hawk's Eyes, from "y-their watchfulnefs to prevent a near approach when fitting. When thefe birds are on the wing, they fly very fwift and irregular, particularly when lingle or in fmall flocks. At Churchill River they are by no means numerous,

They exally correfpond with the bird aefcribed by Mr. Pennant, except that they are much longer, but I have feen them in fuch large flocks at York Fort in the Fall of one thoufand feven hundred and feventy-three, that Mr. Ferdinand Jacobs then Governor, Mr. Robert Body Surgeon, and my-felf, killed in one afternoon as many as two men could conveniently carry. They generally feed on infects, and are at all times good eating, but late in the Fall are mofl: excellent. They are by no means equally plentiful in all years; and at the Northern fettlements in the Bay they are not clafled with thofe fpecies of game that add to the general flock of provilions, being only killed as a luxury; but I am informed that at Albany Fort, feveral barrels of them are annually falted for Winter ufe, and are efteemed good eating. This bird during Summer reforts to the remoteft Northern parts; for I have feen them at the Copper River, though in thofe dreary regions only in pairs. The young of thofe birds always leave their nefts as foon as hatched, and when but a few days old run very faft; at night, or in rainy weather, the old ones call them together, and cover them with their wings, in the fame manner as a hen does her chickens. Black Gui- Black Gullemots, known in Hudfon's Bay lemots. jg name of Sea Pigeons. Thofe birds frequent the lhores of Hudfon's Bay and Straits in confiderable numbers; but more particularly the Northern parts, where they fly in large flocks; to the Southward they are only feen in pairs. They are of a fine black, but not c, lofly, with fcarlet legs legs and feet; and the coverets of the wings are marked with white. They are in weight equal to a Widgeon, though to appearance not fo large. They ufually make their nefts in the holes of rocks, and lay two white eggs, which are delicate eating, but not proportionably large for the fize of the bird. My friend Mr. Pennant fays, they brave the coldeft Winters in thofe parts, by keeping at the edge of the ice near the open water; but as the fea at that feafon is frozen over for feveral miles from the fliore, I believe no one's curiofity ever tempted him to confirm the truth of this; and it is well known they never make their appearance near the land after the froft becomes fevere.

Northern Divers. Thefe birds, though com-jjorthem mon in Hudfon's Bay, are by no means plentiful; divers. they are feldom found near the fea coaft, but more frequently in frefli water lakes, and ufually in pairs. They build their nefts at the edge of fmall illands, or the margins of lakes or ponds; they lay only two eggs, and it is very common to find only one pair and their young in one fheet of water; a great proof of their averlion to foci-cty. They are known in Hudfon's Bay by the name of Loons. They differ in fpecies from the Black and Red throated Divers, having a large black bill near four inches long; plumage on the back of a glofly black, elegantly barred with white; the belly of a lilver white; and they are fo large as at times to weigh fifteen or fixteen pounds.

pounds. Their flefli it always black, hard, and fifliy, yet it is generally eaten by the Indians. Black Black-throated Divers. This fpecies are

Divers. morc beautiful than the former; having a long white bill, plumage on the back and wings black, elegantly tinged with purple and green, and prettily marked with white fpots. In lize they are equal to the former; but are fo watchful as to dive at the flafli of a gun, and of courfe are fel-dom killed but when on the wing. Their flefh is equally black and fifhy with the former, but it is always eaten by the Indians. The fkins of thofe birds are very thick and ftrong, and they are frequently drefled with the feathers on, and made into caps for the Indian men. The (kins of the Eagle and Raven, with their plumage complete, are alfo applied to that ufe, and are far from being an unbecoming head-drefs for a favage. Red threat- Red-throated Divers. This fpccics are alfo cddivers. 2Led Loous in Hudfon's Bay; but they are fo far inferior to the two former, that they feldom weigh more than three or four pounds. They, like the other fpecies of Loon, are excellent divers; they always feed on fifli, and when in pur-fuit of their prey, are frequently entangled in fich-ing-nets, fet at the mouths of creeks and fmall rivers. They are more numerous than either of the former, as they frequently fly in flocks; but like them make their nefts at the edge of the water, and only lay two eggs, which, though very rank and fioiy, are always eaten by Indians and Englifh.

Englifli. The legs of thofc three fpecies of Loon are placed fo near the. rump as to be of no fervice to them OQ the land, as they are perfectly incapable of walking; and when found in that fitua-tion (which is but feldom) they are eafilv taken, though tiiey make a ftrong refinance with their bill, wiiich is verv hard and fharp.

-TTT r,. 1 r 1 J-r TT jr Whltcgulls vvHftE Gulls. 1 hele birds viht rludlon s Bay in great numbers, both on the fea coafls and in the interior parts, and probably extend quite acrofs the continent of America. They generally make their appearance at Churchill River about the middle of May; build their nells on the iflands in lakes and rivers; lay two fpeckled eggs, and bring forth their young in June. Their eggs are generally efteemed good eating, as well as the flefli of thofe in the interior parts of the country, though they feed on fi(h and carrion. They make their ftay on Hudfon's Bay as long in the Fall as the froft will permit them to procure a livelihood.

Grey Gulls. Thefe birds, though common, Grey cuii, are by no means plentiful; and I never knew their breeding-places, as they feldom make their appearance at Churchill River till the Fall of the year, and remain there only till the ice begins to be formed about the fliores. They feldom frequent the interior parts of the country. They are not inferior in fize to the former, and in the Fall of the year are generally fat. The ilefli is white and very good eating; and, like moft other

F f Gulls,

Guils, they are a moft excellent fliot when on the wing.

Eiackguiis. Black Gulls, ufually called in Hudfon's Bay, Men of War, from their purfuing and taking the prey from a lefier fpecies of Gull, known in that country by the name of Blackhead. In fize they are much inferior to the two former fpecies; but, like them, always make their nefts on iflands, or at the margins of lakes or ponds; they lay only two eggs, and are found at a conliderable diftance from the fea coaft. The length of their wings is very great in proportion to the body; the tail is uniform, and the two middle feathers are four or five inches longer than the reft. Their eggs are always eaten, both by the Indians and Englifh; but the bird itfelf is generally rejected, except when other provifions are very fcarce.

Black Black-heads. Thefe are the fmalleft fpecies

Hudfon's Bay in fuch vaft numbers, that they are frequently feen in flocks of feveral hundreds; and I have known bufhels of their eggs taken on an ifland of very fmall circumference. Thefe eggs are very delicate eating, the yolks being equal to that of a young pullet, and the whites of a femi-tranfparent azure, but the bird itfelf is always fifhy. Their afieclion for their young is fo ftrong, that when any perfon attempts to rob their nefts, they fly at him, and fometimes approach fo near as to touch him with their pini CDS J and when they find their lofs, will frequent- ly follow the plunderer to a ccmficlerablc diftance. and exprefs their grief by iiiaking an unufual fcreaming noile.

This bird may be ranked with the elegant part of the feathered creation, though it is by no means gay. The bill, legs, and feet are of a rich Icarlet; crown black, and the remainder of the plumage of a light afli-colour, except the quill-feathers, which are prettily barred, and tipped with black, and the tail much forked. The flight, or extent of wing, in this bird, is very great, in proportion to the body. i hey are found as far North as has hitherto been vifited, but retire to the South early in the Fall.

Pelicans. Thofe birds are numerous in the Pelicans. interior parts of the country, but never appear near the fea-coaft. They generally frequent large lakes, and always make their- nefls on ifiands. They are fo provident for their young, that great quantities of fifli lie rotting near their nefts, and emit fuch a horrid ilench as to be fmelt at a con-fiderable diftance. The flefli of the young Peii- can is frequently eaten by the Indians; and as they are always very fat, great quantities of it is melted down, and preferved in bladders for Winter ufe, to mix with pounded flefh; but by F f 2 keeping, ! n the Fall of 1774, whn I firft fettled at Cumberland Houfe, the Indians impof-d on me and my people very much, by felling us Pellcaa fac for the fat of the black bear. Our knowledge of the delicacy of the latter induced us to refetve this fat lor paiticuu. r purpofts; but when we came to open the bladders, it was little fuperior to tiain oil, and waicn- keeping, it grows very rank. The Pelicans In thufe parts are about the fize of a common goofe j their plumage is of a delicate white, except the quill-feathers, which are black. The bill is near a foot long; and the bag, which reaches from the outer-end of the under-mandible to the breaft, is capable of containing upwards of three quarts. The fkins of thofe birds are thick and tough, and are frequently drelted by the Indians and converted into bags, but are never made into clothing, though their feathers are as hard, clofe, and durable, as thole of a Loon. Coofanjeis GoosaNDERs, ufually Called in Hudfon's Bay, Shell-drakes. Thofe birds, are very common on the fea-coaft, but in the interior parts fly in very large flocks, The bill is long and narrow, and toothed like a faw; and they have a tuft of feathers at the back of the head, which they can erect at pleafure. 1 hey are moft excellent divers, and fuch great deftroyers of fifh, that they are. frequently obliged to vomit fome of them before they can take flight. Though not much larger than the Mallard Duck, they frequently fwallow fifli of fix or leven inches long and. proportiona-bly thick. Thole that frequent the interior parts of the country prey much on crawfifh, which iy eatable by a few of my crew, which at thst time confifted only of eight Englilhmen and two of tiie home Indians from York-Fort.

Ciiiiibtrland Hoiiie was the firll inland fct. lement the Company made from i. idion's Fort; and though begun on ib imali a Icale, yet upon it ana i: ud. en's Houli, which is fituated beyond it, upwards of feventy men werenovv employed.

are very numerous in fome of the hallow ftony rivers. In the Fall of the year they are very fat, and though they always feed on fifh, yet their flefh at that feafon is very good; and they re-main in thofe parts as long as the froft will permit them to procure a fubfiftence.

Swans. There are two fpecies of this bird swans. that vifit Hudfon's Bay in fummer; and only differ in fize, as the plumage of both are perfed-ly white, with black bill and legs. The fmaller fort are more frequent near the fea-coaft, but by no means plentiful, and are moft frequently feen in pairs, but fometimes fmgle, probably owing to their mates having been killed on their paflage North. Both fpecies ufually breed on the iflands which are in lakes; and the eggs of the largor fpecies are fo big, that one of them is a fufficient meal for a moderate man, without bread, or any other addition. In the interior parts of the country the larger Swan precedes every other fpecies of water-fowl, and in fome years arrive fo early as the month of March, long before the ice of the rivers is broken up. At thofe times they always frequent the open waters of falls and rapids, where they are frequently fliot by the Indians in confi-derable numbers. They ufually weigh upwards of thirty pounds, and the lefter fpecies from eighteen to twenty four. The flefh of both are excellent eating, and when roafted, is equal in flavour to young heifer-beef, and the cygnets are very delicate.

Ndt-

Notwithftanding the fize of this bird, they are o fwift on the wing as to make them the moft difficult to flioot of any bird I know, it being frequently neceitary to take fight ten or twelve htt before their bills. This, however, is only when flying before the wind in a brilk gale, at which time they cannot fly at a lefs rate than an hundred miles an hour; but when flying acrofs the wind, or agairift it, they make but a flow progrefs, and are then a noble fliot. In their moulting ftate they are not eafily taken, as their large feet, with the afliftance of their wings, enables them to run on the furface of the water as fail: as an Indian canoe can be paddled, and therefore they are al-vays obliged to be (hot; for by diving and other manoeuvres they render it impofiible to take them by hand. It has been faid that the fwans vvhiflle or ling before their death, and I have read fome elegant delcriptions of it in fomeof the poets; but I have never heard any thing of the kind, though I have been at the deaths of feveral. It is true, in ferene evenings, after Sun-fet, I have heard them make a noife not very unlike, that of a French-horn, but entirely divefted of every note that conftituted melody, and have often been forry to find it did not forebode their death. Mr. Lawfon, who, as Mr. Pennant juftly remarks, was no inaccurate obferver, properly enough calls the largefl: fpecies Trumpeters, and the leiler. Hoopers. Some years ago, when I built Cumberland Houfe, the Indians killed thofe birds birds in fuch numbers, that the down and quills might have been procured in confiderable quantities at a trifling expence; but lince the depopulation of the natives by the fmallpox, which has alfo driven the few furvivors to frequent other parts of the country, no advantage can be made of thofe articles, though of confiderable value in England.

Geese. There are no lefs than ten different ocefe. fpecies of Geefe that frequent the various parts of fludfon's Bay during Summer, and are as follow: Firft, The Common Grey Goofe. Second, The Canada Goofe. Third, The White, or Snow Goofe. Fifth, The Blue Goofe. Sixth, The Laughing Goofe. Seventh, The Barren Goofe. Eighth, The Brent Goofe. Ninth, The Dunterj and Tenth, the Bean Goofe.

Common Grey Goose. This bird precedes ". qj," every other fpecies of Goofe in thofe parts, and in fome forward Springs arrives at Churchill River fo early as the latter end of April, but more commonly from the eleventh to the fixteenth of May 5 and in one year it was the twenty-fixth of

Mr. Pennant, in treating of the Whirling Swan, takes notice of the formation of the Windpipe; but on examination, the windpipes of both the fpecies which frequent Hudfon's Bay are found to be exadly alike, thililgh their note is quite different. The breag-bone of this bird is different from any other I have feen; for inftead of being (harp and folid, like that of a goofe, it is broad and hollow. Into this cavity the windpipe paftes from the valve, and reaching quite down to the abdomen, returns into the chert, and joins the lungs. Neither of the fpecies of Swan that frequent Hudfon's Bay are mute: but the note of the larger is mikh louder and harlher than that of the fmaller.

May before any Geefe made their appearance. At their firft arrival they generally come in pairs, and are fo fond of fociety, that they fly ftreight to the call that imitates their note; by which means they are ealily (hot. They breed in great numbers in the plains and marfhes near Churchill River; and in fome years the young ones can be taken in cpnhderable numbers, and are eafily tamed; but will never learn to eat corn, unlefs fome of the old ones are taken with them, which is eafily done when in a moulting ftate. On the ninth of Augull one thoufand feven hundred and eighty-cne, when I redded at Prince of Valess Fort, 1 fent fome Indians up Churchill River in canoes to procuie fome of thofe Geefe, and in the afternoon they were feen coming down the river with a large flock before them; the young ones not more than half-grown, and the old ones fo far in a moulting ftate as not to be capable of flying: fo that, with the affiftanceof the 1 nglifli and the Indians then refiding on the plantation, the whole flock, to the amount of forty-one, was drove within the ftockade which inclofes the Fort, where they were fed and fattened for Win= ter ufe. Wild Geefe taken and fattened in this manner are much preferable to any tame Geefe in the world. "When this fpecies of Geefe are full-grown, and in good condition, they often wfigh twelve pounds, but more frequently muc lefs. cr. nada C AN ADA Goose, or Piflv-a-fifli, as it is Called by the Indians, as well as the Englifli in Hudfons Bay. This Ipecics do not differ in plumage from the former, but are inferior in fize; the bill is much fmailer in proportion, and the flefli being much whiter, of courfe is more efteemed. Tliey are by no means fo numerous as the former, and generally fly far North to breed; but fome few of their eggs are found near Churchill River. It is feldom that either of thefe fpecies lay more than four eggs; but if not robbed, they ufually bring them all forth.

White or Snow Goose. Thefe are the moft white or numerous of all the fpecies of birds that frequent ' the Northern parts of the Bay, and generally make their appearance about a week or ten days after the Common Grey Goofe. In the firftpart of the feafon they come in fmall parties, but in the middle, and toward the latter end, they fly in fuch amazing flocks, that when they fettle in the marflies to feed, the ground for a confide-rable diftance appears like a field of fnow. When feeding in the fame marfli with the Grey Geefe, they never mix. Like the Grey Geefe, they fly to the call that refembles their note; and in fome years are killed and falted in great numbers for Winter provilion; they are almoft univerfally thought good eating, and will, if proper care be taken in curing them, continue good for eighteen months or two years. The Indians are far more expert in killing Geefe, as well as every other fpecies of game, than any European I ever law in

Hudfon's

Hudfon's Bay; for fome of them frequently kill upward of a hundred Geefe in a day, whereas the moft expert of the Englifli think it a good day's work to kill thirty. Some years back it was common for an Indian to kill from a thoufand to twelve hundred Geefe in one feafon; but latterly he is reckoned a good hunter that kills three hundred. This is by no means owing to the de generacy of the natives; for the Geefe of late years do not frequent thofe parts in fuch numbers as formerly. The general breeding. place of this bird is not known to aihy Indian in Hudfon's Bay, not even to the Efquimaux who fre–uent the remoteft North. The general route they take in their return to the South in the Fall of the year, is equally unknown; for though fuch multitudes of them are fetn at Churchill River in the Spring, and are frequently killed to the amount of five or fix thoufand; yet in the Fall of the year, feven or eight hundred is confidered a good hunt. At York Fort, though only two degrees South of Churchill River, the Geefe fea-fons fluctuate fo much, that in fome Springs they htve faked forty hogflieads, and in others not more than one or two: and at Albany Fort, the Spring feafon is by no means to be depended on 5 but in the fall they frequently fait fixty hogf-heads of Geeie, befides great quantities of Plover. The retreat of thofe birds in Winter is equally unknown, as that of their breeding-places. I obferve in Mr. Pennant's Ardic Zoology, that about about Jakutz, and other parts of Siberia, they are caught in great numbers, both in nets, and by decoying them into hovels; but if" thefe are the fame birds, they muft at times vary as much in manner as they do in fituation, for in Hudfons Bay they are the fhyeft and moft watchful of all the fpecies of Geefe, never fuffering an open approach, net even within two or three gun-fliots: yet in fome of the rivers near Cumberland Houfe, and at Bafquiau, the Indians frequently kill twenty at one fliot; but this is only done in moon-light nights, when the Geefe are fitting on the mud, and the fportfmen are perfectly concealed from their view. Though the plumage of thofe Geefe are perfectly white, except the quill-feathers, which are black, the fkin is of a dark lead-colour, and the flefli is excellent eating, either frefh or fait. They are much inferior in fize to the Common Grey Geefe, but equal to the Canada Geefe.

Blue Geese. This fpecies are of the fame fize Blue Oeefe. as the Snow Gce(c; and, like them, the bill and legs are of a deep fiefh-colour, but the whole plumage is of a dirty blue, refembling old lead. The fkin, when ftripped of its feathers, is of the fame colour as the Snow Goofe, and they are equally good eating. This fpecies of Geefe are feldom feen to the North of Churchill River, and not very common at York Fort; but at Albany Fort they are more plentiful than the White or Snow Geefe. Their breeding-places are as little known known to the moll accurate obferver as thofe of the Snow Geefe; for I never knew any of their eggs taken, and their Winter haunts have hitherto been undifcovered. Thofe birds are frequently feen to lead a iock of the White ones; and, as they generally fly in angles, it is far from unplea-fant to fee a bird of a different colour leading the van. The leader is generally the object of the firft fportfman who fires, which throws the whole flock into fuch confufion, that fome of the other hunters frequently kill fix or feven at a fliot. Horned HorNED Wavey. This delicate and diminu-

Wavcy. j, g fpecies of the Goofe is not much larger than the Mallard Duck. Its plumage is delicately white, except the quill-feathers, which are black. The bill is not more than an inch long, and at the bafe is lludded round with little knobs about the lize of peas, but more remarkably fo in the males. Both the bill and feet are of the fame colour with thofe of the Snow Goofe. This' fpecies is very fcarce at Churchill River, and I believe are never found at any of the Southern fettlements; but about two or three hundred miles to the North Weft of Churchill, I have feen them in as large" flocks as the Common Wavey, or Snow Goofe. The flefli of this bird is exceedingly delicate; but they are fo fmall, that when I was on my journey to the North I eat two of them one night for fupper. I do not find this bird defcrib-ed by my worthy friend Mr. Pennant in his Arctic Zoology. Probably a fpecimen of it was not fent fent home, for the perfon th; it commanded at Prince of Wales's Fort at the time the colleclion was making, did not pay any attention to it.

Laughing Goose. This elegant fpecies has a i. auphing vhite bill, and the legs and feet are of a fine yel-"'"' low colour J the upper part of the plumage is brown, the breaft and belly white, the former prettily blotched with black. In fize they are equal to the Snow Goofe, and their fkins, when ftripped of their feathers, are delicately white, and the flefli excellent. They vifit Churchill River in very fmall numbers; but about two hundred miles to the North Weft of that river I have feen them fly in large flocks, like the Common Waveys, or Snow Geefe; and near Cumberland Houfe and Baquiau they are found in fuch numbers, that the Indians in moon-light nights frequently kill upwards of twenty at a hot. Like the Horned Wavey, they never fly with the lead of the coaft, but are always feen to come from the Weftward. Their general breeding-places are not known,"though fome few of their eggs are occa-fionally found to the North of Churchill j but I never heard any Indian fay that he had feen any eggs of the Horned Wavey: it is probable they retire to North Greenland to breed; and their route in the Fall of the year, as they return Southward, is equally unknown. They are, 1 believe, feldom feen on the coaft of Hudfon's Bay to the Southward of latitude 59 North.

Barren Geise. Ihefe are the iargeft of all Barren the'"''

Mr. Mofes Norton.

g A JOURNEY TO THE the fpecles of Geefe that frequent Hudfons Bay, as they frequently weigh fixteen or feventeen pounds. They differ from the Common Grey Goofe in nothing but in fize, and in the head and breaft being tinged with a rufty brown. They never make their appearance in the Spring till the greateft part of the other fpecies of Geefe are flown Northward to breed, and many of them remain near Chur(: hill River the whole Summer, This large fpecies are generally found to be males, and from the exceeding fmallnefs of their tefti-cles, they are, 1 fuppofe, incapable of propagating their fpecies. I believe 1 can with truth fay, that I was the firft European who made that remark, though they had always been diainguiflied by the name of the Barren Geefe; for no other reafon than that of their not being known to breed. Their flefh is by no means unpleafant, though always hard and tough; and their plumage is fo thick before they begin to moult, that one bird ufually produces a pound of fine feathers and down, of a furprifmg elafticity. Brent Brent Geese. 1 his fpecics Certainly breed in

"- the remoteft parts of the North, and feldom make their appearance at Churchill River till late in Auguft or September. The rout they take in Sphng is unknown, and their breeding-places have never been difcovered by any Indian in Hudfon's Bay. When they make their appearance at Churchill River, they always come from the North, fly near the margin of the coaft, and are never feen in the interior parts of the country.

In lize they iire larger than a Mallard Duck, hut inferior to the Snow Goofe; and though their fieih appears delicate to the eye, it is not much elleemcd. In feme years they pafs the mouth of Churchill River in prodigious numbers, and many of them are killed and fervcd to the Company's fcrvants as provilions; but, as I have juft obferv-ed, they are not much refliflied. When migrating to the South, they generally avail themfelves of a ftrong North or North Wefterly wind, which makes then fly fo fwift, that when I have killed four or five at a fliot, not one of them fell lefs than from twenty to fifty yards from the perpendicular fpot where they were killed. Like the White, or Snow Geefe, when in large flocks they fly in the (hape of a v edge, and make a great noife. Their flight is very irregular,- fometimes being forty or fifty yards above the water, and in an inftant after they fldm clofe to the furface of it, and then rife again to a confiderable height; fo that they may jufl: ly be faid to fly in feftoons.

The DunTER Gef. se, as it is called in Hudfon's q" Bay, but which is certniiiiy the Eider Duck. They are common at the mouth of Churchill River as foon as the ice breaks up, but generally fly far North to breed; and the few that do remain near the fettlement are fo fcattered among fniau iflands, and fea-girt rocks and ftioals, as to render it not worth while to attempt gathering their down. Their eggs, when found, are exceeding good eating; and in the Fall of the year the flefh is by no means unpleafant, though they are no-torioufly known to feed on fifli.- r Bean Goose. This fpecies is feldom found in

Beangock.

any part of Hudfon's Bay, as in all my travels I have only feen three that were killed. This bird never came under the infpeclion of Mr. Graham, or the late Mr. Hutchins, though they both contributed very largely to the coiledion fent home to the Royal Society.

Species of Waier-Fowl uek9.

Ducks of various kinds arfe found in thofe parts during Summer; fome only fre-quenting the fea-coaft, while others vifit the interior parts of the country in aftonifhing numbers. The fpecies of this bird which is found moft commonly here are, the King Duck, Black Duck, Mallard Duck, Long tailed Duck, Widgeon, and Teal. The two firft only vifit the fea-coaft, feed on fifh It is, however, nolefs true, that the late Mr. Humphry Martin, many years Governor of Albany Fort, fent home fevcral hundred ipecimens cf animals and plants to complete that colkdion; but by fome miftake, nothing of the kind was placed to the credit of hi. s account. Even xtiy re-= fpeded friend Mr. Pennant, who with a candour that does him honour, has fo generoufly acknowledged his obligations to all to whom he thought he was indebted for information when he was writing his Arlic Zoology, (fee the Advettifement,) has not mentioned his name; but I am fully per-fjaded that it entirely proceeded frim a want of knowing the peifon; and as Mr. Hutchins fucceeded him at Albany in the year 1774, every thing that has been fent over from that part has been placed to iiis account.

and fifli-fpawn; and their flcfli is by no means elleemed good, though their eggs are not difa-greeable. The Mallard and Long failed Duck, vilit Hudfon's Bay in great numbers, and extend from the fea-coaft, to the remoteft Weftern parts, and near Cumberland Houfc are found in vail multitudes. At their firll arrival on the fea-coaft, they are exceeding good eating; but when in a moulting ftate, though very fat, they are in general fo rank tliat few Europeans are fond of them. At thofe feafons the difference in flavour is eafily known by the colour of the fat; for when that is white, the flefti is moft afturedly good; but when it is yellow, or of an orange colour, it is very rank and fifhy. This difference is only peculiar to thofe that frequent and breed near the fea-coaft; for in the interior parts I never knew them killed but their flefli was very good; and the young Mallard Duck before it can fly is very fat, and moft delicate eating. The fame may be faid of the Long-tailed Duck. Neither of thofe fpecies lay more than fix or eight eggs in common, and frequently bring them all forth,

Widgeon. This fpecies of Duck is very un-"'=' "-common in Hudfon's Bay; ufually keeping in pairs, and being feldom ken in flocks. TJiey are by no means fo numerous as the two former, and are moft frequently feen in rivers and mar-flies near the fea-coaft. Their flelh is generally efteemed; and the down of thofe I have examined is little inferior in elafticity to that of the

G ST p: jder.

Eider, though much fhorter. The fame may be faid of feveral other fpecies of Ducks that frequent thofe parts; but the impoflibility of col-ieding the down in any quantity, prevents it from becoming an article of trade. Teal. Teal. Like the Mallard, they are found in coniiderable numbers near the fea-coaft; but are more plentiful in the interior parts of the country, and fly in fuch large flocks that I have often killed twelve or fourteen at one fliot, and have feen both Englifh and Indians kill a much greater number. At their firfl arrival they are but poor, though generally efteemed good eating. This diminutive Duck is by far the moft prolific of any I know that reforts to Hudfon's Bay; for I have often feen the old ones fwimming at the head of feventeen young, when not much larger than walnuts. This bird remains in thofe parts as long as the feafon will permit; for in the year one thoufand feven hundred and feventy-five, in my paffage from Cumberland Houfe to York Fort, I, as well as my Indian companions, killed them in the rivers we pafled through as late as the twentieth of Oftober. At thofe times they are entirely involved in fat, but delicately white, and may truly be called a great luxury.

Befides the birds already defcribed, there is a great variety of others, both of land and water fowl, that frequent thofe parts in Summer; but thefe came not fo immediately under my infpecli-on as thofe I have already defcribed.

Of the Vegetable Produftions.

The vegetable producllons of this country by no means engaged my attention fo much as the animal creation; which is the lefs to be wondered at, as fo few of them are ufeful for the fupport of man. Yet I will endeavour to enumerate as many of them as I think are worth notice.

The GooscbiirRieS thrive beil in ftony and "f'- beriies.

rocky ground, which lies open and much expof-cd to the Sun. But in thofe lituations few of the buflies grow to any height, and fpread along the ground like vines. The fruit is always moll plentiful and the finefi: on the under-fide of the branches, probably owing to the reflecled heat from the ftones and gravel, and from being fheltered from all cold winds and fog by the leaves. I never faw more than one fpccies of Goofeberry in any part of Hudfon's Bay, which is the red one. When green, they make excellent pies or tarts; and when ripe are very pleafant eating, though by no means fo large as thofe produced in England.

Cranberries grow in great abundance near cranbcuie Churchill, and are not confined to any particular fituation, for they are as common on open bleak plains and high rocks as among the woods. When carefully gathered in the Fall, in dry wea-

G g 2 ther, ther, and as carefully packed in cafls with moift fugar, they will keep for years, and are annually fent to England in confiderable quantities as pre-fents, vhere they are much efteemed. When the fnips have remained in the Bay lb late that the Cranberries are ripe, fome of the Captains have carried them home in water with great fuccefs. Heath T Heathberries are in fome years fo plen- btincs. jfyj jg Churchill, that it is impoffible to walk in many places without treading on thoufands and millions of them. They grow clofe to the ground, and are a favourite repafl: of many birds that migrate to thofe parts in Summer, particularly the Grey Goofe; on which account the Indians di-ftinruifh them bv the name of Nifhca-minnick, or the Grey Goofeberry. The juice of this berry makes an exceeding pleafant beverage, and the fruit itfelf would be more pleafing were it not for the number of fmall feeds it contains.

Bethago-tominick, as it is called by the Indians, or the Devv-ater-berry of Mr. Dragge. I have Qtn this berry as far North as Marble Iliand, and that in great abundance. It flourifhes beft, and is mod: productive, in fwampy boggy ground covered with mofs, and is feldom found among grafs. The plant itfelf is not very unlike that of a Strawberry, but the leaves are larger. Out of the center of the plant (hoots a fingle ftalk, fome-times to the height of feven or eight inches, and each plant only produces one berry, which at fome diftance refembles a Strawberry; but on exami- toiiiinick.

examination they have not that conical form; and many of them are only compofed of three or four lobes, while others confill of near twenty. The flavour of this berry is far from unplcafing, and it is eaten by our people in confidcrable quantities during the feafon, (which is Auguft,) and, like all the other fruits in thofe parts, is fup-pofed to be wholefome, and a great antifcorbutic.

CurRANS, both red and black, are common cunans. about Churchill River, but the latter are far more plentiful than the former, and are very large and fine. The bufhes on which thofe currans grow, frequently exceed three feet in height, and generally thrive beft in thofe parts that are moift but not fwampy. Small vallies between the rocks, at fome little diftance from the woods, are very favourable to them; and I have frequently obferved that the fruit produced in thofe fituati-ons is largrer and finer than that which is found in the woods. Thofe berries have a very great eftect on fome people if eaten in any confiderable quantities, by acling as a very powerful purgative, and in fome as an emetic at the fame time; but if mixed with Cranberries, they never have that effecl.

Juniper-berries are frequently found near the""- ' new fettlement at Churchill River, but by no means in fuch plenty as in the more Southern and interior parts of the country. The buih they grew on is fo fimilar to the creeping pine, that one half of the Company's fervants refiding berries.

454 A JOURNEY TO THE in Hudfon's Bay do not know one from the other. Like the Goofeberry bufhes in thofe parts, the fruit is always moft plentiful on the under-fide of the branches. They are not much efteemed either by the Indians or Englifh, fo that the few that are made ufe of are generally infufed in brandy, by way of making a cordial, which is far from unpleafant. Etrav Strawberries!, and thofe of a confiderable fize and excellent flavour, are found as far North as Churchill River; and what is moft remarkable, they are frequently known to be more plentiful in fuch places as have formerly been fet on fire. This is not peculiar to the Strawberry, but it is well known that in the interior parts of the country, as well as at Albany and Moofe Forts, that after the ground, or more properly the underwood and mofs, have been fet on fire, that Rafp-berry-buflies and Hips have fliot up in great numbers on fpots where nothing. of the kind had ever been feen before. This is a phasnomenon that is not eafily accounted for; but it is more than probable thatnature wanted fome afliftance, and the mofs being all burnt away, not only admits the fun to act with more power, but the heat of the fire mufr, in fome meafure, loofen the texture of the ioii, fo as to admit the plants to fhoot

The Indians call the Junipcr-herry Caw-caw-cur-minick, orthe Cro-v-berry.

f The Oteagh-ir. inick of the Indians, is fo called, bccaufe it in fome neafure refenibies zkrrt.

ihoot up, after having been deep-rooted for many years without being able to force their way to the furface.

Befides the Berries already mentioned, there are three others found as far North as Churchill; namely, what the Indians call the Eye-berry, and the other two are termed Blue-berry and Partridge-berry by the Englifti.

The Eye-berry grows much in the fame man-Eye-bcny. ner as the v"trawberry, and though fmaller, is infinitely fuperior in flavour. This berry is found in various fituations; but near Churchill River they are moil plentiful in fmall hollows among the rocks, which are fituated fome diftance from the woods; but they are never known to grow in fwampy ground, and I never faw them fo plentiful in any part of Hudfon's Bay as about Churchill River.

The Blue-berry is about the fize of a Hur-"-"y-tleberry, and grows on bulhes which rife to eighteen inches or two feet, but in general are much lower. They are feldom ripe till September, at which time the leaves turn to a beautiful red; and the fruit, though fmall, have as fine a bloom as any plum, and are much efleemed for theplea-fantnefs of their flavour.

The Partridge-berry is nearly as large as the te. y"""' Cranberry imported from Newfoundland, and though of a beautiful tranfparent red, yet has a difacreeable tafte. Thefe berries are feldom ta-ken, either by the Indians or Englifh j and many of the latter call them Poifon-berries, but feveral birds are fond of them. They grow clofe to the ground, like the Cranberry, and the plant that produces them is not very unlike fmall fage, either in fhape or colour, but has none of its virtues.

I had nearly forgotten another fpecies of Berry, which is found on the dry ridges at Churchill in confiderable numbers. In fize and colour they much referable the Red Curran, and grow on bufhes fo much like the Creeping Willow, that people of little obfervation fcarcely known the difference; particularly as all the fruit is on the under-fide of the branches, and entirely hid by the leaves. 1 never knew this Berry eaten but by a frolickfome Indian girl; and as it had no ill effeci:, it is a proof it is not unwholefome, though exceedingly unpleafant to the palate, and not much lefs fo to the fmell.

Hips of a fmall fize, though but few in number, are alfo found on the banks of Churchill River, at fome diftance from the fea. But in the interior parts of the country they are frequently found in fuch vaft quantities, that at a diftance they make the fpots they grow on appear perfeft-ly red. In the interior parts of Hudfon's Bay tliey are as large as any I ever remember to have feen, and when ripe, have a moft delightful bloom; but at that fcafon there is fcarcely one in ten which has not a worm in it; and they fre-queatly act as a ftrong purgative.

With

Hips.

With refpecl to the fmallcr produions of the vegetable world, I am obliged to be in a great meafure filent, as the nature of my various occupations during my refidence in this country gave me little leifure, and being unncquainred with botany, I viewed with inattention things that were not of immediate ufe: the few which follow are all that particularly engaged my attention.

The Wish-A-CA-pucca, which grows in moft "iiii-a-ca- r 1 1 r pucca.

parts of this country, is faid by lome Authors to have great medical virtues, applied, either inwardly as an alterative, or outwardly dried and pulverifed, to old fores and gangrenes. The truth, of this I much doubt, and could never think it had the leaft medical quality. It is, however, much ufed by the lower clafs of the Company's fervants as tea; and by fome is thought very pleafant. But the flower is by far the moft delicate, and if gathered at a proper time, and carefully dried in the fliade, will retain its flavour for many years, and make a far more pleafant beverage than the leaves. There are feveral fpecies of this plant, of which fome of the leaves are nearly as large as that of the Creeping Willow, while others are as fmall and narrow as that of the Kofemary, and much refembles it in colour; but all the fpecies have the fame fmell and flavour.

Jackashey-puck. This herb much refembles J.-J " Creeping Box; and is only ufed, either by the Indians or Englifli, to mix with tobacco, which makes it fmoke mild and pleafant 5 and would, I

Grafs, 438 A JOURNEY TO THE am perfuaded, be very acceptable to many fmokers in England. Mofs. Moss of various forts and colours is plentiful enough in moft parts of this country, and is what the deer ufually feed on.

Grass of feveral kinds is alfo found in thofe parts, and fome of it amazingly rapid of growth, particularly that which is there called Rye-grafs, and which, in our fliort Summer at Churchill, frequently grows to the height of three feet. Another fpecies of Grafs, which is produced in marflies, and on the margins. of lakes, ponds, and rivers, is particularly adapted for the fupport of the multitudes of the feathered creation which refort to thofe parts in Summer. The Marfli Grafs at Churchill is of that peculiar nature, that where it is mowed one year, no crop can be procured the next Summer; whereas at York Fort, though the climate is not very different, they can get two crops, or harvefts, from the fame fpot in one Summer. Vetches are plentiful in fome parts as far North as Churchill River; and Burrage, Sorrel, and Coltsfoot, may be ranked among the ufeful plants. Dandelion is alfo plentiful at Churchill, and makes an early falad, long before any thing can be produced in the gardens. In facb, notwithftanding the length of the "Winter, the feverity of the cold, and the great fcarcity of vegetables at this Northern fettlement, by proper attention to cleanlinefs, and keeping the people at reafonable exercife, I never had one . yi. rr . 1 , A,,

Myv. A,,;,. J Ar. Jrrr I ;.,., ,;,,, ff fUI . fju.

I ,O- ,, r yjr rff-

U fw (7lf man under me who had the lead fymptoms of the Icurvy; whereas at York Fort, Albany, and Moofe River, there were almoft annual complaints that one half of the people were rendered incapable of duty by that dreadful dif-order.

I do not wifli to lay claim to any merit on this occaiion, but I cannot help obferving that, during ten years I had the command at Churchill River, only two men died of that diftemper, though my complement at times amounted in number to fifty-three.

The Foreft Trees that grow on this inhofpita- Trees. ble fpot are very few indeed; Pine, Juniper, fmall fcraggy Poplar, Creeping Birch, and Dwarf Willows, compofe the whole catalogue. Farther Weftward the Birch Tree is very plentiful; and in the Athapufcow country, the Pines, Larch, Poplar, and Birch, grow to a great fize; the Alder is alfo found there.

THE END.

DIRECTIONS TO THE BINDER,

A PLAN exhibiting Mr. Flearne's Tracks in his own Journies for the Difcovery of the Copper Mine River, in the Years 1770, 1771, and 1772, under the Direftion of the Hudfon's Bay Company. To face the Title-page.

Plate I. A North Weft View of Prince of Wales's Fort in Hudfon's Bay, North America. Igface Page i

Plate II. Indian Implements. To face P. 98

Plate III. Plan of the Copper Mine River.

To face P. 164

Plate IV. A Winter View. in the Ath apusco w Lake.

To face P. 248
Plate V. Indian Implements Jt the End,
Plate VI. Plan of Albany River in Hudfon's Bay.
Jt the End.
Plate VII. Plan of Moose Rives, in Hudfon's Bay.
Jt the End.
Plate VIII, Plan of Slude River.- Jt the End.

Lightning Source UK Ltd.
Milton Keynes UK
08 March 2010

151089UK00002B/68/P